New Masters of Flash

The 2002 Annual

Jonathan Gay
Yugo Nakamura
Vas Sloutchevsky
Samuel Wan
Marc Stricklin
Chris Andrade
Gabriel Mulzer
Brian Limond
Pete Barr-Watson
Mickey Stretton
Josh Levine
Jessica Speigel
Hoss Gifford
Manuel Tan
Amit Pitaru
Ross Mawdsley
Erik Natzke

friendsof

DESIGNER TO DESIGNER™

NEW MASTERS

New Masters of Flash

The 2002 Annual

friendsof

DESIGNER TO DESIGNER™

NEW MASTERS

Published by friends of ED Ltd. 30 Lincoln Road, Olton, Birmingham. B27 6PA
Printed in USA
ISBN 1903450365

Credits

Authors
Jonathan Gay
Yugo Nakamura
Vas Sloutchevsky
Samuel Wan
Marc Stricklin
Gabriel Mulzer
Brian Limond
Pete Barr-Watson
Josh Levine
Mickey Stretton
Jessica Speigel
Hoss Gifford
Amit Pitaru
Chris Andrade
Ross Mawdsley
Manuel Tan
Erik Natzke

Flash Consultant
Sham Bhangal

Author Agents
Gaynor Riopedre
Jeremy Booker

Project Administrator
Fionnuala Meacher

Copyright Research
Fionnuala Meacher
David Spurgeon

Translation
Zoe Keep
Europa Technical Translations

CD Design
New Media Works
3rd Floor, Lupus House
11-13 Macklin Street
Covent Garden
London WC2B 5NH

Content Architect
Mel Orgee

Editors
Mel Orgee
Alan McCann
Dan Britton

Graphic Editors
Deborah Murray
Katy Freer

Technical Reviewers
Sham Bhangal
Garrett Carr
Simon Gurney
Vicki Loader
Glain Martin
Eric Mauro
James Penberthy
Gabrielle Smith
Jake Smith
Kev Sutherland
Phill Taffs
Gobhi Theivendran
Peter Walker
Andrew Zack

Proof Readers
Kristian Besley
Jeremy Booker
Simon Collins
Joanna Farmer
Ciara McNee
Fionnuala Meacher
Sunny Ralph
Joel Rushton

Index
Simon Collins

Cover Design
Deborah Murray

Contents

Contents

Flash and Relativity – initiating some spacetime sanity on the Web.

In 1884 a mathematician called Edwin Abbott wrote a treatise on what it might be like to live in a 2-dimensional world. He called that world Flatland. What he described, more than a century ago, is uncannily like the user experience of the HTML web. On encountering a being from the three-dimensional real world – an individual or a group or a business – the two-dimensional citizen can only ever be aware of a single slice at a time. So getting a feeling for relative size and context is near impossible.

A year ago, the Jacobean tendency was to declare that 99% of Flash is bad, in exactly the same way that Abbott's Flatlanders violently rejected their first visitors from the inconceivable three-dimensional realm. But Flashers have begun to prove through great design and intuitive usability that Flatlanders have no reason to be scared. The third dimension that Flash brings to the party isn't the z-plane to complement the x and y. It is the dimension of time.

A realm that recognizes time is more usable than one that doesn't.

That is a polemical statement and it is the gauntlet thrown down by Flash.

It's yet to be proved on the Web, because the true potential of Flash design is still unfolding. But think of another realm – the human brain, say – and it's not in the least bit provocative. A mind unconscious of the temporal context of reality is known to the psychiatric profession as manic. And sure, mania is fun for a while, but it pretty much always ends in tears.

Dot.bomb depression. We propose that HTML was the cause.

Get sane. Use Flash.

The Flash world has moved on a little since the first New Masters book, and the keywords now are *integration* and *ActionScript*. Whether you're integrating surreal images created in Photoshop with the motion graphics of Flash, or using a Flash front end with a remote database, you're mixing Flash with something else, and moving into powerful new territory. The increasing use of ActionScripting is nothing to be afraid of because it allows us to create totally interactive or non-linear animations and effects – designers are no longer tied down to a timeline.

Initial ideas
Flash needs cool new ideas before it will create cool new stuff – look at Ross Mawdsley for the graphic side of things, or Erik Natzke for the ActionScript-heavy stuff. Look and learn from the New Masters.

Basic scripting
Vas Sloutchevsky's chapter adds a little ActionScript-heavy pixie dust to Flash's basic animation and drawing tools, using a deceptively simple idea to spice up basic tweens. He creates a whole new button-less navigation scheme with just a few short lines of scripting. Like us, you'll be fuming that you didn't think of it first...

Combining graphics and scripting
Of course, despite all that new scripting stuff, Flash is still a visual tool. Marc Stricklin and Hoss Gifford epitomize the seamless integration of scripting and graphics. Marc's surreal Photoshopaholic world looks like the product of an over-imaginative mind, brought to light and to life by some equally imaginative coding. Meanwhile, by controlling a few simple brush-stroke graphics, Hoss creates the ability to draw and save your own masterpieces in his pen and ink online guestbook.

Flash 5 objects
For an easy to follow but ingenious introduction to incorporating Flash's predefined multimedia objects, look at Mickey Stretton's piece on the nature of time.

Masking
Too few people use masking in Flash, but now you need look no further than Limmy and Chris Andrade to see how it can be used to create some eye-catching effects. Based on a similar masking trick, they show how two differing creative directions can produce starkly different end results.

3D
Flash and 3D have a love-hate relationship, but Gabriel Mulzer and Josh Levine show us a few ways to get Flash to play ball via a mix of cheating (faux 3D) and honest scripting (3-axis 3D).

Total ActionScript
There are those who have taken the route of ignoring the timeline-based approach and gone for an ActionScript-heavy solution. Samuel Wan looks at a structured programming route, then it's on to Amit Pitaru and experimental ActionScript, before Manny Tan's butterflies show us how scripting isn't just about number-crunching, but total control of the graphic environment.

Flash front ends
Finally, once you've mastered ActionScript, server-side scripting and remote access is the next stage. Take a look at Jessica Speigel and Pete Barr-Watson for an introduction into this fast-moving field.

Whatever your Flash needs, front-end, back-end, code or design, there's a New Master in these pages just waiting to inspire you.

Vas Sloutchevsky

Vas Sloutchevsky is the creative director and vice president of Firstborn Multimedia in New York City. He co-founded Firstborn Multimedia in 1997, using Flash on the day-to-day basis since version 2 (he actually has a few .spa files in his archives). He and his team have created high-profile digital designs for Calvin Klein, Redken, L'Oreal, The Beatles, Madonna and many other well-known names. Vas comes from a family of artists. Being convinced that Flash is just another art form, he likes to characterize his work as "digital canvas, where technology merges with art". He is passionate about creating new navigation systems and aims to simplify the way data is presented to the user in elegant, stimulating interfaces. "There is nothing wrong with being too cerebral when it comes to designing an interface", says Vas. His work for Yigal-Azrouel.com was recently awarded at the Flash™ Film Festival in categories of Motion Graphics and Navigation, and MadonnaMusic.com in the Design category.

Samuel Wan

Samuel Wan was generating his own computer graphics several years before his introduction to commercial graphics software. His main passion is to communicate through technology, and he currently pursues graduate-level studies in Human-Computer Interaction at the University of Michigan's School of Information, covering subjects such as usability evaluation, user interface design, information architecture, and social systems. As an independent developer, he has contributed to the development of cutting edge Flash solutions for various studios. Samuel also writes books, speaks at conferences, and conducts large workshops on the ActionScript language. He contributes to the design community as a moderator for the We're Here forums, and his experimental storytelling (samuelwan.com) has been featured at the London Flash Film Festival.

Marc Stricklin

Marc Stricklin spends most of his time pumping out work as creative director for engineroominteractive.com. While not plugging away at the corporate side of interactive life he spends most of his time working on his personal site, brittle-bones.com. Maybe it's the completely organic navigation that keeps people coming back to brittle-bones.com? Maybe it's the disturbingly intracate Photoshop work that it has become notorious for? One thing is for sure, people can't seem to get enough of this dark playground. It just so happens that it has become one of the most popular sites on the Web today.

Chris Andrade

Christopher Andrade is the creator behind Fifth Rotation, a personal site geared towards new media design and art by communicating ideas through the medium of Flash. Before his involvement with design and the Web, he was pursuing a career in art for feature animation and films. When he's not glued to his computer screen doing work or surfing the Web, he spends time with his wife Sena, plays Capoeira, and enjoys reading.

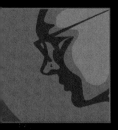

Gabriel Mulzer

Born the last days of 1969, grown up at various places in southern Germany. '89 moved to Berlin after leaving school. Periods of working on computer animations, drawings, illustrations, half starving and dawdling, caring for kids, running a shop... From 1997 working employed as multimedia animation and screen designer, senior designer and art director. Freelancing as a designer today, focusing on Flash, motion and game design.

Brian Limond

Brian Limond is a Flash developer from Glasgow, Scotland, and is best known in Flash backslapping circles for That Flash Site with the Dancing Guy and the Sam Fox Come Again Thing, Limmy.com. He works best when working on happy things and thinking happy thoughts, which consist of a mix of memories of mum and Misty the cat; dreams of future with the lovely Lynn McGowan; looking forward to the next delicious glass of Hoegaarden; childhood adventures in Millport (pictured); and the prospect of creating something that will put a smile on someone's face out there in Internet land.

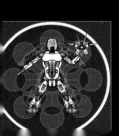

Pete Barr-Watson

Pete has been around since the good old days of web design when Flash didn't exist and site were coded by hand. The closest thing you got to 'cool' was a few dodgy Java Applets (Pete would like it known that he is NEVER used the 'ripple' applet as gratuitously as is suggested in certain circles). Times have changed and new technologies have emerged and it is this, along with an insatiable appetite for learning (oh, and the photographic memory he is cursed with) that have kept him in this industry and not bumming around the world doing mad things.

About the Authors

Mickey Stretton

After graduating from University with a graphic design degree, Mickey Stretton did on freelance job designing a magazine cover before swapping CMYK for RGB and finding a jc as an interactive designer. He currently works as Senior Designer at Digit in London whe his clientwork includes projects for Sony, Motorola, 007.com and the award winning MTV web site. He has spoken at various events around Europe and America includingFlashForwar and has contributed his opinions for magazines such as CreateOnline and Dazed ar Confused. Mickey's ambitions include upgrading his 56k modem and establishing a regula sleep pattern.

Josh Levine

Josh Levine is a digital artist, and founder of AlphaB2 Media, an award winning Flash stud and idea factory in New York City. His current projects include original entertainment conten 12D billboards, and e-cemeteries. In 1999, Josh established himself as one of New York premiere Flash instructors, training many of New York's most prestigious creativ departments. Josh loves digital video and has a passion for Datsuns. When he is bored, Jos makes giant sails out of garbage bags and duct tape, and he flies away.

Jessica Speigel

Born and raised in Seattle, WA, Jessica Speigel is co-founder of We're Here Forums. We're Her has existed as a haven for knowledge-seeking Flash designers since the release of Flash We're Here is a sharing community where members have developed their creative an technical skills among each other, many of whom have become recognized professionals i the web industry. Her passion is building attractive user interfaces with ActionScript tha integrate typography, dynamic content, and motion graphics into a fluid, user-friend experience for visitors. In her spare time, Jessica shapes webstyles.net, her personal proje and portfolio site.

Hoss Gifford

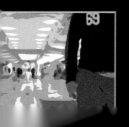

Hoss is one of the founding directors of Flammable Jam (www.flamjam.com), and curator o his personal site www.h69.net. He regularly sponges his way around the world, getting fre flights in exchange for talking at new media seminars, including Flash Forward and Milia. H inspirations include Paul Daniels, Ron Jeremy, and the number 69. Hoss reckons we should a take this stuff a bit less seriously, and be happy with making 'quite nice things that entertai people for a wee while' as can be seen from his other two sites www.katakanaguestbook.co

Manuel Tan

Manuel Tan started college studying Engineering but graduated from the University at Buffalo with a degree in Communication Design. At his present day job at Rare Medium, Inc., Manny designs for clients like Tutopia, Apollo Management, The New York Times, Knoll and a variety of financial services institutions. In his spare time, Manny updates his personal site at uncontrol.com, an online space for him to create interface and behavioral experiments. His site has been linked to countless "site of the day/week/month/year" webzines like k10k, surfstation, and more recently, Macromedia's shocked site of the day. Manny was nominated for best interactivity at the NYC Flash Film Festival, created a Flash exhibition for the OFFF.org in Barcelona and exhibited work at the Art Directors Club New York. Manny, age 25, currently resides in Queens, New York, building Japanimation models. He also likes mountain biking and bidding on Post-Modern furniture from Ebay.

Amit Pitaru

A Flash artist and musician, Amit combines the two crafts through his creative outlet: pitaru.com .Beyond producing/performing music and freelancing as a Flash designer, Amit is a faculty member at the Pratt Institute, teaching for the CGIM Academic Graduate Program, and also delivers workshops for such companies as Miramax, Sony, and MTV. Amit recently completed a collaborative work with James Paterson (presstube.com) for the CODEX.SERIES.3 project, and is currently planning his first gallery exhibition. He currently lives in NY with his wife Makiko, and is expanding his work into the realm of software design and physical computing.

Ross Mawdsley

Ross Mawdsley is a graphic artist/multimedia producer living and working in Liverpool. By day he works for IKDA, designing and producing web sites for a variety of clients from around the world, and by night he designs Simian, an experimental Flash web site which deals with the darker side of life. He describes his style of work as "the offspring of Jackson Pollock meets Stanley Kubrick".

Erik Natzke

When it comes to challenges, Erik will take on anything. He enjoys giving form to intangible ideas. A natural aesthetic and knowledge of programming give him an edge when it comes to creating work. His play site natzke.com allows him to constantly challenge himself. Erik also enjoys passing on his knowledge so others may begin to explore. Erik's work isn't all play either. In August of 2000, he started Fourm Design Studio with three classmates from the Milwaukee Institute of Art and Design. His partners are Craig from miniml.com, JD from Infourm.com, and Ty from soundofdesign.com. The studio is located in Milwaukee, WI.

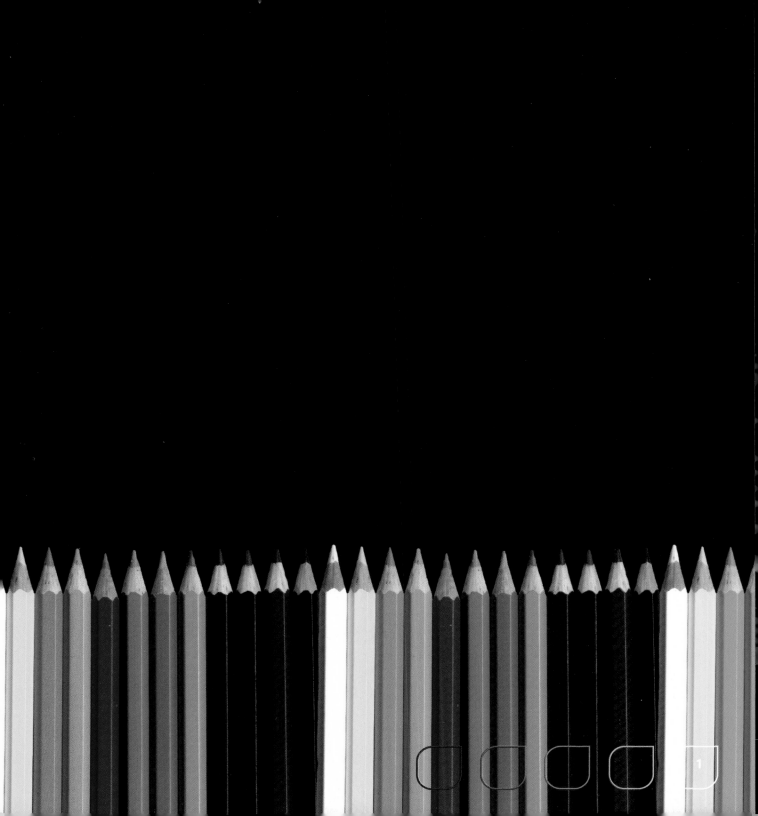

Pencils

When people ask what I do in my work, there are many answers I can give. There are mundane sounding activities like sitting in meetings, typing code, writing e-mail, reading documentation, and reviewing lists of bugs. Those are all pieces of what I do, but I actually like to think I do something a bit more romantic. I build pencils.

Your first reaction might be to say that a complex piece of software, created by a large team of people and containing hundreds of thousands of lines of code is nothing like a pencil but I do aspire to create pencils. A pencil is a simple tool that many people use to communicate to express ideas and their creativity. It's a tool that provides the basic capability for making marks on paper but it doesn't enforce a policy for making those marks. A pencil can be used to create a precise engineering drawing, a freeform sketch, a love letter or a child's story. A pencil *does* impose constraints: it only supports a single color, it draws lines very well, and it requires a bit of creativity to fill in large areas of color. Despite those constraints, a pencil can be used to create an image that represents any idea. We work hard to capture the spirit of the pencil in Flash. We build a tool that gives people freedom to express their ideas and provides constraints to focus their creativity. To me, the most interesting computer software is about communication. Effective communication is one of the biggest needs and challenges of people all over the world. We see this in the importance of communications tools such as language, writing, paper, television, telephones, and e-mail. A pencil is a communications tool. It's a very good tool for capturing ideas, information and emotion on paper. Flash is a bit like that. Flash helps designers capture ideas, information and emotion on a computer screen.

Creation is an act of communication. It's capturing an idea in a concrete form. When I was a child, I loved to build things with Lego. The square blocks imposed tremendous constraints with their limited shapes and numbers, but they also provided tremendous freedom because you got results quickly and you could keep changing and rebuilding until you captured the idea that you wanted. As I grew older, I dreamed of becoming an architect, thinking that building would be a great way to capture ideas and communicate. Buildings are an expression of the way that people live. It's a powerful idea. I quickly learned that although I could use my drafting board and pencil to capture these ideas, I didn't get much opportunity beyond building a shed and garage to see if these ideas would work. I understood that even when I grew into adulthood buildings are expensive and I would only get to create a few. I discovered that with computers and software an individual teenager could start with an idea, write the code, and refine it until it worked. (As it turns out commercial software is big and expensive and I only get to build a few products.) I find it wonderful that Flash has been so successful at providing a tool for individuals to start with an idea, execute and deliver that idea to millions of computer screens all over the world in a few days or weeks. That is a powerful act of communication.

When Robert Tatsumi, Charlie Jackson, Michelle Welsh and I started building SmartSketch, a drawing program that provided the foundation for Flash, our vision was to make drawing on a computer as easy as drawing on paper. It was 1993 and we wanted to take advantage of a new revolution in computer technology: the Pen Computer. I felt that the ability to draw directly on a computer screen with a pen would enable us to create a new user interface for drawing that captured the freedom of drawing on paper while providing the power of the computer for precision, editing and duplication. We wanted to build a smart pencil in software. We built a good technology, but Pen Computers failed in the marketplace. You still see the technology created for SmartSketch in Flash's drawing tools today. It's the reason that Flash was the first vector

rawing tool with an eraser. After all, what good is a pencil that you can't erase?

ur challenge was to let people capture drawings on a omputer screen that they would eventually print on aper. When the Internet started to gain visibility in 1995, 'e realized that a new medium might appear. People ould easily distribute information to be displayed on a omputer screen. We did our best to think about how a omputer screen is a different medium than paper. There 'e obvious things. Computer screens have much lower esolution than paper, so we needed anti-aliasing to make nes smooth. Color on a monitor is free, so we added ood gradients. It's a dynamic medium, so we included nimation and interactivity. Modems are slow, so we ocused on building small files and a small player. These 'e some of the ideas that we tried to capture in Flash1 nce we had that foundation in place, we had a chance to sten to the Flash community and evolve with it. In ash 2, we added sound and better support for images nd photographs. In Flash 3, we added better interactivity vith movie clips. In Flash 4, we added basic ActionScript nd the ability to send data to and from web servers. With lash 5, we took ActionScript to a new level and provided etter tools for talking to servers.

o me, the progression is clear. Flash is evolving from a mple technology for drawing in black and white to a latform that brings drawings, color, images, motion, ound and behavior to the computer screen. With each ersion the Flash team, Macromedia and the Flash ommunity gain a better understanding of the computer nd of the Internet as a communications medium. As reat as the things that have been created with Flash are, here are more steps to come in the evolution of Flash as medium. With Flash 5, ActionScript and XML Sockets, ve're beginning to move beyond thinking of the Internet

as just a way to distribute content and realize that it's a way to build and deliver content and applications that have behavior and talk to computers across the network I am looking forward to participating as that progression continues over the next few years. We're all part of the birth of a new medium and it's still evolving.

When we released Flash 1, I understood and tried to understand that there are people who use a software package, and that listening to and understanding the needs of those users is important. When I first came to Macromedia, I heard people talk about how important the community of Director users is to the success of Macromedia Director but I didn't really understand that concept. As I've watched the community of Flash developers grow, I now understand the power of a community of people who support each other and become part of Flash's success in the process. The richness of the Flash community amazes me. Individual Flash developers, small Flash development companies, Flash community web sites, books written about Flash, classes taught about Flash, and people who enjoy Flash content are all part of the Flash community. These elements of the community are just as important to Flash's success as the team at Macromedia building the Flash code.

The best part of being part of the Flash community i seeing how people use it and how designers have grown with Flash as a medium. It's very easy to use a pencil fo the first time, but the real art of a pencil lies in the techniques for using it. Do you write in block letters o cursive? Do you sketch free form or with a ruler and a drafting table? The magic of a pencil is in the skill of the people who use it, and in the power of the ideas the express. So learn as I have from the New Masters of Flash Learn from their techniques, their ideas, their passion and their inspiration.

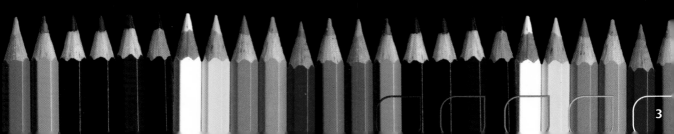

An incredible number of people are all working away at a furious pace in an ever-increasing number of places all round the world. Everybody is looking at each other's work and influencing each other and although when somebody comes up with a brilliant new technique or piece of technology, they are given credit for it, at the same time new ideas get appropriated, adapted and used to produce other new things. And all this is happening at a breathtaking pace. That's just how the Web is at the moment. It's an exciting high-speed environment that nobody has seen before. But at the same time it's an ephemeral world with some aspects that we just have to accept.

A designer friend of mine once commented that when he produces something he wants it to make an impact as fresh and new, and he has a keen hope that it will continue to be appreciated for a long time. Anybody who tries to express themselves or produce anything creative resumably has much the same hopes. But the relentless pace of the Web doesn't leave room for such leisured aspirations. He may have spent a lot of time and a lot of effort developing his own new technique or a unique style of expression, but the moment he has uploaded his ideas into the server they are out there to be mercilessly consumed. The all-important originality, which in his own small way he has produced with a lot of thought, is then cannibalized down to the bone in hardly any time at all. Before his very eyes it is washed away into a sea of anonymity. And the speed at which that happens is just breathtaking. But, he laments, if that's how the Web works, can he really create anything inspiringly new, something which can leave a lasting impression? Surely it's impossible....

Anybody with a web site, even the most meek and humble of individuals, has an equal opportunity with everybody else to express themselves and fill PC screens in all four corners of the globe with their own messages. And that a wonderful thing about the Web. But before we get carried away with the wonder of it all, picture my friend drifting forlornly on what has depressingly turned from world of expression into a sea of high-speed consumption. I suspect that everybody has felt such feelings, which can almost make us give up.

However, even though I half agreed with him, I could still reply with conviction "No, that's not how it is". And the reason I was able to do so is simple. When he referred to "something inspiringly new, which can leave a lasting impression", I recognized that I've seen that sort of thing a number of times on the Web. I've been astounded, and it really has left a lasting impression.

When I think back to a number of sites that I've found beautiful and which have left a really lasting impression, I realize that they've all had something in common. A distinctive style alone isn't enough to gain my respect, and I'm not impressed by sophisticated techniques in themselves. No, with me what *does* leave a deep and lasting impression is what lies beneath the surface. It's the interest to be found, the freshness, the aesthetics of the approach or the concept itself. And at a deeper level still there's the passion.

The design techniques and styles found on the Web have been advancing, have been developing at the speed we've now become used to, and we can assume that they will continue to do so for some time to come. Anybody who produces anything for the Web is destined to continue to follow the trends and keep up with them. If we view the situation from the outside it can seem like nothing more than an endless and pointless race to keep up. However

To: friendsofed

from YUGO

Introduction:

それぞれが互いに評価し合い、影響し合いながら切磋琢磨し、誰かの編み出した素晴らしい技術や手法に感嘆しながらもそれを貪欲に取り込み、応用し、また新しい何かを生み出していく。そういった行為が世界中の数え切れない人々によって、信じられないようなスピードで延々と展開している。それが今現在、私たちが置かれている Web の世界である。それはいまだかつて誰も体験しなかったエキサイティングな連環的世界であるが、同時に、ある種の諦めを伴う刹那的世界でもある。

自分の創ったものが人々にとって新鮮であって欲しい、そして願わくば出来るだけ長い時間の中で評価され続けていたい。これは、何かを創り、表現しようとしている人々にとっては、とても自然で率直な想いであろう。しかしながら、Web の圧倒的な速度は、そんなのどかな淡い期待など一顧だにしてくれない。長い期間と労力を費やしてようやく独自に編み出した新しいテクニックやユニークな表現スタイルは、それがサーバにアップロードされた瞬間から、圧倒的な消費の場に投げ出されることになる。ささやかながらも思い入れをもって育んできた自分の大切なオリジナリティは、あっと言う間に骨の髄までしゃぶり尽くされ、見る見るうちに匿名性の海の中に溶かし切られてしまう。それはもう見事としか言いようが無いスピードで。果たして自分は、こんな状況の中で、新しい感動を与え、何か人の心に残るようなものを創ることができるのだろうか？　いや、おそらく無理だろう‥‥。

これは、ある友人のデザイナーが私に漏らした言葉である。どんなにちっぽけな個人でも、自分のサイトさえ持てば、みな平等に世界各地の PC スクリーンを自分の表現やメッセージで占有することができる。web はそのような素晴らしい世界だ。しかし、そのような謳い文句を信じ込んでいざ飛び込んでみると、そこには現実世界よりさらに絶望的に高速化された消費の海の中でただただ彷徨う自分の姿があるだけであった‥‥。そんな諦めに近い気持ちは誰しも感じたことはあるのではないだろうか。

しかしながら、僕はそんな友人の気持ちに半分くらいは共感しつつも、彼に「そんなことは全く無いよ。」と当たり前のように答えることが出来る。理由は単純明快だ。なぜなら、彼の言っている「新しい感動を与え、そして心に残っていく何か」に僕は WEB の中で何度も遭遇し、驚き、そしてそれらを実際に心の中に残しているからだ。

そういった、幾つかの「ずっと心に残る美しいサイト」といったものを自分の中であれこれ思い返してみると、其処にある種の共通点が存在していたことに気付く。
今まで単なる見栄えのスタイルだけに感動してきたわけでは無かったし、高度な表現テクニックだけに驚いてきたわけではなかった。そうではなく、自分の心に深い印象を落としてきたのは、表面的な表れの奥にある、ある一貫した「アプローチ」や「コンセプト」の面白さ、新しさ、美しさ、それ自体であった。そしてそのさらに背後にある、「情熱」と呼ぶほかに無いような代物、なのであった。

web にまつわる表現技術やスタイルはこれまで常にあるスピードで進化、発展してきており、これからもその流れはしばらく続いていくことだろう。web の世界で何かを作る人々は、この流れをずっと追いかけ、それと付き合い続ける運命にある。全体を俯瞰すると、ただ延々と不毛な追い掛けレースをしているだけように見える。しかしながら、こういった流れに巻き込まれながらも、他とは明らかに区別される新鮮な印象を残せている仕事というものは必ず

5

there are some people who, even though they are swept along in this stream of events, nevertheless come up with work which leaves a fresh impression and clearly stands out. If we look at their work closely what comes through is a very individual creative approach and worldview. They also fuse the latest techniques into unique forms, and both the content and what meets the eye on the surface are highly rewarding.

This book New Masters of Flash The 2002 Annual is firstly intended to explain Flash, which is a powerful tool for personal expression. It's probably not necessary to describe Flash here from first principles. Flash is simply an authoring environment that came along and dramatically simplified web animation and interfaces which had previously required various complex and strange techniques.

Although it was initially an easy-to-use animation tool, Flash too gradually acquired a greater level of sophistication and a fully-fledged scripting environment, and became more compatible with the web environment, so that the range of expression that Flash allows was drastically increased.

However on the downside, the authoring environment, which had initially been laughably simple, gradually became more and more complex and required a degree of familiarity and training. This isn't the place to go into the rights and wrongs of that, but what can't be denied is that it brought about a situation where many designers and creative people started channeling all their energy into trying to use the available functions to the fullest. A pointless race just to keep up had started in this arena too.

Fortunately, however, just like everywhere else, there were still people striving to create work that left a lasting impression. This book contains pieces written by fifteen authors who assimilated the best elements of such work. These authors use Flash with complete freedom. They have a deep knowledge of a very large number of techniques, and are keen to learn more. They also have an extremely polished style of expression. However, this isn't the most important thing. What distinguishes their work from others is not any superficial technique or style but the beauty of their individual concepts and design approaches which run consistently beneath the surface. It's also the passion that translates their concepts and design approaches into beautiful inspired forms, while at the same time forming the basis of their techniques and styles.

And that's where the second, no the *real* aim of this book lies. While you're finding out more about the techniques that these experts use, the greatest benefits will come if the book succeeds in giving you an insight into the way they think and what they are influenced by as they produce their very different creations. And they could hardly have any better reward than if that feeds back into your own future work.

If you do get inspired by any of the authors in this book and manage to come up with something new, you could try mailing that particular author directly. The author might be able to give you feedback and advice. There again, the author might actually be inspired by what you have done. It's through precisely this sort of exciting interchange of ideas that the Web will continue to flourish.

あり、それらをつぶさに観察してみると、そこに見えるのは、その作者独自のアプローチや世界観であり、さらにそれらが最新の技術とユニークな形で融合し、表面的な表れとその内容を、より豊かにしている姿なのである。

この本「NewMasterOfFlash2」は第一に、Flashという表現技術に関する解説本である。Flashについてはここで改めて説明するまでも無いだろう。これまで様々な複雑怪奇なテクニックを駆使してやっとこさ実現していたWEBアニメーションやインターフェースを、呆れるほど簡単に編集できるようにしてしまったオーサリング環境、それがFlashである。

当初はとても簡単便利なアニメーションツールだったFlashも時を経るごとに次第に高度化し、スクリプティング環境を充実させ、ネット環境との親和性を増していくことで、Flashで可能な表現範囲は格段に広がった。

しかしながら、その一方で、当初は笑ってしまうぐらいシンプルなものであったオーサリング環境は次第に複雑化し、それなりの知識と習練を必要とするものとなってしまった。その是非は特にここでは問わないが、多くのデザイナー、クリエイターが、その機能を単に使いきることで精一杯になってしまう状況をもたらしてしまったことは否めないだろう。不毛な追っ掛けレースは、ここでも行われているのだ。

しかし、幸いなことに、このような状況の中でも、心に残る仕事を常に続けている人達はやはり相変わらず存在してくれている。そして、そういった人達の中から最良の部分をピックアップしたのが、この本に参加している20名弱の著者たちなのである。

彼らはFlashというツールを完全に自由自在に使いこなす。非常に多くのテクニックについて深く知っているし、その習得には非常に貪欲だ。そしてさらにその表現のスタイルも非常に洗練されている。しかしながら、そんなことは実は大して重要なことではない。彼らの仕事を他から区別するものは、そういった表面的なテクニックやスタイルではなく、その奥に一貫して流れる、彼ら独自のコンセプト、アプローチの美しさなのである。そしてそれらを様々なテクニックとスタイルを駆使しながら独自の美しい形へ昇華していくまでの、情熱それ自体なのである。

この本の第二の、いや、本当の狙いはここにある。彼らの持つテクニックについて学ぶのと同時に、彼らが、一体どんなことを考え、どんなものに影響されながら、何を、どのように創っているのか、そういった彼らの思いを、是非感じとって欲しい。そしてそれが今後、あなたが作ることになる何かの為の糧となれば、彼らにとってこれ以上のことは無いだろう。

もしこの本の中の誰かに刺激されて、あなたが新しい何かを作ったとしたら、是非一度、彼に直接メールしてみて見せてみたらどうだろうか。色々な感想やアドバイスが聞けるかもしれない。あるいは彼自身が逆にあなたから刺激を受けてしまうかもしれない。そんな風にそれぞれが作用しあいながら互いに発展していくのだ。WEBはそんなエキサイティングな連環的世界なのだ。

YUGO
MONO*crafts
http://yugop.com/

"Soon we'll see an absolutely incredible paradigm, where art will become truly interactive."

Vas Sloutchevsky
www.firstbornmultimedia.com

To most people the cursor is just a functional accessory – a means of getting from A to B. But in Flash the cursor takes on a new meaning. It is a very sharp, sometimes deadly object. You can use it as a sword, scalpel, or simply to smear some butter. You can also conceal it to secretly poke holes in people's minds, causing them to step back, disoriented and amazed. Let's face it, that's all we've got. The cursor connects us with the computer; it lets us explore and interface with the machine world in a human intuitive way. So let's pretend that little arrow is the most powerful thing in the universe.

© Vas Sloutchevsky, 1993

This chapter isn't going to become an Ode to Cursor. We'll return to the cursor later, in the tutorial, but before we do, let me roll back in time and remember what originally made me a graphic designer and, subsequently, a cursor-obsessed Flash designer.

When I studied graphic design at college, I had a very specific idea about what I wanted to do in the future. I loved logos and corporate identity. Typography was my other obsession. I was also pretty good at illustration, for which I guess I can thank my mother, a children's book illustrator, and my father, a college professor of design. (I even helped my mother a little on one of her books when she wasn't meeting her deadline - I had to imitate her style so that the editors wouldn't notice.) There was no doubt in my mind that my career was going to be associated with print. Nothing could prepare me for what happened next.

What happened? I bought a computer and discovered the Internet. With my traditional print background I never considered myself to be technically inclined, but all of a sudden, I discovered an absolute fascination with bytes and pixels. And slowly I started living within that 640x480 space (which has since become 1600x1200).

Now, when I think about it, my intimate relationship with the pixel began long before I bought my computer. In my drawings I was always subconsciously trying to break their fabric into the smallest possible elements. Then I was obsessively building my drawings out of those little bricks. This gave my illustrations a great amount of detail...

But, back to the Internet, where I was finding my way through the clutter of information. At first I liked it. What an incredible abundance of styles! It seemed like every site was trying to win your attention by organizing their content in their own, unique way. But, little by little, I came to realize that their differences were becoming nominal, as some invisible and powerful Web Standard was emerging. This was largely dictated by the limitations (and convenience) of HTML – ruler of the Internet for many years. Rigid, table-based graphic design was shaping the minds of designers around the world. The clutter of commercial text-based 'high-traffic' sites was starting to irritate me more and more. To this day, the Web behemoths like Yahoo, AltaVista and Ebay have no plans of abandoning their 'well-tested' formats.

Today I can safely say that Flash has 'undone' all the damage the HTML standard did to my brain. It's interesting to observe how different designers and artists turn to Flash, each bringing something new to it. Video artists try to exploit its cinematic abilities, basically creating interactive AfterEffects movies; sound designers and musicians team up with ActionScript gurus to create incredible interactive music; traditional animators find it very compelling to use Flash to deliver their vector-based cartoons to millions; programmers and scientists build intricate interactive toys and 3D models... And all this is possible with the same software! I think we're now seeing the first crop of traditional artists catching up with Flash. Sites like www.presstube.com and www.cmart.design.ru are only the beginning. Soon we'll see an absolutely incredible paradigm, where art will become truly interactive. We'll see the DaVincis and Michelangelos of today turning to Flash. What's more important is that the Internet connects all of us together, and we all influence each other in some way.

So, what do identity designers (like me) do with Flash? When I created the first version of firstbornmultimedia.com (way back in Flash 2!) it was as interactive as it could be at that time but I was then mostly treating Flash as an animation tool. For firstborn's second site, which I simply called *Square*, the square interface was comprised of four smaller squares, each containing a symbol. Each symbol becomes an animation when the user rolls over and fills up the whole interface when they click. Every section is color-coded with four bright colors, making it very easy to navigate the site. In essence, it's an interactive identity system, very simple and very unpretentious. But for me, it was a very important exercise leading me to new ideas in interface design.

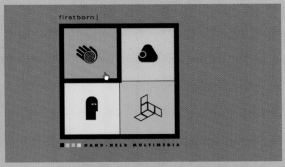

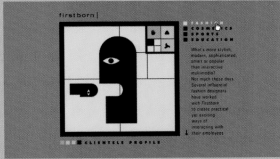

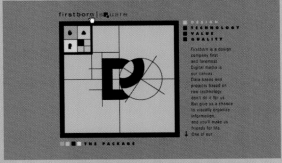

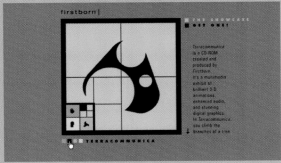

www.firstbornmultimedia.com/popup.asp?swfname=015

13

Slide

A major inspiration has to be New York. When I first came to New York I was stunned by the contrast of unparalleled grandeur of its architecture and the coziness of some of its streets, by the noise and quiet, by the lavishness and distress. Now I'm living in Manhattan, in the middle of the Big Melting Pot. The city is on the top of my list of influences. This is where I suddenly come up with my ideas, whether I'm rollerblading in Central Park, or crossing busy streets near Times Square (where my office is located). Sometimes a beer or two at Rudy's will work better for inspiration than two hours at Guggenheim. When I was working on the *Square* site I was energized by New York. New messages bombarded my eyes and ears from all directions. The city's insane, overcaffeinated pace excited my senses. The visual mess that surrounded me directly (or indirectly) inspired the site's images (whether it's obvious or not). Maybe it was my way out of the chaos of the urban lifestyle. I was subconsciously looking for order and simplicity in my designs.

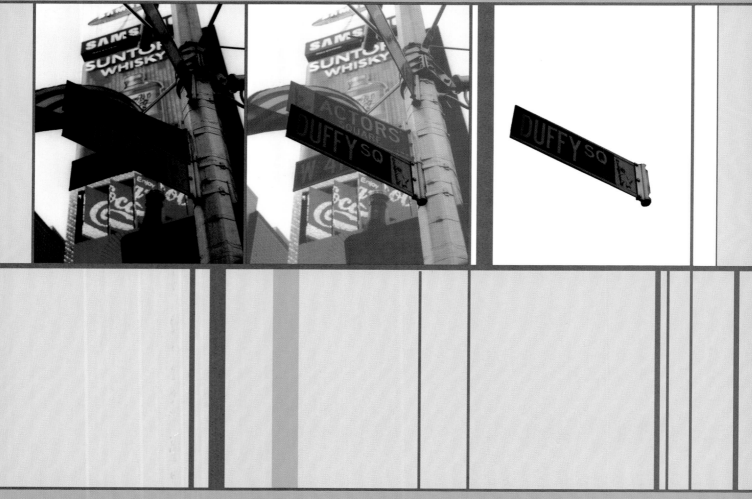

I was beginning to reassess the meaning of design. I was trying to understand my own, intimate definition of 'good design'. With so many currents and movements it's never easy. The *Ray Gun* phase that swept so many web sites and magazines in the 90s failed to impress me, as did the 'techno' look that so many designers are obsessed with today, repeating themselves and each other, implanting abstract 3D shapes and dubious 45-degree angles in their work. These were not the styles for me. Sometimes it takes seeing something that's *not* yours to realize what *is*. I was looking for the way out of the chaos and clutter of the Internet. The 'garbage' look was capitalizing on information overload, looking for the aesthetic in things that the brain isn't capable of processing. It was fun to look at, but it wasn't suitable for my vision of the interface. I turned for help to the timeless legacy of my favorite designers.

My really big influence in graphic design is Neville Brody. He was never afraid to break new ground in design and yet he managed to keep his designs incredibly simple and classy. He was as fascinated with the computer ten years ago as I am with Flash today. He felt like he was on the verge of discovering something important and unprecedented. That fascination propelled his art to mind-boggling heights and keeps him going till this day (you may know him by his expressive box art and splash screens commissioned by Macromedia).

Also my major influences include the apostles of design: El Lissitzky, Massimo Vignelli, Ivan Chermayeff and Milton Glaser. My goal is to always stay fresh like them.

Now I'm a big fan of minimalism in design (and mottos). My motto is: **Hide**. I have to confess that I wasn't always completely true to it (just look at my old illustrations!), but with my interface work I'm trying as much as I can to simplify and distill my work to a concentrate. With commercial clients it's not always easy. That's why it's bliss to have a client that has already adopted this philosophy. I mostly work with fashion design clients, because some of them, like Calvin Klein, have a very strong visual aesthetic built into their corporate culture. They have already designed mountains of beautiful and professional print and TV campaigns. With clients like CK, being graphically minimal is easy. It's kind of expected from you.

© Neville Brody

New Man From Victory Over the Sun (Sieg Uber der Sonne) El Lissitzky
© Philadelphia Museum of Art/CORBIS

But designing an interface is very, very different from designing for print. One has to design an information structure that branches rather than a linear, cover-to-cover piece. The trick is to present it in the most logical way without sacrificing design integrity. Many multimedia interfaces of today still borrow their 'GUI' devices (like pull-down menus, sliders, and buttons) from the operating systems and applications of yesterday. A good designer finds a way to free his mind from visual standards that are offered by software engineers and create something truly unique. (Or, if he's on a tight deadline, he can at least try being elegant.) With interfaces I have to apply the same minimalist principles of print design, yet take advantage of all interactive possibilities. The other challenge, of course, is to save precious 'real estate'. Eventually the revised Mantra for the Minimalist Interactive Designer becomes:

Hide as much as possible but keep it accessible.

Let me explain my theory with a simple example. Let's say you're standing in front of an apple tree. You can't see all the apples at once, but you can definitely see more than one apple at a time. Now, let's say you want to reach for an unusually big apple. It's more than likely that you won't make an error. Your brain registers and compares the size of the apples and almost unmistakably delivers the result to your hand. All this happens instantly and automatically, without you 'thinking' about it. Now imagine, it's dark and you only have a flashlight to search for the giant apple. You have to inspect the apples consecutively, one by one, catching them in the spotlight. Needless to say it's going to take you forever, and it's likely that the apple that you think is the biggest will turn out to be just big. Your brain is cooling down faster than you need, it doesn't give you enough time to remember and compare.

This is the best analogy that I can find for the current state of web design. Many web sites overwhelm us with choices without giving us the whole picture. My ideal interface should be both *simple* and *intuitive* – in other words 'brain-friendly'.

But staying simple isn't always easy. John Singer Sargent, an English painter, once said, "An artist painting a picture should have at his side a man with a club to hit him over the head when the picture is finished." What he meant was: don't cook it for too long or you'll ruin it. The key for every designer is to know when to stop.

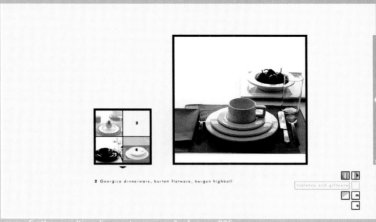

2 Georgica dinnerware, burton flatware, bergen highball

tabletop and giftware

www.firstbornmultimedia.com/popup.asp?swfname=006

Now back to our cursor.

At some point in my Flash career, I came to the conclusion that creating a successful interface usually means the reduction of unnecessary mouse moves. The less obvious your navigation is, the more time the user spends on an irritating search, pointlessly wandering around your otherwise beautiful creation. I've seen quite a lot of intriguing graphical solutions completely spoiled by an overly smart (or overly stupid) nav.

So one day it dawned on me: what if I exploit the user's tendency to chaotically explore the interface by providing content and navigation while they're doing so? While mousing around, the user should actually build their own content. This should happen before they realize that they were tricked into something. The goal is to prevent them from prematurely, and angrily, clicking the Close button. I asked myself: "Can the cursor 'paint' animation, or indeed my whole interface?" "It sure can," was the answer. "I'm gonna harness that little cursor, no matter what."

And then this Flash idea of ideas came to me – convert the cursor's pixel coordinates into frame numbers. Here's my train of thought. Let's say your stage is 400 pixels wide. That means that your x mouse coordinate will always be between 0 and 400. So theoretically, if you build an animation that's 400 frames long, you can issue a Goto command and simply use your x mouse coordinate as a frame number. This should cause the play head to skip to any frame depending on the horizontal position of the mouse.

Back then (a little less than two years ago), I was sure I was the first one to use this idea. I'm not so sure about it now. I remember jealously guarding my secret from anybody who asked me how I did it. Even though the idea was quite simple, it was a little trickier to track the cursor position in Flash 4 than in Flash 5. It involved creating an empty movie clip and dragging it invisibly. The other caveat was creating that infamous two-frame loop to dynamically dump the value into a variable. So the whole recipe wasn't very obvious. I don't know if I'm going to surprise any of you with that idea now, but I'll try to concentrate on the creative aspect of my discovery.

Vas Sloutchevsky

Yigal-Azrouel

One thing I was sure about is that the possibilities are endless. The key is to use your imagination. My brain was pulsating with excitement. Imagine some incredible mechanism where one simple motion causes it to work, stopping when you stop. Any animation can become mouse-controlled. Essentially this principle works like my childhood toy penguin. It had wheels and flapped its wings and shrieked when you dragged it around. You can control so many properties by cursor position: transparency, color, rotation, scale, and sound – you name it! Sure, you can control all those things programmatically, but it's so tedious. Best of all you have control over a frame-based timeline. You can have as many layers in one movie clip, as you want. They can all do different things, but only one single line of code controls it all. Absolute power!

For my first 'machine', I invented a clock-like mechanism, where gears and numbers were moving and interacting with each other, depending on where you drag a horizontal slider. The 'machine' (I dubbed it Retroscope), was useful, as it provided links to our portfolio. Navigation was built around a 'peapod' that displayed different items depending on the slider's position. I styled it as a blueprint schematic, and provided a 'secret level' button that you only discover after viewing the first part of the portfolio. So this is how the idea to create navigation for the Yigal-Azrouel site was born. We have all those beautiful model shots, but how do we show them so that the user is not bored with clicking "Next, Next... ", or by watching a self-running slide show or animation? What if we make that wobbly chaotic cursor do the work? Let the user control the animation! Then I pondered the idea a little bit more. "Hmm, the motion of the cursor is two-dimensional – we have x and y to play with. What if I throw in another layer of complexity, and combine a horizontal animation with a vertical animation, weaving them together?"

In this tutorial I'm going to explain in detail how I achieved the mouse-controlled 'cinematic' effect. This is the first time I'm going to talk about it, though I have been asked numerous times. The Yigal-Azrouel site has become widely popular thanks to the FlashForward Film Festival (where it won in Navigation and Motion Graphics categories), and 'inspiration' sites, like www.linkdup.com. I think it's time to reveal Yigal's secrets.

Slide

For this tutorial we'll recreate the Trends module of the site. It will contain two movie clips – one that responds to the *x* motion of the mouse, and one for the *y* motion. The tutorial essentially covers two things: creating a cinematic animation with masked images and assigning code to a movie clip so that it can be controlled by mouse movement.

You can find the source file for what we'll recreate on the CD that comes with this book. It may be an idea to open yigal-azrouel.fla in a separate window and use it for reference. We can also use this file's Library to drag and drop items into our recreated file. Using the Open as Library option on the File menu we can import the yigal-azrouel.fla Library into our new, blank Flash document.

We'll begin by setting up the movie at 700 by 480 pixels, at 64 frames per second, and with a black background. A high frame rate will ensure that the site will run smoothly (although not too fast) on faster machines.

First, name the default layer graphics. Add the text graphic symbol from the imported Library, at the top of the screen to identify the Trends section. Add the back button in the lower left corner. Then, let's make a mask layer, called, you've guessed it... mask, that will contain a rectangle (704x300). It will become a 'letterbox' for our site.

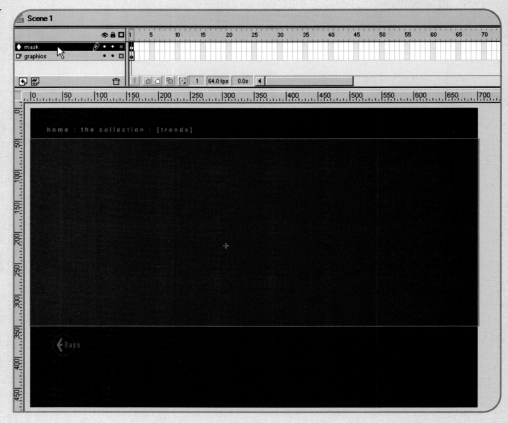

Add a new layer called background, place it under the mask layer and make a background rectangle. This background rectangle needs to be slightly bigger than the rectangle on the mask layer, so that it inherits the exact dimensions of the letterbox mask. The actual dimensions of the background rectangle don't matter, as long as it's larger than the mask.

Next, we'll make the crosshair, consisting of a horizontal and vertical hairline, both of which will follow the cursor position to form a large crosshair cursor. Add a new layer between the background and mask layers and call it crosshairs. Add crosshairs to it by dragging horizontal line and vertical line from the Library.

It's not important where you place them on the stage since they are controlled by code, but I found it convenient to put them outside of the rectangle on the mask layer. I added Contact and Home buttons to make my crosshairs a little more functional.

The crosshairs will move independently from each other. The vertical line will assume the x position of the cursor, and the horizontal one the y position. To add this behavior, click the horizontal line instance and attach this ActionScript:

```
onClipEvent (enterFrame) {
    _y = _root._ymouse;
}
```

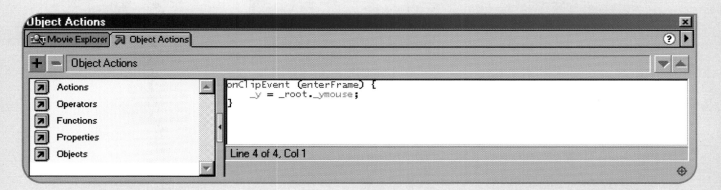

Attach the following line to the instance of vertical line:

```
onClipEvent (enterFrame) {
    _x = _root._xmouse;
}
```

Now we're ready to create the movie clip that will host the horizontal animation. It will contain six images and six masks that we'll animate by motion tweening. The images and masks are graphic symbols. We begin building our horizontal animation by creating a new layer over background (it becomes masked automatically). Call this layer animation x and drag Bitmap 01 from the Library onto the stage.

Make sure the bitmap is the only object selected, select Insert>Convert to Symbol, make the bitmap a graphic symbol and call it image01. Delete this symbol from the stage – we're going to use it shortly in a movie clip.

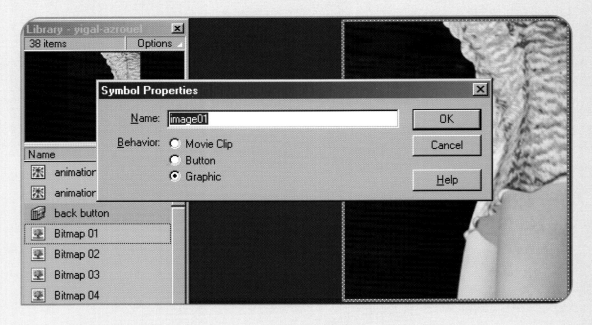

Select Insert>New Symbol, and create a movie clip called animation_x. Make a new layer within animation_x, call it code, and on the very first frame add a Stop action. This is very important because it will ensure that the movie clip doesn't play by itself, and lets us add some mouse-driven actions to it.

I always reserve the uppermost layer in movie clips and the main timeline for code, since it's always easier to access (no need to scroll), and it's also more convenient to have all the actions in one place. By the way, Flash 5 allows you to use another advanced technique to accumulate all the code in one place. You can create an empty controller clip that, on `enterFrame`, addresses all the movie clips in the movie based on their current frame. Thus, in our example, you can tell animation_x to stop if its current frame equals 1. However, to keep things clearer, we'll use frame actions.

Make animation_x 700 frames long by using Insert Frame at frame 700 (in this example, in order to keep it simple, we'll 'trade' one pixel your mouse moves for one frame). Now we'll use these 700 frames to create a tweened animation where the image will move from right to left, gaining full opacity towards the middle of the tween, and reducing alpha to 5% at both ends.

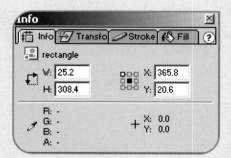

Make a mask layer, named mask, under the code layer, and place the symbol rectangle (from the imported Library) onto the mask layer. This symbol should, at this point, fill the whole layer. Adjust the values within the Info panel so that they match what you see here.

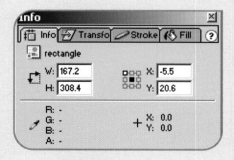

Make a keyframe at frame 61, and put the following size, and position, in the Info panel.

23

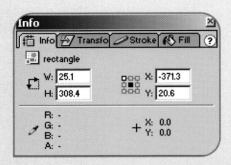

We now need to create a motion tween between frames 1 and 61. Next, create a keyframe at frame 129, and a blank keyframe at frame 130 (we want this mask to end at frame 129). Add another motion tween between frames 61 and 129, and set the Info panel properties of frame 129 like this:

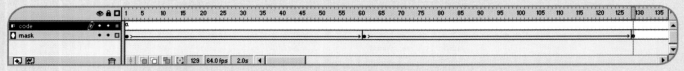

This clip now has the mask starting narrow on the right, widening as it gets to the middle, and then narrowing again as it gets to the left of the stage.

We'll now add a layer below the mask, called image 01. Make a keyframe at frame 12 of this layer and drag the symbol image01 from the Library onto the stage. We're going to have this image moving across the stage, from right to left, gaining full opacity in the middle, but having alpha set to 5% at both ends. This should create a great effect when combined with the mask we've just made. Position image01 on frame 12 with the coordinates x = 103.0, y = 0. Reduce the symbol's alpha to 5%. Next, make a keyframe at frame 61, and change the alpha of image01 at this frame to 100%. Move image01 to x = 0.5, y = 0, and make a motion tween between the two frames.

We want the image to end up on the left side of the stage, so we'll make another keyframe at frame 107. We need to reduce the alpha here to 5%, and move the image to x = -103.5, y = 0. Then create a motion tween between frames 61 and 107. We want this part of the movie clip to end at frame 107, so create a blank keyframe at frame 108.

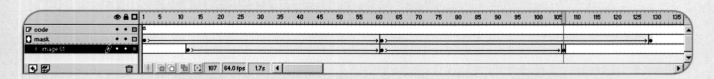

Drag the play head back and forth to test your animation, tweaking it until you're happy with it. Once you're done with the mask and satisfied with the results, you can add outlines that will define the edge of your mask. Outlines are optional; I use them because, in combination with the crosshair (which uses the same line style but moves in the opposite direction), they create an interesting rhythmic effect. To add outlines, simply copy all the frames of the mask layer and paste them in a new layer above it. Change the status of this new layer from mask to normal, and name it outline. Click on the first frame of outline, then click the Duplicate Symbol button in the Instance panel, and name the new symbol rectangle outline.

Double-click on it. Use the Rectangle tool to add an outline to the rectangle (hairline, light gray, 40% alpha), and remove the fill.

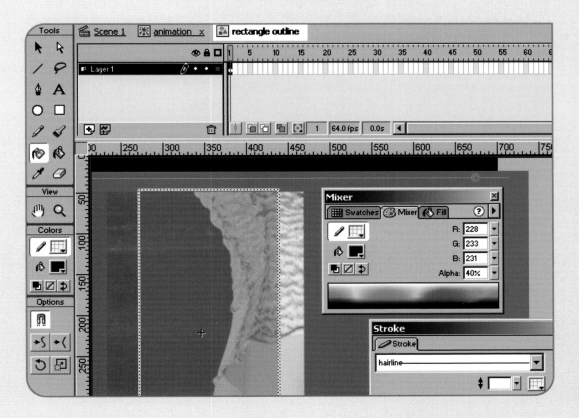

Next, we'll go back to animation_x. We need the symbols on the keyframes at frames 61 and 129 of the outline layer to be rectangle outline as well, so change these instances.

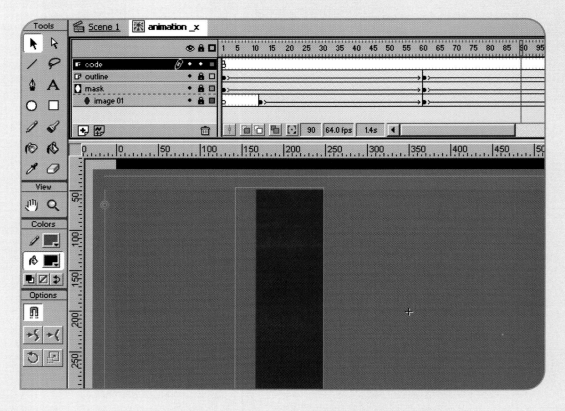

Repeat the same techniques that we've applied with image01 to image02, image03, and so on, up to image06. Scatter these mini-animations at different points along the timeline. To do this, just choose different keyframes for the start, midpoint, and end of each animation. Don't make your animations exactly the same – use your imagination. Some irregularity will add character to the final animation. It's still important, though, to make sure to keep all the animations within the 700-frame timeline. You should end up with six image layers, six masks, and six outlines.

To simplify things you can combine some of the layers. You can do this on layers where animations won't overlap due to their position on the timeline. Make sure you only combine like with like (images with images, masks with masks, outlines with outlines).

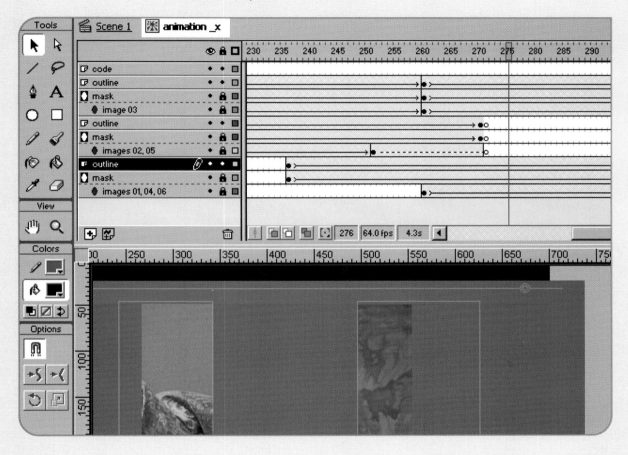

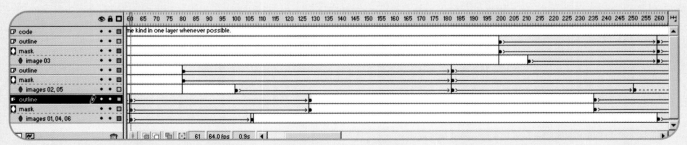

We now need to go back to the main scene and put animation_x on frame 1 of the animation x layer. I've placed it just to the right of the main scene's mask.

We've now finished making animation_x, so we can go onto animation_y. Make a new layer on the main timeline between animation_x and background, and call it animation_y. Drag bitmap 07 onto the stage from the Library. Select Insert>Convert to Symbol, and make a graphic symbol called image07, and then delete this symbol again. Now choose Insert>New Symbol, select movie clip, and name it animation_y. Add a Stop action to the first frame of the default layer, which we'll again name code, and make the movie clip 300 frames long using Insert Frame at frame 300 (I will explain this number later). We have three graphic symbols for this animation – image07, image08, and image 09. They should move from bottom to top, and the masks move in the same direction, but a little bit faster. We'll use the same techniques that we used in animation_x to achieve this.

This time in each mini-animation, the images and masks move from the bottom of the screen upwards (rather than right to left). I won't take you step-by-step through how to do this, because you already know! It's exactly the same as the technique use in animation_x.

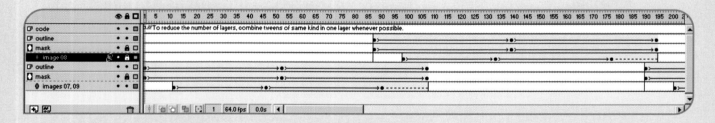

Once you've created animation_y, place it onto frame 1 of the main timeline's animation y layer. I've placed it under the mask area, just so it's out of the way.

Now that we have two independent movie clips, one with horizontal, the other with vertical animations, we can apply all the necessary code. Click on animation_x, and attach the following code to the instance:

```
onClipEvent (enterFrame) {
    gotoAndStop (Math.ceil (_root._xmouse));
}
```

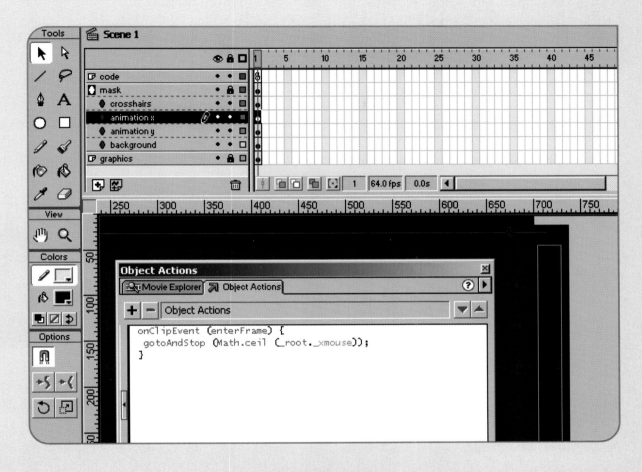

This simple code tells the timeline to react to horizontal mouse movement – one frame for one pixel. The expression has to yield an integer, because it translates into a frame number. Since the `Int` function was deprecated in Flash5, we're using the `Math.ceil` function to round a number to the closest integer. `Math.ceil` is always greater than the current number so it excludes 0, making a better choice than the similar action `Math.round()`, which rounds to the nearest integer irrespective of whether it is higher or lower (thus including zero in the range). A Flash timeline cannot have frame 0.

Slide

Publish your work to a SWF. The horizontal animation works perfectly!

Click on animation_y, and attach this code:

```
on ClipEvent (enterFrame) {
    gotoAndStop (Math.ceil (_root._ymouse) -50);
}
```

Remember, the length of the animation_y is 300 frames. Even though the vertical dimension of the site is 480 pixels, our horizontal animation is offset from the top edge by 50 pixels. The vertical dimension of the 'letterbox' is 300 pixels. So, subtracting 50 from a current mouse position will yield a correct frame number. The remaining 130 pixels don't produce any animation, so we can cut off the clip's duration at 300 frames.

Test your work. We now have both *x* and *y* motion generating a dazzling cinematic effect!

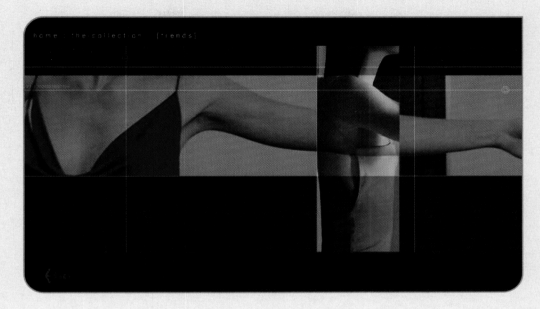

You can also use this method with fewer frames. For instance, the following expression will cause the animation to move one frame for every four pixels your cursor travels:

```
onClipEvent (enterFrame) {
    gotoAndStop (Math.ceil (_root._xmouse)/4);
}
```

The higher the number, the jerkier the motion is. I've learned from my experience that you can achieve pretty smooth motion dividing xmouse by 2. This will save you half the frames on the timeline, subsequently cutting down the size of your SWF.

In conclusion, I should say that despite its simplicity this method could yield some unusually complex results. For example, you could enhance this basic formula by adding complex math. Or mouse-controlled movie clips that can contain other movie clips that also react to the mouse. I hope that this example will jump-start your creativity.

Headnotes

The yigal-azrouel and shameless sites convert *x* and *y* mouse position to frame position in two movie clips.

In Vas's examples, the two movie clips contain a number of time-unrelated photos. By linking the frames timewise, a number of new effects and even narratives can be created;

ROTATION MOVIE

car web site
The cursor's *x* position controls rotation of the

Cursor x-position →

main car image allowing the potential buyer to see exactly what the bodywork looks like. The movie clip seen here was created by moving a videoCam around the car (or rather, car-shaped pencil sharpener).

Different y-movieclip "filmreels" are selected via hotspots in the map. rolling over WARSAWA would bring up the film reel I took whilst in Warsaw.

vroom

vroom!!

The use of the cursor position to simultaneously show two filmreels visually describing the car in both 3D and in close-up provides an intuitive and transparent method of navigating through motion graphics completely describing this and any other product.

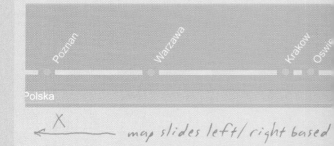

Poznan   Warzawa   Krakow   Oswie

Polska

X

← *map slides left/right based on x-cursor position.*

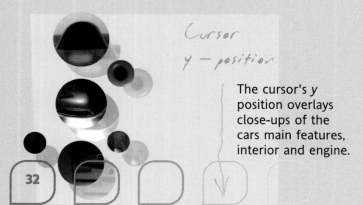

Cursor y-position

↓

The cursor's *y* position overlays close-ups of the cars main features, interior and engine.

travelogue
By using a map for the *x* movie clip, the mouse *x* position now represents distance into a journey. Hotspots on the map (created via transparent buttons) can be used to switch between several y movieclips that show a up-down sliding filmreel for each location.

In this way, the mouse position is now being used to tell a story. The broadband site specified here would illustrate pictures taken by myself during a car journey across Eastern Europe soon after the Berlin wall came down...

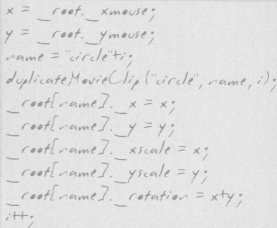

```
x = _root._xmouse;
y = _root._ymouse;
name = "circle"+i;
duplicateMovieClip ("circle", name, i);
_root[name]._x = x;
_root[name]._y = y;
_root[name]._xscale = x;
_root[name]._yscale = y;
_root[name]._rotation = x+y;
i++;
```

Weird vector art Flash toy

instance "circle", hairline stroke

smorgasbord

By applying the *x*, *y* and even *x+y*, *x*y*, or any other combinations of mouse *x,y* position, you can create some weird and wonderful Flash effects, toys, and various other diversions...

The *x* and *y* mouse positions don't neccessarily have to create movement in the *x* and *y* directions... Try making the mouse position do other things, such as varying tint (via the color object), rotation or scaling.

Breathe new life into the ageing side scroller idea by making it a four way scroller, with two streams of content (such as graphics and text) being controlled by the mouse position...

JB — Map must slide in opposite direction to mouse.
—position selects between a number of y-position movieclips

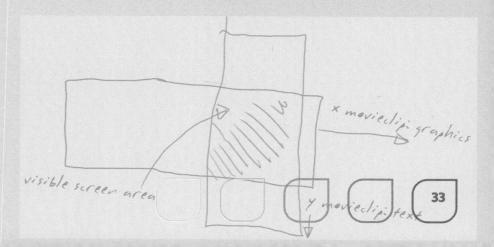

x movieclip: graphics

visible screen area

y movieclip: text

33

"ActionScript is a human language, designed to be written, read, and easily learned by anyone with a creative intent. It provides a bridge between the streaming media capabilities of Flash and the logical dexterity of programming."

Samuel Wan
www.samuelwan.com

Pollen

My first experience with computer graphics occurred during high school, when a casual conversation with an older student introduced me to three simple concepts of graphical programming. These basic notions planted seeds in my mind which lay dormant throughout college – until, that is, I discovered Flash.

One day in the high school library, I was fiddling with a text-based menu written in QBasic. QBasic was an introductory programming language built into every PC until a few years ago, but my QBasic class only covered graphics to the extent of printing text on the monitor. A senior student by the name of Dewey happened to notice the code on my screen as he walked by. Dewey offered to show me a 'cool trick' in QBasic, and he began to explain the concept of pixels and color palettes. In retrospect, I think he saw me stuck in the world of text and decided to pull me out of it. I gave him my seat and watched him type five lines of code into the editor:

```
SCREEN 13
FOR x = 1 TO 63
        PALETTE x, x + (x * 256) + (x * 65536)
        LINE (50 + x, 60)-(50 + x, 110), x
NEXT x
```

The screen went dark, and then it quickly drew a series of parallel lines on the screen, forming a shaded rectangle from black to white. This was the first computer graphic I actually understood from the inside out:

The process of translating an idea from plain text code to visual graphic was stark; the graphic itself was sleek, beyond human even. The smoothness of gradations between darkness and light transcended what I could achieve with a sketchpad. To top it all off, the fact that anyone could generate such a smooth gradient in five lines of code simply blew my mind. I asked Dewey to write down his explanation on a piece of paper, and spent the evening studying his formulas.

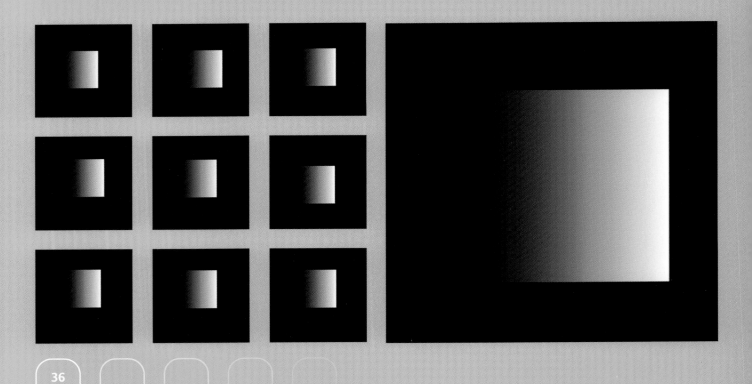

We had two subsequent conversations in the library before Dewey graduated from high school. The second 'cool trick' used simple equations to draw and stretch gradient shapes on the screen. Only several years later did I realize that he'd taught me the basics of vector graphics.

Our third conversation started with a crude version of the gaussian blur algorithm, where the value of one pixel changed in relation to its surrounding pixels, and the lesson ended with a simple fractal. I started combining pixel filters with controlled randomness and gradient shapes, resulting in very textured and unearthly images on screen. Over time, these experiences opened up a whole new world of computer-generated art.

The great thing about having curious friends is that you're never asked why you're doing something. When I showed these computer visuals to my schoolmates, the most frequent question was, "Can I get a copy of that code? I'd like to see what would happen if I wrote it like this." Today, that question is asked every day around Flash communities such as the We're Here forums.

All of my other studies suddenly became relevant: light, sound, and motion from physics; shapes and behaviors from mathematics; color and composition from art; and not least, a certain amount of single-minded obsession from my classical music training!

This synthesis of ideas into visual expression was my creative outlet and a source of inspiration for a long time. The whole experience gave me a fundamental understanding of computer graphics that came in handy several years later. Unfortunately, screen captures from those old projects aren't available because I lost track of all my code after high school. In fact, I pretty much forgot about computer graphics during the last year of high school and throughout most of college.

He wrote f

"You can't let the little pricks generation-gap you," Molly said. Case nodded, absorbed in the patterns of the Sense/Net ice. This was it. This was what he was, who he was, his being. He forgot to eat." - William Gibson, Neuromancer. Publisher: Penguin Putnam, 1984

Around the time I realized that bio-engineering wasn't the right choice of career, the Web started to pick up momentum. Low bandwidth and primitive browsers encouraged autobiographical narratives to emerge as the web's first form of pop-culture. Some of my favorites, such as anthology.net, have disappeared, but sites like fray.com, glassdog.com, and afterdinner.com still exist. Narrative web sites left a deep impression on my view of the web because the story always came first. All other graphical or audio elements were secondary enhancements to the experience. The narrative could be an autobiographical vignette, an urban legend, or a simple diary. Whatever the subject matter, these early sites demonstrated that storytelling can be meaningful when it evokes both a sense of familiarity and discovery for the reader.

My last year of college also happened to coincide with the last days of Flash 3. When I followed the Gabocorp URL from a news magazine article, the discovery of a whole Flash community rekindled the same passion in computer graphics that I'd forgotten four years ago. In that final college year, the first generation of Flash pioneers provided a year's worth of quiet motivation as I slowly climbed back into the digital world. Some of my heroes (a few whom I've since met in person) included Joen Asmussen, Yugo Nakamura, Manuel Clement, David Emberton, Irene Chan, Todd Purgason, Colin Moock, Branden Hall and many others. It was a very intense year of personal research into every aspect of programming and design. However, my focus was entirely technical; I couldn't seem to recapture the creativity of earlier days...

Pollen

I was on my way to a management internship at one of the nation's largest healthcare organizations when I ran into an old friend and fellow violinist/violist. We had played together at gigs and orchestras, so we spent the entire plane ride talking about our respective career choices and her life as a musical artist. If I could define the moment that revived my creativity, it was when my bohemian friend lifted her viola in the central hub of the Midway Airport and fearlessly played passages from Hindemith loud enough to echo down the terminals. Her notes had such refined intensity that bystanders actually paused to listen and applaud.

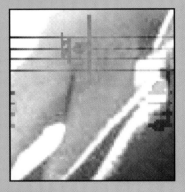

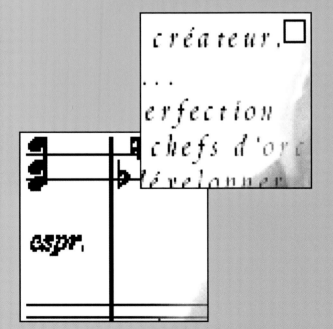

I composed Expression by Proxy to tell the rest of this story, and the Flash narrative consequently earned a nomination at the London Flash Film Festival. In my project, the reader unwraps the story by interacting with text, imagery, and music, but the narrative flow relies entirely on ActionScript to keep the interaction natural and unobtrusive. This kind of programming wouldn't have been possible if I hadn't invested so much time studying the technical aspects of Flash.

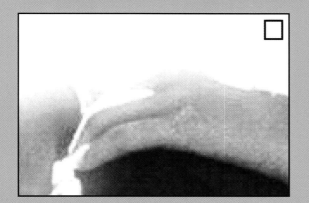

The point I'm making is that opportunities for expression are unexpected because inspiration is unpredictable. However, if you spend the effort to master an instrument – whether it's digital or analog – then you'll be prepared to translate your inspiration into a shared experience at any given moment.

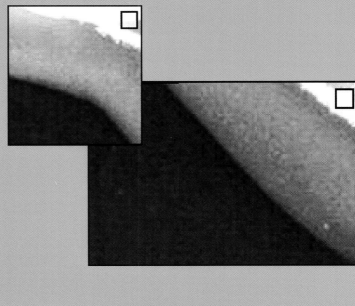

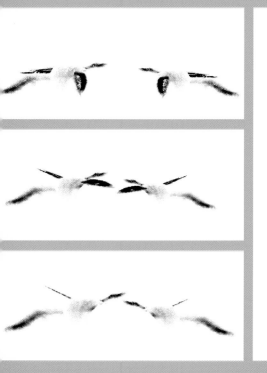

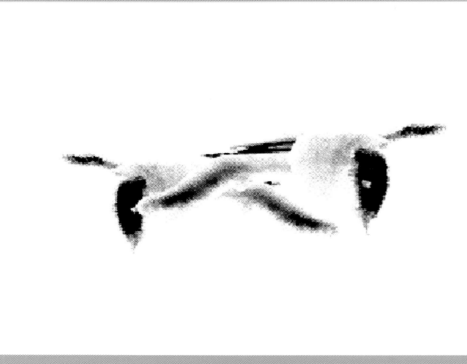

After graduation, I got a message from my friend David Emberton. He was stuck at home in Australia, so he asked me to stand in for him at a web conference in Seattle. I had performed for larger audiences in concert, but this was my first time teaching ActionScript to two thousand professional designers. Fortunately, my co-speaker was Eric Wittman from Macromedia, who kept me cool during the presentation. After we received a standing ovation, my name started appearing next to the word *ActionScript*, which brings us to the question: "Do I consider myself a designer or a programmer?"

Whenever I speak at conferences or participate in online discussions, people often ask me this question. More often than not, I think the people who ask are actually asking themselves which subject they should study next. This question would hardly have been raised in the Flash community a year ago, if not for the fact that Flash 5

features a new object-oriented ActionScript language. Programming wasn't a serious consideration in Flash 4 because its syntax was non-standard compared to other languages, and extremely awkward to use. Only the truly elite (or madly obsessed) such as Yugo Nakamura or Joshua Davis could twist the old ActionScript into performing complex tasks, either through the application of old skool math tricks, or trial-and-error experimentation. Even though interactive programming has been around for a long time, bringing the rich realm of computer science into the limited scripting language of Flash 4 was like trying to play Jimi Hendrix on a ukulele. The introduction of an object-oriented ActionScript really threw open the door between the new world of experimental media and the more mature world of programming. These two worlds have very different cultures and learning curves. As a result, the new range of

Proxy by expression. Balance is difficult,
Its achievement satisfying in itself.
Beyond the pursuit of being the best,
It's best simply to appreciate the experience of being.
The IRONY: I found my true self in this ether,
In the ether, discovered an inverse blueprint for living.
So I walk away to look past the 17" screen.
Without regrets, without expectations,
To appreciate the gift of bittersweetness,
A wonderful flavor of life,
And the gift of you, humanity,
Who stare at these cathode words without seeing.
After two years, I am back where I started,
With a smile on my face.

-2-

possibilities with Flash technology can sometimes overwhelm a designer's creative instinct.

In the first weeks of Flash 5 beta-testing, it became trivial to port algorithms from other languages to the new ActionScript. As soon as that realization hit me, I spent every day and night of that summer re-educating myself on programming concepts instead of celebrating my graduation. The floor around my computer was tiled with printouts from the ActionScript manual, Netscape's JavaScript documentation, and even some of my "Intro to C" homework from freshman engineering.

My experience with the outdated QBasic language also came into play because it was an interpreted language rather than a compiled language. An interpreted programming language is easy for humans to read, but it requires the computer to translate your commands into machine language. Even though you can make changes and instantly visualize your results on screen, the translation process eats up a lot of processing power, causing your instructions to run more slowly than compiled code. Out of necessity, I learned to optimize my code for speed because my old QBasic filters took forever to render on screen. Placing a high priority on optimization applies equally well to ActionScript, which also happens to be an interpreted language. When you publish a Flash 5 movie, your ActionScript commands are compressed into bytecode for size, but the structure of your commands doesn't change at all. Macromedia's Flash plug-in acts like an interpreter between your commands and the machine instructions of the computer. Two layers of processing actually take place, so the fact that the Flash player interprets ActionScript at such high speeds is an awe-inspiring feat of engineering!

I describe interpreted languages in order to point out that ActionScript is not a machine language. ActionScript is a human language, designed to be written, read, and easily learned by anyone with a creative intent. It provides a bridge between the streaming media capabilities of Flash and the logical dexterity of programming.

Think of it in terms of a conversation: you think of an idea, you form the sentences in your mind, and then you verbalize the sentence. The sentence is a chain of words that follow the rules of grammar to say something meaningful. Likewise, ActionScript is also a set of descriptive words [diction] chained together according to the rules of grammar [syntax] in order to express an idea [ActionScript]. In the object-oriented paradigm, nouns are represented as objects, verbs as object methods, and adjectives as object properties. In fact, the term *expression* in computer science refers to a set of commands that follow the rules of the programming language. Therefore, in the hands of a designer, ActionScript can be used as a language of expression.

Like any other language though, Flash 5 ActionScript is easy to learn, but difficult to master. Take the English language for example - people essentially share a common set of words as their vocabulary, but you can combine those words to say anything your imagination can think of. The difference comes from the fact that anyone can learn how to write a simple sentence in English like "See Spot run, run Spot run", but it takes a lot more learning and innovation to write something on the level of Shakespeare. The more words and rules you learn in any programming language, the richer your expressions become; not because you're bound by more rules, but because you've identified more structures that can be built upon later.

Pollen

Sometimes you can have too much structure, but spending the past year as a graduate student has been an eye-opening experience in many ways (including how to manage a double life in industry and academics). At the University of Michigan's School of Information, I've had the good fortune of being introduced to the tip of the iceberg in human-computer interaction research; a glimpse at branches of study in user-centered design, information visualization, social systems, and other fields which preceded the current state of information technology. I've learned to appreciate the significance of user-centered design, and consideration for the social context.

My workflow has evolved with the realization that user-centered design of interfaces can also apply to the user-centered design of ActionScript source code. Whether you're assigning simple commands to a button, or building an XML converter as part of a larger Flash application, it's not enough to crank out something that works. Many commercial projects require a collaborative effort these days, especially for freelancers, so it helps to think beyond the source code at hand, and look at the overall context of a project from the perspective of both colleagues and clients. When I've got to integrate my complex chunk of Flash into the larger framework of something like a server application, I try to avoid potential headaches by keeping in mind the technical and social context of the work. For example, source code is often re-used between portions of a project, and Flash is often integrated with other technologies like Java on the server-side or JavaScript on the client-side. Knowing this, I package Flash movie clips into independent objects as often as possible, so that each movie clip contains a flexible yet complete set of functions. These functions can either be re-used or 'hooked' into external systems by another developer.

Detail of Dandelion Seed Clock
© Chinch Gryniewicz; Ecoscene/CORBIS

Dandelion Seeds
© Robert Pickett/CORBIS

From a social context, source code can also take on the same characteristics as organizational memory. This is especially true within the Flash community and its vast archives of tutorials and forums, where people from all over the world share their knowledge. The discussion of organizational memory is beyond the scope of this chapter, but it's important to remain aware that your Flash source files exist in a world where collaborators may come from another language, another time zone, another background, or a different programming style. So before I send my code out into the real world, I spend a lot of time reviewing the structure to make sure it's flexible enough to adapt to external forces, such as shifting client needs, new project specs, and maybe even future evolutions of Flash.

I began this chapter by demonstrating how text-based code can be interpreted by the computer into visual graphics, to form a picture of what's happening behind the curtain of graphics software. However, the whole purpose of graphics tools such as Freehand or Photoshop is to help designers avoid the need for programming, so we can transfer our ideas directly onto the screen without having our creative flow disrupted by the chore of talking directly to a machine.

When it comes to interactive design, complex interactions between human and computer still require some amount of programming. My favorite strategy for interactive design is to approach programming from an angle that makes the source code transparent to the design process. In other words, don't let programming get in the way of your idea; make your source code as easy to use as possible. The second half of the chapter uses an example of 'pollen seeds' to illustrate fundamental concepts in bringing design and programming together. Hopefully, the ideas will also plant a few seeds in your mind for the future, as the art of interactive design evolves along with technology.

The key to this strategy is a concept called *modular programming*, where each *component*, or *module*, in a system contains all of the necessary code to exist on its own. Modular programming allows you to make changes to one module without affecting all the others. It also allows you to manipulate a module through simple commands without having to mess around with complicated code, and to re-use the modules in later projects.

To demonstrate these concepts, we'll use a simple sketch of dandelions that uses both the timeline-based animation and ActionScript-driven animation. The end result simulates the effect of blowing pollen seeds from one flower tip to another.

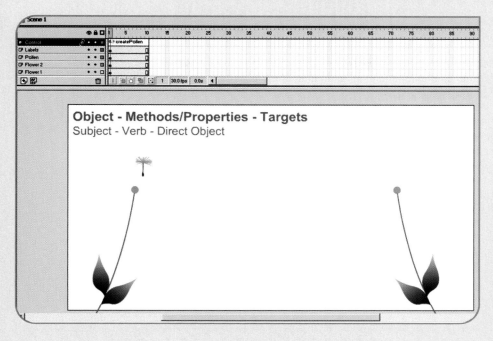

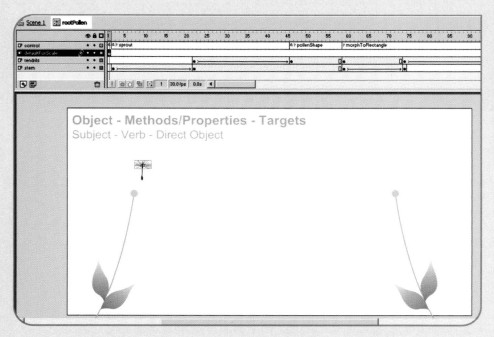

Open the Flash source file named `PollenSeed.fla`, and test the movie. Try brushing your mouse cursor against the dandelion pollen seeds to 'blow' them across the screen. Look at the source file again, and you'll notice that the main timeline contains no motion or shape tweening. The movement of pollen seeds from one flower to another is driven entirely by ActionScript. However, try double-clicking on the pollen and you'll see that the morphing animation between pollen seed and blue petal action uses both motion tweens and shape tweens.

Pollen

Before we discuss the ActionScript code to blow the pollen seeds, let's break down the events in this movie:

1.   Pollen seeds sprout from the flower's stem tip.

2.   The pollen seeds can be triggered to fly from one flower to another.

3.   The pollen seeds can morph into a new shape.

4.   The pollen seeds can re-orient themselves into a new formation.

Here, you can see that the events of the movie can be broken down into regular grammar structures of plain English. The *subject* in each sentence is highlighted in blue, *verbs* are highlighted in red, and *direct objects* are highlighted in green. The subject refers to something in real life; in this case, the subject is a pollen seed. The verb is an action performed by the subject, and the direct object is the target of the action; for example, the other stem tip is the target of a flying pollen seed as it travels across the screen.

I previously mentioned that ActionScript is a language of expression, so our goal is to implement these four sentences with ActionScript code. Unfortunately, ActionScript isn't sophisticated enough to understand simple English sentences, so we have to build some intelligence into a movie clip so that its functions can be triggered by simple commands.

For the next step, we'll start building movie clips that contain ActionScript code that can be triggered by commands. But first, I want to link our pollen effect to *object-oriented programming*.

Object-oriented programming is like modular programming, only much more structured and well-defined. In ActionScript, object-oriented code usually consists of three concepts: objects, methods, and properties.

An *object* is an abstract representation of something in reality. It's a thing, or the grammatical equivalent of a noun. In Flash, movie clips can be considered objects, though not in a strict academic sense. In this demo, the object is a movie clip called rootPollen, which contains animation to morph between a dandelion pollen and translucent petal.

A *method* is the equivalent of a verb. In this demo, the methods are functions defined in the Actions panel of the pollen movie clip. Each function contains ActionScript to do things like flying, swinging, and turning.

A property is the equivalent of an adjective. It describes some aspect of an object, such as the object's position on the screen, or its size and color. Our pollen movie clip contains many properties, such as its *x* and *y* coordinates on screen, its degrees of rotation, and most important of all, a property called *state*. The state of an object describes what the object is currently doing. In our case, the pollen movie clip contains a state called `action`, which describes whether it's in the process of flying, turning, or waiting for the mouse to trigger it.

Let's go back and look at the FLA. Take a look at the basic pollen movie clip, rootPollen, which contains animation to tween from dandelion pollen to a blue petal, and then back to a pollen.

The rootPollen movie clip will be our noun and our main object for this project. It's also the original movie clip from which we'll duplicate many more, to create the effect of having several independent objects moving on the screen at the same time.

Pollen

Next, we have to set up the pollen clips in a circle. In order to arrange them into a formation, we'll need an anchor to provide the center of the circle. The anchor for the first flower on the left is the gray circle movie clip at the tip of the stem. The gray tip on the left has an instance name of stemtip1 and the tip on the right side is given an instance name of stemtip2. They are both instances of the stemtip movie clip, which is a blank movie clip with a small gray circle aligned in the center.

Using stemtip1 as the center of the circle, our next step is to duplicate a certain number of pollen movie clips and position them around stemtip1. You can find the ActionScript to perform these initial tasks by double-clicking on the first keyframe of the Control layer in the main timeline.

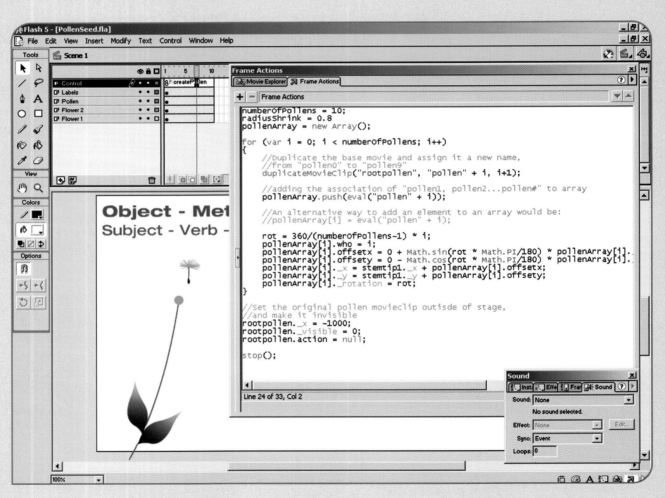

The first line of code in this keyframe declares a variable called `numberOfPollens`. This variable defines how many times we want to duplicate the original pollen movie clip, and we can change this to reflect the number of pollen particles that we want. The `radiusShrink` variable defines how far each duplicated movie clip is positioned from the center of the stemtip1 clip. The array structure `pollenArray` holds a reference to each duplicated movie clip. It's a handy way to execute the same code against several target movie clips by providing an index, and is known as an `associative array`.

Next, we have a `for` loop which executes the code between its curly braces for as many times as the value held within the `numberOfPollens` variable (in this case 10). The code inside the loop duplicates the original movie clip, which has an instance name of rootPollen, and gives the new movie clip a name of pollen1, pollen2, pollen3, and so on until the loop ends. After each duplicate is created, the `pollenArray` is given a new reference to the duplicate. For example, `pollenArray[2] = pollen2`.

Rotating and positioning each duplicate pollen clip requires the use of trigonometry. For the rotation, a circle has 360 degrees, so we divide the circle into 'slices' by dividing 360 by the `numberOfPollens`, and then multiply the angle of a slice by how many times the `for` loop has looped through the code.

The variable `rot` contains the angle of a 'slice' of the 360 degrees in a full circle:

```
rot = 360/(numberOfPollens-1) * i;
```

Near the bottom of the code, we set the rotation of each duplicate pollen clip to the value of `rot`:

```
pollenArray[i]._rotation = rot;
```

Once the loop has finished duplicating movie clips, the original movie clip, rootPollen, is moved off screen, and set to invisible.

```
rootpollen._x = -1000;
rootpollen._visible = 0;
```

Without bogging you down in math (it's not the aim of this chapter!), the rest of the trigonometry algorithm basically uses the angle of one slice (the value of the `rot` variable) to calculate the *x* and *y* position of the newly duplicated movie clip.

Pollen

Now that we've examined the code that produces the pollen, experiment on your own. Try to move the stemtip1 movie clip to another position on the screen before you publish the movie, or even in the SWF, and see what happens to the duplicated pollens.

All of the important ActionScript for object-oriented programming resides in the event handlers of the rootPollen movie clip, so that's where we'll go next. Select the rootPollen movie clip on the stage, and open its Actions panel.

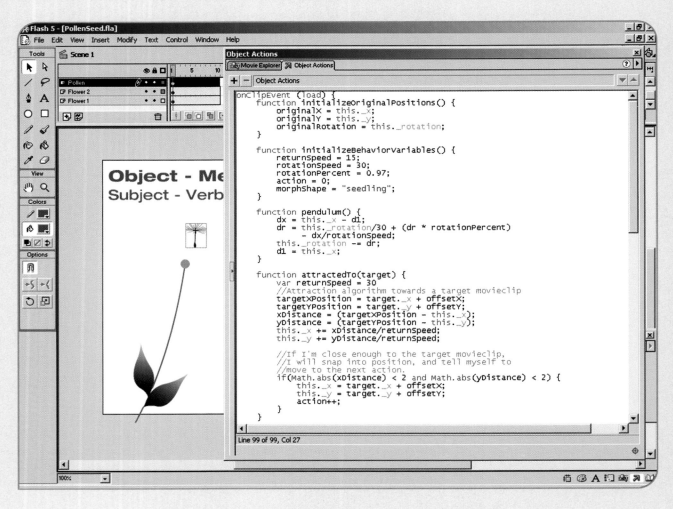

For this demo, we use two event handlers to assign code to the rootPollen movie clip: the load event, and the enterFrame event. ActionScript assigned inside event handlers only exists for instances of a movie clip dragged from the Library. This means that if you delete a movie clip and drag from the Library again, the ActionScript on the first movie clip instance will have disappeared. However, if you duplicate the movie clip using duplicateMovieClip (or do it manually on the stage via copy/paste), the duplicates will also have the code attached to them.

All code written between the curly braces of the load event executes as soon as the movie clip has completely loaded into the timeline. All code written between the curly braces of the enterFrame event will execute repeatedly as fast as the frame rate of the Flash movie, as long as the movie clip exists in its parent timeline.

```
onClipEvent (load) {
    //All the ActionScript code here is executed ONCE and ONLY ONCE
    //after the movieclip has completely loaded, and we are
    //using this
    //event to initialize our variables and functions.
}//onClipEvent (load)

onClipEvent (enterFrame) {
    //All code here will be executed repeatedly
    //as fast as the movie's framerate, as long as
    //the movieclip exists in its parent timeline, and we are using
    //this event to continuously work out what the pollen should be doing
    //next, and animating its movement via ActionScript.
}//onClipEvent (enterFrame)
```

You might have noticed that I add a comment of //onClipEvent (eventname) at the end of every event handler. Commenting the end of a chunk of code helps you figure out where your eyes are positioned on the code if your ActionScript is especially lengthy and complex.

As soon as the movie clip loads, we want to define the pollen movie clip's properties such as its original position on screen, original rotation, speed of movement, speed of rotation, and degrees of rotation. The original position and original rotation are stored as variables so that the pollen knows how to return to its original state. The speed and rotation constants are stored so that the pollen knows how fast and how much to rotate. The action variable defines what the pollen movie clip is doing, and the morphShape specifies what the current shape of the pollen seed should be.

Pollen

In order to prepare the pollen movie clip, we have to define two things: properties and functions. The properties store information about the movie clip, so in terms of language, properties of a movie clip act as an adjective. Functions are also part of a movie clip, but they're like verbs, which we build with all the ActionScript logic needed to do a particular task. Such a task might be flying towards another flower stem tip or swinging in the wind like a pendulum.

All of these properties and functions must be defined as soon as the movie clip loads, so we put the code inside the onClipEvent (load) event handler, with two notable functions at the top:

```
onClipEvent (load) {
  function initializeOriginalPositions() {
     originalX = this._x;
     originalY = this._y;
     originalRotation = this._rotation;
  }

  function initializeBehaviorVariables() {
     returnSpeed = 15;
     rotationSpeed = 30;
     rotationPercent = 0.97;
     action = 0;
     morphShape = "seedling";
  }
```

These two functions contain code to set the position and speeds of the pollen movie clip, so they act as verbs that initialize the movie clip when they're called. Once all the other functions have been defined (we'll get to them next), the initializing functions are called at the bottom of the onClipEvent (load) handler:

```
  //INITIALIZE VARIABLES
  initializeOriginalPositions();
  initializeBehaviorVariables();
}//onClipEvent (load)
```

Now, if you're going to tell the pollen to wait for the mouse to collide with it, you have to define the verb *wait*. Also, if you're going to tell the pollen to be attracted to another flower's stem tip, you have to define the verb *attract,* or attractedTo. Therefore, our next step will involve the definition of several verbs as functions inside the `load` event handler so we can call upon them later at our convenience.

Written inside the `load` event handler, the pendulum function is defined to make the pollen seed swing from side to side, as if gravity and inertia existed.

```
function pendulum() {
    dx = this._x - d1;
    dr = this._rotation/30 + (dr * rotationPercent)
        - dx/rotationSpeed;
        this._rotation -= dr;
        d1 = this._x;
}
```

The calculations for this swinging motion work in three parts. Firstly, in the last line of the function, the variable `d1` records the last position of the movie clip on screen. In the first line of the function, the distance between the movie clip's current position (`this._x`) and its last position (`d1`) is assigned to a new variable named `dx`. You may note that `d1` isn't defined the first time the function is run. This could be added, but doesn't change the end effect.

Pollen

The second part is on the second line of the code, which uses the variable `dr` to determine how far to rotate the pollen seed as it swings. Check out this calculation:

```
this._rotation/30 + (dr * rotationPercent) - dx/rotationSpeed;
```

The section `this._rotation/30` takes the current rotation of the pollen movie clip and divides it by 30. The second section `(dr * rotationPercent)` multiplies the last value of the variable `dr` by the decimal value (a number between 1 and zero) to produce a fraction of the previous `dr` value. The last section – `dx/rotationSpeed` subtracts the distance of `dx` divided by the value of `rotationSpeed`.

In the third and final part, we subtract the value of `dr` from the current rotation of the movie clip, so that it swings in one direction by several degrees.

So what does this all mean? If the pollen seed is moving very fast, the distance between its current position and its last position will be proportionally long, so the faster the pollen seed is flying across the screen, the more it's rotated every time the pendulum function executes itself. By adding a fraction of the previous rotation value, we can give the pollen seed an extra 'boost', like giving your friend a push on a playground swing to swing higher. The end result is a swinging motion that will swing high if the pollen seed will move fast, but that will also gradually slow down if the pollen seed isn't moving at all.

The function `attractedTo(target)` basically finds the location of another movie clip as a target, and then gradually moves the pollen movie clip towards that target by closing the distance between the two movie clips. In the case of our demo, the target movie clip is the stemtip2 movie clip.

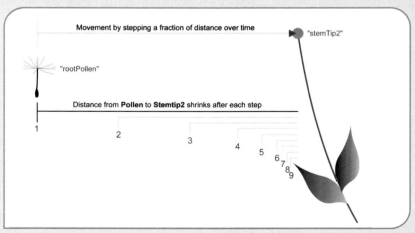

```
function attractedTo(target) {
  //Attraction algorithm towards a target movieclip
  targetXPosition = target._x + offsetX;
  targetYPosition = target._y + offsetY;
  xDistance = (targetXPosition - this._x);
  yDistance = (targetYPosition - this._y);
```

In the first few lines of the function, `targetXPosition` and `targetYPosition` capture the position of the target movie clip, which is referenced as a parameter when this function is called. The `offsetX` and `offsetY` are insignificant variables, which slightly adjust for the shifting effect of rotating a movie clip off-center. Then `xDistance` and `yDistance` are given the distance between the pollen movie clip and the target movie clip.

```
  this._x += xDistance/returnSpeed;
  this._y += yDistance/returnSpeed;
```

Next, the pollen movie clip moves a fraction of the distance between itself and the target by adding the result of the distance divided by `returnSpeed`. Take another look at that last diagram, and you'll see that the fraction of movement for each step towards the `stemtip2` movie clip shrinks each step, so that movement towards `stemtip2` gets slower, and slower, and slower until the distance shrinks to less than 2. Once the horizontal and vertical distance are less than 2, the following lines of code 'snap' the pollen movie clip to the same location as the target movie clip, and increases the `action` variable by a value of 1:

```
  //If I'm close enough to the target movieclip,
  //I will snap into position, and tell myself to
  //move to the next action.
  if(Math.abs(xDistance) < 2 and Math.abs(yDistance) < 2) {
    this._x = target._x + offsetX;
    this._y = target._y + offsetY;
    action++;
  }
}
```

59

Pollen

As soon as the pollen movie clip has snapped to the target movie clip, the `action` variable increases by a value of 1, so the next function to be called is the `reorient()` function. We'll get into the whole purpose behind the `action` variable, but for now, let's look at the code:

```
function reorient() {
    rotationDifference = originalRotation - this._rotation;
    this._rotation += rotationDifference/rotationSpeed;
    if(Math.abs(rotationDifference) < 2) {
        action++;
    }
}
```

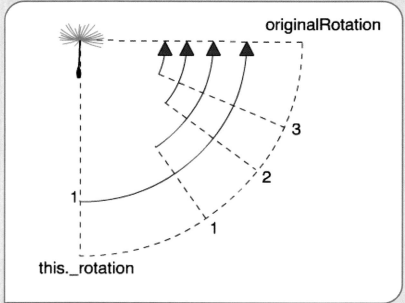

Notice that for each step in turning the movie clip, its rotation becomes smaller and smaller. Here, the concept works in a similar fashion to the `attractedTo(target)` function, where the difference between two values is calculated, and a fraction of the result is applied to the first value. In this case, `rotationDifference` is assigned the difference between the current rotation of the pollen movie clip, and its original rotation that we had recorded in the `initOriginalPositions()` function. Once `rotationDifference` has been calculated, we add a fraction of its value to the current rotation of the movie clip, so that the movie clip gradually returns to its original angle.

The final function that `onClipEvent (load) calls` is `triggerAction`. When the `triggerAction` function is called, it runs a `hitTest` to see if the mouse overlaps the movie clip. If it does, the pollen movie clip goes to the frame with a name that corresponds to the `morphSequence` variable, and the value of `action` is raised by 1.

```
function triggerAction(morphSequence) {
    if (hitTest(_root._xmouse, _root._ymouse, false)) {
        gotoAndPlay(morphSequence);
        action++;
    }
}
```

Now that we've set the stage, defined the properties, and defined all the variables, we can give a simple command to each duplicated pollen seed movie clip and have the movie clip's internal functions figure out how to do its task. This is done through the `enterFrame` event handler.

In order for the movie clip to know which function it should be calling, the variable `action` contains a number which the movie clip can check using an `if` statement. If the action matches a specific number, a specific function will be called. For example, consider the excerpt from the rootPollen movie clip below:

```
onClipEvent (enterFrame) {

if (action == 0) {
   triggerAction("morphToRectangle");

} else if (action == 1) { //attracted to the second stemTip
   pendulum();
   attractedTo(_parent.stemtip2);
}
```

Although this `onClipEvent(enterFrame)` is incomplete, you can see how a series of `if-else-if` conditional statements can check the value of the `action` variable, and then call the corresponding function. The `enterFrame` event handler executes all code inside its curly braces repeatedly, as fast as the movie's frame rate. As a result, the pollen movie clip can repeatedly check to see whether the value of the `action` variable has changed.

The first conditional statement, `if (action ==0)` checks to see if `action` is equal to zero, and if so, then the `triggerAction` function is called, with a parameter of `morphToRectangle`. This parameter tells the pollen movie clip to begin playing at a frame labeled `morphToRectangle` so that the graphic slowly transforms into a rectangular flower petal. Once the `triggerAction` function is called, then the function's internal code bumps up the value of the `action` variable to 1.

The next time the `enterFrame` event handler executes its code, it checks the value of `action`. Now that `action` has a value of 1, it executes the functions `pendulum` and `attractedTo(_parent.stemtip2)`. Calling these two functions causes the pollen clip to start moving towards the stemtip2 movie clip on the other flower, while swinging back and forth, according to how fast it's moving. Looking back at the function definitions, you can now see why `action` is increased by one every time the flower reaches within two pixels of its target movie clip, or when the pollen seed has rotated to within two degrees of its original angle.

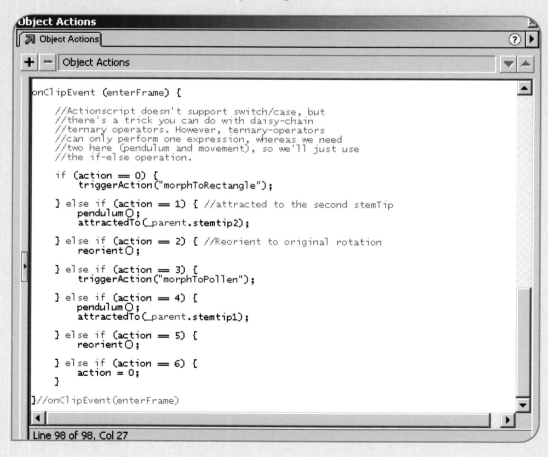

```
Object Actions

  Object Actions                                              ?  ▶

  +  −    Object Actions                                      ▼  ▲

onClipEvent (enterFrame) {                                       ▲

    //Actionscript doesn't support switch/case, but
    //there's a trick you can do with daisy-chain
    //ternary operators. However, ternary-operators
    //can only perform one expression, whereas we need
    //two here (pendulum and movement), so we'll just use
    //the if-else operation.

    if (action == 0) {
        triggerAction("morphToRectangle");

    } else if (action == 1) { //attracted to the second stemTip
        pendulum();
        attractedTo(_parent.stemtip2);

    } else if (action == 2) { //Reorient to original rotation
        reorient();

    } else if (action == 3) {
        triggerAction("morphToPollen");

    } else if (action == 4) {
        pendulum();
        attractedTo(_parent.stemtip1);

    } else if (action == 5) {
        reorient();

    } else if (action == 6) {
        action = 0;
    }
}//onClipEvent(enterFrame)                                       ▼

  ◄                                                          ►

  Line 98 of 98, Col 27
```

By simplifying all the complex algorithms into smaller functions, we can use the functions as verbs for our new sentences, with the rootPollen movie clip as the object, and either stemtip1 or stemtip2 as the target.

Firstly, wait and check to see whether the mouse has collided with this movie clip. If so, go to the frame morphToRectangle to begin animation, and move on to the next action.

```
if (action == 0) {
  triggerAction("morphToRectangle");
```

Make the pollen seed swing like a pendulum while it flies towards the stemtip2 movie clip on the other flower. Once the pollen seed has reached the other flower, move on to the next action.

```
} else if (action == 1) { //attracted to the second stemTip
  pendulum();
  attractedTo(_parent.stemtip2);
```

Start re-orienting the pollen seed so that it rotates towards its original angle. Once the angle is reached, move to the next action.

```
} else if (action == 2) { //Reorient to original rotation
  reorient();
```

Wait and check to see whether the mouse has collided with this movie clip. If so, go to the frame morphToPollen to begin transforming back into a pollen seed instead of a blue flower petal. Move on to the next action.

```
} else if (action == 3) {
  triggerAction("morphToPollen");
```

Start swinging and flying towards the stemtip1 movie clip on the first flower. Once this movie clip reaches stemtip1, move on to the next action.

```
} else if (action == 4) {
  pendulum();
  attractedTo(_parent.stemtip1);
```

Pollen

Start re-orienting the pollen seed back towards its original angle of rotation. Once it's done, move on to the next action. Since the next action sets itself back to zero, the whole sequence of actions starts all over again from zero.

```
} else if (action == 5) {
  reorient();

} else if (action == 6) {
  action = 0;
}
```

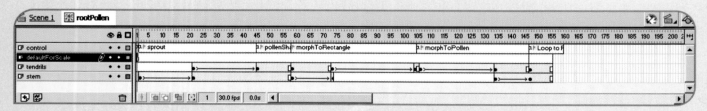

The behaviors of these duplicated pollen seed movie clips are now contained inside complex functions, and each function can be easily called in the `enterFrame` event handler according to the `action` variable in the `if-else` sequence. Since each duplicated movie clip contains all of its own properties and functions, we've met the goal of writing modular and object-oriented ActionScript. Like the English language, every verb or command has its own meaning, and these commands can be chained together into a series of events to form a sentence, or several sentences.

I encourage you to experiment with this demo... try re-arranging the action sequences to see what happens. You can also add new target movie clips for the pollen seeds to fly towards, or change the `initializeBehaviorVariables` to modify how fast, or slow, a pollen seed will fly and swing.

As a bonus, I've included a more complicated but unpolished version of this flower demo, with a 3D engine and a reactive spider. Both the 3D engine and spider were written during the first days of Flash 5, but I recently found out that an earlier Flash 4 version of the insectoid crawling effect was built by Geoff Stearns at www.deconcept.com.

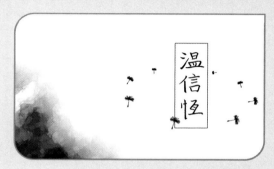

During the research for this chapter, I found a few of my old QBasic graphics programs. Feel free to visit www.echotap.com or www.samuelwan.com for both Flash 5 and Java versions of my graphics experiments. Both sites should be updated by the time of this publication.

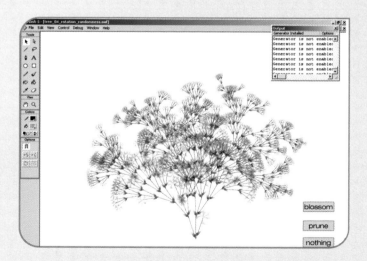

Samuel's tutorial shows how the new Flash 5 programming constructs can be used to create a modular approach. Although the code is separated into several distinct functions, the actions of each one merge into a single overall animation effect.

Because the code is totally modular, we can make a large number of changes by adding new functions...

repulsive mouse effect 'blows' pollen away.

How about writing a game where you have to blow the pollen to a place where the seed can grow, avoiding landing in spider webs, water and all sorts of obstacles...

blow on the pollen

Rather than use collision/over events, try emulating blowing on the pollen by making the pollen tend to move away from the mouse, based on a 'the closer I am to the mouse, the greater the effect'. The effects of the mouse would be offset by a weaker force that tends to make the pollen stay where it is. The interaction of strong distance based forces and constant but weaker forces can be used to create many natural effects.

do it in 3D

By adding scaling of the
petals as well as all the other
animation effects, you can make
them float into the distance.

Because Samuel's code is
modular, you could even
make the pollen move back
and forth throughout a whole
garden of flowers...

use the real thing

Finally, Samuel's FLA uses a rather oriental
drawing style, but for those of us who want
to add another flavor ino the mix, the easiest
way is to scan real petals and trace them into
vectors ready for shape tweening.

A quick trip outside into the garden and
five minutes on a scanner gave me these
pretty candidates...

"Find out what it is you'd like to accomplish and dive in. Sure, you'll screw up along the way, but when you finally get it right you feel like you're ready to tackle most anything."

Marc Stricklin
www.brittle-bones.com

Flower

I always knew that art would play a big role in my life. From as far back as I can remember I've had an affinity for illustration. It was a passion that stayed with me throughout my younger years and into my early teens. It wasn't until the came time to choose a career path that I decided just how big a role it would play in my life. I had chosen to pursue becoming an illustrator as a career, but how exactly to go about it was what was bothering me.

I knew I wanted to use my ability as a form of expression and most importantly (at the time) to generate income. I had no interest in being a starving artist who was determined to remain true to his art and not compromise. I wanted to find a way to make dream become reality. The bottom line was I needed formal training, so I took the next obvious step. school. After a brief stint in traditional college, I decided I would be better suited for a school that would help me hone my specific talents without all the peripheral studies getting in the way. I needed more focus, more inspiration and fewer keg parties. I chose to attend the Portfolio Center in Atlanta. At the time it had a flawless reputation and was dishing out amazing talent left and right. I went in with the full intent of being the next M.C. Escher. That lasted about three months. Illustration was my passion, but I wasn't quite ready to limit myself to being the guy that sat in front of a drawing board all day and experienced zero interaction. Instead it turns out I became the guy that sits in front of a computer monitor all day and experiences zero interaction. Oh, the irony.

After concluding I would abandon my life-long ambition of to become an illustrator, I switched my major to art direction – all the while knowing that I could still pick up the pens and pencils when I had the urge. After switching to art direction a whole new world opened up. I was overwhelmed by what programs like Photoshop, Illustrator and Quark had to offer. I was also introduced to the conceptual side of art. The advertisement, the printed piece. A tangible piece of work that held within it all the self-gratifying attributes of my illustrations. The Web was merely crawling at this point and web sites were just pitiful pages of blue-underlined text.

There was no graphical content worth mentioning and my God, it was a slow, dull experience. I had zero interest in the Web and couldn't imagine the possibilities of what it would become merely a few years later.

From the Portfolio Center I went on to work as an art director for ad agency after ad agency. I enjoyed the work and was beginning to become very proficient at an array of programs. I liked conceptualizing, art direction and execution, but what intrigued me the most was the software. I wanted to have a working knowledge of every program I came across. That was a little ambitious. I never seemed to have the time to learn all I wanted. I had read a few blurbs about Flash and was interested enough to go to the Macromedia site and download a trial version of Flash 3. I was hooked.

Flash 4 came out weeks later so I went ahead and purchased it along with every book on Flash I could get my hands on. Things moved along rather quickly for me and after a couple of months of experimentation I was ready to start actually constructing a web site. After learning the basics, I created my first Flash project for my interactive company, Engine Room Interactive. Looking back it wasn't an awful first attempt, but left a lot of room for improvement. Ironically, the problem I was having at that time was that I was using Flash the way it was intended to be used – as a vector-based program. Considering that I've never been very good at conforming to the rules, I decided to start using Flash to achieve what I wanted.

Quickly, my work began to reflect the realism that has always been my passion. In the earlier stages of my Flash explorations, I had thought it might be hard to get that vivid, all-too-real look that I had become so accustomed to in my illustrations. As Flash is a vector-based program and I'm a realist at heart, it seemed ludicrous to think this program would give me the canvas I needed to portray my art. Another concern was whether Flash would be able to hold the resolution and detail that is the mainstay of the art I create.

Flower

I began to view Flash as a kinetic, motion-driven canvas for the art I create in Photoshop, and I all but abandoned traditional art after realizing that I wasn't creating art for its tangible value but for a way to convey emotion.

The Web is the perfect place for me to reach people all over the world and gain many perspectives on how my creations are perceived in many different cultures. I was finally able to get to reach everyone I wanted to, in a fashion that was in no way sacrificing the quality of the work I created in Photoshop and on canvas. Finally, I was creating in a fashion that I deemed worthy. Not brilliant, but worthy nonetheless.

As time went by, I managed to achieve a fairly firm grasp on what Flash could do for me and my art. I would by no means consider myself a master of ActionScripting. I know what I can pull off in Flash and how to go about it most of the time. That's what it's really all about, once you've established a working knowledge of almost any program. Find out what it is you'd like to accomplish and dive in. Sure, you'll screw up along the way, but when you finally get it right you feel like you're ready to tackle almost anything. I begin with conceptualizing the idea and from there figuring out if this can be accomplished in Flash. Usually it's just a matter of how badly I want to pull off the desired effect. And for me, about 99.9% of the time, it'll bug the hell out of me until I figure out a way to make it work.

I continued to improve my technical command of Flash while becoming comfortable with my new-found approach to its use as a canvas for my art. Soon after, I got the idea for www.brittle-bones.com as something to serve as my corner of the Web – a place where I could showcase my work. I wanted it to be different from anything else out there. I wanted the navigation to be very organic and serve *only* as the navigation, and felt that by making some space-age, souped-up nav element I would only be stealing the thunder of the graphics. After all, the graphics were to be the highlight of the site.

It took weeks for me just to finish manipulating the illustrations and photos before I even started the Flash work. I wanted each individual space in www.brittle-bones.com to be a different experience for the viewer, a kind of cocoon that could almost suck the viewer into a place where they can just dream away. It was also important that while the viewer was waiting for the next page to load, the wait would be cushioned by the indelible impression the prior page had left. To me, if that were to work, I would have created something worthwhile. I always try to keep rotating the first page of brittle-bones with some of my alarming imagery. It's my way of saying, "Hey, now's your chance to get out and run for the hills because from here it only gets better". That first image has always been a way for me to set the precedent – a way to get all the nonsense out the way and get to the real grit. If I can hold people after I've given them a bit of a shock then they're the people who need to be there. I've even found that those who aren't ardent fans of the site are still intrigued to go just that one step farther to find out what it's all about. Even though the intro page is of great importance, it's more important not to let the rest of the site fall down. I want it to be one slap in the face after another. This is what I mean when I say indelible. This is what keeps people coming back for more. This is also what stirs emotion and arouses curiosity. This is why I do what I do and enjoy it so much.

Flower

I get a lot of e-mails referring to me as brilliant. Nothing could be further from the truth. What I do with Flash is fairly basic, and could probably be accomplished by just about anyone who is willing to build a set of basics. For me, the basics first came with learning my way around the main stage and learning the tools and what limitations or boundaries these would have. I read just enough about ActionScripting to be able to pull off simple things such as mouse events, drags, tell target and other simple commands. I also learned what type of files would best display my work in Flash and how to keep them of decent quality without too large a file size.

Everything I was learning in Flash was shaped by my background as an artist. It seems that from the beginning of my career I've had an intense love for ultra-realist pen and ink drawings, and for some reason have always preferred drawing older people's faces. The character lines and wisdom that those faces held always made amazing subject matter. Over the years, I've accumulated tons of old illustrations, and one day got the idea to scan them into Photoshop for archiving purposes. Because I have an immense respect for realism in art, I've always had a hard time straying from that vein, but I was astounded

by the effects I was achieving through the manipulation and reconstruction (or deconstruction) of these images, particularly when I placed them in this exciting, workable environment. I was able to give my illustrations new life by adding filters and shading and gradients.

Over the years, I have become a very accomplished Photoshop artist, and to this day it's still my strong suit. Photoshop has actually re-shaped how I went about working with pen and ink. Whereas before I worked out every minor detail directly on paper, with Photoshop I was given the relief of being able to add in so much of what would have taken hours to produce by hand. With cutting and pasting I'm able to replicate many of the details within an illustration and save tons of time. I can even take a small portion of an illustration or photo and tweak it until I've created some whacked-out looking image that fits perfectly into my portfolio. Long before I discovered Flash, I often wished Photoshop would allow me to move past the static world of print and allow me to infuse my work with motion. Suddenly, my wish came true. The shackles came off; there were no limitations and I could give my work more of a televisual-realist feel.

always with your head in the clouds
never with the clouds

All scripting on this page courtesy of Geoff Stearns He's the guy God calls when he needs scripting done.
contact: geoff@dconcept.com

"I hope this guy has managed to purge some of his personal demons by building this site."

Those were the words of one concerned citizen I stumbled upon in a news forum. Well, to address his concern directly, I'd have to say no. Personal demons were in no way taken into consideration when I began the process of piecing together brittle-bones. I understand that brittle-bones could easily be misconstrued as a much

deeper dive into the dark than it actually is. I can only say that it's merely a showcase for my art. The art isn't sunflowers and grandmas. It's faces aged with character and burdened with emotion. The emotion is what I wanted to convey. I wanted people to leave the site thinking. Thinking about what they've just seen and how it made them feel. If the site were to do anything, I wanted it at least to evoke an emotion.

Flower

So on September 15 2000, I started what would come to be known as www.brittle-bones.com. I set out to create an absolute first. I wanted to explore a use of Flash and the Web that hadn't been touched on much at the time. It was of high importance that I didn't lose sight of the art by letting the kinetic aspects take too much precedence. I wanted it to be experimental in every sense of the word. But I also wanted the experiment to be a success.

Since my first loves were illustration and film, it was all but predetermined that I would derive inspiration from a myriad of artists such as H.R. Giger, Leonardo da Vinci, Stanley Kubrick, Terry Gilliam, and Christopher McQuarrie,

to name just a few. With inspiration of that kind you can probably see where the root of brittle-bones got its start. Da Vinci's sketches were what first inspired me to begin illustrating with pen and ink. His early sketches, such as *Grotesque Head of Man* and *Study of Woman's Hands*, were so full of emotion and life that from that point on, I was determined to try to emulate the purity and rawness that he seemed to capture in his sketches. I guess it wasn't until the mid-80s that I was introduced to my other inspiration, H.R. Giger. Now here, I thought, was a man hell bent on conveying every morsel of himself through art. A man possessed by art and the emotion it had to offer. At this point I was pretty much hooked.

Film also played an important role in shaping my career. The first movie that blew me away with aesthetic brilliance and black comedy was Terry Gilliam's *Brazil*. That surreal, dark, and at times futuristic feel that Terry Gilliam accomplished inspires me to this day. Although I tend to be one of those that likes the Web 'just the way it is', I am extremely attracted to what the Web will offer in the future for people who want to branch of more into the directing realm of things.

The Web at this time is a difficult place to convey emotion through art – it's hard to pull off. Download times and image quality tend to hinder the experience a bit. Film, on the other hand, is the ultimate canvas. There are no limitations from conception to reality. That vast, unbounded quality is what has always intrigued me so much with film. Just being able to take the dream and watch it evolve into the same vivid moving pictures you once had in your mind is amazing. I'm sure the Web will continue to evolve into a much more friendly canvas for film makers, but until then we'll have to continue to produce quality work with the limitations that are set.

Yugo Nakamura first inspired me to push the envelope with Flash, and I've tried to stay one step ahead of the expected ever since.

Flower

In this tutorial, we're building a freak on a leash, a common or garden spider-baby. It will consist of a body (the baby), surrounded with eight feet (flowers), which will each be connected by a leg (string) to the body. Let's lay out what we'll need to begin coding our creation.

First the baby will need to control the flowers around it, and also control the lines connecting each one of these flowers. We want the user to be able to interact with the baby and drag it around the stage, so we'll put a button inside it that the user can grab on to.

Next we'll need some the flowers that 'float' around the baby, and some strings to connect the baby to each one of the flowers.

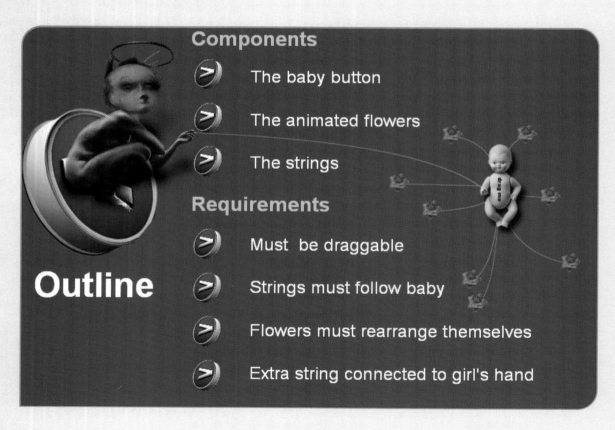

Components

> The baby button

> The animated flowers

> The strings

Requirements

Outline

> Must be draggable

> Strings must follow baby

> Flowers must rearrange themselves

> Extra string connected to girl's hand

Lastly, let's take a look at what will be on our main timeline, or how we want to contain our baby on the main stage. I like to keep things as modular as possible, so I can take this baby and just drag it out of the Library and drop it on the stage wherever I want and it will work. For that reason we'll create the entire thing inside another movie clip.

Now that we've decided what we'll need to create this spider-baby, let's look at how we want the baby to move and behave. We want it to sit still until the user moves the body around, so all we have to worry about is keeping the flowers close to the body when the user moves it around the stage. To accomplish this, we'll set up a clip event on the baby that will check the distance of each flower from the baby, and if it's past a certain distance, move the flower to a new random position near the baby. We also want the flowers to stay in the same area relative to the baby, that is, have the flowers below the baby to stay below (or at least close by). We want the flowers that start at the top of the baby to stay near the top. This will keep a fairly even balance to the baby so all the flowers won't end up on one side.

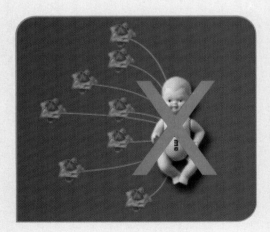 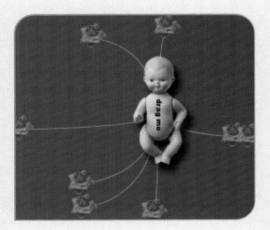

The very first thing I do when I start a new project in Flash is to set up the stage and my working area, so let's get started and build that spider-baby.

Flower

Go ahead and open a fresh movie in Flash. Open your movie properties from the Modify menu. Set the stage dimensions to 900px wide by 600px tall. Then set the frame rate to 20 frames per second to give it a nice smooth look. We also want the movie background to be a nice dark gothic gray.

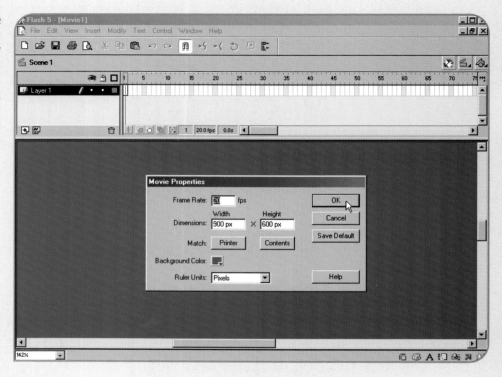

Now that our stage is set up, let's set some basic actions in the first frame. I always like to keep all my actions on one layer so that it's easier to keep track of where I put things. Rename Layer 1 actions. At the outset we also decided that the baby would be contained in its own movie clip. We want to keep things as organized as possible, so create a new layer specifically for the baby and name that layer baby.

Go back to the actions layer, and we'll determine what we need for actions on the first frame. Open the Frame Actions window, and make sure it's set to Expert mode – we need it in Expert mode for some of the advanced ActionScript we'll be adding later. In most of my movies I like to place an fscommand("allowscale", false); on the first frame. This will keep the movie from scaling and stretching while I test it. Also, since the movie is only going to have one frame on the _root timeline, you'll want to place a Stop action on the first frame too.

Now the main stage is all set up, and we're ready to begin building the parts of the baby.

We'll turn our attention to the main part of the baby first. Start by creating a new graphic symbol, called g-baby in the Library. I'm in the habit of placing this g- in front of the name of all my graphic symbol names to keep my Library clean and organized. We'll also want to reuse the name baby and since Flash doesn't allow duplicate names in the Library, we need to use some way to distinguish the baby graphic from the baby movie clip.

I've already created a movie clip that has the loop of the baby animation for you to use. The animation consists of the baby with a sequence of interchanging heads. The heads are interchanged by using the whiteflash image in the baby.fla Library. By tweening the alpha setting of the whiteflash, I was able to create the head-switching effect. If you want to know more, you can simply open up the changing baby movie clip from the Library and play around with it.

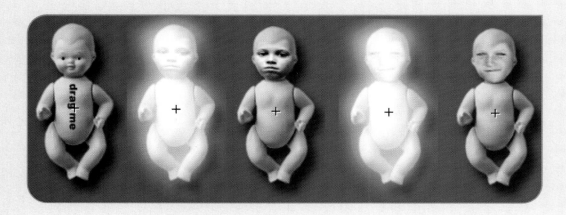

Import the Library from the completed baby.fla file and drag an instance of changing baby into the g-baby graphic. The movie clip and all its associated files will now have been copied into your new movie's Library.

Flower

We also want to center it on the stage, so bring up the Align panel. Making sure your baby is selected on the stage, select the Align to Stage option and then click the Align to Center button for vertical and horizontal.

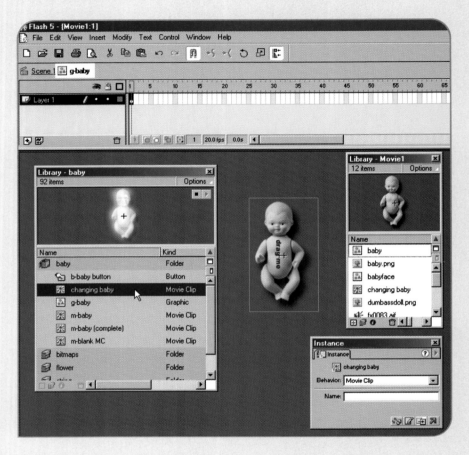

Now we have the graphic for the body, we still need a button so the user can drag the baby around. Create a new symbol again and this time call it b-baby button. Choose Button as the behavior. This will give us a new button symbol in the Library, so open it for editing.

Since we already have the visible part of the baby done, we want our button to be invisible. To do this, select the hit frame in the button's timeline and press F6 to create a keyframe. Then use the Oval tool again to draw an oval on the stage about the size of the baby. Since this won't be visible, the color isn't important, but we want the size to be a little bit larger than the baby. Once you have the oval on the stage, align it to the center of the stage in the same way you did the baby. Now we have the graphic and the button, so we're ready to put them together in a movie clip that will be our baby movie.

Create another new symbol, this time a movie clip, and name it m-baby. Rename the default Layer 1 to graphic and create a new layer called button. Then select frame 1 in graphic and drag the g-baby symbol out of the Library and onto the stage and align it to the center. Select the first frame in the button layer and drag the b-baby button from the Library onto the stage and center it.

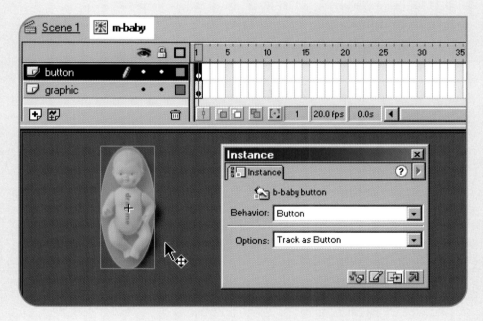

We'll put the actions on our button later when we put the rest of the actions on the baby. We need one more thing here: a blank movie clip that we'll use to position the line connecting the girl's hand to the baby. We'll just use an empty movie clip to make placement of this line easier. Create a new movie clip symbol and name it m-blank MC.

Now it's time to build the flowers. Since we'll be using clip events to make them move around, we need to plan out the best way to handle this. Since you can only attach clip events to a movie clip that's on a stage, we'll need to create a 'holder' clip, place the flower movie inside that movie clip, and then put the actions on the movie clip inside our holder clip. Sound confusing? It is, but don't worry, you should understand what I'm saying as we build it.

For the animation, I've placed nineteen different PNG files that I created earlier onto the timeline in sequence. These nineteen frames are what make up the flower movie. I've dragged the last keyframe (19) out to frame 61 in order to give the movie a bit of time when there will be no movement. I've told the last frame to go to and play frame 1, so it will continuously loop.

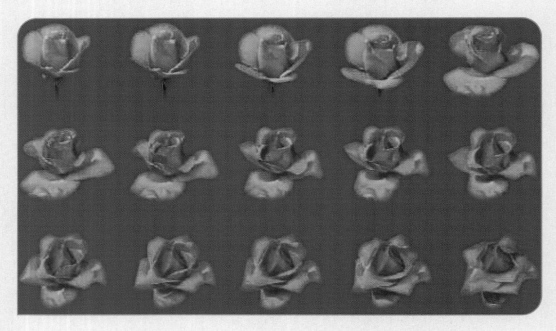

Although I've supplied this for you in the `baby.fla` Library as m-flower animation, feel free to create your own, or even import your own from another project. That's one of the best aspects of this tutorial; although I'm showing you specifically how to create a spider-baby, the modular nature of the whole process means you can take out the baby animation, the flowers, anything, and replace them with your own animations and graphics to create a completely different FLA with the same cool effect.

Let's continue with the spider-baby for the moment. You already have the flower animation, so create a new graphic symbol and name it g-flower. Put the flower animation inside the g-flower graphic and create another symbol, this time a movie clip called m-flower.

Now drag the g-flower graphic from the Library, and place it on the stage *inside* the m-flower movie clip we've just created. Center it on the stage.

As I said before, Flash 5 will only allow you to attach clip events onto a movie clip that's on the stage. Since we want to contain our code in one place instead of eight different places (clip events for each flower), we'll need to place the m-flower movie clip inside another movie clip.

Create a final movie clip, name it m-flower holder, and place the m-flower symbol inside it, again centering it on the stage. That's it for the flower. We'll add the actions to it once we get all our parts ready to go. Your final movie clip should look like the screenshot from the final `baby.fla`.

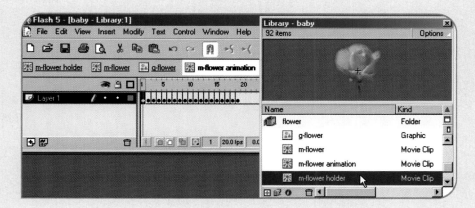

If you look back at our outline at the beginning, there's just one final component to create – the strings.

We're going to attach the strings from the Library using the `attachMovie();` method. This means our string needs to be a movie clip, although it's good practice to make all your raw graphics actual graphic symbols, as opposed to just drawing a line inside a movie clip. Usually when I work with movie clips, I consider them to be containers for holding multiple graphics or buttons, or other movie clips.

So we'll start our string off by creating a new graphic symbol, calling it g-string. The way I draw these lines in Flash is by creating a 45-degree angle line, making that line 100 pixels tall by 100 pixels wide – this is because we'll be adjusting the `_xscale` and `_yscale` properties of the line to stretch it between our two points (the baby and each flower). Since `_xscale` and `_yscale` work as a percentage, we'll make our line movie clip 100 pixels square.

Flower

With that in mind, draw a diagonal line, starting at the center point of the stage, and going diagonally down and to the right. You can hold the SHIFT key to have Flash force the line into a 45-degree angle, and the size doesn't have to be perfect because we'll use the Info palette to size it exactly.

Once you have the line on the stage, open your Info panel. On the Info tab set the line's width and height to 100 pixels. We also want to align our line so the top left corner is at the (0,0) coordinates of the g-string graphic, so in the Align tab align the left edge and top edge relative to the stage.

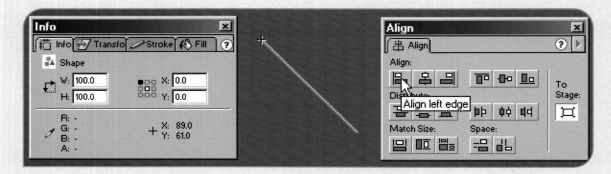

We also don't want our string to be straight, so to add a slight curve to the strings, we'll bend the line. First de-select the line on the stage, then hold your mouse over the center of the line, grab it and drag it down until the line bends slightly. Now, since we'll be attaching this line from the Library, we need to place it inside a movie clip.

Create a new symbol and name it m-string. Drag the g-string graphic from the Library and align the top left corner to the (0,0) coordinates.

Now that we have our string movie clip, let's set up the linkage for the `attachMovie();` call. Right-click or CTRL-click on the m-string movie clip in the Library, and choose Linkage.... In the linkage dialog box, choose Export this symbol and for the Identifier, type string and click OK.

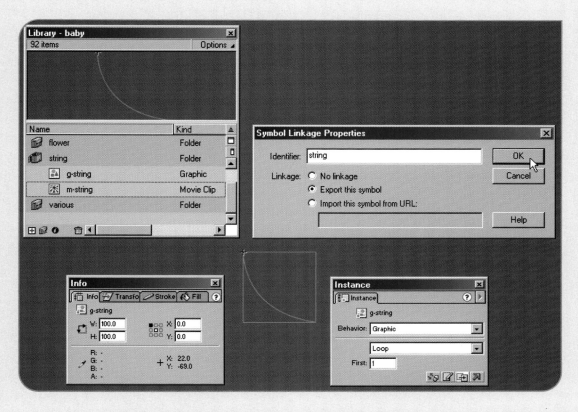

We're all done creating the parts for our baby. Now it's time to put it all together.

First we'll take care of the flowers. The actions here are pretty simple and straightforward. We'll use clip events and some movement code to slide the flowers to their new position each time the body tells them to move.

We'll also place the code to maintain the amount of offset each flower has from the baby. This is to keep each flower in the same general area that it started out in – that is, flowers that start under the body will stay roughly under the body, and flowers that start above the body or to the left of the body will stay above or to the left. So let's write some code to move our flowers.

Start by double-clicking the m-flower holder movie clip in the Library. This will open that movie clip on the main stage, and show the m-flower movie clip within it. Open your Instance panel and name it flower. Right-click on the m-flower movie clip on the stage and choose Actions from the menu. Now let's go over the code that we'll need.

Flower

First, we'll go through and set up some of our variables – including the 'offset' variable which will contain the information needed to keep each flower in the same general area in which it started. You can follow the code in more detail by looking at the comments included throughout. Enter the following ActionScript into the Actions window:

```
onClipEvent (load) {
  // — - set up variables
  // — - "a" controls how fast the flowers move, a lower
  ➡number will make them slide faster
  var a = 3;
  var newX = _parent._x;
  var newY = _parent._y;
  var xSpeed = 0;
  var ySpeed = 0;
  // — offset is the distance of this movie clip to the baby
  var xOffset = _parent._x -_parent._parent.baby._x;
  var yOffset = _parent._y-_parent._parent.baby._y;
}
```

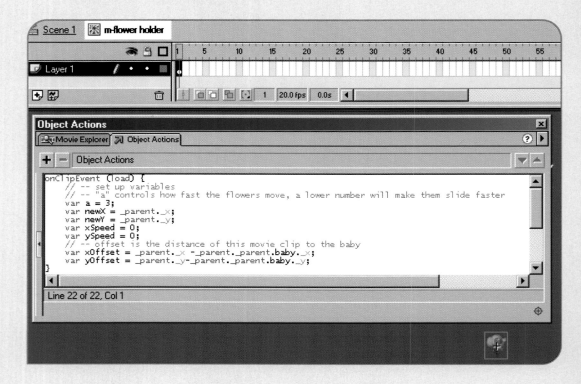

Here we use an onClipEvent (load) to set up the variables that we'll be using – the offset variables simply check the distance between the flower and the baby. This will be used below to maintain the spacing between each flower and the baby. Next we'll use an onClipEvent (enterFrame) to continuously update the position of the baby:

```
onClipEvent (enterFrame) {
   // - Calculate the speed each frame
   xSpeed = (_parent._x-(newX+xOffset))/a;
   ySpeed = (_parent._y-(newY+yOffset))/a;
   // - adjust parent movie clip position
   _parent._x -= xSpeed;
   _parent._y -= ySpeed;
}
```

Imagine that you have two points – a current location and a new location that you are heading to. Each time this code executes, it checks your position (_x), then your new position (newX), divides that amount by a certain number (a), then updates your position by that amount. This gives the movement a nice 'easing' effect, so the flower starts out fast, then slows down as it nears its new position.

We'll now set up the code that will control when our flowers will move, but first, we'll need to place our body inside another movie clip so we can keep it contained on its own, and also place the flowers on the stage.

Create another new movie clip and name it m-baby (complete). Now find the m-baby clip in the Library, drop it on the stage inside m-baby (complete) and name the instance baby. Also, align the m-body movie clip to the center of the stage, just to keep things tidy.

Next create eight new layers (one for each flower) and rename each layer flower1, flower2, flower3, etc. Then drag the m-flower holder movie clip onto the stage eight times, placing them around the baby in a circle, and selecting a new layer each time. We'll also need to name each instance on the stage - flower1 through flower8.

Flower

We'll also need to drag the blank 'line end' movie clip onto the stage somewhere below the baby. We'll adjust the location of this clip later when we place the baby on the stage, but for now add one more layer, name it line end and drag the m-blank MC movie clip onto the stage.

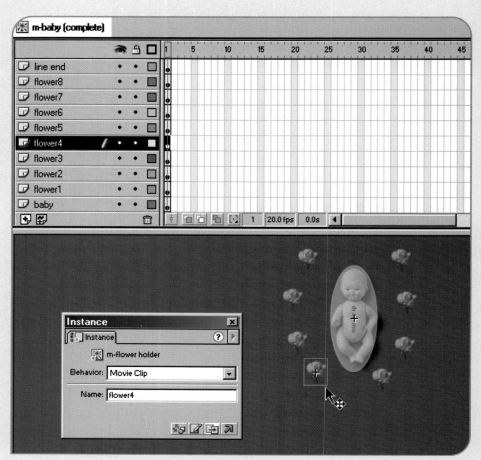

You should now have ten layers in total; one layer with the body, eight with an instance of m-flower holder on each, and a layer for the end of the tether string.

Now let's create our actions for the body. First we set up the variables we'll be using – we need to tell the baby how many flowers we have (8). Since we'll be using the `attachMovie()` method to 'attach' our strings to the baby, and we want the baby to be in front, or on top, of our strings, we'll need to change the depth of the baby and the flowers.

We do this by calling the `swapDepths()` method to put the movie clips on a higher level than the strings. Once we've done that, we'll set up some other variables needed to control how the flowers follow the baby.

We have `walkDist` and `maxDist`. The variable `walkDist` is the maximum possible distance a flower will move when it's told to update, and `maxDist` is the maximum distance a 'leg' can be from the spider-baby before it's told to update its position. We initially set this variable to 0 because it will change each cycle to give the flowers a more random-looking movement. Lastly we'll attach all the strings we'll need from the Library, using the `attachMovie()` method. First we loop through eight times (once for each flower), and then once more to attach the baby to the hand of our girl on the stage (which will really be attached to our empty movie clip positioned over the hand of the girl).

Once you're comfortable with the explanation above, add the following code to the body of the baby (an instance, baby, of the m-baby movie clip). Again, the code is full of comments, so you know exactly what part performs which function, and how:

```
onClipEvent (load) {
  // — this tells the baby how many flowers we have
  var flowers = 8;
  // — first swap the depths of the baby to place it above
  the strings (This is only a cosmetic change)
  this.swapDepths(1000);
  // — swap the depths of the flowers so the lines are
  behind them
  for (i=0;i<=flowers;i++) {
    _parent["flower"+i].swapDepths(i+2000);
  }
  // — set up the variables
  // — walkDist is used as a base number to keep the
  flowers close to the baby
  // — the higher this number is, the further the strings
  will be allowed to travel
  // — from the baby
  var walkDist = 60;
  var maxDist = 0;
  // — attach the strings from the library and name them
  for (i=1; i<=flowers; i++) {
    _parent.attachMovie("string", "string"+i, i+100);
    }
    // — attach the main string that connects the baby to
the hand
    _parent.attachMovie("string", "mainString", 200);
}
```

Flower

Now it's time to build the *brain* of our project. I worked on this section with Geoff Stearns (of deconcept.com), so special thanks to him for being the brain behind this brain that we're about to build. I'll go through the logic of this first to help you see what's happening, and then we'll go through the code together line by line to see what's happening.

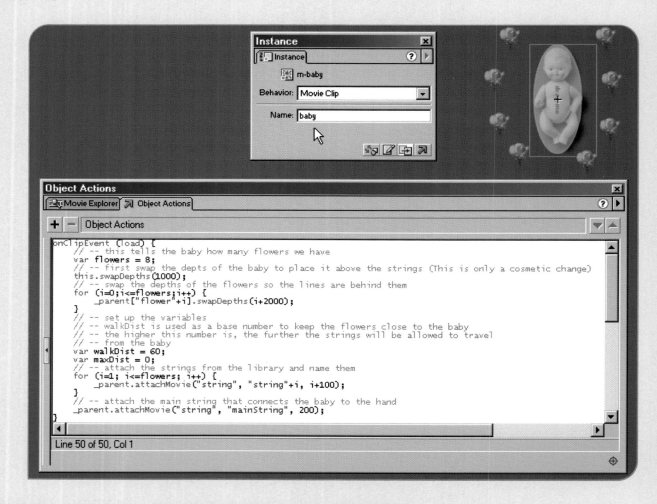

```
onClipEvent (load) {
    // -- this tells the baby how many flowers we have
    var flowers = 8;
    // -- first swap the depts of the baby to place it above the strings (This is only a cosmetic change)
    this.swapDepths(1000);
    // -- swap the depths of the flowers so the lines are behind them
    for (i=0;i<=flowers;i++) {
        _parent["flower"+i].swapDepths(i+2000);
    }
    // -- set up the variables
    // -- walkDist is used as a base number to keep the flowers close to the baby
    // -- the higher this number is, the further the strings will be allowed to travel
    // -- from the baby
    var walkDist = 60;
    var maxDist = 0;
    // -- attach the strings from the library and name them
    for (i=1; i<=flowers; i++) {
        _parent.attachMovie("string", "string"+i, i+100);
    }
    // -- attach the main string that connects the baby to the hand
    _parent.attachMovie("string", "mainString", 200);
}
```

Line 50 of 50, Col 1

We start off with another loop – this tells the baby to do this action eight times, once for each flower. First it checks the distance between the baby (`this._x`) and the flower (`myFlower._x`). Then we set the `maxDist` variable – notice that this is inside the loop, so we get a new number for each flower. Then we check to see whether the _x distance between the baby (this._x) and the flower (myFlower._x) is more than the maximum distance allowed (maxDist). If it is, we choose a new random *x* and *y* position for our flower by setting the newX and newY variables in the flower itself, then let the flower move itself to the new position using the code we attached to it earlier.

```
onClipEvent (enterFrame) {
   // — loop through each flower and check its distance
   from the baby
   for (i=1; i<=flowers; i++) {
      myFlower = _parent["flower"+i];
      xDist = Math.abs(myFlower.flower.newX-this._x);
      yDist = Math.abs(myFlower.flower.newY-this._y);
      maxDist =
Math.floor(Math.random()*walkDist)+walkDist;
      // — if the distance is farther than a certain
amount, tell that flower to move
      if (xDist>maxDist || yDist>maxDist) {
          myFlower.flower.newX =
this._x+Math.floor(Math.random()*walkDist)-walkDist/2;
          myFlower.flower.newY =
this._y+Math.floor(Math.random()*walkDist)-walkDist/2;
       }
```

Next we need to draw the lines or 'strings' that will connect the flowers to the baby. We attached the strings to the stage when the baby was loaded above. Now we just need to position the _x and _y position of the strings to the _x and _y of the baby, then set the _xscale and _yscale to that of each flower. Since _xscale and _yscale work as a percentage and our lines are 100px by 100px, they'll be stretched perfectly to the points we specify.

```
      // — adjust the "strings" each cycle (the lines)
      myString = _parent["string"+i];
      myString._x = this._x;
      myString._y = this._y;
      myString._xscale = myFlower._x-this._x;
          myString._yscale = myFlower._y-this._y;
      }
```

The last thing we need to do is position the line that connects the baby to the hand of the girl. When we place the baby on the main stage, we'll edit it in place, and position the blank lineEnd movie clip over the hand of the girl, then use this code, which is roughly the same as the above code for drawing the strings that connect the flowers to the baby.

```
// — draw a line from the bottom of the baby to the hand
_parent.mainString._x = _x;
_parent.mainString._y = _y + 30;
_parent.mainString._xscale = _parent.lineEnd._x - _x;
_parent.mainString._yscale = _parent.lineEnd._y -
➡ (_y+30);
}
```

Object Actions

Movie Explorer | Object Actions   ? ▶

\+ \- | Object Actions   ▼ ▲

```
onClipEvent (enterFrame) {
    // -- loop through each flower and check it's distance from the baby
    for (i=1; i<=flowers; i++) {
        myFlower = _parent["flower"+i];
        xDist = Math.abs(myFlower.flower.newX-this._x);
        yDist = Math.abs(myFlower.flower.newY-this._y);
        maxDist = Math.floor(Math.random()*walkDist)+walkDist;
        // -- if the distance is farther than a certain amount, tell that flower to move
        if (xDist>maxDist || yDist>maxDist) {
            myFlower.flower.newX = this._x+Math.floor(Math.random()*walkDist)-walkDist/2;
            myFlower.flower.newY = this._y+Math.floor(Math.random()*walkDist)-walkDist/2;
        }
        // -- adjust the "strings" each cycle (the lines)
        myString = _parent["string"+i];
        myString._x = this._x;
        myString._y = this._y;
        myString._xscale = myFlower._x-this._x;
        myString._yscale = myFlower._y-this._y;
    }
    // -- draw a line from the bottom of the baby to the hand
    _parent.mainString._x = _x;
    _parent.mainString._y = _y + 30;
    _parent.mainString._xscale = _parent.lineEnd._x - _x;
    _parent.mainString._yscale = _parent.lineEnd._y - (_y+30);
}
```

Line 50 of 50, Col 1

Finally, add the actions to the button that will allow us to drag the baby around the stage. Find the m-baby movie clip in the Library and double-click it for editing. Add these actions to the button inside:

```
on (press) {
    this.startDrag();
}
on (release, releaseOutside) {
    stopDrag();
}
```

That should be it for the coding. Now let's get to the main stage by choosing Edit Movie from the Edit menu, and drag and drop the m-baby (complete) movie clip onto the stage. Make sure you have the baby layer selected when you do this.

To finish the effect, drag the 'girl' – affectionately named `freak2.png` – from the `baby.fla` Library onto the main stage.

Once the girl is sitting on the main stage, we need to place our lineEnd movie clip in the correct position over her hand. So double-click on the baby on the main stage, then select the lineEnd clip instance, and place it over the hand of the girl. That should be it. All that's left is to test the finished baby!

As I said at the start, the underlying effect and the code are the same whatever graphics and animations you wish to use. You can see in the final `baby.fla` file that I've added lots more design elements and images to spice up the overall scene. It's entirely up to you how your completed movie looks and feels.

Much of Marc's output is not so much a Flash web site designed to illustrate some other content (as are most product/service based commerical sites), but rather a set of motion graphics-based art pieces that use Flash as the medium of expression.

This is a recent application of Flash, brought on not by the graphic capabilities so much as the underlying scripting that allows a high level of interactivity.

use a dummy

Instead of using a "holder" movie clip so that you can attach movie clip events to symbols in the library, you can create a "dummy". This is a blank movie clip with nothing in it.

Place it inside any other movie clip in the library that you want to attach event-based scripts to, and then attach the scripts to dummy. This can be better than using holders because you only need one dummy clip in the library.

Flash for art's sake

The basis of the brittle bones piece illustrated here is collage, or to give it the proper digital term, compositing. Like the Simian stuff, this is based on bitmaps as much as vectors, but Marc is actually using the png format not just as a 'super bitmap' format that comes with a 'mask', but rather using the masking feature to composite or selectively add images together.

This isn't discussed in the tutorial, but if you have a look at the additional baby faces in the 'various' folder, you can see how masking has been used to cut the faces out of photographs so that they will fit onto the doll's head.

select your freak face here...

NB — As usual, if using bitmaps in this way, remember to keep them small otherwise Flash will slow down...

"It's great to see that Flash is at the forefront of this constant state of evolution, empowering designers to change the way we all interface with the Web, and pushing the design potential of us all, along with the art that we create, to the limit"

Chris Andrade
www.fifthrotation.com

Axis

Life experiences have a tremendous impact on my design and thought process. Life events are something that we can all associate with, so, like most designers, I draw from the stimulus around me to try and create ways for users to engage easily in my designs. The way I emotionally react to events in my life triggers a thought, that thought is turned into an idea, and that idea eventually becomes the starting point of my artwork. Every day is filled with new experiences to provoke thought and inspiration. Sometimes they're a little too obvious; you meet someone new, you feel a breeze flow through your hair, your boss throws a pile of work on your desk that you have to get done by tomorrow morning. For me, the inspiration that I get from these comes from both the experience itself and my response to it, the way it makes me feel. I get angry, I feel elated, I'm saddened – most of the work I try to create emerges from the relationship between a particular experience and these feelings that it invokes.

Hopefully, this chapter will initiate a new experience for both you and I – the passing of knowledge from one person to another. Mine will be sharing and passing over some of the insight that I've attained by the graciousness of others in the Flash community, and yours, one of gaining insight into one artist's methods and techniques.

My hope is that through this you'll get a better understanding of how you can take what I've done and go on to even higher levels. As we go, on you may find that that we're amazingly similar as far as inspiration and creativity goes. If that's the case, it will make this experience much more meaningful.

It's intriguing how everything we perceive the Web to be will be taken apart and changed within a matter of minutes. Boundaries and barriers are being broken each day as the technology that defines the Internet evolves – all the time designers and developers are able to touch users in new interactive ways, rich media is more readily available and distributed and interfaces are becoming more engaging and exciting. It's great to see that Flash is at the forefront of this constant state of evolution, empowering designers to change the way we all interface with the Web and pushing the design potential of us all, along with the art that we create, to the limit. Flash 5 ActionScript has opened up unlimited scope for us to sharing interactive experiences. We can emulate an experience that we encounter in the real world by capturing the qualities of it (motion, color, atmosphere) with graphics and ActionScript and use our art to communicate with our audience.

A BOY AND HIS CAMERA
A INDIVDUAL PERSPECTIVE OF FF2K1 SAN FRANCISCO

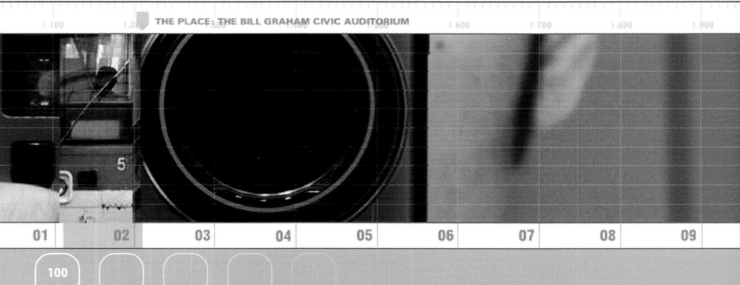

THE PLACE: THE BILL GRAHAM CIVIC AUDITORIUM

1.100   1.200   1.600   1.700   1.800   1.900

01   02   03   04   05   06   07   08   09

Great designers such as Yugo Nakamura, Joshua Davis, Andries Odendaal, and Erik Natzke have pushed interface design to make experiences much more tangible on the Web. We're now working within an environment where to capture a user's attention we need to provide for them a truly interactive and engaging experience. Our talent to create rich media, tying in motion graphics, good design and interactivity will allow users to relive the experiences and emotions that led us to create the piece originally.

I feel that the most successful designers on the Web today are ones who communicate messages through whole web events. They know that we often share in the same types of everyday occurrences so they exploit them with the intent of stimulating a reaction from us. The impact of eye candy and graphics will only stimulate a surprise element but I feel that it takes a lot more from us to engage users in a true experience. I remember seeing the collective efforts of the artists at SubMethod for the first time. One particular visual piece which engaged me contained images of a person wielding a gun with type in the foreground stating *Washington DC is full of culture; Hello, I'm going to kill you.* The visuals coupled with the design clearly communicated to me the message and the experience involved with the piece – what the creator must have felt emotionally in order to create that work.

Although stimulus in everyday life is at the core of my inspiration, creative ideas also stem from my peers and the idea of what the Internet will become in the future. I can imagine that some day soon the Internet will be something beyond what you sit down and log on to from home or work – it will become something that you're constantly connected to and communicating with whether you're walking, driving, or traveling – an experience in itself.

If you'd asked me two years ago what I wanted to do for a career, Flash development and animation would never have crossed my mind. At that time, I considered web development as just a job, not a career. My primary career focus while I was in school was animation film. Whether it was traditional 2D/3D animation, compositing, art direction, it didn't matter – I just wanted to be part of that field. It's what I fell in love with and dreamed of doing since I was a kid. I always wanted to take part in feature film or special effects animation and help create the magic that enchanted me in my youth.

Web development and design was pretty much comparable to any other job you have while going to school and I treated it as such. I learned as much as I needed to stay current in technologies, but didn't fully immerse myself in all its possibilities, even multimedia and animation. I felt that if I'd done that, it would've detracted me from my original career goals and I would have ended up in some nine-to-five work environment looking at code for the rest of my life. As my job responsibilities evolved in my workplace, little by little, so did my view of the Internet. I really had no other choice but to immerse myself in as much of the technology as I could handle, so I started to dabble here and there in Flash. As with other technologies, I never took it as seriously or pursued its total potential. I just did it because the tweening seemed simple enough and I could put rich media on the Web. It was only till I stumbled upon the online design community that I started to take developing animation in Flash much more seriously.

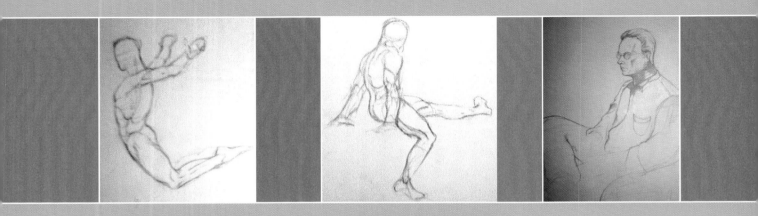

Originally, my first art influences came from Greek and Roman antiquity, the Renaissance, and Neo-classicism. I loved viewing the works of artists such as Carravaggio, Michaelangelo, and David. Since life drawing was important to my career goal, I kept my focus solely in those categories. In college, however, I was being exposed to more art that was outside of my perspective field. In an Art Issues class I took one semester, I was forced to confront art that I had previously and consciously stayed away from. I had conditioned myself to believe that art encompassed only the traditional and not the experimental. Expression was in a different category so I never acknowledged other art forms. But through that experience I began to embrace other forms of artistic expression. My perspective scope opened as I figured out that I couldn't put confines on what art was. It was everything and anything all at the same time. I became highly influenced by the art of Barbara Kruger. Her art has had a significant impact on my design and art philosophy and I thoroughly enjoy how effectively she communicates her social and cultural ideas through her artwork. Her command of type and images convey her opinions clearly. I feel strongly about that core fundamental of design. Despite the technology used to create a design, it must, for me, effectively communicate a message. The technology only supports and strengthens the communicative goal of the work.

© Barbara Kruger, 'Untitled' (A Picture is worth more than a thousand words) 1992. Courtesy: Mary Boone Gallery, New York.

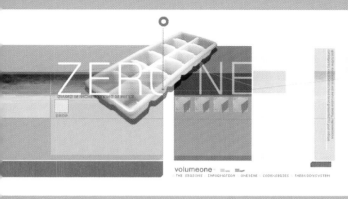

© www.volumeone.com

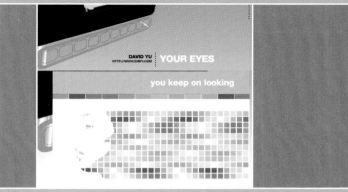

© www.dhky.com

Flash and web design impacted me at a time when I was exploring art and what it meant to me as well as what I thought about my career goals. I was being influenced by what I was seeing online from designers like Matt Owens, David Yu, Lee Misenheimer, and Jimmy Chen and also from what I was being exposed to in school. One piece specifically was an exhibit on DHKY named *Love is a four-letter word*. It showcased the work of several designers and the narratives they created based on that theme.

The online design community has also played a significant role in influencing the way I approach design. Since I was aspiring to become an animator, design wasn't one of my core competencies in art. I took the required foundation classes in 2D and 3D design that I needed to satisfy my requirements in school, but never really had an outlet to apply them. I began to view the design that many talented artists on the Web were creating and that helped to mold what I felt I wanted to emphasize as I was producing my own work. For example, the interactive experimentations from MONO*Crafts and visual narratives from Volume One helped sculpt my style and techniques in design. The more active I was in exploring the community, the more I wanted to express myself through design. I can't emphasize enough how the community is a source of inspiration for all who are part of it. I don't feel it necessarily means that we rip off one another, but we do influence each other. There's so much to explore and see from other individuals design perspectives, so I try and keep part of that alive with the work that I create. I've tried to find my niche with others whom I've looked up to and admired.

© www.yugop.com

© www.destroyrockcity.com

Axis

With this newfound direction, I began to actively explore the possibilities of Flash. I began experimenting with ideas in art, design, and typography. I didn't start exploring other possibilities in interactivity with ActionScript, other than the basics, until I stumbled upon praystation and MONO*crafts. Once I'd been exposed to these great interactive elements, I began to understand that programming could re-inforce my ideas and my work and thus become an integral part of my design process. I began to read up on tutorials and downloaded as many open source FLAs as I could, trying to develop my skill set in ActionScript. I quickly got to the point that I needed to understand more so I also began reading math, physics, and game programming tutorials so that I could understand the principles behind the interactivity that others were creating. I never wanted to feel that I couldn't create the interactivity I wanted on my own. As I read more and more about math and how to apply it through programming I found that I was creating art as well.

For a long time I figured that science and art were two completely different things. On the contrary, I now feel that they are closely coupled together. A lot of art created in traditional media is trying to emulate things that we perceive in the real world. Those perceptions of the real world are explained and studied through science. For example, when animators learn and practice the principles of squash and stretch, they're trying to emulate principles of physics, but through drawings. The same can be said for artists and painters creating landscapes and sunsets, linear perspective, and light and shadow.

Through a few months of diligence and a few late nights, I was able to build my skill set in Flash ActionScripting. I now view ActionScript as part of my media kit just as much as the pencil, fill, or eraser tools in Flash. It's all a part of the toolset that delivers the message of your design – just in a different form. It's only a tool and just like any other tool, whether it be a brush, pencil, or pen, there's a set of techniques and rules that apply to its proper use. The thing that I feel is great about ActionScripting is that you can apply many different interactive elements, which enrich the engagement and association of emotions and responses even more. I try to associate the interactivity with what we see in the real world that can be associated with a feeling, mood, or experience, and emulate that in my Flash work.

When I started Fifth Rotation, I tried to bring all of these things together and explore ways to communicate utilizing Flash. Each exhibit has an idea. Sometimes it's narrative; sometimes it's a fragment of a thought. It's all geared towards exploring new concepts of communication and expression. Whenever I approach the point where I get ready to draft my ideas, I keep to a pretty systematic approach. I try to personify the idea I have with drawn shapes, type, and imagery that can usually be directly associated with the message or experience I'm trying to convey. Lately, I've been sticking with more vector art rather than raster or rendered images. I find that this allows me to work more freely in Flash. In my personal work I've also been trying to stick with basic colors and values. My friend Maurice Wright from Moluv.com asked me once, "Why grayscale?" My answer was that if I could communicate with what I considered the bare minimum and people understood the message I was sending, then I've come closer to communicating more effectively.

When I created the *My Life is Falling Apart* exhibit, I tried to relay my feelings of stress and work through the clutter of words and type with the physical motion of the image breaking apart. The key to finding the whole message in the piece is by dropping the blocks in an orderly fashion, with a balance, which I feel is the key to handling the everyday stress we come across. I feel this is a good example of a combination between design and interactivity that helps communicate the idea.

Chris Andrade

Another work of mine that I feel tries to convey an experience is the exploratory 3D navigation. 3D can fully immerse a user in an experience because the environment has the feeling of depth, as if they could actually be a part of the environment. This is something that has always intrigued me. A while ago I ventured into what designers like Yugo Nakamura, Thomas Noller, and Andries Odendaal were doing with ideas and concepts in 3D ActionScripting and navigation. I was immediately hooked and began experimenting. *Exhibit 6* was a playground and sketch environment for an upcoming Kaliber10000 issue that I was creating at the time. The issue was showcasing designers in the community and I wanted the interface to simulate an environment with depth, as if you were in the same room with these people and you could move around and talk with them.

Over the next few pages in my tutorial, we'll be jumping into some more 3D ActionScripting and build the 3D perspective zoom experiment that I created on *Exhibit 6* of my site. If you're like me, you will have learned some great 3D ActionScripting techniques from the work of Andries Odendaal, a designer I respect enormously, but here we'll be focusing more on the areas of translation transformations and perspective projection. Don't be intimidated by the names of the concepts; in my opinion they're actually easier than rotation transformations. We'll also be jumping into some OOP techniques to build custom objects with Flash 5 ActionScript.

Have fun.

Axis

This tutorial covers many advanced topics and involves the use of some 3D mathematics. I'm briefly going to describe the mathematical logic behind the 3D scripting that we're going to perform and then present the formulae you need to create the effect. At the end of the tutorial, I'll provide resources where I learned the techniques and principles behind the 3D programming we use, that will be of use to you if you decide this is an area you'd like to understand in more detail. Secondly, this tutorial will hopefully give you a real feel for the programming possibilities in Flash and get you really familiar with OOP in ActionScript.

We're going to go through the processes I used to build the object that I used for my experiment so that you can get some experience building objects from scratch. You can find all the working and completed files on the CD with this book, so you can both build and troubleshoot your work at the same time. I've simplified the file and removed those things that aren't necessary to the core functionality, in order to allow you to focus solely on creating the effect.

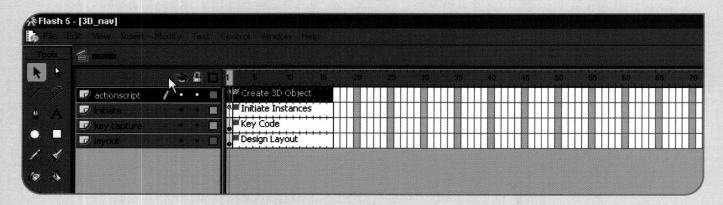

Let's get started. Open up the working file. In our root timeline, create a layer called actionscript. This is where we'll store our code for creating our 3D object, or class, that all of our instances will follow.

Now, we'll begin the process of creating an object that has properties and methods pertaining to 3D calculations. The properties will include data such as (x,y,z) coordinates and the methods will calculate functions that render our object in 3D space. This will give us a set of reusable code that we can apply to all our movie clips easily and effectively. The first step in creating our object is to build a *constructor* function. The constructor function assigns a name for our object and initializes the names of its properties and methods.

In your actionscript layer, click on the Actions panel and type the following code:

```
function threeDObj(mc,x,y,z,d,s,oX,oY,i){
  _root.attachMovie(mc,"object"+i,i);
  this.c = _root["object"+i];
  this.x = x;
  this.y = y;
  this.z = z;
  this.d = d;
  this.s = s;
  this.oX = oX;
  this.oY = oY;
}
```

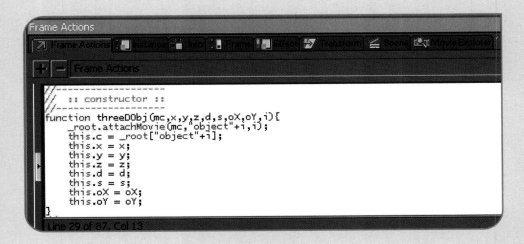

Kind of scary at first but don't worry, we'll make this easier to understand. As I said just now, in OOP, this is what we refer to as our *constructor*. When this function is called, it initializes a new instance of our 3D object and sets up all of its properties. You'll see that in our parentheses we have a bunch of different arguments, or data, passed into our function. These arguments are what our object's properties will be based on. Here's what they stand for:

That's the data we pass into our function that is needed to create our 3D object. To avoid taking up too much space and to keep our code compact, I named each property by the first letter of its actual name. For example, for depth I named the property d, for origin *x* I named it oX and so on. The next block of statements goes about taking the data or arguments that we passed into the function and building our object's properties from that information. We use this in our syntax because it means we're applying this data to the object we're creating.

ARGUMENTS PASSED INTO OUR CONSTRUCTOR FUNCTION

function threeDObj(mc,x,y,z,d,s,oX,oY,i){

mc	= the movie clip which we want to replicate and render in 3D
x	= our object's x-coordinate in 3D space
y	= our object's y-coordinate in 3D space
z	= our object's z-coordinate in 3D space
d	= our object's depth value or the distance of our eye to our view plane
s	= our object's size value to evaluate with perspective
oX	= the x-position of our origin
oY	= the y-position of our origin
i	= is used for the attachment of our movie clip. It specifies the depth and name of our object on the root timeline.

```
_root.attachMovie(mc,"object"+i,i);
this.c = _root["object"+i];
this.x = x;
this.y = y;
this.z = z;
this.d = d;
this.s = s;
this.oX = oX;
this.oY = oY;
```

Now you can see that the function is creating a set of properties for our object that are pretty much the same as the arguments you passed into the function, except for the first two statements. The first statement attaches the movie clip we want to render by using the attachMovie() method which allows us to attach any movie clip in our Library that has been given an Export identifier as its linkage property.

The next statement creates a property called `c` which holds the movie clip instance name on the root timeline and allows us to modify the clip's properties, things like `_alpha` as well as `_x` and `_y` position, with our 3D calculations.

Now we'll continue to build our object by adding methods to give actions to our object, so it's not just a lump of data. The methods we create will perform calculations for rendering our object in 3D. There are two ways to create methods for objects. The one I used is to attach a function directly by using the `prototype` property of our object. The `prototype` property stores all the properties and methods that all instances created from our class inherit.

So below our constructor function type the following code:

```
// -------------------
// :: methods ::
// -------------------
threeDObj.prototype.getRadians = function(theta){
    this.sin = Math.sin((Math.PI/180)*theta);
    this.cos = Math.cos((Math.PI/180)*theta);
}
Line 29 of 87, Col 13
```

```
threeDObj.prototype.getRadians = function(theta){
    this.sin = Math.sin((Math.PI/180)*theta);
    this.cos = Math.cos((Math.PI/180)*theta);
}
```

We've created our first method for our 3D object. We first typed the name of the constructor, accessed its `prototype` property, created a name for our method (`getRadians`) and then set it equal to a function. The function passes a degree angle to be converted into radian measure so Flash can find our appropriate sine and cosine values. Radians are another way to measure angles. This method performs the conversions from degrees to radians we need, finds the appropriate Sine and Cosine values, and then stores them as two new properties for our object, `sin` and `cos`. These values are necessary for performing our z-axis rotation transformations.

Axis

If you know Andries Odendaal's work well, the next few methods will already be familiar to you. The methods perform our rotation transformations about each of the three axes. These formulae simply calculate the new location for our points in space as the angle of rotation of our points around one of the three axes gets bigger or smaller.

These methods are purely supplemental to this chapter, except for the getRotationZ() method. I've included them so that if I wanted to use them for experimentation I'd have them readily available. Having them here also makes our 3D object more complete if we want to create rotations around the other two axes.

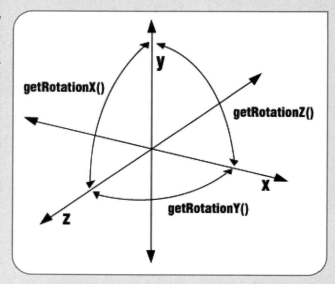

Type the following code in your Actions panel:

```
threeDObj.prototype.getRotationX = function(){
    tmpy = this.y;
    tmpz = this.z;
    this.y = (this.cos*tmpy)-(this.sin*tmpz);
    this.z = (this.sin*tmpy)+(this.cos*tmpz);
}

threeDObj.prototype.getRotationY = function(){
    tmpx = this.x;
    tmpz = this.z;
    this.z = (this.cos*tmpz)-(this.sin*tmpx);
    this.x = (this.cos*tmpx)+(this.sin*tmpz);
}

threeDObj.prototype.getRotationZ = function(){
    tmpx = this.x;
    tmpy = this.y;
    this.x = (this.cos*tmpx)-(this.sin*tmpy);
    this.y = (this.sin*tmpx)+(this.cos*tmpy);
}
```

Here's the breakdown of the methods. It first grabs the current points position and places it in a temporary variable. Then it performs the calculations to find its next point and sets the (x,y,z) properties equal to the new location.

The next method we construct is what calculates the perspective projection of our object. Perspective projection is a way of rendering depth perception on a 2D surface, that surface being your screen. Examine the diagram to see how it works.

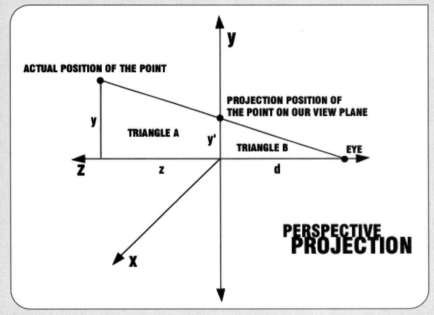

Both d and z are properties of our object. We created those properties with our constructor. We'll now use those properties to calculate our projection.

Let's dig into a little bit of math. What we're trying to achieve is to find the position of our object on our view plane, which is denoted on our diagram as y^1. If you notice on our diagram, we have two triangles: A and B. Looking at both of these triangle, you can see that there's a similarity between the two, – their sizes are proportional. From that, we can assume these ratios between the two triangles:

$$(d+z)/y = d/y^1$$

Now to find our location to project our point, which we denote as y^1. Once simplified, our equation will look like this:

$$y^1 = y*d/(d+z)$$

We've now found the formula to project our point onto its correct position on our view plane. The same formula would arise if we were solving for a projection point on the x-axis:

$$x^1 = x*d/(d+z)$$

Let's simplify even further. You can see that both equations have in common the calculation $d/(d+z)$. So we assume that in order to find a point's new *x* or *y* position on our view plane $(x1,y1)$, we multiply the actual *x* or *y* position by d and divide it by $d+z$.

113

Thus we arrive at the formula:

perspective projection = d / z+d

where

d = center of projection or the position of our eye to the view plane

and

z = an object's z-coordinate

The calculations are represented in the following code. Type this in your Actions panel:

```
threeDObj.prototype.getPerspective =
➡ function(){
      this.p = this.d/(this.z+this.d);
      this.sc = this.p*this.s;
}
```

This method yields two new properties for our object: its projection value, which we denote as p, and the value that we'll use to evaluate its scale proportions (sc). Our scale proportion is evaluated by taking the scale value of our object at the origin, which is our property s, and multiplying it by the perspective ratio.

Now that we have methods to compute our 3D math calculations, we can construct a method that will create the x and y positions of our movie clip in respect to our 3D calculations.

Type in this ActionScript:

```
threeDObj.prototype.getProjection =
➡ function(){
      this.xp = (this.x*this.p)+this.oX;
      this.yp = (this.y*this.p)+this.oY;
}
```

Remember how we stated before that in order to find our new *x* and *y* positions on the view plane we need to multiply its current *x* and *y* position by our perspective formula (p=d/(z+d))? Well, here's where that happens. We perform the multiplication, then add the origin coordinate for each axis, oX and oY. This method will yield another set of two new properties, xp and yp, which are the values to which we set our movie clip's _x and _y positions.

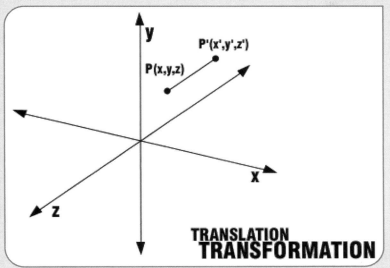

TRANSLATION TRANSFORMATION

Next, we construct a method that provides the translation transformations we'll need to make our objects zoom back and forth in 3D space. Translation transformations simply move the points of an object to a new specified location in space. For example, the translation transformation of a point P(x,y,z) to a new position point P'(x',y',z') is as follows:

```
x' = x + tx
y' = x + ty
z' = x + tz
```

where

tx = translation displacement for the x-axis
ty = translation displacement for the y-axis
tz = translation displacement for the z-axis

See, not so tough! We're just placing our points in a newly specified position by adding a new value to each coordinate. No math object functions involved. We represent this with this ActionScript:

```
threeDObj.prototype.setTranslation = function(tx,ty,tz){
     this.x += tx;
     this.y += ty;
     this.z += tz;
}
```

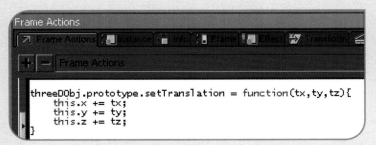

Our method takes our current (x,y,z) properties and adds whatever translation displacement values we pass into the function for each coordinate property respectively. The last method we need is one that combines all the calculations we created and applies them to our movie clip to render our objects in 3D space.

Axis

Click on your Actions panel and type the remaining code:

```
threeDObj.prototype.setTransformation =
➡ function(){
    this.getPerspective();
    this.getProjection();
    this.c._x = this.xp;
    this.c._y = this.yp;
    this.c._xscale = this.sc;
    this.c._yscale = this.sc;
    this.c._alpha = this.sc/2;
}
```

What does this method do then? Well, in order to complete our transformation we first access two of the methods we constructed earlier, `getPerspective()` and `getProjection()`, which are crucial to setting the final transformation. We then use the `c` property of our object – the property that holds our movie clip name – to set the clip's properties to the calculations we just made.

OK, now you can relax. You've created our 3D object. I know that was tough, but you know what's good about it? You never have to go through the process of creating 3D code for each clip or movie you create. You just declare a new instance of this object and voila, it inherits all these calculations. What may have seemed tough at first has just made our lives a whole lot easier. This code is also reusable and can be ported over into other projects where you'd like 3D elements involved. To do that you just export that code as an `.as` file by pressing CTRL+O while you're in the Actions panel; you can then load that into any other project where you may want to use it.

Now it's time to put our code to work and create our effect. The next portion of this tutorial is going to concentrate on duplicating the clips that we want to render in 3D. Before we do that, let's start by creating a movie clip that'll work together with our scripting.

Create a blank movie clip and name it capture. Then create a layer called key capture. Place the movie clip on your root timeline in the key capture layer and give it an instance name of capture. This movie clip will evaluate our key down events and initiate our zooming effect. We're going to leave this movie clip alone for now but we need it on our stage for some steps later on, which you'll see as you read on.

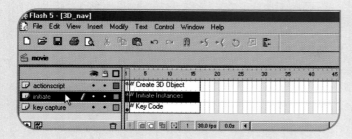

Create another layer underneath your actionscript layer and label that initiate. Frame 1 will encase the code that creates our instances of the 3D object and places them in space.

Now click on the frame and add the following ActionScript:

```
for(i=1;i<=10;i++){
    rX = random(20)-10;
    rY = random(20)-10;
    rZ = i*-50;
    oX = capture._x;
    oY = capture._y;
    this["obj"+i] = new threeDObj
    ➡ ("object",rX,rY,rZ,600,30,oX,oY,i);
    this["obj"+i].c.gotoAndStop(i);
    this["obj"+i].setTransformation();
}
```

This code is what initiates our 3D objects and sets them in their preliminary position in 3D. We use a `for` loop to loop through this block of statements ten times, ten being the number of objects we want to create in our movie. We've created three variables that are refreshed on each iteration of the loop: `rX`, `rY`, and `rZ`. These variables create a random `x` and `y` coordinate for our object and a `z` coordinate based on our current iteration count value times -50. This will place each of our objects progressively farther away on our coordinate grid. The next statements create the origin coordinates (`oX` and `oY`) of our grid that we need for our objects.

Remember that capture clip we created before we started hacking away? We're using that clip's `x` and `y` position on our movie as the origin for our objects to reference. Wherever you move the capture clip to, all your objects will revolve and be placed around its `x` and `y` coordinates on the root timeline.

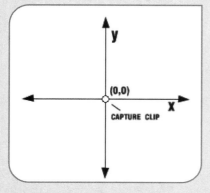

The last statement actually creates our new instance of the 3D object and creates a new name for it on our stage. It will name our object `obj` plus the value of `i`, so if `i` is equal to 1 our first object will be called `obj1`. When `i` is equal to 2 our second object will be called `obj2`, and so on.

To create a new instance of our object, we first type `new` and then the constructor function which creates our object. You use `new` whenever you want to create a new instance of any object. Now when we create our instances, we pass on the variables we previously created into the constructor function. Next we have to render these in perspective. The next statement does that by invoking our method `setTransformation()`.

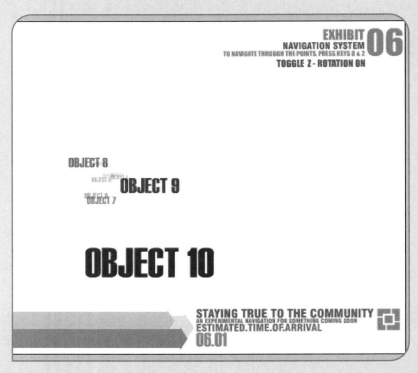

We have just created our objects and rendered them. If you export the movie you'll see all our clips in perspective. But now we want to be able to zoom in and out and move our objects closer or farther away from us. Let's go back to the neglected little clip on our stage, `capture`.

`capture` will now switch from being an idle clip on our screen to a very important part of our process for moving our objects back and forth in 3D space.

With the advent of Flash 5 ActionScript, we no longer need buttons to perform our key captures. We can now use `onClipEvent(keyDown)`. We'll be using the `onClipEvent` action like crazy, so get ready!

Let's start coding. Click on the your capture clip, then go to the Actions panel and type in this code:

```
onClipEvent(load){
        zrot = true;
}
```

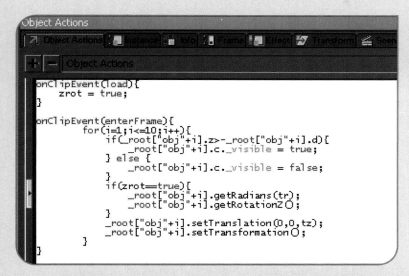

This initiates variables when our clip is first loaded in the movie. It sets the variable controlling our z-axis rotation (zrot) equal to true. This will mean that the z-rotation toggle is on.

Type in this next block of ActionScript:

```
onClipEvent(enterFrame){
        for(i=1;i<=10;i++){
            if(_root["obj"+i].z>_root["obj"+i].d){
                _root["obj"+i].c._visible = true;
            } else {
                _root["obj"+i].c._visible = false;
            }
            if(zrot==true){
                _root["obj"+i].getRadians(tr);
                _root["obj"+i].getRotationZ();
            }
            _root["obj"+i].setTranslation(0,0,tz);
            _root["obj"+i].setTransformation();
        }
}
```

Axis

This performs our zooming actions. It will perform our set of statements every time it passes through this frame. It's the equivalent of the old method of setting up an action clip and having it loop back and forth between two frames. The code first uses an `if/else` conditional to check whether our objects z-position is greater than its depth amount. If it is, it renders our clip's visibility to false – because what's the use of it being visible if it's past us, right?

Next it translates (or increments) our object's z-coordinate by a value `tz`. The translation will move our objects closer to us or farther from us depending on the value of `tz`. Once the translation is calculated, we call our `setTransformation()` method to render our object with its updated `z` value.

We also check to see whether `zrot` is true or not for a z-axis rotation added. If it is, we first send a degree value `tr` through our `getRadians()` method, which will return the proper `cosine` and `sine` values needed for our `getRotationZ()` method to produce our rotation effect.

We now need code that will capture our key press and send the correct value of `tz` and `tr` to our `enterFrame` actions. The value of move is controlled by which key is pressed; 8 on our keypad or keyboard controls the forward movement, and 2 controls our backward movement.

```
}
onClipEvent(keyDown){
    if (Key.getCode()==50||Key.getCode()==98) {
        tr = 5;
        tz = 10;
    }
    if (Key.getCode()==56||Key.getCode()==104) {
        tr = -5;
        tz = -10;
    }
}

onClipEvent(keyUp){
    if (Key.getCode()==50||Key.getCode()==98||Key.getCode()==56||Key.getCode()==104) {
        tr = 0;
        tz = 0;
    }
}
```

Line 38 of 38, Col 1

Under the `onClipEvent(enterFrame)` code type in the following:

```
onClipEvent (keyDown) {
    if (Key.getCode()==50||Key.getCode()==98) {
        tr = 5;
        tz = 10;
    }
    if (Key.getCode()==56||Key.getCode()==104) {
        tr = -5;
        tz = -10;
    }
}

onClipEvent (keyUp) {
    i                                                            f
(Key.getCode()==50||Key.getCode()==98||Key.getCode()==56||K
ey.getCode()==104) {
        tr = 0;
        tz = 0;
    }
}
```

When the viewer presses either the 8 or the 2 key, the `keyDown` clip event first checks to see which key was pressed by retrieving the key code value. It then passes the value of `tz` and `tr` accordingly. When a key is released, the `keyUp` clip event retrieves the key code once again and checks to see whether it's 8 or 2 and sets the value of `tz` and `tr` to `0`, which stops all movement.

If you exported the movie now, you'd see that we have a fully functional movie. The only thing lacking is that we don't have control over whether or not the z-rotation takes effect.

Let's create another clip called toggle. This clip will control whether or not the z-rotation effect is on or off, combined with our perspective zoom effect. In this clip, create two layers, one called stops and the other called text. For both layers, create two keyframes. In the first keyframe of your text layer type the words *toggle z-rotation on* and in the second keyframe type *toggle z-rotation off*. Next, add a `Stop` action for each keyframe in your stops layer. This will allow us to toggle back and forth between keyframes, like turning a light switch on and off.

Once you've created the clip, place it on the root timeline in a layer called layout.

Open up that clip and add the following code to frame 1 and 2 on the stops layer, before the Stop action.

Frame 1
```
_root.capture.zrot = true;
```

Frame 2
```
_root.capture.zrot = false;
```

This will pass the value of zrot to our capture clip and dictate whether or not the z-rotation is in effect. Let's go back to our root timeline and click on the toggle clip to add one last action:

```
onClipEvent(mouseDown){
    gotoAndPlay(_currentFrame+1);
}
```

All this does is to move our toggle clip's frame back and forth to create the on/off switch effect.

Now our movie is complete, and you'll see if you export it that you've got a nice perspective zooming movement and a z-axis rotation added to it that you can turn off and on.

All that's left is the list of resources that I promised for the avid 3D enthusiast, so that you can learn more about the subject of 3D programming.

Brandon Williams (a.k.a. Ahab) is a moderator for the Mathematics forum at www.were-here.com. I would say I learned about 50% of my 3D knowledge from him. His tutorials provide an excellent resource for learning not only the principles behind 3D math, but also how to implement them in Flash. He is, in my opinion, by far the best resource for Flash designers wanting to learn 3D programming. You can view his tutorials and work here:

www20.brinkster.com/ahab/index.htm

Here are some other good links for 3D programming:

www.gamedev.net
www.geocities.com/SiliconValley/2151/graphics.html
members.nbci.com/3dcoding/index.html

I hope that this tutorial has given you some insight into 3D ActionScripting possibilities, as well as OOP principles that you can implement the next time you start an interactive Flash project. There was a lot of information to digest, but I suggest that if you study the code again and play around and experiment with rotating around the other axes or setting different rotation and translation increments, you'll soon get the hang of it all.

Some of you may have noticed that Chris's effect is similar to Limmy's. There is of course one important difference; artistic direction. Both are using the masking effect in different ways such that a non-Flash ActionScript expert would not be able to see the similarity.

There are two main areas we can play with Chris's photo journal in our quest to develop it; we can change the content or the effect itself.

content

Obviously, the photo journal can be used to show any sequence of images (such as an online portfolio), but remember that you can also substitute the current content for animated movie clips. To do this, you would also have to make sure that the movie clips only started animating when they were selected to maintain a decent frame rate.

You could also alter the format of your content by including (say) multiple versions of the slideshow in a related order. The sketch on the left is one idea. By making selections in each of the middle two slideshows, you can select between the red skirt and the yellow blouse or the red skirt and the blue blouse. The advantage of this setup us that it shows the potential customer how their selectionof clothes will look together. Just the thing for a fashion kiosk!

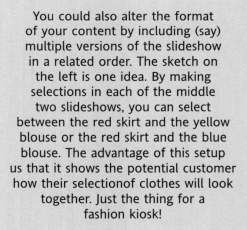

Add Vas's mouse position trick for an even swisher interface; simply click and drag left—right to change each garment — something to consider if you get to do the next seasons Yigal—Azrouel site!

effect

There are several cool variations you can make simply by changing the mask. By changing the mask from a solid rectangle to a closely spaced 'venetian blind' shape as shown on the right, you can mix the thumbnail pixels with the currently selected full picture in a way that is more interesting than the overused (and processor intensive) alpha method.

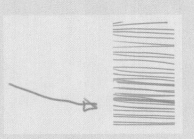

Although animated masks are difficult to implement, you could always spice the static images up by overlaying parts of the journal with animated movie clips. A personal favorite with static photos is the 'old film effect', complete with scratches and random dots and dropouts.

Alternatively, make the bitmaps into movie clips (by inserting them into a clip each). You then inherit the ability to do any of the transitions you could do with a standard movie clip.

You could for example, use the brightness effect (or the color objects setTransform command if you're an ActionScript junkie) to simulate a camera flash 'whiteout' transition effect between slides.

chapter 1
chapter 2
chapter 3
chapter 4
chapter 5
chapter 6
chapter 7
chapter 8
chapter 9
chapter 10
chapter 11
chapter 12
chapter 13
chapter 14
chapter 15

"Often it's only when you happen to view something from a different angle that you're inspired with an idea you never expected."

Gabriel Mulzer
www.voxangelica.net

Depth

The last movie Jean Cocteau ever made, *Orpheus' Will*, seemed to be all about himself: a portrait of Jean Cocteau by Jean Cocteau, an iconic summary of his own work and life. So at one level we have the story of his life's work, but if you're in the mood to perceive something invisible and imaginary behind this, for me it's about something slightly more poetic. This is all compressed into one short moment of the movie, one short moment that I've never managed to get out of my head: the petals from an hibiscus are unfolded from blank bare hands, and put together one by one until they form a beautiful blossom. For me this stresses the idea that something beautiful is created out of nothing, and nothing you see had existed before.

You could think and wonder about this, relate it to life, love, beauty, existence and creation.

Finally, all you find yourself left with is a mystery. A very beautiful mystery indeed.

I find mysteries and beauty, which is a mystery in itself, very appealing. The images I love the most are those that have been created around clear themes. The atmosphere surrounding the images, the symbols and meanings I find within them relate in different ways to different thoughts and personal things, moods and memories. Then they start to have a special meaning to me that I can't share with or explain to anyone else. Some of the images that are most important to me are those created by Max Ernst, in particular *Eve, La Seule qui Nous Reste*. If you've ever seen it, you may have been struck by the air of mystery that surrounds this image. Even if it doesn't have the effect on you that it has on me, I hope you agree that it contains something you can't express verbally, something that you can't quite put your finger on.

Depth

Of course, I pick up tiny grains of an idea from all around me, just as I'm sure that you pull ideas and snippets from here, there and everywhere when you work on projects. These can be pictures from films or other media, but equally it can be very simple things you might see every day. Often it's only when you happen to view something from a different angle that you're inspired with an idea you never expected. You may one day look at an old iron statue that you pass every day on the way to work and see there a shape you hadn't spotted before that's exactly what you need for that new logo you're working on. You can be looking at a casual or random arrangement of dried flowers and find yourself admiring the inspirational beauty of the natural forms. While you're engrossed in looking at it, you may unexpectedly discover the stimulus for new ideas. Perhaps one day by chance you'll see a dead pigeon on the street. This really mundane image sinks into your mind and stays in your memory. Once there it combines with all your other experiences and memories from the past, picking up associations that make it into more than an image of a dead bird. But you're hardly ever conscious of how or when this has happened. At some point, that pigeon will come to mean more to you than just a dead bird. It will conjure up a mixture of emotions and form a partnership in your head with other images to provide you with exactly what you're looking for to express a particular message or theme.

We all see design ideas everywhere around us and we can't help continually picking up influences from everything we look at. Of course, this seldom happens consciously. The image adds itself to all the other memories that are hidden away somewhere, lying dormant in the dark corners of our minds. At the right moment, those shadowy memories begin to emerge from the darkness to form links with other subconscious influences to give birth to something new. They turn into the mystery that is creativity and to some extent remain hidden from our conscious stream of thought. Of course, it's rather difficult to examine this process more closely, not only because what's at work here is a unique personal experience, but also because it's impossible to say in the end exactly where all these things, which have combined into something new, have come from.

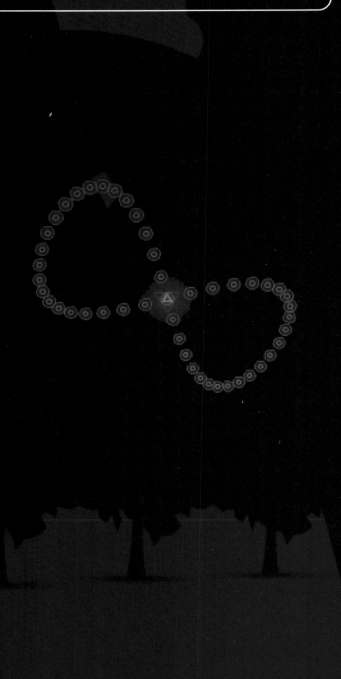

Depth

The idea of space is important to me, especially on a screen. I don't want to show any coloured pixels on a flat monitor. It's much more important to me to let the screen disappear and to have the viewer enter the space behind it. A space, which only exists in my head, is usually so vague that to begin with I have to work on it to discover exactly what kind of a world it is. In some ways this is similar to what happens in Maurice Sendak's *Where the Wild Things Are*, when the walls of the room disappear and it turns into a forest. Max enters the forest and the world on the other side, which is actually an unimaginably immense vastness, somewhere where he has to travel a frightening distance before he gets anywhere at all. He is reassuringly quickly returned from this strange world, in spite of the enormous spatial and transitory dimensions, which separate this place from his home.

Sometimes I escape to the world of computer games and comics. Apart from the fact that I never have enough leisure time to play the games properly, for me it's not the game itself that is the attraction. It's enough for me just to watch players over their shoulders because I enjoy just engaging with the world and the atmosphere surrounding the games. I have to say, though, that most of the time this illusion of entering a different dimension quickly falls apart for me.

I engage with comics in a similar way — the individual pictures and the moods fascinate me rather than the stories themselves. I actually used to draw comics myself, though they mostly didn't have any text and words, or even an actual story. Needless to say, they were never going to be a great success. Mind you, that's going back a good while. At the time I was also already working to develop my animation skills using outrageous, self-designed software.

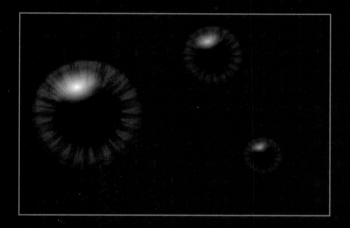

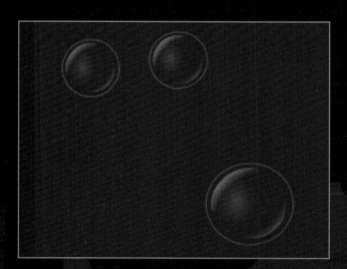

Years later when I began working with Flash for the first time, I was immediately fascinated by its simplicity compared to the software that I'd been using previously. Disappointingly, the company I was working for at the time had hardly any use for Flash, so, funnily enough, I used it mostly as a pure vector drawing programme. I would even use it as an interactive notepad for navigational structures, occasionally even to draw short animations which then found other uses in other software packages.

I'm still fascinated by the impact that the simplicity and limitations of Flash have on my work. Of course, the biggest limitation is the file size issue, which forces me to reduce the size of my graphics as I work. A second limitation for me is that in Flash I'm forced to draw with clear sharp lines. When I draw with a pen or pencil, my sketches can be softer, giving a subtle hint of the theme I'm trying to convey. I do what I can to use Flash to create semi-realistic impressions by only using simple forms and keeping some details blurred. I like to keep a certain gap between what viewers can actually see and the pictures that develop in their heads. I feel I've succeeded if what they see in their mind's eye isn't actually what's on the screen.

The simplicity of Flash as a medium is fascinating, because its limitations force us to make the most of our creativity by staying within them, or by trying to find a way around them for a solution. Over the next few pages I'll take you through how I use perspective distortion to create the feeling that you're entering a whole new world, as you watch some of my effects at voxangelica.com and a project that I've just completed at freshfroot.com.

Depth

Probably the most obvious way to create depth in a movie is to use motion and shape tweens. I've used them to make logos, which is quite simple, but when I'm working on larger-scale projects I find it's not the most flexible or time-efficient method.

An alternative approach to creating depth is to move, scale, and tints objects following the rules of *perspective distortion*. The perception of depth is mostly created by motion, where objects are moving whilst changing their appearance in accordance with these rules at the same time.

Whilst there are these different approaches, and I can't promise my home-grown methods are the best, the basics of what I'm using are really very simple. When I was thinking over what to write this chapter about, I considered which of my Flash pieces I could use. I had used the technique I'm going to show you in one of my favorite Flash pieces – *The Lake*. Unfortunately this piece was created in Flash 4, so is not within the scope of this chapter. *The Ice Queen* was the first movie I created in Flash 5, but it contains some unnecessary, and confusing Flash 5 features that I thought it wouldn't be smart to use – not the best subject for a tutorial like this then! (If you want to see *The Lake* and *Ice Queen* you can find them on my web site – www.voxangelica.net.)

So I've set up a new, basic tutorial file, which I hope will give you some ideas. The concept is not so detailed that it is confined to a specific purpose. You can build upon it, play around with it, and change it to suit your own ideas.

To scale and position movie clips in a way that looks to be in perspective, we first need to have a quick look at this 'virtual space' onto which we're going to place our objects. This two-dimensional space is commonly described in a two-axis coordinate system, where a pair of values (*x,y*) describe the location of a point on the 2D surface. For a third dimension, a third axis is needed, and this is commonly named *z*.

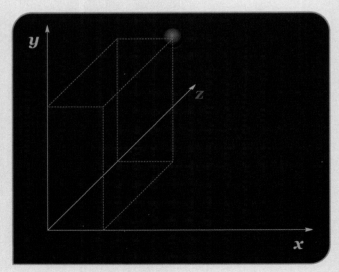

Take the base FLA, `simple_1.fla`, and save it as `simple_2.fla`. We're doing this so that we can later return to the base FLA to take it in a different direction to what we're doing in `simple_2.fla`.

Go back into the edit mode of the viewer movie clip. On the bg layer delete the rectangle outline and draw a horizontal line 365 pixels long, with a gray hairline stroke. Center this line – it's going to act as our horizon in the end effect. Create a new layer above the bg layer, and name it button. Guess what's going on this layer! We now need to create the button. Select Insert>New Symbol, choose the Button option, and name our button invBigButton. You should now be in the edit mode for this button.

Draw a rectangle as we did for the bg layer of our base FLA (400x300, gray hairline stroke, no fill, centered). We want to create the effect that you often find on a camera's viewfinder – with the four corners intact, but most of the sides missing. To do this we need to delete the center part of each of the rectangle's four sides. I'll now show you one way of doing this. An alternative is to show the grid on the stage and crop the lines using the sanp to grid function.

Draw another rectangle with the dimensions 360x320 above our outline rectangle (if they overlap, the lines of the first rectangle will be accidentally erased). Align this to the center of the stage horizontally, and then vertically (the order in which you do this *does* matter). We now need to deselect the rectangle, select it again, and then delete it. The process of deselecting and reselecting the rectangle is necessary to make sure that our lines are actually erased.

To finish off the viewfinder effect, make another rectangle to the left of our outline. Set its dimensions to 440x280, and then center it – this time vertically first and then horizontally. Deselect, select and delete this new rectangle. We should now have our viewfinder.

Depth

Insert a keyframe on the hit frame and delete the viewfinder. Draw a 480x300 red rectangle (no outline), and align this to the center. Now go back to the viewer movie clip's edit mode and place our new button onto the center of the stage on frame 1. This button spans the movie clip's timeline. We now need to add a couple of actions to the button. Select the button on the stage, and open up the Object Actions window. Add these lines of code:

```
on (rollOver) {
     inside = true;
}
on (rollOut) {
     inside = false;
}
```

These actions mean that when we add our mouse actions to frame 1, they'll work when the mouse rolls over the button (hence true), but not when the mouse is not over this area (hence false).

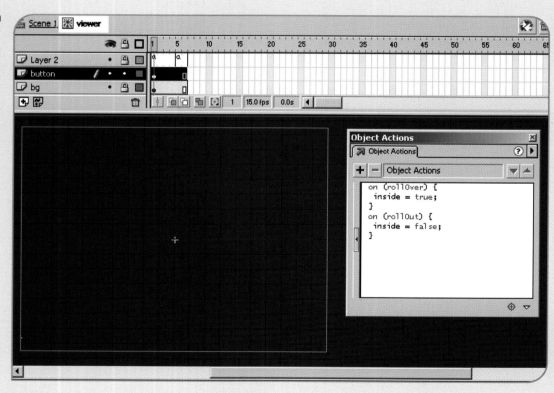

To finish our modifications of the viewer movie clip, we need to edit the actions on Layer 2. Let's start with frame 1. The simplest thing to do here is to copy the code from the version of simple_2.fla on the CD, as there is a lot of it!

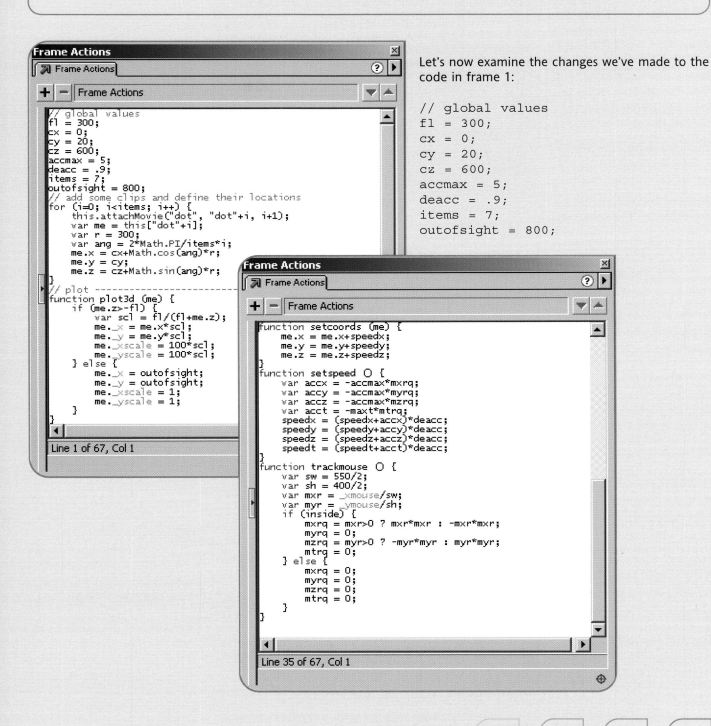

Let's now examine the changes we've made to the code in frame 1:

```
// global values
fl = 300;
cx = 0;
cy = 20;
cz = 600;
accmax = 5;
deacc = .9;
items = 7;
outofsight = 800;
```

Frame Actions window 1:

```
// global values
fl = 300;
cx = 0;
cy = 20;
cz = 600;
accmax = 5;
deacc = .9;
items = 7;
outofsight = 800;
// add some clips and define their locations
for (i=0; i<items; i++) {
    this.attachMovie("dot", "dot"+i, i+1);
    var me = this["dot"+i];
    var r = 300;
    var ang = 2*Math.PI/items*i;
    me.x = cx+Math.cos(ang)*r;
    me.y = cy;
    me.z = cz+Math.sin(ang)*r;
}
// plot ----------------------
function plot3d (me) {
    if (me.z>-fl) {
        var scl = fl/(fl+me.z);
        me._x = me.x*scl;
        me._y = me.y*scl;
        me._xscale = 100*scl;
        me._yscale = 100*scl;
    } else {
        me._x = outofsight;
        me._y = outofsight;
        me._xscale = 1;
        me._yscale = 1;
    }
}
```

Line 1 of 67, Col 1

Frame Actions window 2:

```
function setcoords (me) {
    me.x = me.x+speedx;
    me.y = me.y+speedy;
    me.z = me.z+speedz;
}
function setspeed () {
    var accx = -accmax*mxrq;
    var accy = -accmax*myrq;
    var accz = -accmax*mzrq;
    var acct = -maxt*mtrq;
    speedx = (speedx+accx)*deacc;
    speedy = (speedy+accy)*deacc;
    speedz = (speedz+accz)*deacc;
    speedt = (speedt+acct)*deacc;
}
function trackmouse () {
    var sw = 550/2;
    var sh = 400/2;
    var mxr = _xmouse/sw;
    var myr = _ymouse/sh;
    if (inside) {
        mxrq = mxr>0 ? mxr*mxr : -mxr*mxr;
        myrq = 0;
        mzrq = myr>0 ? -myr*myr : myr*myr;
        mtrq = 0;
    } else {
        mxrq = 0;
        myrq = 0;
        mzrq = 0;
        mtrq = 0;
    }
}
```

Line 35 of 67, Col 1

Depth

Our focal length and center y coordinate have been slightly altered. These are just minor adjustments that will change the way we see the final effect. For example, our final effect has trees in it, so we need to make these changes to stop the trees from flying into the air! We've also changed the number of items, because we don't want our forest to be too dense!

We've also added three new variables: `accmax` (maximum acceleration), `deacc` (deceleration), and `outofsight`. In this movie there will be an element of mouse-responsive movement. So we've added these variables to regulate the consequences of mouse movement. We'll see these variables in use shortly.

```
// add some clips and define their locations
for (i=0; i<items; i++) {
      this.attachMovie("dot", "dot"+i, i+1);
      var me = this["dot"+i];
      var r = 300;
      var ang = 2*Math.PI/items*i;
      me.x = cx+Math.cos(ang)*r;
      me.y = cy;
      me.z = cz+Math.sin(ang)*r;
}
```

This section of code appears exactly the same as it did in our base FLA. We still want our objects to be drawn in a circle around the center point. Our reduced number of items will obviously impact on the size of angles and the number of repetitions of this loop. This is where the mathematical placing of objects comes into its own: our objects will be evenly spaced around our circle regardless of the number of items, and this code does it all for us!

The advent of mouse-controlled motion in this exercise has led to us changing our `plot3d` function to an `if` statement:

```
// plot ------------------
function plot3d (me) {
      if (me.z>-fl) {
            var scl = fl/(fl+me.z);
            me._x = me.x*scl;
            me._y = me.y*scl;
            me._xscale = 100*scl;
            me._yscale = 100*scl;
      } else {
            me._x = outofsight;
```

```
        me._y = outofsight;
        me._xscale = 1;
        me._yscale = 1;
    }
}
```

If the `if` condition is satisfied, then the function will act exactly the same as the `plot3d` function in `simple_1.fla`. In plain English, this means that our objects will be plotted using the original `plot3d` function if we're viewing the scene from in front of the movie clip. If we've gone past the movie clip in our virtual world, the `else` statement will kick in. The effect of this is that the movie clip's *x* and *y* coordinates will be equal to `outofsight`. When we chose the value of `outofsight`, we were really just choosing a value that will take our coordinates off the visible stage. This can create the effect that we've gone past the object, or that it's not in view. As the clip will be off the stage if the `else` statement is triggered, the scaling isn't important so I've set it to the fixed value of 1, rather than our variable factor that achieves perspective distortion.

Note that as we're moving around our virtual world in this example, trying to create depth, the scaling of objects becomes more important than in our static base FLA, and this is where the `scl` variable really becomes useful.

The purpose of our next function is to change the global center coordinates of the group dependent on any mouse movement (we'll define the `speed` variable later in the code):

```
function setcoords (me) {
    me.x = me.x+speedx;
    me.y = me.y+speedy;
    me.z = me.z+speedz;
}
```

To give a realistic feeling of steering through our 3D arrangement, we need to define functions that will keep track of the relative position of the mouse, and to derive speed from this. The further away from the center of the stage the mouse goes, the faster I want our speed to be. In the center itself I want all motion to stop, and let us stand still and admire the view.

The `setspeed` function is defined first in our code, but to give us a better understanding of what's going on, we'll look at the `trackmouse` function first:

```
function trackmouse () {
    var sw = 550/2;
    var sh = 400/2;
    var mxr = _xmouse/sw;
    var myr = _ymouse/sh;
    if (inside) {
        mxrq = mxr>0 ? mxr*mxr : -mxr*mxr;
        myrq = 0;
        mzrq = myr>0 ? -myr*myr : myr*myr;
        mtrq = 0;
    } else {
        mxrq = 0;
        myrq = 0;
        mzrq = 0;
        mtrq = 0;
    }
}
```

Firstly, this function stores the stage width and height in the `sw` and `sh` variables. It would usually make more sense to store these variables with the other global variables, but it's easier to explain what we're doing here if we keep them in the place where they're needed. Our next variables, `mxr` and `myr`, take our mouse position and divide it by the stage width/height. This will produce a value between −1 and 1. The value in the center will still be 0. Why do I want this conversion? One advantage is that the result will always be a value in the same range from −1 to 1, no matter whether we use a movie of 1000 pixels by 10 pixels, or one 300 by 200. The second advantage is that in the next step we multiply this value by itself, so the result will be closer to 0 for smaller values, but still be in a range from 0 to 1.

Once again, the next step takes the form of an `if` statement. When we added our object actions to our button we stated that `inside` would only be `true` when the mouse was over the button (which corresponds to the same area as our viewfinder). Hence, if the mouse isn't within the viewfinder, the `else` statement is run and all values equal 0.

Here's the one piece of code within this `if` statement that could be confusing:

```
mxrq = mxr>0 ? mxr*mxr : -mxr*mxr;
```

This line represents a kind of `if` statement, it's known as a *ternary conditional operator*. If `mxr>0` is true, `mxrq` takes the value between `?` and `:`, which, in this case, is `mxr*mxr`. If it's false then `mxrq` takes the value of the equation to the right of `:`, which is `-mxr*mxr`. This statement could also be written as:

```
if (mxr>0) {
        mxrq = mxr*mxr
    }
else {
        mxrq = -mxr*mxr
    }
```

We now have all our variables to use in the `setspeed` function:

```
function setspeed () {
    var accx = -accmax*mxrq;
    var accy = -accmax*myrq;
    var accz = -accmax*mzrq;
    var acct = -maxt*mtrq;
    speedx = (speedx+accx)*deacc;
    speedy = (speedy+accy)*deacc;
    speedz = (speedz+accz)*deacc;
    speedt = (speedt+acct)*deacc;
}
```

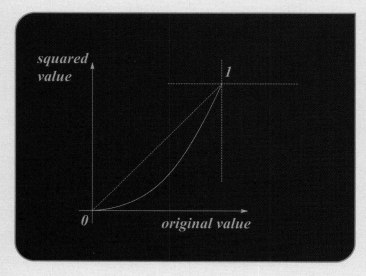

This function pulls together a number of variables that we've previously defined, and uses them to define our speed and acceleration values. Not real world physics inertia exactly, but it will do for a softer and more natural motion.

Depth

In order for our new functions to take effect, we also need to replace our `Stop` action in frame 5 with:

```
trackmouse();
setspeed();
for (i=0; i<items; i++) {
        var me = this["dot"+i];

setcoords(me);
        plot3d(me);
}

gotoAndPlay (_currentframe-1);
```

We've now called our functions and our virtual world is nearly complete. The final thing we need to do is modify our dot movie clip to produce a more lifelike effect. Go into the edit mode for dot. Change Layer 1 from a normal layer to a guide layer:

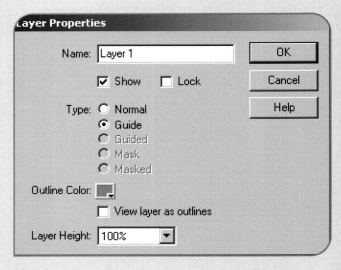

Now, insert a new layer above Layer 1. In frame 1 of this new layer we're going to create a tree. You can create your own, or just copy and paste the tree image on the CD version of `simple_2.fla`. Whichever you choose to do, make sure the tree is about 125 pixels in height. Place the base of the trees trunk over the triangle on the guide layer. Test the movie – when you press the mouse button and move the cursor you should get the impression of walking through the trees. Adding a background image above the horizon line, or changing the trees or the ground, could easily jazz up this piece. Have a go – you've now got the tools to create your own 3D Flash world.

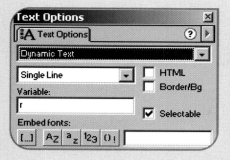

Let's now return to our saved `simple_1.fla`, and save it as `simple_3.fla`. I'll now show you a different purpose that we can use this for – a menu. Again we're going to leave the main timeline alone, and go into the edit mode for the viewer movie clip. This time we want the movie clip's timeline to be 10 frames long, so we'll insert a frame at frame 10 of the bg layer. Make a new layer above bg, and change it to a guide layer. On frame 1, make a textbox anywhere within the outline rectangle, and with the text color set as something light, to contrast with our dark background, put a 0 in it. With the textbox selected, open the Text Options panel and change to the Dynamic Text option. Set the variable name as r.

Now, we need to edit the actions layer, layer 2. Start by dragging the actions for frame 1 onto frame 2 on the timeline. Next, put the following actions onto frame 1:

```
linklist = new Array();
linklist[0] = "<a
➥href='asfunction:_parent.openurl,www.freshfroot.com'>fresh
froot</a>";
linklist[1] = "<a
➥href='asfunction:_parent.openurl,www.voxangelica.net'>vox
➥angelica</a>";
linklist[2] = "<a
➥href='asfunction:_parent.openurl,www.dasdeck.de'>das
➥deck</a>";
linklist[3] = "<a
➥href='asfunction:_parent.openurl,www.friendsofed.com'>
➥friends of ed</a>";
linklist[4] = "<a
➥href='asfunction:_parent.openurl,www.freshfroot.com'>fresh
➥froot</a>";
linklist[5] = "<a
➥href='asfunction:_parent.openurl,www.freshfroot.com'>fresh
➥froot</a>";
linklist[6] = "<a
➥href='asfunction:_parent.openurl,www.freshfroot.com'>fresh
➥froot</a>";
linklist[7] = "<a
➥href='asfunction:_parent.openurl,www.freshfroot.com'>fresh
froot</a>";
function openurl (murl) {
    murl = "http://"+murl;
    getURL (murl, "_blank");
}
```

This code has created a new array, and populated it with the items that will later be called to fill our menu. In this case we've got web site addresses. We don't want our links to replace the menu movie when clicked on, so we've used an undocumented function that had been pointed out by Branden Hall – one of the innumerable gifts he has given to Flash users. Instead of our URL being handed to the browser, we've defined an ActionScript function to handle it. We've specified in this `openurl` `(murl)` function for the `http://` prefix to be added to the address, and for it to open in a new window. The `linklist` array will be called by our code in frame 2 when we modify this.

We now need to modify our code that is now in frame 2:

```
//
fl = 300;
cx = 0;
cy = -80;
cz = 150;
//
maxt = Math.PI/60;
deacc = .9;
r = 1;
//
targetr = 150;
```

Once again we're changing some of our global values so that our end product is viewed from the right angle. We've again introduced some variables that will be used to define our speed and acceleration (`maxt, deacc`). You'll also see two other variables have been defined as global variable: `r` and `targetr`. The variable `r` (radius) has been placed here, instead of its previous location in the `for` statement, because it's associated with our new variable `targetr`. These two variables are referenced in the frame 5 actions that we'll add.

In order for the links that we defined in our frame 1 array to work in the movie, we need an HTML text field to write the links into:

```
//
items = linklist.length;
//
for (i=0; i<items; i++) {
    this.attachMovie("dot", "dot"+i, i+1);
    var me = this["dot"+i];
    me.txt = linklist[i];
}
```

You'll notice that our items variable is now defined as the number of items in our frame 1 array. This means that we can create as many variables as we want in that array, and all of the variables will be automatically in the loop. You might also be wondering where all our glorious trigonometry has gone. Fear not, it's still here - we've just moved it into a new `buildcircle` function:

```
//
function buildcircle () {
        twist = twist+speedt;
        for (i=0; i<items; i++) {
                var me = this["dot"+i];
                var ang = 2*Math.PI/items*i+twist;
                me.x = cx+Math.cos(ang)*r;
                me.y = cy;
                me.z = cz+Math.sin(ang)*r;
                me._alpha = 100-Math.sin(ang)*50;
        }
}
```

We've split the duplicating of the clips and the calculation of the coordinates into two different `for` statements, because our circle will spin, and our coordinates will therefore need refining constantly. We've introduced an `alpha` variable into this loop, and its value depends on its depth within the circle. Clips at the front will be clearer than those in the background; hence we can create the illusion of depth. You'll also see a new variable called `twist` that's used towards calculating our angles.

As in `simple_2.fla`, we've added a `trackmouse` function:

```
function trackmouse () {
        var sw = 400/2;
        var sh = 300/2;
        var mxr = _xmouse/sw;
        var myr = _ymouse/sh;
        var inside = (mxr*mxr<1 && myr*myr<1);
        if (inside) {
                mtrq = mxr>0 ? mxr*mxr : -mxr*mxr;
        } else {
                mtrq = 0;
        }
}
```

Depth

As we don't have a button in this example, we've defined `inside` here. This time, the variable `inside` is true if the squared values of `mxr` and `myr` are less than 1. By default, it's false if the squared values are equal to 1 or more. Since all of our values of `mxr` and `myr` are between -1 and 1 (see the previous example for why this is so), the squared values will always be equal to 1 or less.

We now pass on our value of `mtrq` and our global variables `maxt` and `deacc`, to a `setspeed` function:

```
function setspeed () {
      var acct = -maxt*mtrq;
      speedt = (speedt+acct)*deacc;
}
```

One thing we don't have to change in our code this time is the `plot3d` function:

```
function plot3d (me) {
      var scl = fl/(fl+me.z);
      me._x = me.x*scl;
      me._y = me.y*scl;
      me._xscale = 100*scl;
      me._yscale = 100*scl;
}
gotoAndPlay ("grow");
```

We've added a `gotoAndPlay` action at the end of our frame 2 code. This will send us to frame 5, which you'll need to label grow. In frame 5 we're going to call the functions we've just defined.

Open up the actions in frame 5. Again, we need to replace the `Stop` action, this time with the code you see in the screenshot here.

```
Frame Actions                                              ⊠
  Frame Actions                                      ?  ▶
  +  −  Frame Actions                               ▼  ▲
  r = r+(targetr-r)/9;

  trackmouse();
  setspeed();
  buildcircle();
  for (i=0; i<items; i++) {
        var me = this["dot"+i];
        plot3d(me);
  }
  //
  var done = int(r+.5) >= targetr;
  if (!done) {
        gotoAndPlay (_currentframe-1);
  }else{
  gotoAndPlay("main");
  }

  Line 17 of 17, Col 1                                ⊕
```

Let's quickly look at what this code does:

```
r = r+(targetr-r)/9;
```

This redefines our radius value, and will be used to define the variable `done`. You'll see that our global values `r` and `targetr` have been used. You can see the purpose of this redefinition if you watch the `simple_3.swf` from the CD. You'll notice that the circle starts in the centre with our globally-defined `r` value of 1, and then expands outward to a fixed size. It's the changing radius that achieves this effect. You might also have guessed that this is why we labeled this frame `grow`.

Our next section of code calls the functions that we defined in frame 2:

```
trackmouse();
setspeed();
buildcircle();
for (i=0; i<items; i++) {
    var me = this["dot"+i];
    plot3d(me);
}
```

This will draw our circle with the initial radius of 1. In order to achieve the radius growth we need some further actions:

```
//
var done = int(r+.5) >= targetr;
if (!done) {
    gotoAndPlay (_currentframe-1);
}else{
gotoAndPlay("main");
}
```

In essence this code means that the variable `done` will be true when we've reached the target radius (`targetr`), and we then go to our frame labeled `main`. Until this value is achieved, this frame will be repeated over and over again, due to the `gotoAndPlay (_currentframe-1)` command. Each time it's repeated our `r` value will be increased by the `r = r+(targetr-r)/9` code.

So, when we've got the radius we want, we go to the frame labeled main. This is going to be frame 9, so go there, make a keyframe, add the label, and write the following code:

```
trackmouse();
setspeed();
buildcircle();
for (i=0; i<items; i++) {
    var me = this["dot"+i];
    plot3d(me);
}
gotoAndPlay (_currentframe-1);
```

Our functions will now run again. Our radius is now at its desired figure, but we've still got the `gotoAndPlay (_currentframe-1)` code. This time the code will keep repeating and redrawing itself to account for rotation, rather than a change in size. It's actually mouse movement that creates the rotation: when we move the mouse to the left the rotation is clockwise, when we're in the center there's no rotation, and when we're on the right, the rotation is counterclockwise. The further we go to either side, the faster the rotation is.

We should now insert a frame at frame 10, so that all the movie clip's layers are the same length. If you now test the movie you'll see our dot symbol duplicated in our revolving ellipse. With just a bit of modification to the dot symbol we can turn the effect into that of a revolving 3D navigation. Let's now do these modifications.

Open up the dot movie clip in edit mode. Delete our triangles symbol that we currently have in the center of the stage. Make a blank textbox on the stage using the Text tool, and align it so that x=19 and y=9.5. With this textbox still selected, open up the Text Options panel and once again change to Dynamic Text. Check the HTML box, uncheck the Selectable box, and set the Variable name as txt. Make sure you have the text color again set as something light, to contrast with our dark background. To finish off, create a new layer above Layer 1, and put a Stop action in frame 1. If you now test the movie, you should see that the names we defined in the frame 1 actions of the viewer clip have replaced our triangle symbol and are now clickable links in a 3D circle. We've succeeded in changing our simple base FLA into a complex-looking navigation, with text that rotates and fades to give a feeling of depth.

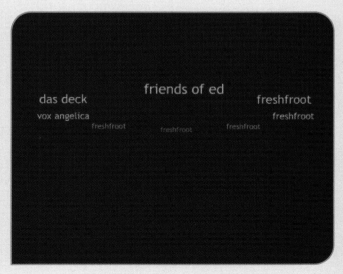

For our final example, let's take a look at the freshfroot web site (www.freshfroot.com) where a purposeful development of our simple technique has been used. On this site you'll see that menu functionality isn't just added for fun – it's vital to the site. While three-dimensional navigation doesn't make sense on every site, on this site it fits the concept perfectly.

freshfroot.com is an inspirational and creative source for motion web designers. It provides links that you often won't find anywhere else on the Web, or at least not in the way they're juxtaposed here!

Each day the freshfroot team looks at the Web from a different aspect, and the findings are categorized under themes. The links range from Shockwave movies and famous paintings you might already know, to strange photographs and cryptic sites, which get you curious about how they ever found them! Twice a week a guest editor chooses the selections, and is interviewed. Great communtiy vibe man!

Take a look at the site and get a feel for the navigation. You'll see that the selections are based on a grid of thumbnail images in the center of the screen. When you mouse over one of these images, you'll see it expand over the whole grid, and the notes will appear.

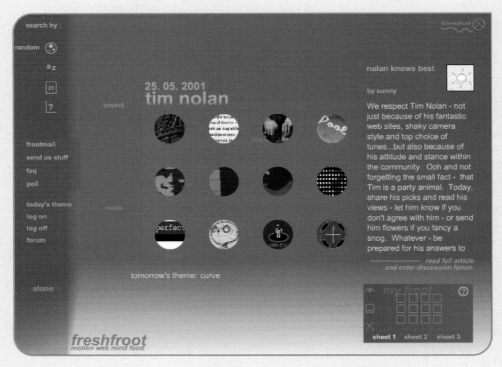

To explain how the freshfroot site works and how I designed it would take a whole book in itself! To explain even one of the movieclips within of would take a chapter or two, so I'm going to pull out the defining aspects of one of these clips to conclude my tutorial. A feature of the freshfroot site is that previous theme names float softly around the site in the background, emerging from an infinite unknown depth, like fish on a pool. If you choose one of these floating themes, it will then load in the grid. I'm going to take you through the movie that contains these floating themes, as it fits the concept of depth that I've been exploring throughout this chapter. Take a look at `freshfroot_themes.fla` on the CD.

The key actions in this movie are on Layer 1 of the viewer movie clip, so this is where we'll focus our analysis.

As in our previous examples, mouse movement defines where the words float on the stage, and at what speed. Play around on the `freshfroot_themes.swf` and you'll notice that the words float in the opposite direction to which you move your mouse when you move left or right. They move closer together when you move the mouse down, and further apart when you move it up.

You'll notice that in the center of the stage there's a rectangle labeled inactive area. This is where the thumbnail grid appears on the freshfroot site. When the mouse is over the grid, the words will become static. We decided that if the words still reacted to mouse movement as the user was browsing the grid, the calm appearance of the words would be destroyed, which could take the viewer's focus away from the grid. So I programmed for this exclusion zone. If you look in the code on frame 24 of Layer 1 you'll see the following code at the top:

```
poolwidth = 720;
poolheight = 520;
pooldepth = 800;
activetop = -90;
activebot = 150;
activelft = -72;
activergt = 88;
```

The `pool` variables refer to the dimensions of our stage. If we go back to our fish analogy you can imagine this as a 3D pool, with the items as fish swimming about. The `active` variables mark the border of the inactive area. So it's these variables that define the inactive area, and not the actual rectangle you see on the movie.

Now that we've seen how the borders of the inactive area are set, we can look at the code that actually makes this region inactive, or conversely, makes the rest of the stage active. You'll find this in the frame 7 ActionScript:

```
// checks if mouse is in active region
// 'inside'actually is outside the defined box in this case :
    var inside = (mx<activelft or mx>activergt) or
➡ (my<activetop or my>activebot);
```

Depth

This code is part of the `trackmouse` function. If you take a look at the `trackmouse` function as a whole, you'll see that there are many similarities with the code we used in our previous examples:

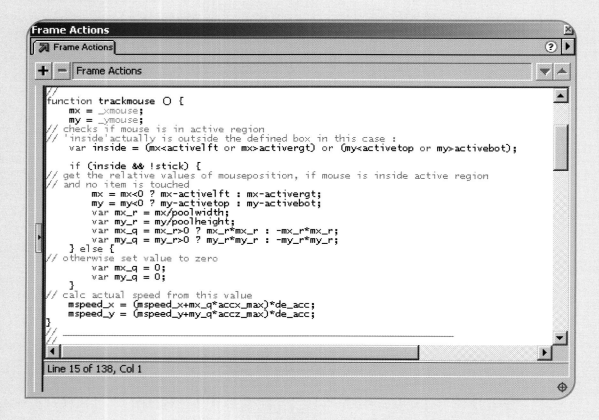

```
function trackmouse O {
    mx = _xmouse;
    my = _ymouse;
// checks if mouse is in active region
// 'inside'actually is outside the defined box in this case :
    var inside = (mx<activelft or mx>activergt) or (my<activetop or my>activebot);

    if (inside && !stick) {
// get the relative values of mouseposition, if mouse is inside active region
// and no item is touched
        mx = mx<0 ? mx-activelft : mx-activergt;
        my = my<0 ? my-activetop : my-activebot;
        var mx_r = mx/poolwidth;
        var my_r = my/poolheight;
        var mx_q = mx_r>0 ? mx_r*mx_r : -mx_r*mx_r;
        var my_q = my_r>0 ? my_r*my_r : -my_r*my_r;
    } else {
// otherwise set value to zero
        var mx_q = 0;
        var my_q = 0;
    }
// calc actual speed from this value
    mspeed_x = (mspeed_x+mx_q*accx_max)*de_acc;
    mspeed_y = (mspeed_y+my_q*accz_max)*de_acc;
}
//
```

Line 15 of 138, Col 1

The `if` statement in this code runs if the mouse is inside the active area (outside the rectangle) and the `stick` variable is `false`. We'll come to what `stick` does shortly. Again you'll see the x and y positions are passed forward in the same fashion to give us our speed. If you follow the math through, you'll see that the further away from the inactive area you go, the faster the words move. If you're interested in how this works, try taking a point near the inactive area, and one on the edge of the movie, and work out the speed values by following the code through.

A problem with our floating themes acting as links is that they could easily just float away when you're trying to click on them – this is where `stick` comes in. To solve this problem we've set `stick` to `true` whenever a theme is rolled over:

```
stick = stick or me.touch
```

The effect of this line of code is that when the viewer touches one of the themes the `stick` function is `true`. We've again used the `me` function as to reference our themes.

So I've briefly defined the key elements of this movie that follow the main concept behind this tutorial. If you're interested, take a look at the rest of the FLA and see how the code as a whole builds up the movie.

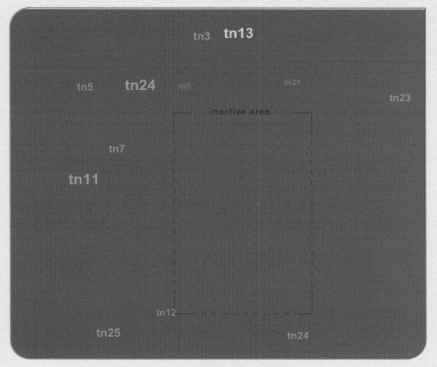

I've finished my quick tour of the 3D possibilities within Flash. You should keep in mind that Flash isn't up to creating a true 3D engine, and to create an illusion of depth or 3D you have to fake a lot of the effect with faux-3D graphics. I hope I've shown you how a simple technique can be developed into a complex navigation, or a simplistic 3D world, with little effort. I hope too that I've inspired you to experiment with the illusion of depth. Go on, have a play, and make your monitor come alive.

True 3D in flash has always been
problematic. The Flash player is
just not fast enough to support the
number of calculations required.

There are a number of ways
around this, and these include;

pre-rendered or faux 3D,
pre-calculating the difficult math before you start,
making only part of your animation 3D.

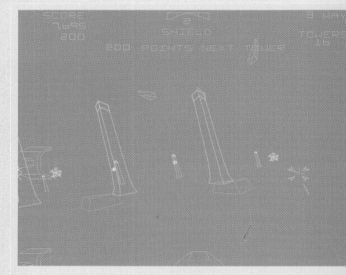

faux 3D

Faux 3D doesn't mean 'you can
tell it is not true 3D', but rather
'you can't tell it is being generated
via pre-rendered objects'. The classic
arcade game Star Wars by Atari has
the most simplistic pre-built 3D
vectors, but it worked because the
game was fast and gave a good
sense of movement.

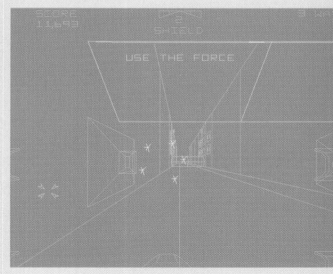

This simple, vector-based 3D is the sort of thing that Flash is very good at working with. By creating pre-calculated vector structures and then scaling them to fit into the current 3D scene, you can create a fast 3D engine.

pre-calculating
If you prefer to create ActionScript-driven 3D, the biggest performance hit is having to calculate trignometric values. By calculating all possible values before the animation, and placing these in an array, you sidestep this number crunching bottleneck by creating something called a look-up table.

combining
By far the most popular option when creating 3D in flash is to mix faux 3D with scripted 3D.

A good example of this is the stuff on the wireframe site.

"Cheap, basic, straight to the point. A quick buzz. Nothing fancy; nothing life-changing; nothing deeply meaningful. And that's what I believe I've done with Limmy.com"

Brian Limond
www.limmy.com

Time

Imagine my surprise when I, Brian Limond, creator of Limmy.com and its grand total of eight pieces therein, was asked by friends of ED to come up with this chapter for New Masters of Flash: The 2002 Annual ! Well actually, you see, without sounding like I'm up my own you-know-what, I wasn't very surprised at all.

For over a year now, ever since my site, with its trademark Glaswegian patter, attracted the first wave of attention, I've been expecting the unexpected. I've been stunned so much by the doors opened to me through my site that I all but shrug my shoulders when something this amazing hits me.

I was invited to talk at the FlashForward 2000 conference in London and the New Media Underground Festival.

We're talking free flights, hotel and dinner with, aye, that's right, free drinks! I was invited to San Francisco, which I couldn't attend through Flammable Jam commitments (FlamJam's my company, by the way) – and I've since been asked over to New York as well.

All because of what? Nothing but what you see on Limmy.com – me dancing on the homepage with eight Flash toys.

You might wonder why I'm putting myself down like this? Why am I talking like I don't deserve to be in this book, at those conferences, or the receiver of back patting? Cos in a way I don't feel that I am. To me, conferences, book writing and back patting is reserved for those who really care about what they do.

From the last book, I've picked up on how the minds of other Flash developers out there work, and when I'm asked by friends of ED to explain who I am and what makes me tick, I think "Aw no, I've got to start sounding like I know what I'm doing, like these other people! I've got to sound like I take this whole Flash game awfully, terribly seriously!"

I can't do it. Ah cannae lie to ye, reader! Chaos theory, maths, juxta-whatever it is... couldn't care less. I'd seriously, honestly and truly rather be down the pub. And whenever possible, I normally am.

Well, either there or in my bed.

So with no architects, painters, designers, poets, writers being foremost in my mind as my influences, how am I supposed to trick you into thinking that I'm important and I deserve to be writing this page rather than reading it? It's probably impossible, but I'll carry on and let you know what makes me tick, in the hope that you'll go away knowing that you too can be invited to Flashy conferences (I'd say "pun intended", but I hate that phrase) all over the world for doing nothing short of being yourself.

Let me tell you how Limmy.com started, where I learned, what I've learned, and just a bit of history. I'll try to keep it reasonably interesting.

Time

I was born in Glasgow, Scotland (is my accent coming through at all!), to Jessie and Billy Limond, and spent the first six months of my life in a council house area called Priesthill in the south side of the city. It's not a place well known for its museums and art galleries but, being under half a year old, I wouldn't have noticed. We then moved to another estate called Carnwadric not too far from Priesthill, and that's where I grew up and lived until a few months ago.

With those beginnings in mind, when I think back to where I hung about, who I hung about with, and the things we did, the word *art* doesn't immediately spring to mind. Neither do the phrases "What's your favourite painting?", "What are you reading right now?", or "Clever design, don't you think?". If I went into an art gallery, it was to make a racket and get kicked out; I couldn't be bothered reading a newspaper never mind a novel, and clever design to me would be a revolving door, because it's got fun and mischief written all over it.

I know what you're thinking. You're thinking: "Brian, how do you feel when contributors from the previous book name painters, animators, and composers as their inspiration?"

I'll tell you – I feel more than a wee bit left out and a little on the ignorant side. I feel like everyone went away on a school trip and learned about art one day, but I couldn't go 'cos I'd been bad, and now everybody's back from the outing, talking about stuff I haven't the foggiest idea about - and it's all my fault!

Well, not quite that bad, but I just don't feel a part of the design world. After dropping out of school when I failed all my exams, I messed about doing absolutely nothing apart from getting drunk and getting into trouble with the law. After about a year of this, I thought it might be good to try for college. So I started a printing course – lithography, screen-printing, learning how to bind a Glasgow Rangers magazine – and one course led to another until I got my degree. Again, throughout all this time I had no real interest in art. I had some Salvador Dali and Gottfried Helnwein postcards up on my wall, but that's yer lot.

Bloody Boys © Gottfried Helnwein
www.helnwein.com

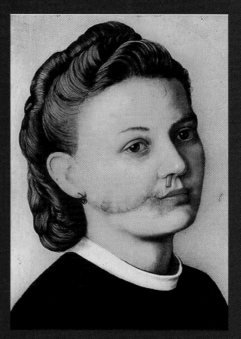

Mother, is it you? ©Gottfried Helnwein
www.helnwein.com

Time

From this, it appeared to me that I was into art that was a spectacle in one way another; art whose meaning was to be found in greater depth, but gave you something you could stare at until you worked out what the painting meant. I began to discover something vaguely resembling what you might call my own 'taste in art'! I was into The Blatantly Obvious.

Dropping out of Uni after failing exams for my post grad, I lazed around yet again and did nothing but get drunk, only this time I wasn't getting in trouble with the law, thankfully. After more than a year of this, I thought it might be good to try for a job – with no Flash skills, little design skills and a basic understanding of HTML. I managed to gain a placement in a design agency in Glasgow, who immediately recognized my inability and unwillingness to do ASP, and so promptly headed me in the direction of junior ASP programmer.

I'm sure you can imagine the sweat that was dripping down my back at that time. I didn't know what I was doing and I was genuinely scared, until I came across www.nrg.be that is! I had never seen anything like it on the Web at that time, and I was gob-smacked. The agency I was working in was at Flash 2 level; I'd never seen anything so alive with Flash as NRG.

I thought "Get a look at the curves! Check the telly flyin' across the screen! Listen to that voiceover man! He he, this is magic!"

It was then I realized that I had to learn Flash or I was out on my arse again. So I guess you could say that you have Peter of NRG to blame for Limmy.com in a way, because he was my first Flash inspiration. Every time I do a motion tween, then slap a keyframe in the centre and make the easing-in -100 in the first frame with the easing-out 100 in the second, I think of Pete. I go all dreamy and glazed over.

After about a year of creating and updating Flash sites with my new skill, I decided to make Limmy.com.

Limmy.com came about for a number of reasons. Firstly, I had enough Flash production under my belt to enable to me to create little Flash toys with little effort. I also realised how bored I was with sites paying more attention to the dark side of life – such as the shootings, heroin, and racism stuff I'd see portrayed in Submethod – rather than the lighter side, such as just having a wee bit of a laugh.

Lastly, well, my nickname Limmy was available as a dotcom!

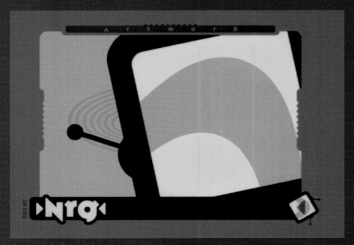

© www.nrg.be

© www.nrg.be

...nt the domain name, and then sat about waiting for ...tion. This time, however, I didn't wait for over a year ...mething to happen; I waited only until the office ...d out that night and began making a splash screen ...ge to say *comin' soon — hoad oan*. I had been ...g about with the office webcam for a week or two ...learned that you could record an AVI from it, put ...Adobe Premiere, and then punt the video out as a ...sequence which could then be pulled into Flash. ...h the office to myself, I stuck on the cheesy Move ...ody by Eiffel 65 and done a quick dance in front of ...nera for the hell of it. I tweaked the contrast a little ...toshop, punted the stills out again for Flash and ...ne image for the homepage, one that I then resized, ...ed, blurred, and sharpened, until I was fairly happy.

...now? What was I going to put in my site? As I said, ...have a lot of enthusiasm for making statements ...how down life can be at times. I wanted to create ...ing that would hopefully give the visitors to my site ...k from the norm; I wanted to present a little light ...inment to all you out there in Internet-land. I

suppose deep down I wanted to get known fo... nothing.

I wanted to present something which was in line with ...of The Blatantly Obvious, but I suppose my thought... what I wanted my site to become can be described ... terms of music.

The sites that I've taken most inspiration fro... Submethod, Gmunk, and Volume One. I was daz... their use of video when I first saw them but, to m... item or project left me either perplexed or no... than before I typed in the URL. I think they're supp... be like that, I guess, but to me there's nothing bett... a laugh, pure and simple. So if these sites I wanted ... clear of are likened to Radiohead, what I wanted to... was the Stock, Aitken and Waterman Hit Factory. ... basic, straight to the point. A quick buzz. N... fancy; nothing life-changing; nothing ... meaningful. And that's what I believe I've don... Limmy.com.

Time

In the future, however, I'd like to head away from Stock, Aitken and Waterman, and head more towards Hardfloor. Hardfloor are a German dance duo that rely mainly on only two instruments; the Roland TB-303 bassline – responsible for all those squelchy acid sounds you may be familiar with – and the Roland TR-909 drum machine. This group, who can use a combination of these two simple machines to produce music that I hear in my head day in day out, are the top of my inspiration list, I'd say. No painting or other work of art has moved me in the way their music does, and it has so little meaning to it other than dance music.

Similarly, all the pieces within Limmy.com are simply ideas I find amusing, cheery, easy for everyone to understand. Life gets confusing and annoying enough for us all to have to endure site after site in an 'expressive style that cannot express itself simply.

I hope my perspective on creation in Flash or otherwise has inspired you to think more simply than before. I hope that rather than creating something tonight, though, you'll put down this book and just spend the night in front of the telly. Thinking too much is harmful and, nine times out of ten for me, it leads to a migraine.

Right, it's tomorrow morning, you've addled your mind with telly all last night and you're sufficiently refreshed. Now, you want your fix of Flash, so I'd better get to it.

The Flash movie I've decided to break apart is a project on Limmy.com called Time.

Your first questions are probably "So what's it all about?", "What's the purpose of this thing?", "What's the message he's trying to convey?"

Well, the simple answer is... nothing, really.

A while back, a site called dplanet.org had a competition. The competition asked you to design an image or a Flash movie based around a topic they'd chosen, and go up against someone else who had done the same. When both competitors had handed their pieces in, they were displayed to the public where they could vote on who gets the glory and who gets the shame.

I went against a guy called Skilla from www.skilla.com, which meant I was up against a top designer type and things could get tough. I retreated to my laboratory and commenced work immediately!

The competition's theme, as you might have guessed, was Time. I had many ideas. Well, now that I come to think of it, I only had one or two, and both of them involved taking a photograph of myself and messing about with some code till I came up with something worthwhile.

For a reason that doesn't spring to mind right now, I shot a photo of myself with my top off, staring into some candles. I think it was because I was a bit stressed out at the time of doing the project, and lying in my bed staring into a flame relaxed me. I'm sure we all do that, right?

One thing I kept in mind when taking the photograph (and you might do this yourself if you're a fan of post-rationalisation) was to include an area of no activity, some empty space I could go back and fill later with whatever effect came to hand.

What I'd like to do now is show you the final file with the final effect, explain to you just what you're seeing when you move the mouse up and down over Time, and the theory behind the code. Then I'll show you how to build it from scratch...

Lazy days : because sometimes Jimmy just can't be arsed

Lazy days : because sometimes Jimmy just can't be arsed

Lazy days : because sometimes Jimmy just can't be arsed

Lazy days : because sometimes Jimmy just can't be arsed

Time

To start with, open the FLA. Before getting into the tutorial, you might want to mess about with the project to put names to faces so to speak, and to familiarize yourself with the various parts. I'll break it down into fine detail so you'll miss nothing.

Take a look at the layers you see in the main timeline.

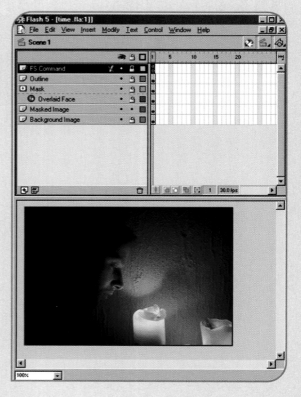

So what are these layers?

The FS Command layer contains the usual lines of code to disallow the scaling of the movie and the right-click context menu.

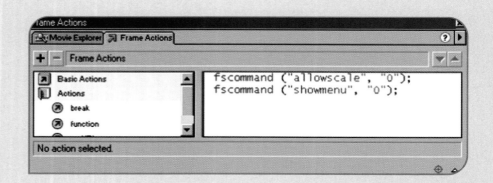

The Outline layer contains an outline rectangle for movie, to make the movie look a little more tidy.

For the Mask and Overlaid Face layers, I decided that I didn't want my effect to cover the whole screen, from the left margin to the right. I preferred my face and body to be unaffected, so I dropped in an instance of the main image here, and created a mask that masked out all but my physical presence.

Masked Image contains a movie instance that has within it the face image (masked by a rectangle) which reveals the text *There are some moments I could live in forever* when the user moves the cursor up and down, dragging the image slowly behind it.

And finally, in the Background Image layer lies the main image, yet again, at the very bottom. This layer does nothing but sit pretty, letting the contents of the layers above do all the work.

Now that I've given you a brief look over the layers, let me show you the principle behind a simple masking effect, and then I'll move on to explain the lot from scratch.

Take a look at the diagram **1a**. This illustrates a movie 500x500 in size, with only two layers on the main timeline: one on the bottom containing a movie instance called image, positioned at x,y (0,0), and one on the top called imageDragged, also positioned at (0,0).

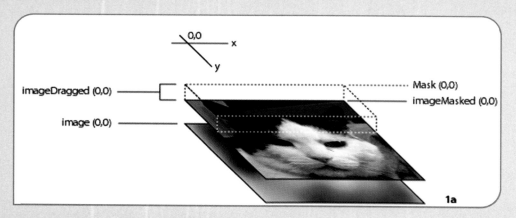

1a

As you can see in the illustration, the instance imageDragged contains a movie instance called imageMasked, positioned at (0,0) and partially masked by a layer called Mask, which is at (0,0) and is 200 pixels high.

So, in short, we have a 500x500 movie, with a 500x500 image at the bottom and a 500x200 image at the top, shortened to this height by the 200-high mask.

Take a look at diagram **1b** to see how this appears to the outside world, running the SWF.

What do I want to do with these pictures of a moody looking cat? I want the layer on top – the clear 500x200 masked image – to follow the vertical y position of my mouse and reveal the puss over the blurred image in the background.

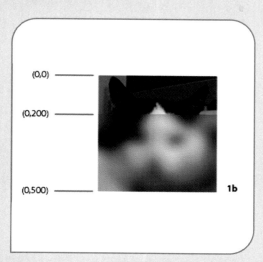

1b

I need to create some code that does two things: positions the *y* of the imageDragged instance at the mouse *y*, and shift the movie instance within (imageMasked) in the opposite direction. Why do this? Well, if we don't then we simply drag up and down a mask of the image of the cat.

Enough of the theory; here's the code that I would attach to imageDragged:

```
onClipEvent (enterFrame) {
    this._y = _root._ymouse;
    imageMasked._y = this._y*-1;
}
```

With the line onClipEvent (enterFrame), I'm telling the actions within the curly brackets to be performed constantly within this movie instance.

The line this._y = _root._ymouse commands the movie to set its *y* position to coincide with the *y* position of the mouse on the main timeline, whilst the line imageMasked._y = this._y*-1 tells the movie instance under the mask, imageMasked, to set its *y* position in the opposite direction to its parent.

Have a look at diagrams **2a** and **2b** to see what would happen if you moved down to (0,300).

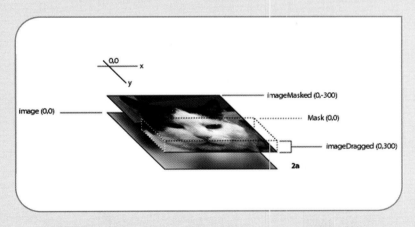

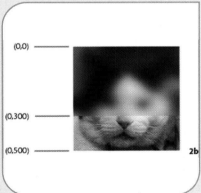

imageDragged moves down towards the mouse at (0,300) and imageMasked within that instance moves faithfully in the opposite direction, placing itself at (0,-300).

And through this, we're able to see the grumpy cat's nose.

Time

Now that you know the basics of masking and moving an image around to create this effect, let's go back to my file and I'll show you how I've created a fluid, watery mask that's a little different from what you'd get with the kitty cat.

I'll start from scratch, as promised. Now that I've explained the theory and shown you my file with all its layers you may already be ahead of me here, but let's just do it one step at a time.

So, where was I? Yes, I was sitting there trying to come up with something to beat Skilla in this competition...

The Beginning of Time

OK, so I had this Flash movie to design, based on the concept of Time. I'll now take you through it from start to finish, showing you how to make your own, using the same techniques I used.

Start by creating a movie at 30fps, enough to get a nice smooth animation. The television standard frame rate is 25fps, so a rate much higher than this can make your animations appear anything from a little smoother to popping out of the screen. Now set your dimensions. I set mine to 376x259, 'cos that's what the guy running the competition wanted – I didn't ask any questions.

Your first two layers are easy enough. The first one, FS Command, contains some code that I explained earlier, and the next – called Background Image – holds the static image on top of which all the magic will happen.

Import your image (in my case Face.jpg) into the Background Image layer using the same dimensions as the movie, and create a movie clip from it called image_mc, placing the bitmap within this clip at (0,0). I always place images, movie clip instances, and so on at (0,0) within their parents. Although sometimes it's not appropriate, for the most part it keeps everything tidy, in its place, and shipshape. Incidentally, for clarity's sake, I always add _mc when I name all my movie clip symbols, so I don't confuse them with the instance names.

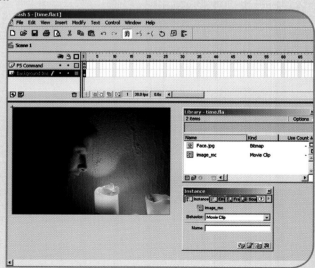

Next, you'll need to add a layer above the Background Image layer to hold the movie clip instance that'll be the *revealed* version of the image below. Since the image we're using is no different from the one in the Background Image layer, other than some text, you can just copy image_mc to the Masked Image layer.

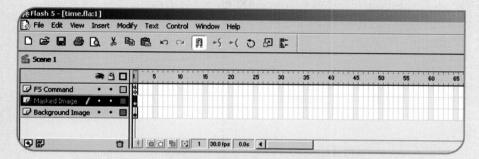

Now create another movie clip from image_mc and call it imageDragged_mc.

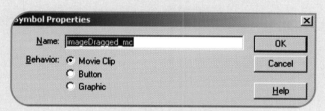

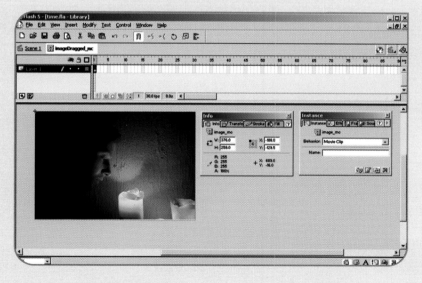

When you go into the imageDragged_mc symbol at this point you'll see that by creating this symbol from the image_mc symbol, Flash has, this time at least, inconveniently aligned the image in the center for us.

As I said before, we want to align the left and top of the contents to (0,0) to avoid any potential problems that may arise from an image being placed at the stupid coordinates (-188, -129.5). So from here on in, for consistency's sake, let's place the top left of our instances and their contents to (0,0).

Align the image_mc symbol within imageDragged_mc to (0,0) and jump out of this symbol to the main timeline to align the imageDragged_mc instance back to (0,0) too, as it's been nudged out by our amendment.

We now need a mask within imageDragged_mc to partially show the image_mc within.

First off, name the layer that image_mc is on in the usual, obsessive-compulsive way we all do – imageMasked – and add a new Mask layer.

Unlock the Mask layer and draw yourself a mask 376 wide and 20 tall, placed at (0,0). I chose a mask of 20 high when I later discovered it to be a good height to reveal just one word at a time in my final movie. In your own Flash projects, the size of your mask will depend on what you're trying to hide.

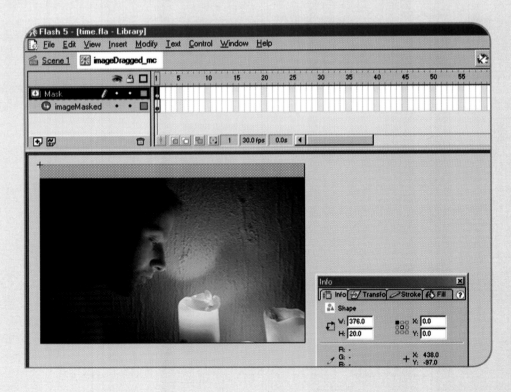

So where do I put these words? Because we've used the image_mc symbol as the image under the mask, any words I put in there will be shown in the identical image_mc instance in the main timeline, so we need to create another movie clip, using this image_mc in front of us.

By highlighting the image_mc instance and choosing Convert To Symbol (F8), create a new symbol called imageMasked_mc.

To control this image later with code, call the instance imageMasked.

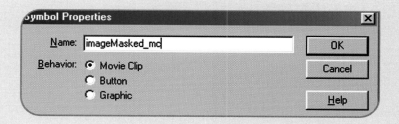

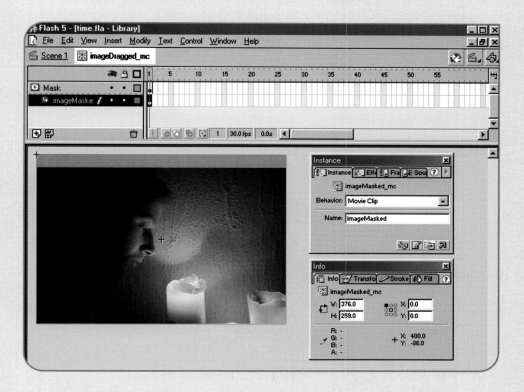

Eeek, but look again. The new imageMasked_mc symbol has aligned its contents, image_mc, to the centre. I want to align image_mc to the top left, so I jump in again, align to (0,0), then jump back out to imageDragged_mc, and align imageMasked_mc to the top left of imageDragged_mc. Believe me, it may be a pain, but it's for the best in the long run.

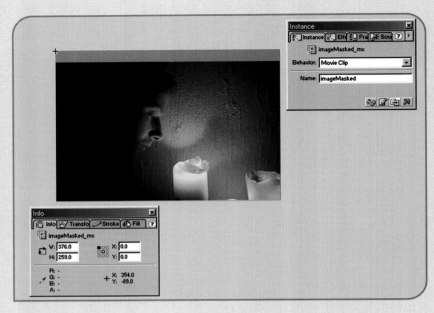

Now to the words we want to place within imageMasked_mc. Back in we go to that instance to create the text that will link this otherwise meaningless image to the topic of Time.

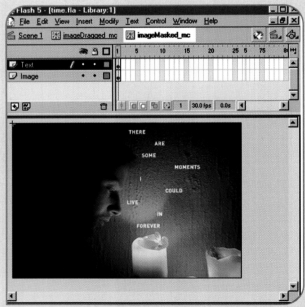

Right, we need a name for the layer with the image – how about Image? Create a new layer above it called Text. I bet you're way ahead of me here – this layer's for the text, so type some in and mess around with the positioning to give a slightly random feel to the location of the words.

To add to the slow-moving, reflective feeling of the piece as a whole, I decided to have the words fade on rather than make a sudden appearance. To make a motion tween for this you need to select all the words and create a symbol from them called words_mc.

A fade-in of one second seems about right, so create empty frames up to frame 30 on both layers, and create a keyframe on frame 30 for our words_mc symbol to be tweened to.

Next, add a simple, no-frills motion tween between the two keyframes, make the words_mc instance in the first frame 0% alpha, and put a Stop action in the final frame to prevent a loop.

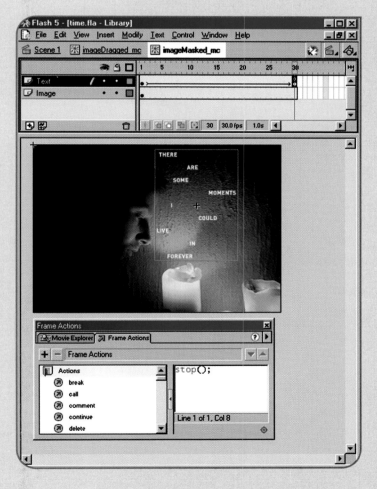

Time

Almost everything's now in place, and all you need to do is drop some code somewhere to make the masking effect happen.

On the main timeline, click on the imageMasked_mc instance and bring up the Actions panel to attach some code.

Remember the theory behind the masking effect with the grumpy cat I described before? Well, just attach this same code to the imageMasked_mc instance:

```
onClipEvent (enterFrame) {
    this._y = _root._ymouse;
    imageMasked._y = this._y*-1;
}
```

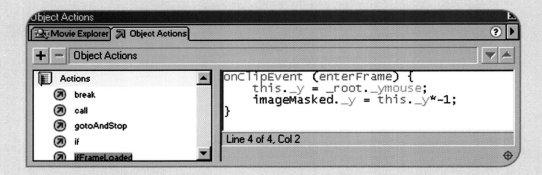

In a moment we'll take a look at how I added a twist to this to make the effect a bit more interesting and see how the code ended up in the final FLA. For now though, as I showed with the cat, this will only give a normal masking effect, where a portion of the imageMasked_mc instance is shown over the image_mc instance, wherever the cursor's *y* position is.

After experimentation in my laboratory, I created a hybrid between this masking code and slow-moving code, which you may already know. I'll explain it in a tick, if you don't.

What if the imageDragged instance didn't immediately set its *y* position to the mouse, but was to take just a little bit longer, and if the imageMasked instance within was to take a little bit longer that that? In other words, I was thinking, "What if the instances were *lazy*?"

So I gave it a shot, and concocted this code to replace the ActionScript that you've just entered:

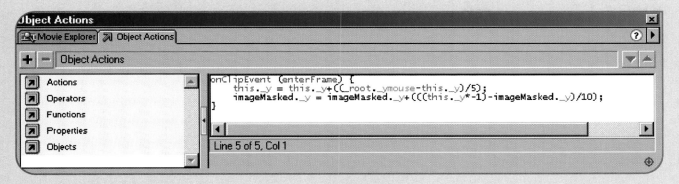

```
onClipEvent (enterFrame) {
    this._y = this._y+((_root._ymouse-this._y)/5);
    imageMasked._y = imageMasked._y+(((this._y*-1)
    ➡imageMasked._y)/10);
}
```

What's this ActionScript doing? Both lines within the enterFrame code have been adjusted in similar ways; they're now taking their time to get to where they previously went to instantly, using this slow-moving code:

```
this._y = this._y+((_root._ymouse-this._y)/5);
```

This line is telling the imageDragged movie, which the code is attached to, to set its *y* position to the sum of its current *y* position and a fifth of the difference between its *y* and the mouse position's *y*. Goodness gracious, what am I on about?

Well, put simply, imageDragged approaches the ymouse the same way you would approach a dangerous animal (someone else's bulldog, for example). You don't want to alarm Rover here, so let's say you'd go a fifth of the way between where you are now and where Rover is. Then, after a moment (or in the next frame, in Flash's case) you would look again from this new position to where the dog is and travel a fifth of the way there. And so on, and so on until you reach the dog, which is where you would stay, as close as you're going to get. At this point you realize you're standing on his tail and you run for your life, but we don't have time to incorporate that into our tutorial!

```
imageMasked._y = imageMasked._y+(((this._y*-1)-imageMasked._y)/10);
```
does a similar thing again, only it looks/travels a tenth of the way each time. Therefore, the image under the mask takes longer to reach its destination than the movie holding it, creating the effect you see in Time.

Once you've added all this code, there you have it. That's the bread and butter of the effect I created.

But wait, there's just one more thing. I didn't want to have this effect happening over my face. No way. I wanted my image to stay static with the stuff happening behind me. Easily done. We just add another instance of image_mc, drop it on top of all that was happening, and mask out all but my face.

Here's how. Create a layer called Overlaid Face above the Masked Image layer, then drag an instance of image_mc onto it, and create a mask layer above it, called Mask.

Using the Pen tool, draw a mask over my face, following my profile reasonably faithfully. (In hindsight, I gave myself a bit of a chop on the hair, which gives it a bit of a Morrissey look, but I'm sure you'll do better!)

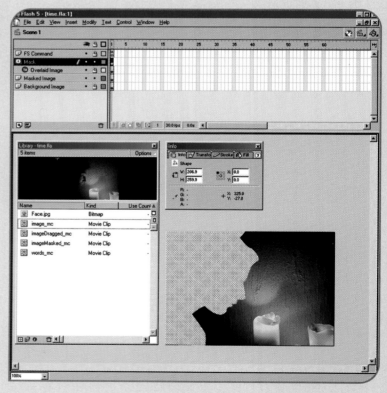

The effect is complete! To cap it all off, you might want to add an outline over the movie to give some definition against an HTML background. Finally, export the lot at a JPG quality of 50, which brings the entire file to just under 10k.

I went on to use this effect in some other projects, including http://limmy.kubrick.org, which was my contribution to a Stanley Kubrick tribute project. If you visit it, you'll see that rather than using words as the masked image, I've used a blurred and enlarged image of a scene from *A Clockwork Orange* to give a magnifying glass look.

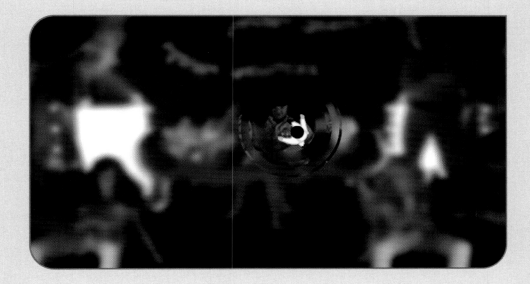

Although this effect is quite easily done, I hope the principles behind it give you some kind of springboard on which to mess about with the tons of experiments that can be based on the file. I've seen far more advanced effects in a similar vein to the one I've demonstrated to you here, but they're a day's mucking about away from Time. If you take the time to sit down and see what you come up with, you'll be surprised by just what you can do, whether your drive comes from inspiration or competition.

(By the way, I won!)

Limmy's effect is based around the clever use of the much under-rated ability to add masking effects. By embedding the masking via movie clips, many effects and transitions are possible...

and

there

are

*some*moments

I

would

rather

forget

the mask is the message
Rather than use a mask to reveal your self-penned poetic angst, try making the mask itself the message. By replacing the red rectangle that Limmy has used in imageDragged_mc, you will see some ghostly text scroll down with the mouse, only to fade slowly when the mouse stops.

when using text as a mask, use chunky fonts otherwise you won't see them.

transition
Embedded masking allows you
to do some fairly complex transitions
and other effects.

Here's a few doodles to get your
creative juices going...

mouse based effects
create a set of circular rings
that when placed together form a
full circle. By making each
mask/picture pair a mouse follower
(in the same sort of way Limmys
picture is) you can create a cool ripple
effect.

time based effects
By creating mask shapes like the ones
shown below, you can create a number
of different image transitions. This
effect is similar to limmys but uses a larger
number of movieclips of the same structure as imageDragged_mc.

"That's the best thing about what we do, it's always growing and evolving into something different, or more advanced. Hell, if the future can't inspire you, what can?"

Pete Barr-Watson
www.kerb.co.uk

Regenerate

Lager, lager, lager, lager, shouting... My Nike MP3 player feeds my imagination as the cold rain and wind makes my face feel deeply clean. The Underworld track reaches a crescendo as, about a mile out to sea, the sun breaks through the clouds, throwing out huge rays like some Japanese sunset image. Cheesy? Sure. But when things really happen like this, you can't fail to be in awe. Living where I do, on an English coastline, is ideal for this kind of excursion. We don't have big hills, but we do have a lot of open countryside to walk around, and very changeable weather, and that is a good thing! Makes for a lot of awe-inspiring moments like this.

I love solitary time. It's rare though, which probably makes it even more special. This is when my imagination can take over and do its thing. My job takes a lot of my time up with 'serious' things, and it's hard to let that go sometimes. Walking across a weather-beaten hillside, with nothing but my thoughts and music to keep me company, normally puts this right, although it doesn't just free up my mind for creativity. Solving technical problems is something I love doing, and being able to free up my mind is instrumental in doing this. A weekend of walking and thinking can develop many ideas on how to sort a problem out, and the problem is solved a lot faster than it would be otherwise.

My inspirational sources are definitely dependent on my moods. The solitude thing is often great when I feel under pressure from home or work. Other times, I find I need the complete opposite. My life tends to be very fast – I have a seven-year-old son for starters! But it's also fast because of my work...and sometimes I just have to go faster to feel at ease with everything. I think this is a very common by-product of our times, of Gen X if you like: the need to multi-task and cram as much information in as possible as quickly as possible. You often hear people complaining about the speed of society today but I think we'd probably go mad if it weren't so fast..

There are two places that I have found fulfill this need to go faster – London and New York. The digital agency that I work for has most of its clients in London, so I'm lucky that I get to visit as much as two or three times a week. New York, unfortunately, is a different story. I was lucky enough to be able to attend FlashForward2000 in NYC last July, and that was my first visit. That week in the city began a love affair for me. The sights, sounds, colors, smells, and people, all came together to provide my biggest inspiration ever. The speed of the city is the biggest thing for me, though. Everyone has a purpose about them, an almost mission-like focus, which propels them through

the busiest streets without hindrance. I've been back a couple of times since, and I'm beginning to realize why some of the best web design agencies have emerged here. Not only is there visual stimulation practically everywhere, but this city is *usable*.

I'm sure there are exceptions to the rule (there always are), but let's say you need to get from W 57th Street to the lower end of Broadway. You could take the subway, a bus, a taxi, or, if you really had the time (and it wasn't snowing!), even walk. I know, sure, you could probably do this in most major cities, but in NYC this kind of

movement is made easier, due to the grid system that the city is built upon. Try doing a similar distance trip in London, and I'm pretty sure you wouldn't find it as easy. The usability goes further than transport, though. Is there something you need? A new pair of Jeans? Or a new battery for your digital camera? No problem, head for CompUSA on fifth – two blocks this way and three blocks that way (yes, I know they don't sell jeans!). The point is you can pretty much obtain almost anything you may need quite easily from somewhere close by. For me, New York is fast, efficient and usable with a creative, inspirational twist. Just like the elusive 'perfect' web site!

The UK is generally behind the USA when it comes to technology, and my visits to New York always manage to feed my biggest weaknesses – new technology, and (my wife's terminology, not mine), gadgets. From MP3 players to the latest wireless Palmtops, New York has it somewhere, and I can be counted on to find it. I have a passion for these things, probably akin to the most serious kinds of addictions. One of the more beneficial side effects, however, is keeping current in the production side of our industry when most of my 'up-time' is taken up with business matters. Whether it's new software, the latest DV technology, or the latest shiny laptop from

Regenerate

Apple, I'm normally up to date with it. I would be less able to advise my clients of the possibilities of their proposed projects if I didn't understand the scripting capabilities of Flash 5 for instance. Or be able to put my CEO's mind at rest over us producing broadcast quality animations from Flash using the latest DV technology, if I hadn't already played around with it beforehand. It also helps to spot the way some things develop in the industry, like the imminent promise of broadband for instance.

I have a major interest in video production at the moment, which has been fueled by awesome sites like heavy.com and atomfilms.com, but also by the potential of broadband to change our industry beyond recognition. I really think that it will continue come to play a greater part in what we do, and because of this, I have really put a major effort into learning as much about it as possible.

I may not have developed the necessary skills to interpret my creative visions into workable presentations just yet, but I may do eventually. And, to be honest, this is probably not a bad thing. Web developers sometimes have too much of a 'keep it in-house' attitude to doing stuff, and with video I think this could be the wrong way to go. There are people and companies out there who have been doing this for TV for a long time and know what to look out for even before a project starts, and are surely better than us crossover novices! I'm sure that Web and TV will continue to crossover, and that people will begin to take on more of the other side's as this happens, but in the meantime I hope we don't find ourselves with the equivalent of the marquee tag and spinning logo hell of recent web years...

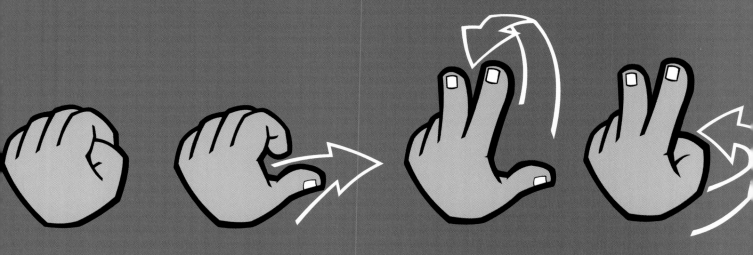

On a recent visit to Hillman Curtis' office in New York, I was inspired to see a similar vein of development happening there too. I remember looking at Hillman's web site (www.hillmancurtis.com) a couple of years ago, and even then he focused on motion graphics rather than plain old web sites. His early work for Macromedia is a living testament to this. But now we're faced with a not too distant broadband future, and he, like us, is gearing up for this right now. There are new skills to be learned, and new technologies to understand, and that is the best turn-on ever. In a recent article in *Creative Review*, Josh Davis states the case for reading books and teaching yourself the stuff that you want to know. If I couldn't do this, I think I'd die of boredom. That's the best thing about what we do, it's always growing and evolving into something different, or more advanced. Hell, if the future can't inspire you, what can?

Despite all of this, even the most creative person (and me) can still have days where the blockage is just too hard to clear. And when this happens, there is nothing better than chatting, e-mailing or just plain abusing your peers (and Hoss from H69 – you know you deserve it!). And this communication is another amazing facet of 'our' world. In what other industry could you be in personal contact with the people whose work inspires you day after day? From the guys who are really well known, to the others who aren't, you can always find someone on the main developers' web sites who can probably help you, and is willing to do so just because they can.

But if you're anything like me, then sometimes you'd just rather keep going at a problem until you've beaten it yourself through hard work and determination. That's the basis of my chapter – simple solutions to potentially complex and costly requests from your clients. It can be a simple element of your development, or a more complex one depending on the facilities you have available to you on the server. At the end of the chapter, I'll list some real-world examples of this method from both ends of the spectrum. Check it out – I hope it'll be of use to you sometime.

Regenerate

What's the simplest and most basic kind of computer file you can think of? Everyone has their own ideas but I'm guessing that your first thought could be a *text* file. And what if you go to the other end of the scale to think of the most complex type? A Flash 5 file could be a good candidate for that accolade. Well, this chapter is going to demonstrate how you can integrate the two to create a web application that is less complex than if it had been built in Flash alone (or more likely Generator). Hopefully you can find a use for it somewhere in your work – our clients certainly seem to like it! Check out www.geri-halliwell.com for a real-world example. Everyone (clients, that is) is aware that regular updates of their sites are important to keep their audience coming back for more, and that the marriage of simple text files with moderately complex Flash apps can offer this without major investment in server technology. I'll take you through a couple of different situations using this method, starting with the bare bones of getting this to work with as little effort as possible, and finishing with the basis of the method we use for creating high score tables on our games sites like www.scooterdeath.com.

OK, let's get working on the first part of the tutorial.

I'm presuming that you have a certain level of knowledge of HTML and Flash, so I'll start with a combination of the two. Did you know that you can display HTML-formatted text within a Flash movie as dynamic text? Only certain formatting is allowed but it's still a good place to start. So, start by opening a new text file, and save it straight away. Let's call it `content.txt`, and bear in mind that for the final application to work it has to be in the same folder as the Flash file we're going to create in a moment.

The format of the text file has to be based on HTML, so the following is a step-by-step guide to doing this. One thing to note before we start with the text file's content: only certain HTML tags can be used in text boxes. These are `<A HREF>`, `<U>`, `<B>`, `<I>`, `<FONT FACE>`, `<FONT COLOR>`, and `<FONT SIZE>`. If you want to create this tutorial's effect, copy the text in the image below into your text file. (If you're using Notepad on a PC, make sure that all the text is on one continuous line. Simple Text on a Mac will automatically wrap the text onto the next line, but Notepad doesn't do this. This is important as it will affect the text layout when we later publish our Flash document.) Alternatively, all the files needed for this tutorial are on the accompanying CD-ROM.

```
content.txt

dynamicText=<HTML><BODY><B>This</B> is where you would place different elements of text that you want to be able
to <I>dynamically</I> update within <A
HREF="http://www.macromedia.com/software/flash">Flash</A>.</BODY></HTML>
```

For the file to be useable in Flash we've had to add one non-standard piece of code right at the beginning. If you're used to coding in HTML you'll have spotted it right away:

```
dynamicText =
```

The reason for this is that the text file will be called into Flash using a method that relies on variables, and we're telling Flash that the contents of this file equals the variable, dynamicText.

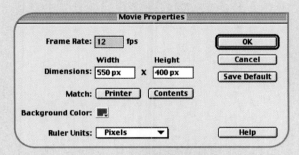

Open a new Flash document and, again, save it straight away as ex_one.fla. The movie properties for this aren't important, but if you want the effect to look the same, mine are in the screenshot.

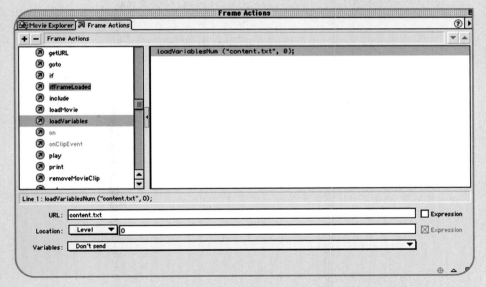

Select the first keyframe (frame 1) on the timeline and open the Actions window. The first thing we have to do is make the Flash movie load the text file that we've just created. To do this we insert a loadvariables action — hence the need to put the variable name right at the beginning of the text file. Go to Actions>loadVariables and in the URL field input the name of the text file, content.txt. You don't need to change the other boxes, Location and Variables, for this exercise.

Regenerate

Now select the Text tool and take a look at the Text Options panel (Text>Options) to make sure that the first drop-down menu is set to Dynamic Text. This is to tell Flash that the contents of the textfield will be coming from somewhere else at run-time. Also make sure that it's set to Multiline, so that Flash knows the contents will be allowed to spill over onto more than one line, and not have to be displayed as one continuous string. Lastly, check the Word wrap box. This allows Flash to make a line of text fit within the dimensions of the textbox as required.

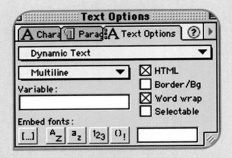

Then drag out a textbox on the stage and make it fit around a quarter of the available space:

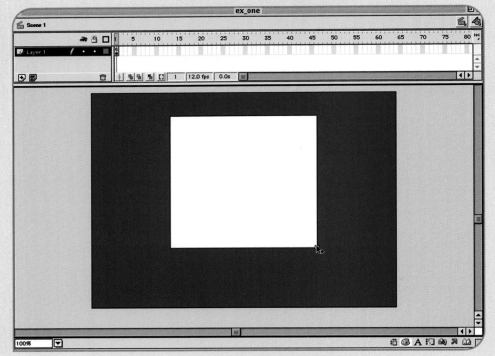

We then need to give it a variable name in the Text Options panel. Let's call it `display`. Make sure that HTML and Word wrap are the only boxes checked.

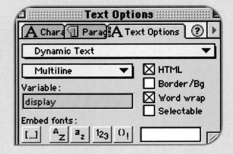

Hopefully you can see where I'm going with this. We want the text from the text file to be displayed in the dynamic textbox that we've just drawn on the stage. So how do we make that happen? Well, there are a few ways of doing this, but for this first example we're going to take the simple way out (see a pattern forming here?), and create a button that'll do it for us.

Create a button symbol (alternatively, use one from the Flash buttons library, or you can use the button from `ex_one.fla` on the CD), and drag an instance of it onto the stage. Select the button and open up the Object Actions window. We'll now add the actions that will make our button work. Go to Actions>set variable and in the Variable box input the name of the dynamic text variable, `display`. In the Value box, input the variable declared in the head of the text file, `dynamicText`.

By the way, Flash automatically attaches the `set variable` action to the button using `on (release)` because it assumes that we'll be using the button in the usual way. For this example this is correct, so leave it as it is. The final thing we need to do in the Actions window is to check the Expression box next to the Value field.

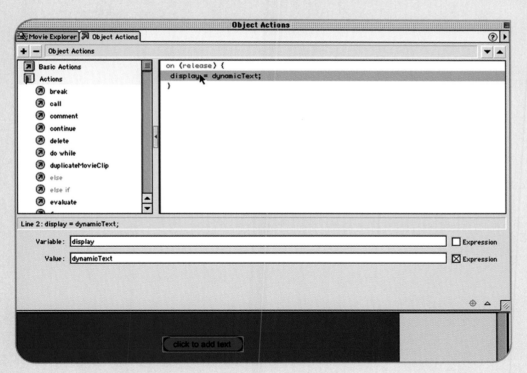

Regenerate

OK, now save your Flash file. We can now export the movie into the same directory as the text file and test it.

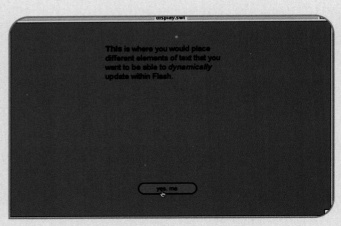

Voila! Dynamically updateable text within Flash, from an HTML-formatted text file. Edit your text file in Notepad (or Simple Text on the Mac), and see how easy it is to update the content of the Flash movie without having to edit the Flash file.

Agreed, this is a very simplistic way of doing things, and it does only update text, but think of the commercial opportunities from this simple procedure alone. If you work by yourself, or for a small web shop, you may have had difficulties in selling Flash sites to smaller clients because of the difficulty in updating the content – you don't any more! It may only update a news headline, or even a price list, but assuming the client can edit a text file according to the guidelines you give, it may help you to get them to use Flash in the first place.

There are limitations to the use of HTML formatting in Flash. In particular, you'll see that any links you put in your text will only be noted by the changing of the mouse pointer to the usual pointing finger. You could get round this by putting `<U></U>` around the link, thereby giving it an underline. It's also worth noting that you don't have to include any kind of HTML formatting in the text file if you so choose. Omitting all HTML references but leaving the variable statement at the beginning will simply result in unformatted text being displayed instead. Check out the list of useable HTML tags at the beginning of the tutorial for more information on what formatting you can use.

Let's now move on to stage two.

The previous example could be useful, but, wouldn't it be better if your client didn't have to edit any text files, and instead simply filled in a form on an HTML page to update the content? Obviously this would need some kind of fancy Content Management System (CMS) wouldn't it? Well, no actually! It wouldn't if you adapted and progressed the method above to include some kind of server-side scripting. I've been in this business for a while now, and I'm pretty good with most kinds of scripting languages, but I wouldn't call myself proficient at the server side of things by a long shot. I'm pretty good at tweaking ASP scripts, but thankfully I have a programming department at my disposal for this kind of thing! In particular, I have a guy called Sermad Buni – a complete Flash ActionScripting god with ASP superpowers too! You can credit all of the ASP stuff here to him entirely, and doubly so for allowing me to give away all of the required scripts for this chapter. Thanks Sermad!

So, in this section we're going to take a basic HTML form and post the contents to an ASP script, which will in turn write out a new text file with the contents of the form in a pre-formatted way that can be used in our Flash movie.

The only requirement for this process is a server which can process ASP scripts such as Windows NT/2000, or a Unix box running Chili!Soft ASP. Most ISPs offer a Windows-based server service for little, if any, additional cost. Most just ask you to specify that this is what you require from the outset. You must also make sure that the permissions are set correctly on the server. You must have SCRIPT ACCESS for the directory that hosts the ASP script, and WRITE PERMISSIONS for the folder containing the text file.

For the purpose of testing that it all works on your local machine, you'll need something like Microsoft Personal Web Server, which is free and widely available from MS and is included on all Windows 98 CDs. Windows 2000 users have the option of installing IIS from the Windows 2000 CD (please read the MS documentation regarding server setup).

Alternatively, the set-up file for the Personal Web Server for Windows 95, Windows NTWorkstation 4.0 and Windows NT Server 4.0 is available for download on the Web. If you're going to download the file, you'll need to go to www.microsoft.com/msdownload/ntoptionpack/askwiz.asp. When this page has loaded, select Option 1 and choose the appropriate download for your operating system from the drop-down menu.

Windows NT Option Pack Download Wizard for Windows NT Server 4.0 ▼
Windows NT Option Pack Download Wizard for Windows NT Server 4.0
Windows NT Option Pack Download Wizard for Windows NT Server 4.0 (Alpha)
Windows NT Option Pack Download Wizard for Windows NT Workstation 4.0
Windows NT Option Pack Download Wizard for Windows NT Workstation 4.0 (Alpha)
Windows NT Option Pack Download Wizard for Windows 95

You then need to select the `download.exe` link at the bottom of the page. There's a choice of saving the program to disk, or running it from its current location. For now, we'll save the program to disk. Follow the instructions to actually run the download executable and install PWS on your system.

Remember, for the PWS/IIS to work, all our files need to be in the chosen home directory, or a subdirectory of this. Also check that the text file's security properties allow Full Control. When you're testing the files in your browser, use the localhost address, rather than the C:\ drive address (for example http://localhost/html_form.htm, rather than C:\Inetpub\wwwroot\html_form.htm).

Mac users will have to use an online ASP server for now (see above for the requirements). This includes me, and yes, it's very annoying! I understand that plans are afoot for a Mac version of the Microsoft Personal Web Server, although I'm not aware of any timescales for it.

Assuming you've now got the software, we can get on with the tutorial! Firstly, we'll need an HTML form. You could create one yourself using the one on the CD as a guide, or even just use that one for now. Then we'll need our ASP script (on the CD too), and lastly, our starting text file, `content.txt`. This time we don't need to write anything into the text file, because the ASP page will do this for us.

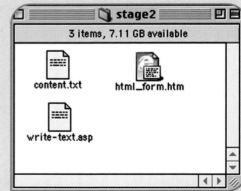

The file `html_form.htm` is a very simple HTML page, which has a form in it to serve two purposes. One is to allow us to type our new content into a textbox, and secondly, it gives us a button with which to write our new content into the text file. The button uses the POST method to send the contents to the ASP page. We use the POST method for a couple of reasons. Firstly, it's a cleaner way of sending variables around. If we used GET, it would append the contents of the form to the URL in the browser, and although there's nothing wrong with this, it's just not as neat. Secondly, if you use GET there's a limit to the number of characters that can be sent from a form, and although that won't (or shouldn't) affect us here, it's worth bearing in mind.

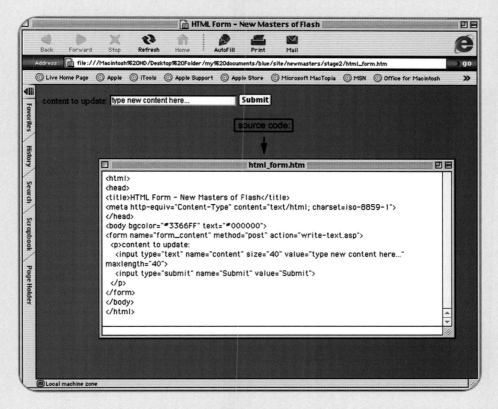

The ASP script receives the contents of the form, and overwrites the existing `content.txt` with a new version containing the updated text. Because we aren't manually editing the text file this time, we don't have to worry about what goes into it. However, if you decide to do this from scratch, you'll have to make sure that your own ASP script formats the resulting text file correctly so that it can be fed into the Flash movie by putting the variable declaration at the top, just as we did in the first stage of this tutorial (`dynamicText=`).

Regenerate

Take a look through Sermad's ASP file, and see how the file is constructed to serve our purposes. It's way too big for me to display all of it here, but here's the beginning:

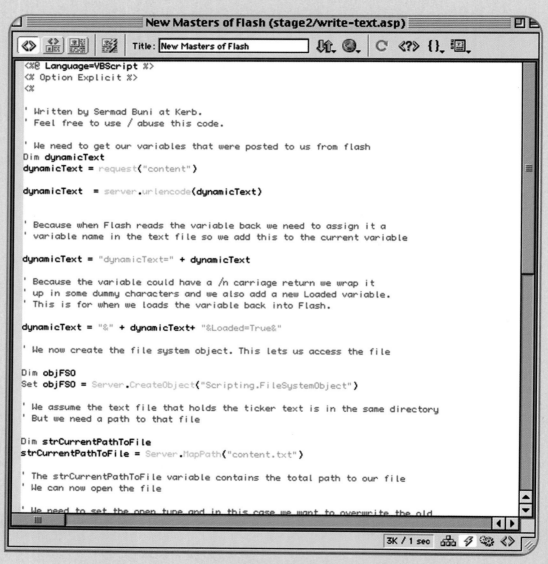

```
<%@ Language=VBScript %>
<% Option Explicit %>
<%

' Written by Sermad Buni at Kerb.
' Feel free to use / abuse this code.

' We need to get our variables that were posted to us from flash
Dim dynamicText
dynamicText = request("content")

dynamicText = server.urlencode(dynamicText)


' Because when Flash reads the variable back we need to assign it a
' variable name in the text file so we add this to the current variable

dynamicText = "dynamicText=" + dynamicText

' Because the variable could have a /n carriage return we wrap it
' up in some dummy characters and we also add a new Loaded variable.
' This is for when we loads the variable back into Flash.

dynamicText = "&" + dynamicText+ "&Loaded=True&"

' We now create the file system object. This lets us access the file

Dim objFSO
Set objFSO = Server.CreateObject("Scripting.FileSystemObject")

' We assume the text file that holds the ticker text is in the same directory
' But we need a path to that file

Dim strCurrentPathToFile
strCurrentPathToFile = Server.MapPath("content.txt")

' The strCurrentPathToFile variable contains the total path to our file
' We can now open the file

' We need to set the open type and in this case we want to overwrite the old
```

Take a look at the rest in `write-text.asp` on the CD.

As for the Flash movie – we'll make this one a little more interesting. We'll still have our dynamic text but let's make it into a ticker this time – like a latest news/info kind of thing.

Open a new Flash file and make the stage 550x68 pixels and then save it right away as `ex_two.fla`. Again, the frame rate and background color aren't important, but I've used the default 12fps and a blue color.

Open the Text Options panel, and make sure that the settings say Dynamic Text, HTML, Single Line, and lastly sure that Include entire font outline is selected – this button is marked [...]. When you're scrolling dynamic text it's best to select this feature, or the scrolling will appear sketchy (if indeed it works at all) on some computers.

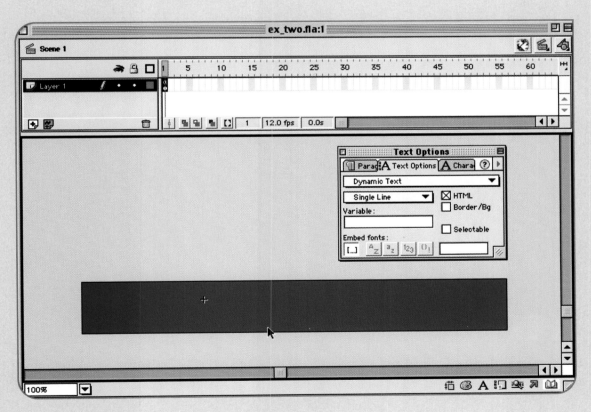

Regenerate

Then, using the Text tool, drag out a textbox on the stage. Make sure that your textbox is selected, and convert it to a graphic symbol called grDisplay.

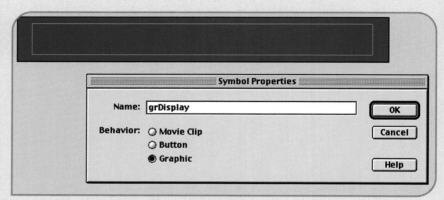

Next, making sure that the only thing on the stage selected is your new symbol, convert it into a movie clip and give it the name mcDisplay.

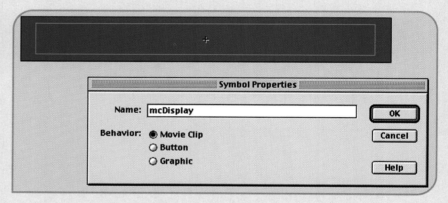

I'm sure that you've been lectured over naming conventions many times before, but it really is important to name your symbols in an ordered fashion. As you may have guessed, I start all of my symbol names with a prefix that denotes what the behavior is: gr for graphic, mc for movie clip, and bt for a button.

The process you've just completed makes sure that you have a dynamic textbox in one symbol, and in turn, that symbol is within a movie clip, which we can, and will, animate to give us our ticker effect.

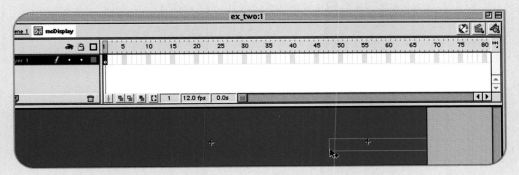

So, open the Library and double-click on the movie clip symbol you just created to bring you into the symbol's editing mode. Select the box (which is actually the graphic symbol) and, holding the SHIFT key to ensure horizontal movement, drag it over to the right.

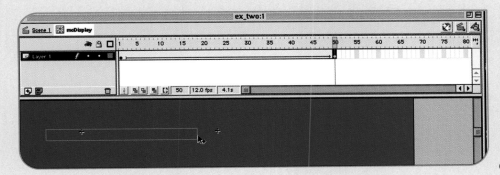

Click on frame 50 of the timeline and insert a keyframe. With that frame selected, drag your box over to the far left (again using Shift for horizontal movement). Create a motion tween between the two keyframes. Check that you've done this correctly by dragging the playhead back and forth - you should see your text box flying from left to right, and vice versa, on the stage in a straight line.

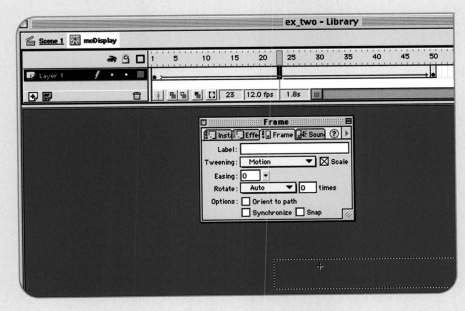

Regenerate

All we have to do now is add our ActionScript to load all the necessary variables. Click on frame 1 of the main scene's timeline and open the Actions window. As we did in the first section, select Actions>loadVariables and enter `content.txt` in the URL box, leaving everything else as it is.

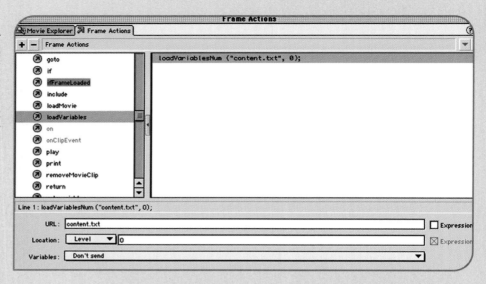

Now, open up the graphic symbol grDisplay in edit mode and select the dynamic textbox within. In the Text Options panel type `_root.dynamicText` in the Variable box. This assigns the value within the variable `dynamicText` (which is from the text file, remember) from the root (base) timeline to the symbol's text box.

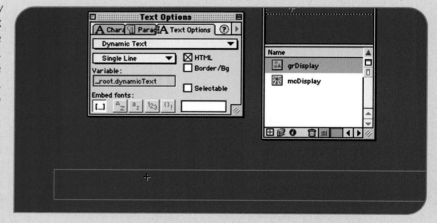

Finally, save the file as `ticker.swf`, into the same directory as the ASP file and the text file. Assuming it's on an ASP-capable server, you can test your application by opening the HTML form page initially to update the text within the text file.

Note that I've added another HTML file to the directory in the CD, which contains the Flash movie and links from the update confirmation page. This is just to display the movie properly and can easily be recreated as necessary.

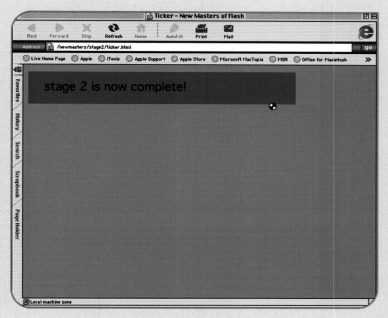

So, there you go – a dynamically updating Flash movie that is updated by a simple HTML form. No messy FTP needed, or costly editing of Flash movies to keep information up to date. We've made a mini Content Management System if you like.

Obviously this system is incredibly scalable, and depending on the resources you have available or your own ASP skills you can create whole updateable web sites using variations of this method. If you're looking at using this kind of thing for any kind of major information management, you'll have to bring databases into play at some stage. This might sound all big and scary, but I urge you to give it a try – it really isn't as bad as it may seem! ASP scripts, text files and Access databases have many common ways of interacting with each other. It's beyond the scope of this chapter to start showing how to integrate databases with Flash in any great detail and it would be remiss of me to try, after all this is a book about Flash mainly. But there are many good resources of information that you can use to help you create Flash-based dynamic applications.

As I mentioned at the beginning of this section, you can adapt this method for many uses, including high score tables. Let's say you've just finished playing your latest amazing Flash game, and as a result you've got a final score. Flash would then pull in the existing high scores from a text file and using ActionScript would check your score variable against all of the values within. If your score variable is higher than, or equal to, any of the other values, we have a high score! We would write your score variable into the right position in the high score table and then output this new version of the table back into the text file, overwriting the previous contents.

There are many uses for this method of dynamically updating textual content within Flash, especially where Generator is overkill but non-dynamic Flash isn't enough. The obvious limitation of this process is that it's only good for text-based content – if you want to update images then you need to look elsewhere. You wouldn't, for example, use a Generator server to update a ticker box on a small web site (I hope!), but likewise you would have difficulty using this method to create a complete e-commerce system within Flash, although it could definitely be used to form part of one. The idea is to take this tutorial and expand on it as you see fit – only you can judge whether this method is useful to you and your project. Hope you can find a good use for it.

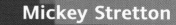

"For many years I didn't wear a wristwatch, preferring instead to be forced into looking around me, taking in my surroundings in search of a clock when I wanted to know the time."

Mickey Stretton
www.digitlondon.com

I'm sitting here wondering how I've come to be writing a chapter for New Masters of Flash. I'm thinking about what interests me, where I draw my inspiration, and how I approach my work, but I'm thinking too about where it all stems from.

I remember when I was ten years old, and how I'd keep myself busy by making small games and programs to run on my Sinclair ZX Spectrum or designing sleeve covers for compilation tapes I had made. sixteen years later, as an interactive designer with a graphic design degree, building Flash movies, I'm doing pretty much the same thing that I was back then.

I don't bother making compilation tapes anymore, and I am lucky enough to get paid to do what I enjoy doing, but things haven't really changed so much.

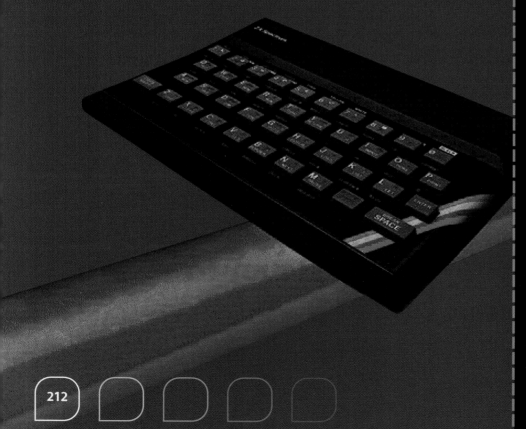

```
MICKEY IS GREAT
MICKEY IS GREAT
MICKEY IS GREAT
MICKEY IS GREAT
MICKEY IS GREAT
MICKEY IS GREAT
MICKEY IS GREAT
MICKEY IS GREAT
MICKEY IS GREAT
MICKEY IS GREAT
MICKEY IS GREAT
MICKEY IS GREAT
MICKEY IS GREAT
MICKEY IS GREAT
MICKEY IS GREAT
MICKEY IS GREAT
MICKEY IS GREAT
MICKEY IS GREAT
MICKEY IS GREAT
MICKEY IS GREAT
MICKEY IS GREAT
MICKEY IS GREAT
MICKEY IS GREAT
MICKEY IS GREAT
MICKEY IS GREAT
MICKEY IS GREAT
MICKEY IS GREAT
MICKEY IS GREAT
MICKEY IS GREAT
MICKEY IS GREAT
MICKEY IS GREAT
MICKEY IS GREAT
MICKEY IS GREAT
MICKEY IS GREAT
MICKEY IS GREAT
MICKEY IS GREAT
MICKEY IS GREAT
MICKEY IS GREAT
MICKEY IS GREAT
MICKEY IS GREAT
MICKEY IS GREAT
MICKEY IS GREAT
MICKEY IS GREAT
MICKEY IS GREAT
MICKEY IS GREAT
MICKEY IS GREAT
MICKEY IS GREAT
```

Using the 48k RAM sitting inside my ZX Spectrum, I was never going to achieve anything special in terms of programming, but Spectrum BASIC, as the language was known, was my introduction to variables, random integers, if statements, and other principles which I now use on a daily basis. Of course, I couldn't write anything in BASIC now, other than...

```
10 PRINT "MICKEY IS GREAT"
20 GOTO 10
```

But the principles, in this case creating a repeat loop with a GOTO statement that is continually re-processed, are exactly the same.

I have even retained some of the same work habits I started all those years ago. When I was making games such as Pontoon or High/Low I would often build the engine, put it aside indefinitely awaiting its graphic treatment, and then start something else entirely! Call it impatience or an over zealous desire to face a new challenge, but it's something that I'm still terrible at.

So perhaps my interest with Flash stems back to my old Spectrum computer. But I'm a designer, not a programmer, right? It's a cliché I know, but my point of entry to Flash, and interactive media in general, is completely from a design background. Eventually the ZX Spectrum got packed up and given away. Perhaps it was when I realized that girls existed or something, but I never saw it again.

As it turned out, I wasn't a pre-pubescent Casanova and soon had to turn my attention elsewhere – it was then that I discovered graphic design. I'd be spending twice as long designing the title pages for my school projects than I would on the project itself, and with nothing else to do would often find myself designing nonsense posters to post around the school, purely for a laugh. (The best one was a public awareness campaign declaring "Ken Hom is the King of Chinese Cuisine".) And the first time I ever saw a Letraset type catalogue and marvelled at the sheer volume of typefaces that actually existed out there, it merely confirmed my suspicions.

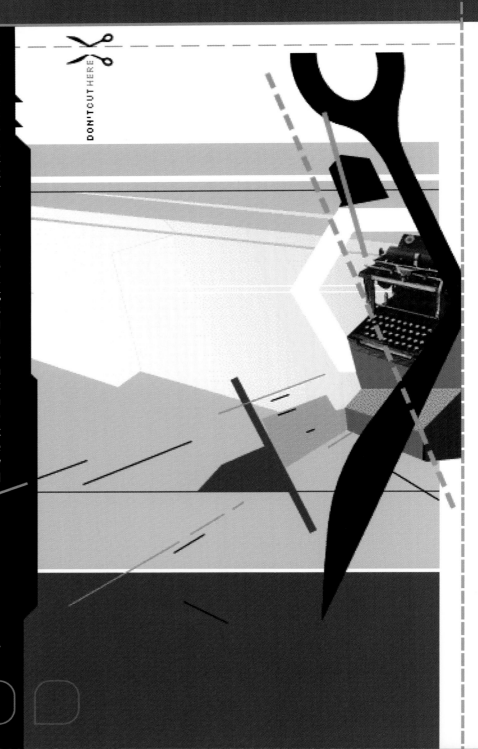

DON'T CUT HERE

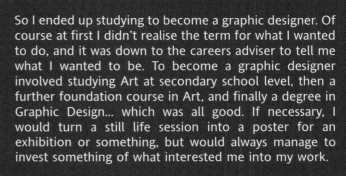

So I ended up studying to become a graphic designer. Of course at first I didn't realise the term for what I wanted to do, and it was down to the careers adviser to tell me what I wanted to be. To become a graphic designer involved studying Art at secondary school level, then a further foundation course in Art, and finally a degree in Graphic Design... which was all good. If necessary, I would turn a still life session into a poster for an exhibition or something, but would always manage to invest something of what interested me into my work.

My interests developed, I learned how to really look at things and not just see what I expected to see, and I began to be open to inspiration and to learn how to use it.

My studies also meant that I would have to study the history of art, which at first did nothing for me but provoke a blank expression. The tutor, known simply as 'Tinleg' on account of his tin leg, did a great job though, and I suddenly found myself wishing I'd paid some attention in Religious Education class as he recounted the tales illustrated in many pieces of Renaissance art. This was perhaps my first encounter with the notion of what I now think of as creating narrative – using symbolism and metaphor to create or infer a story or context – and it is something that I still think about whilst I'm working.

Andy Warhol's Campbell's Soup Poster
© Bettmann/CORBIS

Roy Lichtenstein and his Painting Whaam!
© Hulton-Deutsch Collection/CORBIS

As we plotted the history of art through to the twentieth century, Tinleg eventually introduced us to the Pop Art movement of the '50s and '60s. Immediately I had an empathy with the work I was learning about. This notion of seeing beyond face value was superbly expressed by Pop artists on both sides of the Atlantic – artists such as Roy Lichtenstein, Richard Hamilton and Peter Blake were using found imagery and the objects surrounding them for inspiration, whilst artists such as Andy Warhol, Mel Ramos and Ed Ruscha were openly using commercial graphic design, logos, branding and typography to inspire their work.

The most captivating aspect of the art for me was the crossing over or confusing of boundaries between fine art and graphic design. As someone who already had a keen interest in graphic design, the very idea that it could be used to make a statement, ask a question or provoke thought was very interesting, and something that convinced me to pursue a career in design.

Today, there are many contemporary designers (or should I call them artists?) who are responsible for the same kind of thought-provoking work that blurs the boundaries of graphic design and art: Tibor Kalman, FUEL (www.fuel-design.com), and The Designers Republic (www.thedesignersrepublic.com) for instance. Both visually and conceptually, I find their work a great source of inspiration. The Designers Republic though, in my opinion, takes the biscuit. If the graphic style, visual innovation and considerate plundering of Japanese pop culture aren't beautiful enough, the bold and brazen attitude of their *For f***'s sake, think for yourself* self-promotion poster will always win it for me.

So, this is how I have come to Flash from a graphic design background. Sort of.

Chronometry

If I'm honest, this is probably how I came to Photoshop or Freehand, but not Flash. Unlike Photoshop or Freehand, which enable the designer to communicate using a two-dimensional visual language, Flash also suggests (and at times insists) that the designer communicate using the third and fourth dimensions of space and time. Whether this is defining a spatial language to create a 3D environment or navigation device, or using time to define animation or an object's behaviour, these factors create a whole wealth of opportunity. As such, I guess I came to Flash as a means of experimenting with these notions of time and space, and to indulge ideas, other influences and inspirations that I previously had no outlet for.

In that respect, I find architecture and urban or industrial landscapes a great source of inspiration – one of the advantages being that you don't have to look far. But you do have to look! For many years I didn't wear a wristwatch, preferring instead to be forced into looking around me, taking in my surroundings in search of a clock when I wanted to know the time. I'd often notice clocks incorporated into beautifully designed buildings built for banks, fire stations or electricity substations and indeed a great many other delights nestling inconspicuously within the landscape that, as a passer-by at street level, I probably wouldn't have noticed before.

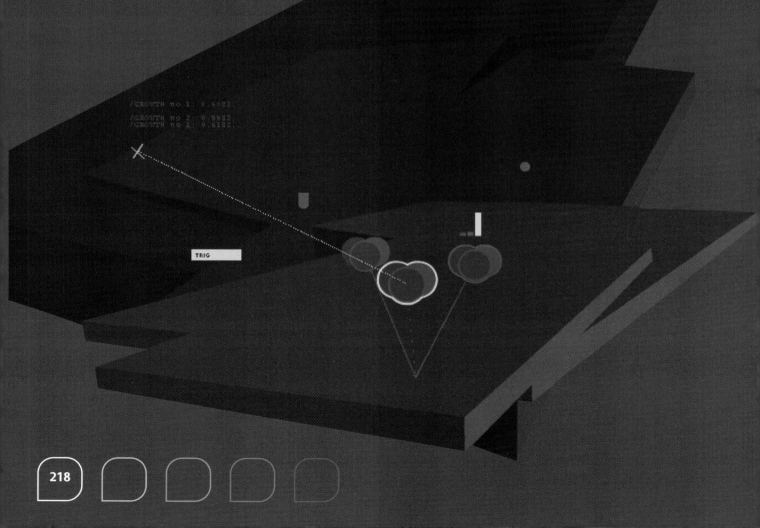

House Sculpture [detail] Rachel Whiteread © Richard Glover/CORBIS

Fading Ad Campaign © Frank Jump; www.frankjump.com

I also have a great fascination for Installation art, such as that of Rachel Whiteread. Whiteread creates sculpture or casts from the negative space within or surrounding an object to suggest the real space that the object occupies, and the spatial language she uses is another great example of looking closer at something to see beyond the expected. Had I a tin-opener close by (not to mention a few extra pages) I would probably open a whole can of worms about using space as a method of communication. I haven't though, so I won't. Besides, the whole issue of time is much more interesting and so with time in mind I'll move swiftly on.

Before I can talk about the works of artists whose use of time I find inspirational and thought-provoking, I guess I must first try to describe what I find so intriguing about the concept of time itself. Whilst I don't let myself lose sleep over it, the whole concept of time poses so many unanswerable questions that I find completely fascinating. How do we understand the notion of time, when we can't see it or feel it? Why does a minute go faster when you're having fun than when you're waiting for a bus? Is time elastic, able to be stretched or otherwise manipulated? What kinds of relationships exist between time and space?

Apologies if you think that last bit got a bit heavy, but stick with me and I'll see if I can explain what I mean. Of any roll of film to come out of my camera, at least four or five shots will invariably be of rusting signs, derelict shop frontages or similar urban typography, so when a friend introduced me to the work of Frank Jump I felt an immediate empathy. Jump is a photographer whose work (www.frankjump.com) concentrates on the ageing ads painted onto the sides of factories or shops around his native city of New York, and reveals a shared preoccupation and fascination with found imagery, typography and urban architecture.

But more than that, the work also relies inherently on the influence of time, and as such provokes thought and begs the question: what story do they tell about the building/advert/product? Is it art or is it graphic design? If it's an advert, then it must be graphic design, but these pieces are often selling products that are no longer on sale and are complete strangers to today's world of commercialism, so surely they must be art? If they are art, how much of their beauty is a result of their age? What did they look like a year ago? A decade or a century ago? Would they have been considered beautiful then?

Chronometry

Jump isn't attempting to answer these questions, but instead just trying to get the viewer to ask themselves the questions it provokes. A couple of paragraphs ago I proposed the question "How do we understand the notion of time, when we can't see it or feel it?" In this case we can visualize time by its effects on the ageing sign, but we can't see time itself – only a vehicle or language that visually represents it. Of course, you could argue that a clock is an adequate way to see time, but even then we are using numbers, in standard measurements of hours, minutes and seconds, as a means to visualize it. And besides, how accurate is a clock as a way of seeing time (they run fast or slow, or stop completely – time never stops, does it?).

With his lover dying of AIDS, and acutely aware of the limited time that they may have together, Cuban New Yorker Felix Gonzales-Torres created *Untitled (Perfect Lovers)* - a work consisting of two clocks, side by side and synchronised to the same time. Placing a set of used batteries (a metaphor for the dying condition of his partner) into one of the clocks, and a fresh set (a metaphor for his own state) in the other, the artist created a piece that would continually change its visual state and meaning as time went by.

The aspect of the work that I find so interesting is that the artist has found a means to question our understanding of how we interpret time. Of course the clocks should run in synch, but for one, time is going slower, even though in reality it isn't! And even the clock that was running on fresh batteries is now running on dying batteries, and so how accurate is that as a true reflection of time? Look deeper and the

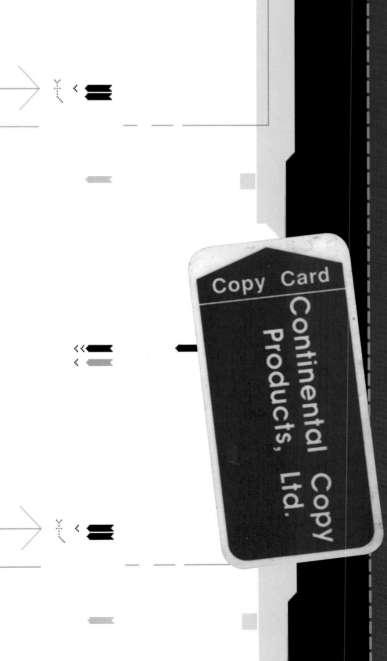

Copy Card

Continental Copy
Products, Ltd.

clocks can even suggest narrative; were I to see the clocks a year later, what would they display? How representative of the lives of the artist and his lover would they be? What would I think if one of the clocks had stopped? I can't answer any of these questions, and that is perhaps why I draw so much inspiration from the work – the appreciation of the fact that it relies emphatically on the visualization of time to stimulate thought and response from within me.

Whilst I've got my arty-farty hat on, let me just take another quick diversion before returning neatly to the subject of Flash. Everywhere I go, I carry around in my wallet a piece of art that I got whilst in New York. OK, so it's not really a piece of art if you look at it in isolation, but this plastic copy card from Continental Copy Products Ltd is one of the dead cells of what I can only describe as a living piece of art. As I climbed the stairs to the second floor of the New Contemporary Museum of Art in New York to visit a recent Tibor Kalman exhibition, I was greeted by an installation created from several plinths. On each of these, often in untitled but classified groups (such as chewing gum, till receipts and cigarette packets) were the items deposited by previous visitors. The description of the installation invited me to leave a personal possession of my choice on one of the plinths and in turn, take one thing from the exhibit.

Essentially it was a guestbook, but not one that would leave the marks of all previous visitors, as the display would be ever-changing, evolving visually and spatially with every user interaction. I took the copy card, and left in its place a British train ticket. As with the work of Frank Jump and Felix Gonzales-Torres, the reason I found myself completely absorbed with the work was its preoccupation with time. Here, time had a direct effect on the piece – the way it looked, the space that it occupied and even the numerous stories that it hinted at, and in this respect time was very much being used as a method of communication.

So, the effect of time on its visual and spatial surroundings and its potential as a form of communication in general holds a great interest for me. But without a brick wall that I feel confident I can return to in a hundred years, or a spare wall and enough friends to explore the themes of the 'living wall', I guess I've had to find other ways of exploring and expressing my inspirations, fascinations and influences.

Which, as promised, brings me neatly back to Flash. Flash is the perfect tool to allow me to indulge myself, not only in providing the perfect canvas to explore visual themes and styles that interest and inspire me, but to explore the other interests that I perhaps don't have the ability to explore via conventional or traditional means.

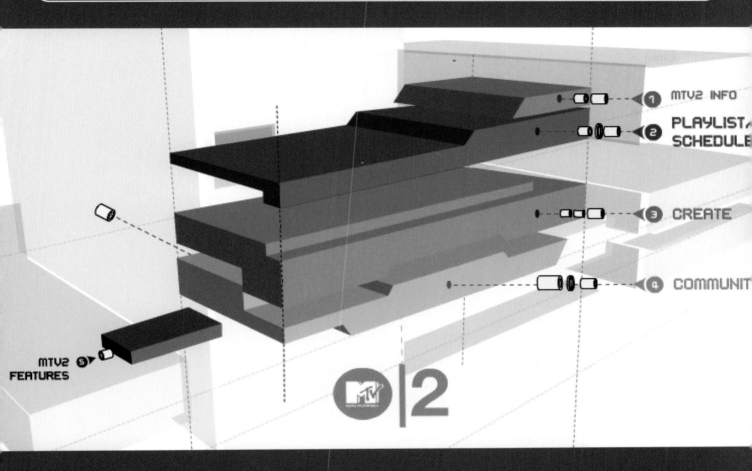

In the end, it's this – the potential of the tool as a means of communication – that has truly brought me to Flash. Using Flash in my job as an interactive designer has enabled me to work with some great people, on great jobs that have allowed me to develop some of these ideas. One of the more interesting Flash projects that I have been involved with was the design and production of the MTV2 web site (www.mtv2.co.uk) which provided the perfect platform to explore the spatial language of design to communicate narrative, environment and community. Subsequently I have found myself looking for ways to pursue the other interests that I have mentioned.

Ideas such as a living web site, that grows healthily or decays over time depending on the user's interaction, or a site that grows spatially as the number of users present increases, all offer a wealth of opportunity that I am eager to wade through. Of course, there is a whole plethora of questions the issue of time is capable of raising. I don't expect to answer any of them, but instead use time as a means to express ideas, raise further questions, and suggest other opportunities. And it's with this in mind that I politely stop talking about myself, add a full stop to the end of the sentence and move onto the next part of the chapter.

I created my personal site, stoprefresh.com, to provide a platform for me to explore the interests, influences and ideas that I've been talking about in the last section. The Flash movie that we're about to build together is a diet version of its interface. The interface itself was the result of a study to see how the components of time can enable and manipulate the visual language of the design, and was an initial exploration into some of the things I've mentioned.

The design of the interface not only allows me to easily populate the site with content over the period of the year, but at the same time creates a visual environment that's easy to use and appears differently at any given second of the year. I've used the units of time and applied them with a particular set of rules or behaviors to the objects of the movie to create the design. As such, the movie that we're about to create isn't 'designed' to communicate visually in the traditional sense – in other words, arranged aesthetically by the trained eye – but is systematically designed by the properties attributed to it by time.

Essentially, by establishing a correlation between the various measurements of time (months, days, hours, minutes and seconds) and the visual properties of our design, (*x* and *y* positions, alpha, height, RGB and hexadecimal values...) we'll use time to *design* the interface for us.

The only consciously designed element in the design is the page layout (see the page layout symbol in the Library of the FLA). This is basically a 12x60 graph, which plots the hours of a 12-hour clock against the 60 minutes of an hour and 60 seconds of a minute. You'll also notice that the markers on the left-hand side of the graph layout appear in bold. These double up to represent not only hours, minutes, and seconds, but also the 12 months of a year plotted against the 28, 30 or 31 days of a month. Accordingly, depending on how we plot our information on the graph, we can illustrate any given hour, minute and second of a day or any given day and

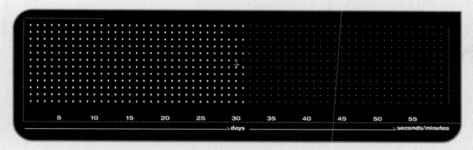

month of the year. The interface design can therefore perform the functions of both a clock and a calendar, and is in itself something of a study into the visual representation of time.

So as not to complicate matters or diffuse the main points of what I'll be talking about, in the tutorial we won't be discussing in too much detail the calendar aspect of the design. If you visit stoprefresh.com online you'll be able to see how this is integrated into the design. Instead, we'll be focussing more closely on the design of the clock elements and see how they're used to create the appearance of the interface.

To build our effect we must do three things. We need to create an engine that provides us with an accurate representation of the current time, create our movie objects, and finally we'll need to establish the behaviors of these objects – the sets of rules we'll apply to them.

Let's start by building the foundations of our movie.

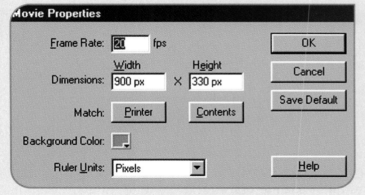

Building the foundations

First, we need to create a new movie set to 900x330 pixels, 20 frames per second frame rate, with a gray background color. These movie properties aren't absolutely vital, but the movie must be at least 800x200 pixels to comfortably accommodate the page layout graphic symbol, which is 765x185 pixels. The 20 fps frame rate is just the setting that I find works fairly well across most machines, while the gray background color will enable us to see our white-colored objects when they're sitting on the stage.

Now let's take the empty blank frame on the layer that we've been given and dive in. I say dive in because we're going to start building our movie by writing the main ActionScript that will provide the engine of the movie. The code and scripting that we'll use for this effect are essentially very simple scripts applied in a logical manner and demonstrate how relatively complex effects can be achieved without the use of Flash's more advanced features, such as smartclips and calling functions. To these ends, this tutorial isn't intended as a programming bible but more as a study into the exploration and realization of an idea.

As the idea behind the effect is to apply the numeric values generated by time to our movie objects, we must first work out what those numeric values are and initialize our variables. We do this by using the `date` object, an ActionScript command that allows the movie to obtain the current day, month, year, hour, minute and second from the local clock (your computer).

Name your default layer scripts and we'll get cracking on writing the script. Click on the blank keyframe on frame 1, open up the Frame Actions panel and click inside the scripting window. I would also suggest that you set the window to Expert Mode, as later we'll be writing scripts in Flash 5 dot syntax. This is only possible when the scripting is written in manually, and can't be added to the window from the drop-down menus provided.

Your first line of script should read like this:

```
date = new Date();
```

This is the 'constructor' of the `date` object, and basically says '*get the full time and date from the local clock, herein referred to as Date*'. The movie has now constructed a `Date` object by retrieving the full date from the computer. Next, we need to retrieve the specific day, month, minutes, and hours values from that `Date` object. We do this by initializing our first set of movie variables, written like this:

```
day = date.getDate();
month = date.getMonth() + 1;
mins = date.getMinutes();
hour = date.getHours();
```

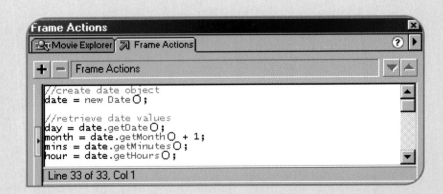

As you can see, each line follows the same format. In layman's terms, and to use the `mins` variable as an example, the command states: *create a variable to be used within the movie called 'mins', and by going to the Date object we've just constructed, assign to it the current 'Minutes' value.* We now have the initial values of day, month, minute and hour that we can use in our design. You'll notice that there's a minor difference in initializing the `month` variable. This is simply because when Flash is asked to return a month value, it starts at 0 for January and ends at 11 for December. Obviously, this doesn't match with how we usually denote the months of the year, so we must compensate for this by adding 1 to the value.

Converting a variable like this, from its existing format to one that we can use more easily within its environment, is called *parsing* and is something that we need to do for some of the variables that we've just created. First, we create mirror variables of our minute and hour values by writing:

```
show_mins = mins;
show_hour = hour;
```

This allows us to manipulate and convert a mirrored minute and hour value for display purposes without changing the original values, which we'll also be using elsewhere. For instance, `hour` will always be a value between 00 and 23 (midnight and eleven o'clock at night), which we'll use. But we also need to know what the `hour` value is in a 12-hour clock format so that we can plot the current hour on the 12x60 graph layout. To do this, the script we've just written allows us to use both variables, `show_hour` and `hour`, even though we'll evaluate one differently to the other. This is exactly what we do with the next lines of ActionScript:

```
if (show_hour == 00) {
        show_hour = 12;
}
if (show_hour >= 13){
    show_hour = (show_hour-12);
    }
```

The first `if` statement states that if our `show_hour` is equal to 00, then it's set to 12, changing the numeric value we'll use for the clock to display midnight from 00 to 12. If this statement is true, the value of `show_hour` is changed accordingly, but leaves the value of `hour` as 00. When true, the second `if` statement also changes the value of our `show_hour` variable. In this case, if its value is equal to or more than 13, it resets its value to its existing value, but minus 12. This is the statement that converts the 24-hour value to the 12-hour value. For instance, if the hour is 18, the value of `hour` is 18, which also means that the value of `show_hour` is 18. But as `show_hour` is equal to or above 13, and therefore the `if` statement is true, we reset `show_hour` to be equal to 18 minus 12, which leaves 6. So, at 6 o'clock in the evening, our movie will return two different hour values: `hour = 18` and `show_hour = 6`.

These aren't the only values that we need to convert in order for them to be used as we would like. Below the previous two `if` statements, write the following scripts:

```
if (day <= 9){
     day = ("0" + day);
}
if (month <= 9){
     month = ("0" + month);
}
```

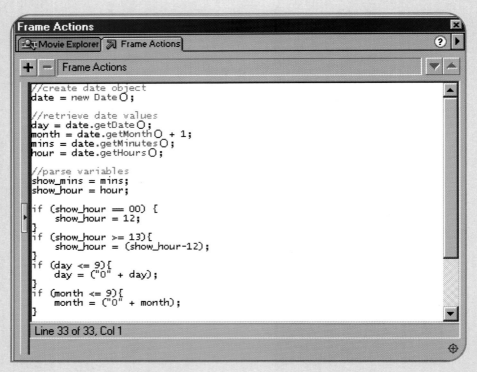

```
//create date object
date = new Date();

//retrieve date values
day = date.getDate();
month = date.getMonth() + 1;
mins = date.getMinutes();
hour = date.getHours();

//parse variables
show_mins = mins;
show_hour = hour;

if (show_hour == 00) {
     show_hour = 12;
}
if (show_hour >= 13){
     show_hour = (show_hour-12);
}
if (day <= 9){
     day = ("0" + day);
}
if (month <= 9){
     month = ("0" + month);
}
```

Line 33 of 33, Col 1

Here we've added two additional `if` statements. These perform similar functions to the two that we've just written: they convert a value generated by Flash into a value that is more compatible with our design. They're simply giving any number equal to or less than 9 a prefix of 0. For example, if Flash returns a `month` value of 3, it will be converted to 03. Of course, this doesn't change the value of our `month` variable, but it does ensure that our values will always be in double figures, something that will be useful later in the tutorial when we discuss applying such values to our objects.

Here I'd like to draw your attention to how we join the two parts of the value together. In the example above, by using the + command, we've joined the literal numeral 0 (as represented by the `""` marks) to the numeric value of 3. This adds the two items by simply joining them one after the other, like Scotch tape, and is known as *concatenating* strings. Were both values numeric and not literal, this example would return a value of 3 (0+3 = 3), and not 03.

The last two lines of ActionScript that we need to add to this first frame are the commands that initialize two additional variables:

```
elapse = 0;
ypos = (show_hour*10) + 100;
```

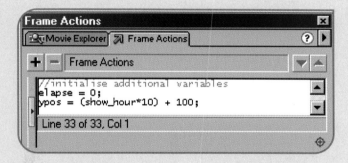

These are variables that we'll rely on later in the movie. We'll be using the `elapse` variable shortly to keep check on how many minutes have expired since the movie commenced, while the variable `ypos` establishes a value that we'll use to set the *y* position of our movie objects. I'll discuss the relevance of this formula later in the tutorial, when we'll be exploring various ways of applying the time values to the different properties of the objects.

Chronometry

Your first frame should now contain a whole lot of ActionScript, and you're well on your way to building the chronometer.

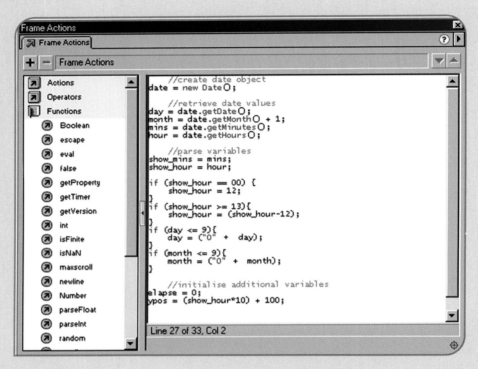

How far have we got? We've written a list of ActionScript that retrieves, and parses where necessary, the day, month, hour and minute information obtained from the local clock. But as this frame is currently the only frame of the movie, the playback head will only ever hit this frame once, perform the commands and calculations and stop. If we're to create an interface that continually changes over the course of time, and as accurately as possible reflects the current date and time (including seconds) we must ensure two things. First we need to create a variable that provides us with a seconds value. We must also ensure that we continually update the numeric values attributed to the respective variables.

In the second frame of the timeline, press F6 to create a new keyframe on our scripts layer. Now return to the Frame Actions panel and enter the following script:

```
show_secs = Math.round(getTimer()/1000)-(60*elapse);
```

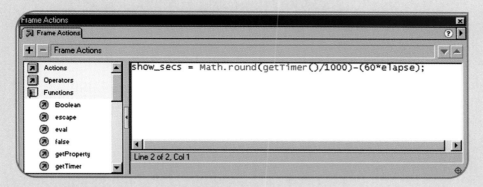

This creates a seconds value to be used in the movie by using Flash's `getTimer` function and attributing it to a variable. In this case we'll call the variable `show_secs`, and assign to it the value returned by the `getTimer` command.

But as you can see, the `getTimer` command is also subject to a few additional calculations. The first part of the equation, `(getTimer()/1000)`, uses `getTimer` to return the total number of milliseconds that the movie has been running, and divides it by 1000. Dividing the number of milliseconds (the only measurement returned by the `getTimer` command, incidentally) by 1000 subsequently gives us our seconds value.

As the name suggests, the `Math.round` command preceding this basically instructs Flash to round the total number that's evaluated between these brackets into a whole number. For instance, if the value returned by `getTimer` was 3247, the equation would divide it by 1000, returning 3.247, then convert it to a whole number, giving us a `show_secs` value of 3.

This leaves the final part of the equation, `-(60*elapse)`. The `getTimer` value returned will continue to increase, and with it, the value of the `show_secs` variable. As this value hits 60, we want it to return to 0, not increase to 61, 62, 63, and so on, so we tell Flash to subtract a multiple of 60 from our `getTimer` total. The multiple that we use is the value assigned to the variable `elapse`.

I guess this is starting to sound a bit complicated so let me give you a *for instance*. If the value returned by `getTimer` is, say, 141234 milliseconds, we first divide it by 1000, giving us 141.234, and then convert it to a whole number, leaving 141. This would indicate that the movie has been running for 141 seconds, or 2 minutes and 21 seconds. The value of `elapse` (as in the number of minutes elapsed) would be 2, so the last part of the equation would be `141-(60x2) = 21`. This calculation therefore will always provide us with a value between 0 and 60 and assign it to the `show_secs` variable.

As before, we'll add an `if` statement similar to those we've just described, that concatenates a 0 to any single numeral and thus always gives us a double figure value:

```
if (show_secs <= 9) {
        show_secs = "0" + show_secs;
    }
```

We now have our final seconds value.

You might at this point be wondering how the `elapse` variable knows to increase its value by one to reflect every minute that's elapsed? Well, we've already initiated the `elapse` variable in frame 1 with a value of 0. Therefore, as our `show_secs` value hits 60, representing the passing of 60 seconds, we must tell the `elapse` value to increment by 1. To achieve this, we would add this ActionScript to our frame actions, but don't type it in just yet:

```
if (show_secs == 60) {
        elapse++;

}
```

This `if` statement simply says that if our seconds (`show_secs`) value is equal to 60, the value of `elapse` needs to be incremented by 1 (using ++). Put simply, this says *'recognize that another minute has elapsed'*. If we also use this opportunity to state that *'if another minute has elapsed, change the value of the current minutes by 1'*, and add this into the statement, the statement looks like this:

```
if (show_secs == 60) {
        elapse++;
        mins++;
}
```

And as we're talking about incrementing the value of our minutes, then hell, let's also say here that *'if the minutes value is equal to 60 (the end of the hour) increase the hour value by 1, and set the minutes back to 0'*. When this is written into the `if` statement, the entire thing looks something like this:

```
if (show_secs == 60) {
        elapse ++;
        mins++;
    if (mins == 60) {
            mins = 0;
                hour ++;
                show_hour ++;
        }
    }
```

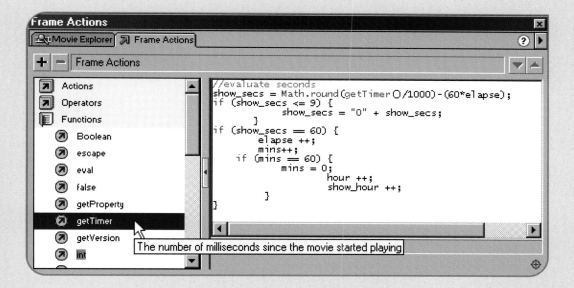

Before we finish the actions for this frame, let's just add another `if` statement that ensures we always have a double-figured minutes value. Again, this is basically the `if` statement we used in frame 1 to concatenate a 0 with any numeric value of 9 or less, and is written as:

```
show_mins = mins;
if (show_mins <= 9) {
        show_mins = "0" + mins;
}
```

Also notice that we re-establish the `show_mins` as a mirror of our `mins` value. This is because, in the scripts we've written above, the value of `mins` will have potentially been updated, so we need to ensure that our `show_mins` value is also updated accordingly. Your actions for frame 2, including additional comments, should now look like this:

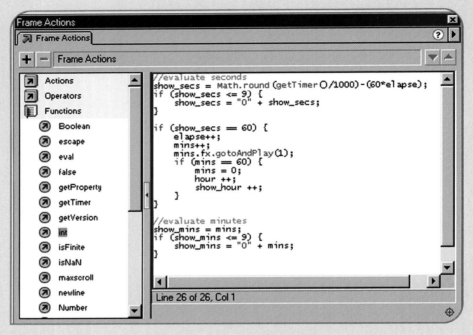

```
//evaluate seconds
show_secs = Math.round (getTimer()/1000)-(60*elapse);
if (show_secs <= 9) {
    show_secs = "0" + show_secs;
}

if (show_secs == 60) {
    elapse++;
    mins++;
    mins.fx.gotoAndPlay(1);
    if (mins == 60) {
        mins = 0;
        hour ++;
        show_hour ++;
    }
}

//evaluate minutes
show_mins = mins;
if (show_mins <= 9) {
    show_mins = "0" + mins;
}
```

So, now we have all the necessary values and calculations to provide us with an accurate representation of the current time. But as I mentioned earlier, we need to continually update the numeric values attributed to the respective variables in order for them to continually represent the current time. We can do this by making sure that we tell the playhead to keep reprocessing the calculations we've just written in frame 2. This is simply a case of adding an action into frame 3 that sends the playhead back to frame 2. Add a keyframe on frame 3, and write a simple `gotoAndPlay` script:

```
gotoAndPlay(2);
```

We now have the movie playhead trapped in a frame loop. It performs the scripts in frame 2, moves onto frame 3 and gets sent right back to frame 2, where it reprocesses the calculations. Onto frame 3, back to frame 2, calculate, onto frame 3 ... you get the idea. Incidentally, we send the movie back to frame 2 every time and not frame 1, as frame 2 systematically updates all the values of seconds, minutes, and hours, so we don't need to go back to frame 1 and ask Flash to retrieve these values from the hard drive. Besides, frame 1 is also where we initialize our `elapse` value of 0, so if we continually returned to this script we would be constantly resetting `elapse` to 0.

All of this means that the main engine of our movie is built.

Even if you stopped building your interface at this point, at least you'd have built a working clock in Flash. But how you do know, without just taking my word for it? At the moment, we have a series of numeric values being calculated by the engine of the movie, but no way to check that they're being processed as we would like. If we wanted to check one single value I would recommend using the `trace` command which would show us the value in the Output window, and include a line of code in the frame actions along the lines of:

```
trace(show_secs);
```

This would show us the value of `show_mins` every time the playback head encountered this script. But as we have several values that we need to check, and these several values would be reprocessed and checked every other frame, our Output window would end up hundreds of lines long, and consequently very difficult to keep track of. Instead, we'll create a symbol that allows us to read these values on the stage – an instrument panel, if you like, that we can use to check the value of each variable and cross-reference them to ensure that our clock mechanism is working bug-free.

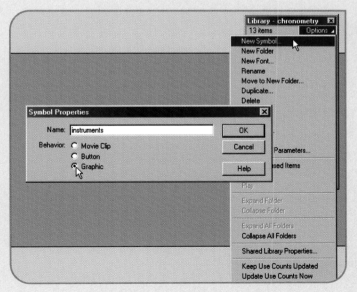

To do this, create a new graphic symbol from the Library and call it instruments. Double-click on it from the Library and let's start to edit it.

Create a textfield and enter month::. Now open the Text Options panel from the Launcher in the bottom right-hand corner and make sure this textfield is set to Static Text. This will see that the textfield always displays what we enter into the field, in this case month::.

Now create another textfield to the right of the last. In this textfield write 00, and this time use the Text Options panel to set the field to Dynamic Text. A dynamic textfield works differently to a static one in that it will display the value of the variable we assign to it. If you've selected Dynamic Text as the option, you'll now see that we now have two more options available to us. Select Single Line as the first option (our values will never be over two numbers, let alone one line), and in the option for Variable type in _root.month.

What we've done here is to create a textfield that will show a default value of 00 until the variable month on the _root of the movie (the main timeline) has a value that we can display. As we've already initialized and parsed our month value in frame 1, the 00 display will change to display our month value; between 01 for January and 12 for December.

This is our first *instrument* reading.

Now, ideally we want to create a whole line of our readings, so we must do this for each of the values that we want to display. As we know, these values are represented by the variables `month`, `day`, `hour`, `show_hour`, `show_mins`, `show_secs`, and `elapse`, so repeat the process described above for each of these variables by creating both a static and dynamic textfield alongside it. Remember also that the variable option for each of the dynamic textfields must reference `_root` before the variable name, as the variables we're asking the textfield to display are on the top level of the movie, not contained within the `instruments` symbol.

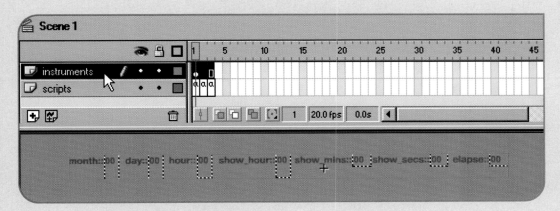

We should now have all of our instruments in the symbol. Arrange the textfields, either by eye, or by using the Align tool so that they all sit neatly and are easy to read in a line. Now return to the stage of the movie, create a new layer and call it instruments. Click in the blank keyframe provided by the new layer and drag the instruments symbol from the Library onto the stage. Making sure that the symbol is present on the stage for all three frames, export the movie and you'll be able to see that our clock mechanism is fully working.

On the stage of the exported SWF you should see something that looks like this:

month:: 05   **day::** 15   **hour::** 19   **show_hour::** 7   **show_mins::** 30   **show_secs::** 11   **elapse::** 0

In this example, we can see that the display tells us that it's 30 minutes and 11 seconds past 7, on the evening of May 15th. Check that your movie is displaying the current date and time correctly, as set by your computer's clock. If you keep your eye on the instruments display for at least a minute you should also see that not only does the seconds display keep itself correctly updated but also that the values of `show_mins` and `elapse` also increase with every minute that passes. You might also want to just check at this point that the scripts we've written to evaluate the correct hours value is also working. To do this, change the current time of your computer's clock to show xx:59 and export the movie again. This time, as the seconds tick away and reach 60, the minutes and seconds values reset themselves to 00 and increase the `hours` and `show_hour` values by 1.

If you're happy that the scripts of your movie are working as they should, let's move on to the next part of the tutorial where we'll create the objects that we want to interact with this information.

Creating the objects
Now that we have a fully functioning clock engine that provides us with ever-changing numeric values for us to play with, we must create the objects that we wish to apply this information to. To achieve our desired effect of creating a uniquely visual representation of any given second, we can do this with just a few symbols, even though we may ultimately reuse one or more of these symbols with different behaviors to achieve different results. For our movie, let's create five different objects; one that displays the current date typographically, another that is a reusable generic color strip, and another three that can each graphically represent hours, minutes and seconds.

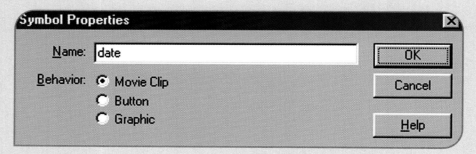

The first object that we'll create is one that we'll use in our movie to show, in text format, the current month and day. Create a new movie clip symbol from the Library and call it date. Now double-click the symbol to edit it, and add a textfield.

Write date into the textfield and make sure that the text in the field is aligned right. As a static textfield this will always display the word date, but we want it to dynamically read whatever the current date is. Change the field to Dynamic Text and enter the name date_txt as the variable. This field will now display the value of

the variable `date_txt`. At this point, though, we haven't created any variable named `date_txt`, so we must create it and give it a value.

Create a new layer within the symbol and call it scripts. We'll now create the `date_txt` variable, so in the Frame Actions window add this ActionScript:

```
monthlist = new Array("january ", "february ", "march ",
➡"april ", "may ", "june ", "july ", "august ", "september
➡ ", "october ", "november ", "december ");
show_month = monthlist[_root.date.getMonth()];
date_txt = show_month + _root.day;
```

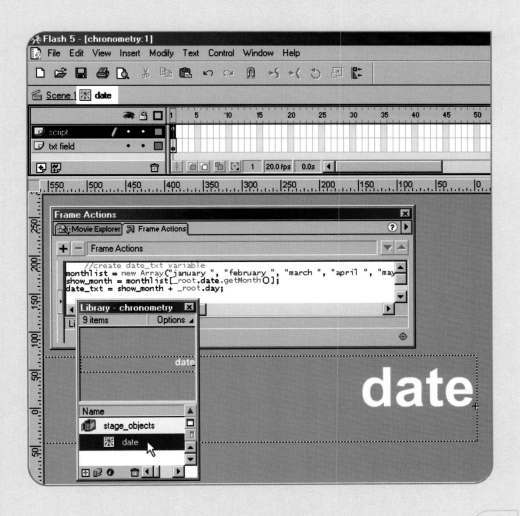

Chronometry

To show the date in a text format we compare the date numerically against an ordered list of month names. The first variable `monthlist` simply creates an array, or list of values — the values being the names of the twelve months.

The second line of code is the script we use to extract the value that we need from the list, and assign it to our variable `show_month`. We know that `show_month` must be one of the values in the list, but how do we know which position in the list? Well, the position that we want is equal to the value returned by the `getMonth` command we used previously, and is contained in the square brackets. We know that targeting the `Date` object we created in the first frame of the movie (`_root.date`) and retrieving the month (`getMonth`) will return a value between 0 and 11 (as I said Flash's date equates January to 0...). And as an array also numbers its values beginning at 0, when the month is, for instance, January, `getMonth` will return a value of `0`, the value occupying position 0 in the list is January, and so the value assigned to the variable `show_month` will be `January`.

The last line of the ActionScript simply concatenates two of our variables to create the `date_txt` variable — the value of which will be displayed in the dynamic textfield. As before, this is achieved by using the + symbol and is simply creating a variable that joins the month is text format (`show_month`) to the day retrieved in frame one of the main timeline (`_root.day`).

With the script in place to give us our first dynamically generated visual element, we're ready to put it on the stage, so return to the stage, create a new layer and add the symbol over the three frames of the movie.

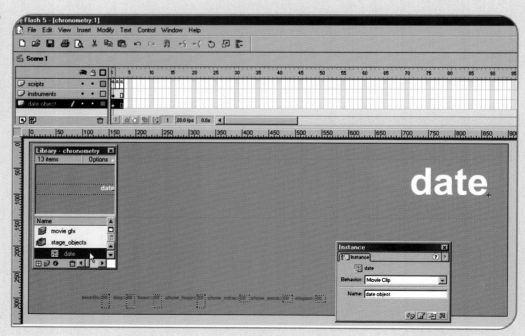

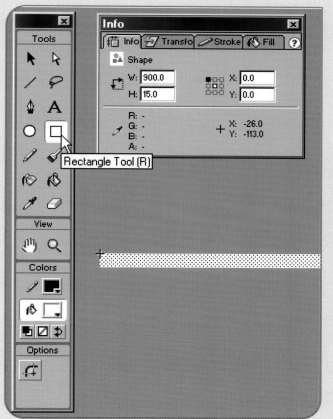

Now we'll create a generic symbol that we can reuse as many times as we require, a symbol that can be made to appear differently for each instance simply by applying different behaviors to it. To do this, first create a new movie clip called rectangle. Add a white rectangle to the center of the stage. This works best if the rectangle has no outline. Now, using the Info panel, set the rectangle to 900 pixels width, 15 pixels height, and set to (0,0) on the stage.

Now create another new movie clip, called fx script, which we'll use to contain our behavior scripts. Later we'll need to edit this symbol, but for now we can leave it empty.

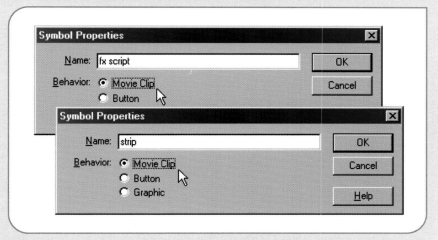

Now that we have our rectangular symbol and the fx script movie clip that we'll eventually use to manipulate it, we must create a new 'parent' symbol to nest these two elements together.

Chronometry

Make a new movie clip symbol called strip, and on the first layer drag our rectangle graphic onto the stage. Then create a second layer and drag the fx script onto the stage. With our two symbols on the stage, set the height of the strip to 3 and align them both top-middle to the stage center. Note that as we haven't yet added anything to our fx script the empty movie is represented on the stage by a white dot, which Flash adds merely as a way of allowing us to see that the symbol is present. The last thing to do is to give each symbol an instance name so that we can talk to them, so use the Instance panel to give our symbols the names stripe and fx respectively.

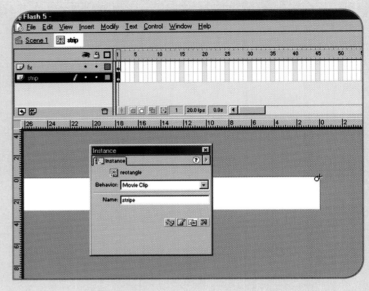

This is effectively all we need to create our generic object. We'll come back to our fx script symbol and its function when we get onto creating our behaviors, but for now our reusable symbol is ready to put on the stage.

So return to the stage and create five new layers. On each of these drag the strip object onto the stage and in turn give each of these strips the following instance names; bg, strip1, strip2, strip3, and (imaginatively enough) strip4. Name the layers accordingly also. The *y* position of these objects on the stage isn't important as we'll use their behaviors to set their *y* property, but do ensure that each strip is aligned to the center of the stage. When set to the desired position, the ends of each object should meet the left and right edges of the stage, covering the entire width of the movie.

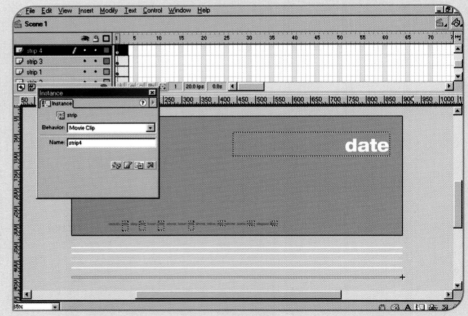

Here we've created five different stage instances out of one single generic object. Not only does this make any future update particularly easy (having only one symbol to edit to ensure all instances get updated) but the duplication will also keep the filesize of our SWF as small as possible.

Now let's create the remaining three symbols of our movie that we'll use to plot our current time on the page layout graph. We'll call them hours, minutes and seconds.

These objects will be very similar to the generic object that we've just made – they'll consist of a plain white rectangle (our rectangle symbol) and the fx script that we'll use to manipulate their appearance. However, the main difference is that we'll also add a dynamic textfield to allow each to display the respective values.

The easiest way to build these objects is simply to create three duplicate symbols of our generic strip object (renaming them hours, minutes and seconds accordingly) and then amending them to add the extra functionality.

Take your newly created hours symbol first. As we've created this movie from our generic strip we already have our rectangle and fx script in place and named. So, all we need to do to turn this into a readout for the hours is to add a dynamic textfield that will display the show_hour value set by the variable on the main timeline. Edit the symbol and do just that, adding a new layer with a dynamic textfield on it. Make sure that the textfield paragraph options are set so that the text will align right (writing a default value of 00 into the text field should allow for easier alignment), and then assign the variable name to the field.

Chronometry

As before, we'll need to reference the variable set at the root level of the movie, so the variable name you need to enter is `_root.show_hour`. We now have our hour symbol that will display our `show_hour` value of between 1 and 12. Align all three elements of the object so that they each sit with their bottom right-hand corners at the center point of the symbol. Also, in the Info panel set the width of the `rectangle` symbol to 200 pixels wide by 22.5 pixels high.

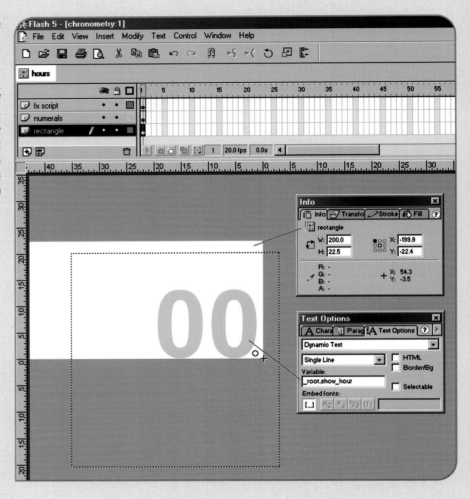

Let's add this to the stage now by returning to the main movie and adding a new layer. Drag the symbol onto the stage and give it the instance name hours. As before, we'll eventually write a behavior that will tell the object how and where we want it to appear on the stage, so don't worry where you place it, as long as you can see it and select it when necessary.

Next we'll edit our minutes symbol. Double-click in the Library to edit and, as with our hours object, add a dynamic textfield onto a new layer. Enter a default value 00 into the field and then give its appropriate variable option, `_root.show_mins`. Again, set the dimensions of the rectangle with the Info panel – this time to 1000x5

pixels, and align the bottom right-hand corner of each symbol to the center point of the stage.

We now have a minutes movie clip that can be used in our movie to display the current minutes value. We need to add this to the stage, of course, so add a new layer to the movie and drag the symbol onto the stage, naming the instance mins.

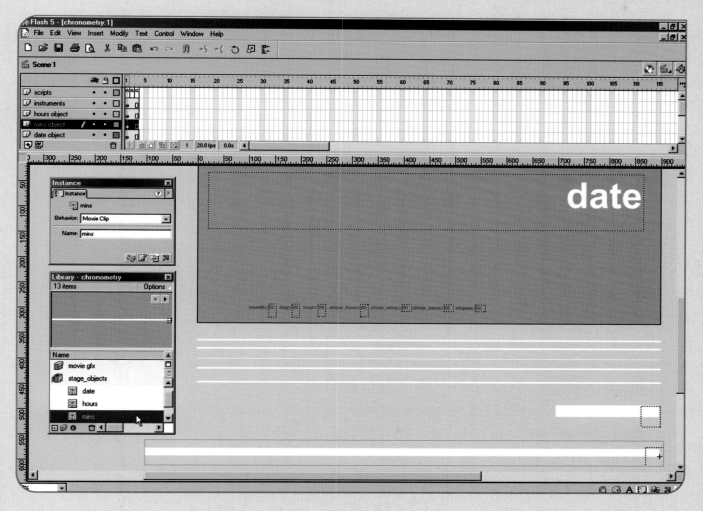

The last of our new *chronometric* objects that we need to create is our seconds. We've already made a duplicate of our generic object to use as the base of our seconds symbol, so let's now edit it. On the timeline of the symbol on different layers we should have the rectangular strip and our fx script. Firstly, let's turn our attention to the rectangle symbol and reset its height and width to 1200x16. Now we need to add our textfield. As we did with the hours and minutes objects, create a new layer and add a dynamic textfield with the default value of 00. Enter the variable we need to call (_root.show_secs) in the Variable field.

Now, press F8 to turn our textfield into a symbol and call it secs_txt and then align all three elements so that their top right-hand corner sits flush to the center point of the stage.

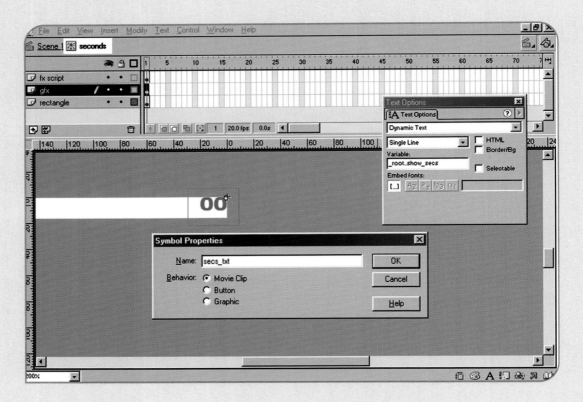

As you can see, this is pretty much how we created our hours and minutes. Of course, the seconds object will work almost the same as the other two 'time' objects but we'll give it slightly different characteristics.

First in the Effect panel, change the white strip by giving it a tint value of your choice:

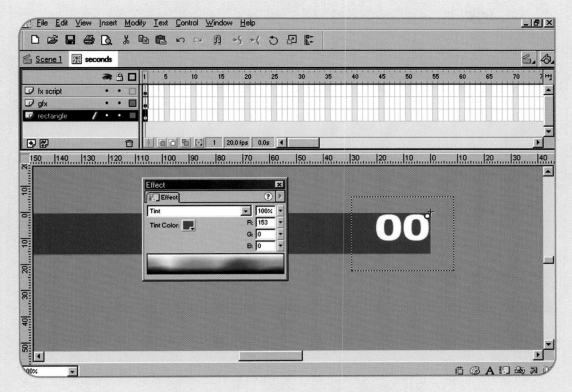

Now, on the layers containing the stripe and secs_txt symbols, add keyframes on frame 3 and frame 10. Make sure that the fx script is on the timeline across all ten frames of our movie clip, but has only the one keyframe in frame 1.

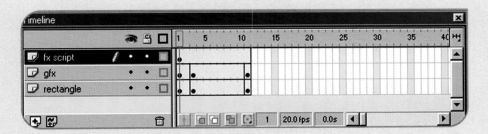

When we create our behaviors for our seconds symbol we'll eventually get the object to move across the stage, plotting the current seconds onto the page layout graph. When this reaches the point on the graph representing 60, we'll need it to return to 00. To have it do this without jumping across the stage we simply get the object to fade out before returning to the start of the graph layout. We could of course do this with our behavior script, but we can achieve this more easily with a motion tween.

Take both the secs_txt and stripe symbols on keyframe 10, move them 100 pixels to the left and set their alpha to 0. Now create a motion tween for each symbol between keyframes 3 and 10. When played back, the symbols should shift off to the left and fade out, and the timeline for the symbol should now look like this:

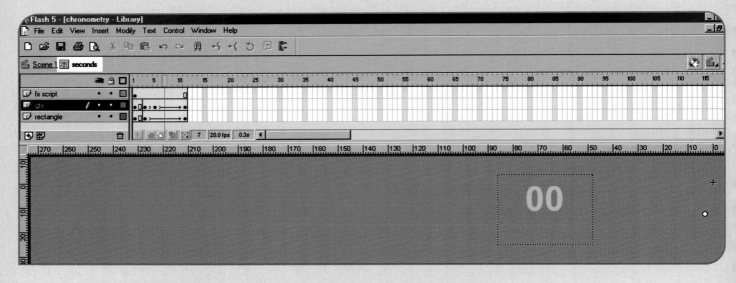

The motion tween we've created here will be used when we need to reset the *x* position of the object back to represent 00. We still need to instruct Flash to only play this part of the movie clip when the seconds reach 60, which we can do when we create the behaviors for the object in the last part of the tutorial. For now, though, we can put the object on the stage. Go back to the stage then and create a new layer for the object, called secs object. Drag an instance of the seconds symbol onto the stage and give it the instance name secs.

Now that we have all of our objects sitting primed on the stage, add the final two symbols already prepared in the Library, page layout and border, giving them each their own layer. The *x* and *y* settings for the page layout symbol should each be set at 100, so that it sits 100 pixels in from the left-hand side, and 100 from the top. The border, by definition, should meet all sides and corners of the movie.

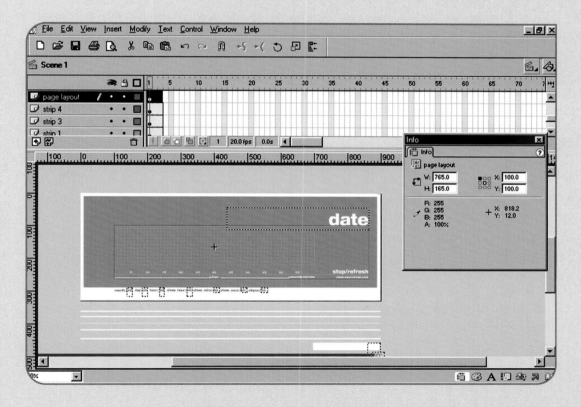

If you were to export the movie at this point, although we have all of our objects on the stage, you would notice that objects are sitting there unaffected, looking exactly as you have placed them. Of course, our 'clock' mechanism is running and is providing us with numeric information that we can use to change the appearance of our layout, but we haven't yet established any relationships between these values and the visual properties of our objects sitting on the stage. So, to get these objects to form a visual representation of our current time, we need to establish these relationships. We'll do this by creating behaviors for the objects.

Creating the behaviors

With our objects built and placed on the stage we can focus our attention to editing the fx script symbol we created earlier, which will be the primary means of giving our objects their different behaviors. As you'll remember, we created the symbol as a means to apply sets of rules to an object but, as yet, we haven't edited the symbol or otherwise given it any functionality.

If we edit the symbol now we'll see its empty timeline. At various points along this timeline, ten frames or so apart, add eight new keyframes. Label each keyframe, giving each one the same frame name as the instance names we gave the objects on the stage earlier; strip1, strip2, strip3, strip4, bg, hours, mins and secs. Our fx script now has several keyframes, each corresponding to an object instance on the stage.

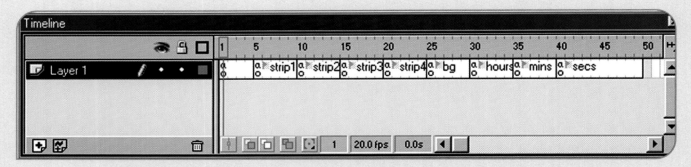

All our objects contain the fx script symbol and each object has a different name. So as long as the fx script knows which instance it's sitting in, we can ask it to jump along to the frame of the same name. As it's a child symbol within the main objects, we can do this simply by getting the fx script to ask its parent what its name is. Add this line of ActionScript to the keyframe on frame 1:

```
gotoAndStop(_parent._name);
```

What this says is, *jump to and stop at the frame that has the same name as my parent*. We've put this script into the first frame, so as soon as it starts playing it will work out the parent's instance name, jump to the corresponding frame, and perform the frame actions. As each instance will jump to a different frame each time, it's in these frames that we write the scripts to create the different behaviors that we'll apply to each of our movie instances.

Click on the first of our labeled keyframes, strip1. In the Frame Actions window add these two lines of code:

```
_parent._y = _root.ypos;
stop();
```

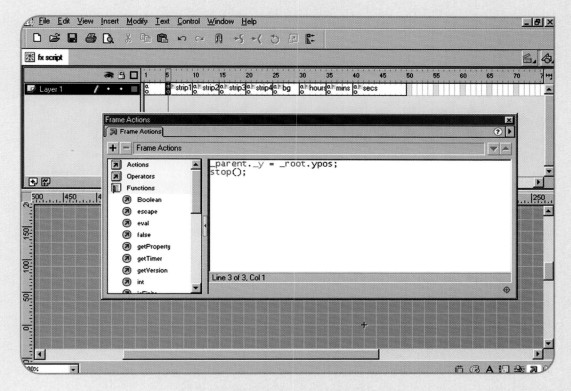

As you can see, we're only asking Flash to perform one command before stopping the playback head. Here we're asking it to set the *y* position of the parent object (our object called strip1 on the stage) equal to the value assigned to ypos at the root of the movie. This is a variable we initialized right back in the first frame of the movie:

```
ypos = (show_hour*10) + 100;
```

The value of our ypos variable is generated by taking our show_hour value, multiplying it by 10, and adding 100. If, for instance, show_hour is equal to 7, our variable ypos would have a value of (7 x 10) + 100 = 170. The behavior that we've just created will then simply tell the parent movie to position itself on the stage at whatever value `ypos` is – in this example 170. The behavior then plots the object `strip1` onto our graph layout to represent the current hour (from the top line of 1, to the bottom line of 12).

Next we'll create another behavior to apply to the instance `strip2`. Click on the keyframe we've labeled `strip2` and enter the following frame actions:

```
_parent._y = _root.ypos;
_parent._height = 200;
_parent._alpha = _root.show_hour*4;
stop();
```

We've added the same scripting as we did for our first behavior, setting the *y* position of the parent to the value of `ypos`, but we've also added another two commands; one setting the parent's height property to 200, and another setting its alpha property. While the height property is always fixed at 200, the alpha property will change depending on the hour displayed, increasing gradually as the value of the variable `show_hour` on the main timeline increases.

A quick flurry of mental arithmetic and you can work out that the alpha property value of our parent will always be between 4 and 48 and always a multiple of 4. This means that the opacity of the object will change over the passage of time, appearing differently at 10 o'clock, for instance, to how it would at 2 o'clock.

The two different behaviors that we've written here show how easy it is to write a self-contained set of rules to manipulate the visual appearance of the parent object. However, what we've written doesn't really fulfill the objective of creating an ever-changing visual aesthetic. For a start, the only value of time that we've called upon so far is the show_hour, and so would appear unchanged and unaffected for an hour at a time. It would also appear the same everyday, so it doesn't go very far in performing how we would like it to.

To do this we will need to create more complex behaviors, creating formulas, which, though quite simple, can supply us with a far wider range of possibilities. There are several different property values that Flash allows us to manipulate. As well as those we've already briefly explored, (y position, height and alpha) there are properties such as rotation angle, scale and color that can be set by ActionScript. In the Frame Actions window for the keyframe strip3, let's write a body of script that will dynamically change the color of our strip3 instance:

```
_parent._y = _root.ypos;
_parent._height = _root.mins + 30;
_parent._alpha = _root.hour + 10;
changecol = new Color(_parent.stripe);
new_rgb = new Object();
new_rgb.ra= _root.day*3;
new_rgb.ga= _root.mins;
new_rgb.ba= _root.month*3;
changecol.setTransform(new_rgb);
stop();
```

As with our previous behaviors, we've first set the *y* position of the object to our `ypos` value. The height of the object is then set by a command that equals its height to the value of `mins` plus 30 (and therefore anywhere between 30 and 90). As this value will be different every minute, it ensures that, however fractionally, the object would appear different for every minute of the hour. The other line of script that you'll recognize is the same command we used before to set the alpha property value of the parent object. This time however, the final value is calculated differently, retrieving the value of `hour` (not `show_hour`) and adding 10. Accordingly, this object's opacity will be set to anything between 10 and 33 when this behavior is applied to it.

The script below these lines are the commands that we need to include in our behavior script in order to apply our factors of time to the red, green and blue color balance of our object. The first line states:

```
changecol = new Color(_parent.stripe);
```

As with our `Date` object that we had to construct in the first frame of the main timeline, we need to create a color object so that Flash knows where or to what to apply the color transform. This line of code basically says *'create a color object called 'changecol' that targets the movie named 'stripe' within my parent movie clip.'* (As you'll probably remember, when we created our objects, each one contained a rectangle named `stripe`.) With the color object established we now have our target to which we can set the new RGB color, but at this point we still don't have an RGB value to apply.

To set an RGB value to our target, we need to construct another color object, this time what we call a *color transform object*, which is written like this:

```
new_rgb = new Object();
```

Here we've created a new object called `new_rgb`. This object will contain the new color information that we apply to the movie clip specified by the `changecol` target. This color information is initialized with the following three lines of code which assign three different values to each of the three color components, `r`, `g` and `b`:

```
new_rgb.ra= _root.day*3;
new_rgb.ga= _root.mins;
new_rgb.ba= _root.month*3;
```

The three components of our `new_rgb` color object are `ra`, `ga` and `ba`, and their values represent the percentage of the red, green and blue components

respectively. As percentages, their values can range from 0 to 100, and so we've created three simple formulas to ensure that we get a wide range of values returned to assign to each component. The first of the three formulae, applied to the red channel, takes the day value set on the main timeline and multiplies it by 3, allowing for up to 31 different values between 3 and 93. The second, assigning a value to the blue component, is similar but this time just takes the mins value 'as is', allowing for 60 different values between 0 and 60 to be returned. As you can see, the third uses the month value multiplied by three to return up to 12 different values between 3 and 36.

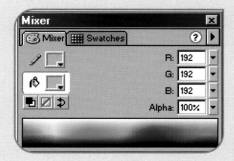

We now have the three different components that make up the new_rbg object. Accordingly, we now have our assembled color transform object that we can apply to our changecol target, and we ask Flash to do that by writing this last line of ActionScript:

```
changecol.setTransform(new_rgb);
```

This simply says, *'go to the target that we set with our changecol color object, and transform it by applying the color information now assigned to the new_rgb color transform object'*. The symbol we originally targeted, our rectangular strip called stripe, will now change from white to the new RGB color combination, calculated using the values of time. Altogether, the number of different combinations that these small equations can create is 22320, which means that from this one behavior alone there are a possible 22320 color combination outcomes, and these are all representative of a particular moment in time.

Using copy and paste, now duplicate the list of frame actions we've just written as the behaviors for strip3 into the Frame Actions window for the keyframe strip4. If we leave the ActionScript as it is, we'll simply have another object on the stage with the same behavior as our last object, so we'll have two objects appearing on the stage with the same visual properties. To change how this object behaves we can simply tweak each of the formulae. There's no hard and fast rule here, so feel free to change the equations to your own settings if you want to. In this example I've changed the formulae so that they read:

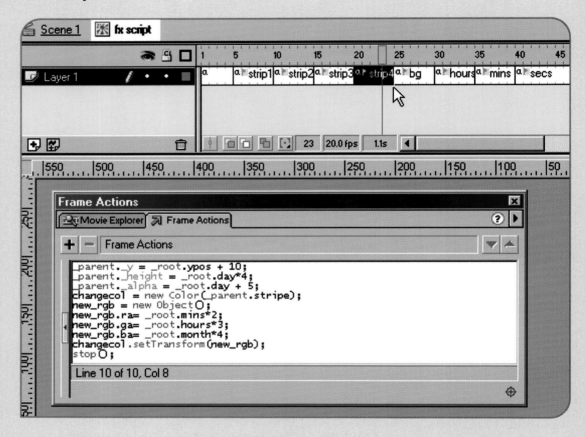

Here I have used the hour value on the root of the movie to assign a value to the green component of the color object, and have also used different multiples to calculate the value of the object's height, *y* position and alpha properties. You'll also see that I've changed how the components of our color object are calculated, but they still ensure a wide a range of outcomes. In theory, these settings could provide a possible 17280 different color combinations so if you haven't realized already, this effect doesn't exactly stick to a web safe palette.

Now we have the behaviors in place for four of our five generic strips, let's create the behavior for the last one, which we've called bg. As you may have guessed, we'll set the properties of this object so that it provides a full-bleed, colored background to the movie. We could set the color properties of this object by using the RGB `setTransform` command we've just been using, but to demonstrate another method of how we can use our time-generated values to change the color of our object, let's take a look at how we can change its hexadecimal color value. In the keyframe labeled bg on the timeline of the fx script symbol, write the following ActionScript:

```
_parent._y = 0;
_parent._height = 330;
_parent._alpha = 60-_root.day;
```

First we ask Flash to set the *y* position of our parent movie (our object named bg on the stage) to 0 pixels – flush with the top of the stage. Next we tell it to set the height of the object to 330, thus filling the full height of the stage, and then we perform a simple calculation to set the object's alpha property. As before, the calculation isn't vital but one that we can use to estimate reasonably what it will return and therefore have a rough idea of how it might behave. Next we need to add the remaining scripts that will create the hexadecimal value that we'll apply to the resized rectangle. We construct the 'color object (to target the symbol we want to transform) as we did before:

```
changecol = new Color(_parent.stripe);
```

And again, as before, we must then construct the color transform object – the object that will contain the color setting information. This time we'll call the object new_hex instead of new_rgb and assign a value to it:

```
new_hex = (_root.mins + 10) + (_root.hour + 10) +
➡ (_root.day + 10);
```

The value that we assign to our new_hex object is literally the two figures of our mins value plus 10, added to the two figures of the hour value plus 10, added to the two figures of our day value plus 10. When these strings are concatenated we're left with a six-figure number, which is exactly what we need for a hexadecimal value. Now that we have our hexadecimal value assigned to our new_hex color transform object we can apply it to our targeted symbol changecol. This is done with the following script:

```
changecol.setRGB(parseInt(new_hex, 16));
```

This is similar to how we applied the color transform of the previous RGB transform, but has the additional command `parseInt` and the value 16 after the `new_hex` value. We talked about parsing variables earlier, and this is exactly the same; the command says *'convert the value assigned to 'new_hex' to a hexadecimal (base 16) value*. This value is then set with the `setRGB` command to the target represented by `changecol`. Finish the actions with a simple `stop();` command and that's our behavior for our movie background object finished.

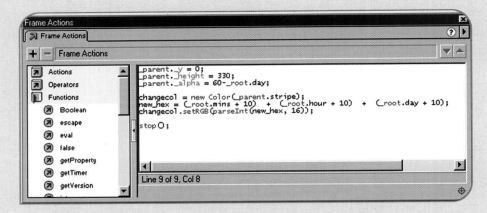

The last objects that we'll add a behavior to within fx script are the hours, minutes and seconds symbols. To add these behaviors we'll reuse some of the scripts we've already used, but amend the equations to give us slightly different results. Still in the fx script movie clip, in the keyframe labeled hours, add this ActionScript:

```
_parent._y = _root.ypos;
_parent._x = 100;
changecol = new Color(_parent.stripe);
new_rgb = new Object();
new_rgb.ra= _root.day*2;
new_rgb.ga= _root.mins*0.75;
new_rgb.ba= _root.month*3;
changecol.setTransform(new_rgb);
stop();
```

As before we've set the *y* position of the object equal to the value our movie variable `ypos`, and the *x* position of the object to 100. The next list of scripting simply resets the color setting of the object according to the formulae we've written, and can be copied and pasted from any of our strip behaviors. You can use these formulae as I've written here, or again you might want to write your own using any of different time values that we have available to us. If you do, remember that the values returned work best when they are between 1 and 100.

To create the behavior for the minutes clip, repeat the process and add the following ActionScript for the keyframe labeled mins:

```
_parent._y = _root.ypos;
_parent._yscale = 70;
_parent._xscale = 70;
changecol = new Color(_parent.stripe);
new_rgb = new Object();
new_rgb.ra= _root.day*3;
new_rgb.ga= _root.mins*0.75;
new_rgb.ba= _root.month*4;
changecol.setTransform(new_rgb);
stop();
```

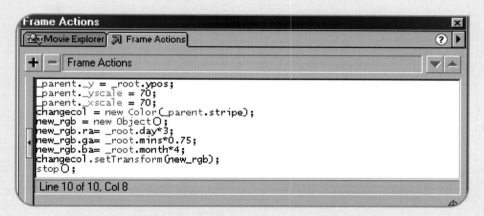

These lines of scripting are more or less what we've written for the hours behavior and perform much the same functions. To make the color of minutes appear differently to that of hours, though, we've slightly changed the values returned from the color object components. We've also introduced a new command that changes the scale of the parent movie clip. The lines...

```
_parent.yscale = 70;
_parent.xscale = 70;
```

...simply tell the movie to set the parent object to 70 percentage of its original *x* and *y* scale, so make our minutes object appear in our movie appear smaller than our hours object. This is introduced merely to help create a visual hierarchy between our clock elements.

Which just leaves the behavior we need to create for our seconds symbol. For the secs keyframe then, write the following script:

```
_parent._y = _root.ypos;
_parent._yscale = 60;
_parent._xscale = 60;
stop();
```

These scripts should be familiar to you by now and so I guess I don't need to go through them in much detail. Note however that the *x* and *y* scale commands reset the object to 60 percent of its original size on the stage which again is to further imply a sense of visual hierarchy.

With these lines of code added to the secs keyframe we should now have behaviors created for all of our object instances. And with this fx script nested within all of our objects and the behaviors written, our movie is almost complete. If you take this opportunity to export the movie you'll see that the simple white strips of the generic object have sprung into life, acting as their behaviors dictate, and thus providing almost any number of unique layouts and color schemes. This fundamentally achieves one of our main aims, which was to see how time can manipulate the visual appearance of the design, so, in that respect, the movie is almost finished.

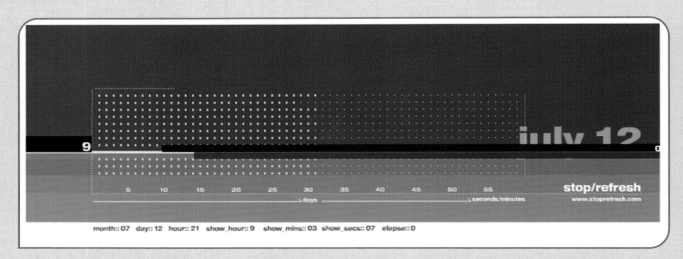

To finish the movie completely, though, we must still create the behaviors that will control the clock function of our minutes and seconds objects. Via our fx script, we now have most of our behaviors in place, using it to set the color, alpha, scale or *y* position properties of our objects. As you'll have noticed, our behavior scripts have been written so that they apply the transformations to the objects and then stop, meaning that these behaviors are only ever applied to the objects once, as the movie starts.

This is entirely sensible – if we were to run each behavior in a loop, continually reprocessing and reapplying the behaviors to our objects, we would probably find our movie running well below its setting of 20 frames per second, and would no doubt eventually crash the machine. Besides, we don't need to continually need to reapply these behaviors anyway; our days, months or hours values aren't likely to change over the course of the movie, so why should we keep asking Flash to perform the same task when the results are likely to be the same?

The only objects that we ultimately need to keep continually updated are the minutes and seconds, which we know *will* change over the course of the movie. And so if we're to get these objects to perform the additional function of accurately representing the current time, plotting themselves accurately onto our page layout graph, we must add to the behaviors we've already written.

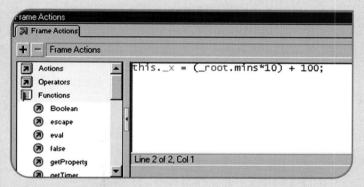

To make sure that the minutes and seconds objects keep themselves updated, and thus plotted correctly along the minutes/seconds axis of the graph, we'll need to keep resetting their *x* position in synch with our clock mechanism. To do this, double-click the minutes movie clip from the Library, and create a new layer, called actions. In the keyframe that has been provided, write the following ActionScript:

```
this._x = (_root.mins*10) + 100;
```

Adding this script to the timeline of the object basically says, '*set the x position of this object to whatever my mins value is, times 10, plus 100*'. If the minutes value is 23, for example, this line of code would position the minutes symbol at (23 x 10 = 230) + 100 = 330. We multiply the mins value by 10, as that is the distance between each marker on our graph, and we add 100 as this the distance from the edge of the movie in which we've positioned the graph symbol. This simple formula then will always set the *x* position of minutes accurately onto the graph to represent the current minute.

Chronometry

Now all we need to do is create a loop on the timeline of this object, by adding a second keyframe and entering a simple `gotoAndPlay(1);` command.

As the script on frame one will continually be re-processed, it will reset the *x* position of the object whenever the `mins` value changes. Use F5 to add frames for each of the fx script, stripe and dynamic textfield layers so that they are present on the stage for both frames and the behaviors for our minutes movie clip are now complete.

This leaves us with just the last of our behaviors we need to create – the *x* positioning of our seconds symbol. As with minutes, we've already applied our scale and *y* position transforms via the fx script, so we now need to add the script that repositions the object along the *x* axis of the graph. Edit the seconds movie clip object from the Library, and create a new actions layer for our additional frame commands. The method we use to ensure that seconds keeps itself updated is similar to that we used for the minutes movie clip – by setting the *x* position of the object in frame 1 and looping the playback head to continually reprocess the script.

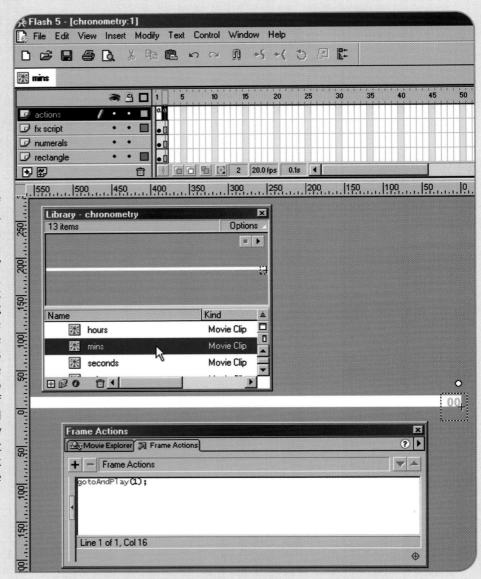

We already have a value, show_secs, that increases from 0 to 60 over the course of a minute that we *could* use to evaluate the correct *x* position, in much the same way we've used our mins value to position our minutes symbol. If we did this, then seconds would jump to the next marker every time our show_secs value increased (in other words, every second). This in itself would provide us with the necessary functionality to plot the object accurately on the graph, but would be rather crude and appear jumpy.

We know that the distance between the first and final markers of the page layout graph (representing 00 and 60 respectively) is 600 pixels, so if we can create a variable whose value increases steadily from 0 to 600 over the course of a minute, we can use this value to plot our seconds movie clip on the graph. This will enable it to move across in a more fluid and less jumpy manner, as it will be moving a pixel at a time not in leaps of 10 pixels.

If you think back to the start of the tutorial where we created the show_secs value, you'll remember that we wrote a script that returned the total number of milliseconds using the getTimer command, divided by 1000. This gave us our seconds value of between 0 and 60 as mentioned above. Let's use that ActionScript again, but this time we'll change the calculation slightly to give us a value of between 0 and 600 over the minute.

Double-click the seconds movie clip to edit it and add a new actions layer to the timeline of the symbol. In the keyframe on frame 1, write the following script:

```
x_secs = Math.round((getTimer()/100)-(600*_root.elapse)+100);
```

Here we've initialized a variable called x_secs and assigned it a value. The getTimer command we've added is exactly the same as the one we wrote to evaluate show_secs, except that we divide the total by 100, not 1000. The value of the elapse variable situated on the main timeline of the movie is still used to evaluate how many minutes have passed. The only addition to the script that we wrote before is the +100 on the end of the formula. This is there to act as a margin, shifting the object 100 pixels in from the left-hand edge of the stage, and thus aligned with the page layout graph which also sits 100 pixels in.

As well as our show_secs value that increases in seconds over the period of a minute, we now have a value called x_secs which increases in tenths of a second, providing a range of values between 100 and 700 (0 to 600, plus 100). With this variable set and a value assigned to it, we simply need to apply it to the object.

Chronometry

Below the script we've just written, add:

```
this._x = x_secs;
```

This command quite simply says *'set the x position of this object to the value assigned to x_secs.'* If you now create a new keyframe on frame 2 and add a `gotoAndPlay(1);` command, we'll create the loop that we need for the seconds clip to keep itself updated. Frame 1 works out what the current *tenth* seconds and x_secs value over the minute is and sets the *x* position of the object accordingly. It then goes onto frame 2 where it gets sent back to frame 1 and reprocesses the command. Onto frame 2, back to frame 1, etc...

The final thing we need to do to complete the scripting of our seconds behavior is to employ the fade down tween we created earlier. As we made this tween to disguise the point where the object resets itself back to 100 (illustrating 00 on our graph) we need to add a command that tells Flash to play the 'fade' part of the timeline. Go back to frame 1 and add into the Frame Actions window:

```
if (x_secs >= 699) {
        gotoAndPlay(3);
}
```

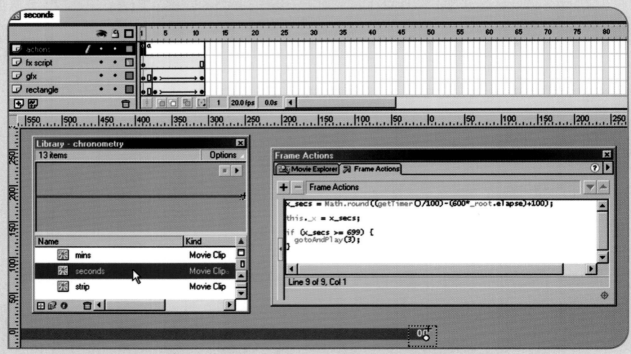

This `if` statement says *'when our* `x_secs` *value is equal to or above a value of 699, go and play frame 3 of the symbol's timeline'*. We know that 700 is the *x* position where our seconds are equal to 60, so, just before our seconds value hits 60 and our `x_secs` value hits 700, the playback head of the symbol jumps to frame 3. Between frames 3 and 10 it plays the 'fade out' tween we created. When it gets to frame 10, the end of the movie clip timeline, it will return to the beginning of the timeline and reprocess the scripting in frame 1, systematically resetting the *x* position of the object back to 100 (or 00 on the graph).

All of which brings us to the end. We've a completed Flash movie that fulfils the criteria we set out with. With all objects built and on the stage and all of our behaviors in place, our interface is now capable of designing itself, and creating a visually unique layout that is representative of our current time.

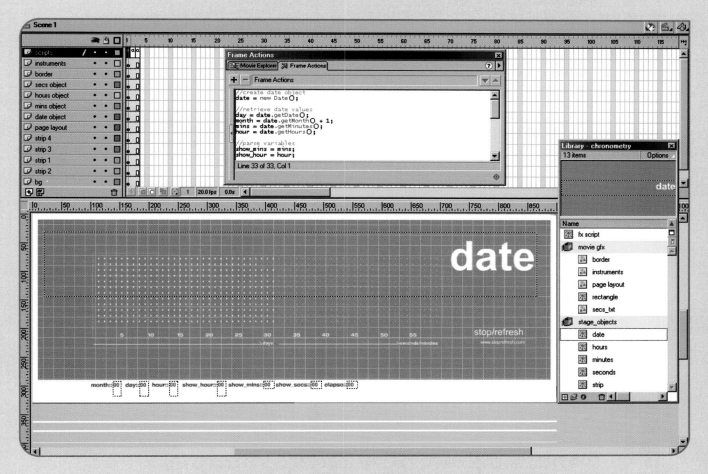

The hours, minutes and seconds objects that we've dynamically colored and positioned against the layout of our graph also give us a comprehensible reading of our current time, and so provide the means to represent the clock functionality. Export the movie now and you should see all of our objects and instances reacting to the behaviors we've written to create our design.

Try testing that the effect fully works by changing the time and date on your computer's clock. As I mentioned earlier, this movie is built so that it will theoretically appear differently for at least every minute of the year (a total that numbers over half a million) and so there will obviously be instances where the differences in its appearance are minimal. But if you try resetting your clock several times you'll see how differently the interface would appear on a summer's morning to say, how it would appear on a winter's evening. Try setting your clock to your birthday for instance. Could we not say that the layout and appearance of the movie is essentially what your birthday *looks* like? The relationship between the information that we use to record that day and that time and the many different visual properties of our objects *designed* what you see in front of you.

To paraphrase one of the people who I admire greatly, Professor John Maeda, this is essentially 'design by numbers'. What we've done is create a system that by using numbers is able to 'design' our interface. We could ask ourselves "Why? What use does it, or could it have?" Of course I can't answer those questions outright, but the potential is surely limitless.

Maybe we could use such a system to infer narrative, for instance an environment that changes as the day passes into night, or the seasons come and go. Or an interface that we can see visibly ageing, decaying over time. Could you create a movie that deteriorates, dying slowly until it grinds to a complete stop? These are some of the more creative and experimental or emotive applications, but maybe there are practical applications for such systems too. Using it to deliver content for example, you could use a similar system to create a content 'watershed', with behaviors that allowed you to view content only before or after a particular time. Or maybe a similar system that displays particular content for a specific time before moving to another area of the movie or site – 'weekly info' content that always displays the up-and-coming seven days for instance. As I said, the potential is limitless, but that potential is there to be explored, studied and experimented with, and I hope that some of what I've talked about and what we have created has sparked off ideas. Now all I'll say is go and have some fun....

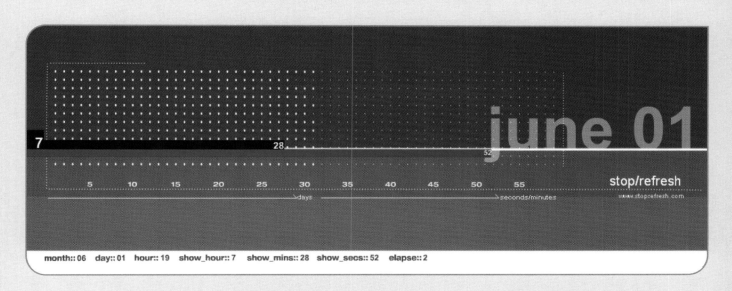

eternal e-greeting card

The new date object can be used to alter the appearance and workings of your final SWF file in many ways, opening up all sorts of new applications...

original scene....   winter...   etc.

Use the date value to vary the color of the sky and ground, and also use it to add seasonal graphics into the mix. Once sent, the e-greeting card will change over time: a card that reflects the changing seasons; Christmas, Easter, and all the ones in between!

date to frame

Rather than use the date to control property-based changes, you could convert it into a movie clip frame number directly.

Just as Vas Sloutchevsky's tutorial converts mouse position into a frame number for one or more movie clips, you could do the same for your own web site, but this time based on the current date. This allows you to totally change your sites appearance over time...

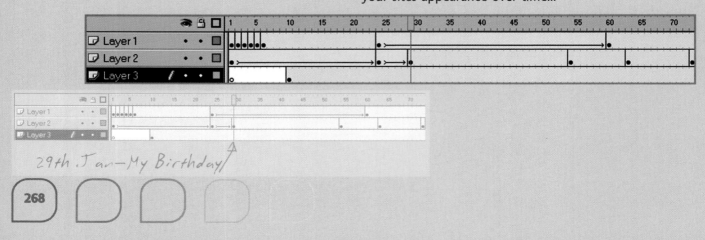

29th. Jan—My Birthday

web wallpaper Flash toy

Some operating systems allow you to use a HTML document as your desktop wallpaper. By using an embedded Flash SWF, you can create all sorts of Flash wallpaper themes that are actually useful. In particular, you could create a simple personal organizer using the date object to find the current date/time.

The SWF would save entries into a local text file.

For those not quite ready for such a task, the simple Flash clock toy might be an easier starting point... don't forget to add some sort of twist to it to keep it interesting to the user!

May	Notes
2001 ___ month ___ **Weekly diary**	
Sun **20**	
Mon **21** *deadline for completing NMOF2 headnotes... DONT be late. MEL Orgee is a cruel woman*	
Tue **22**	
Wed **23**	
Thu **24**	
Fri **25**	
Sat **26**	
Notes	

pen handwriting effect created by using a handwriting font in a blue ink color.

269

"Web sites are very similar to cars — they run at different speeds, need maintenance, security, and sometimes crash."

Josh Levine
www.alphaB2.com

Driven

I'm inspired by the summer sky over the Grand Canyon's North Rim, by Billy Joel's *The Stranger* LP, and by a tall cup of coffee in the morning.

It doesn't take much to inspire me because the world is so full of fascinating details. It's the experience of life that I find most inspiring. I feel lucky to be around during a time of so much innovation. It feels only natural to be part of it!

I'm an explorer. Some say it's the Gemini in me, others that it's just Attention Deficit Disorder, but the more my attention wanders, the more questions arise. I guess I just never was able to accept someone else's notion of the way things are, and the way things can be. I had to learn lessons to move on, make decisions to reveal new choices, and make mistakes to learn new lessons. I had always felt that the benefits of my projects and schemes would eventually present themselves, but I was in it for the journey itself, the search for answers, and the adventure along the way. Mine starts in New Jersey.

I began drawing with charcoals and a hand-me-down 1950s drawing book by the artist Jon Gnagy. I was in awe of the almost photographic realism in the artwork. I always loved looking at images in magazines and encyclopedias, and now I had the power to make images of my own. I began with the cube and sphere, and graduated to a drawing of a train. The feeling I remember about charcoal drawing is that of rubbing the tips of my

© *Charcoal Drawing* Jon Gnagy

fingers into the charcoal and paper, for the purpose of shading and softening. It wasn't just the pencils; I was delivering realism from my fingertips, onto the paper. I enjoyed getting dirty with the artwork.

Eventually reality would prove to supply only very limited content, and I naturally began searching my imagination for imagery. I spent my allowance at the art store, and drew elaborate futuristic scenes and people with pencils and ink. This was the age of the CPM computer, Made-for-TV nuclear war movies, and the Space Shuttle's inception. There was a whole lot to think about!

Staring at walls, TV, and movies also helped to spawn my imagination.

In the opening sequence of Hanna Barbara's *Thundarr the Barbarian*, a runaway planet goes astray and flies between the earth and the moon. The moon cracks into two perfect halves, and the gravitational pull of the earth is affected, mutating all living creatures who then splinter off into groups to survive. Though in cartoon form, these images of the future were enough to set my mind off in countless directions, rearranging the details, adding my own, finding new adventures, and silently living them out in my head.

Robot Appears On "Gilligan's Island"
© Bettmann/CORBIS

C3PO and R2D2 in a Scene from Star Wars, 1977
© Bettmann/CORBIS

Road Leading to Devils Tower
This was the filming site of the motion picture
Close Encounters of the Third Kind.
© Joseph Sohm; ChromoSohm Inc./CORBIS

Land of the Lost and *Gilligan's Island* set in motion many fantasies about living self sufficiently in seclusion, leading to a fort in my backyard! After seeing movies like *The Black Hole*, *Star Wars*, *Close Encounters*, and *ET*, I began a fascination with aliens and outer space, leading to many nights in the fort in the backyard, with a busted Speak 'N Spell, communicating silently with Obi Wan Kenobi.

It was after being mesmerized by the Terry Gilliam film *Time Bandits* that I realized ideas don't need to have rigid boundaries. It was so surreal, full of adventure, and it introduced me to the concept of messing with Time, which I'm still fascinated with. The glowing blue 2D portal into time and space is today's web browser, and we are the midget warriors!

I was never interested in classroom Math, and would use the time to visit dreamland. I would have failed all four years of high school Math, but my Senior Year Math teacher had a better idea. He knew I delivered pizza, and told me that if I delivered 2 extra-large everything pizzas on this one particular night, he'd give me a D- as my final grade for the year. It was the old $F+2\pi=D-$. He let me know in subtle fashion that he could tell I was a mechanical thinker, and that I'd be alright. That was very inspiring!

I attended Film School for two years at City College, San Francisco. Luckily, it was primarily a technical school, so I didn't have to bear with lots of theory. I just wanted to know how to do it. I studied every detail about the cameras, editing equipment, optical printers, and film types, and I made several films. I was inspired by the technology, practically unchanged from the Thomas Edison days, and beautiful in its simplicity.

Later when I discovered Flash, I found a similar freedom each time I expanded my technical understanding of the program, seeing it as a tool to deliver my ideas.

Driven

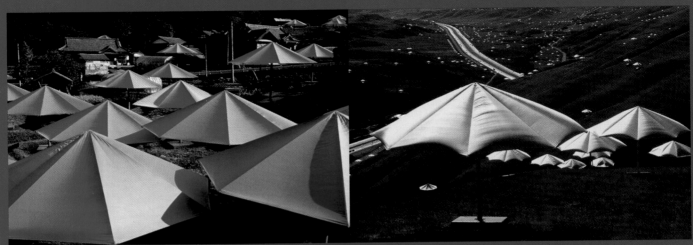

California, USA Site.

Ibaraki, Japan Site.

Christo and Jeanne-Claude: The Umbrellas, Japan - USA, 1984-91. 1,340 blue umbrellas in Japan and 1,760 yellow umbrellas in USA. Each umbrella: 6 meters (19 ft. 8 inches) high. Diameter: 8,66 meters (26 ft. 5 inches) Photo: Wolfgang Volz. © Christo 1991.

In Film School, part of the journey was to find my own way to tell a story, and to use the editing process to help convey the idea. During that process, I was introduced to the art of Christo and Jeanne Claude, and my whole perception of art changed. For me, it was a milestone, a lesson with a simple premise, think big. They had just completed *The Umbrellas* project in southern California. It was such a grand display of color and shadow, infinite combinations depending on perspective. I loved the idea that creativity could be so boundless.

In my last project at City College, I attempted something that set the tone for all future endeavors. I would attempt to take something old, and make it new. It was the production of the opening scene of a short film I was shooting on the outdoor balcony of The Stinking Rose restaurant in San Francisco. After some research, I obtained four helium filled 4-foot diameter balloons, tied them to a cheap super-8 camera and a line of loose kite string tied to a post. I directed the actors to reverse their actions, essentially to act backwards as I pressed record and let the camera go.

The camera faced downward as it lifted up and sideways according to the wind in San Francisco's North Beach

district. After the film cartridge ran itself out, I reeled the camera back in to some difficulty, retrieving and developing the film. Using an optical printer, I transferred the frames in reverse order to 16mm film. The film begins in the sky, and slowly descends to an outdoor balcony active with people on a glowing evening in San Francisco.

I felt an urge to define my creative identity at 21, and concurrently started work at Kinko's, graveyard shift.

Just before the Web began, some friends and I started a paper-based 'zine called the *Gortday Review*, which we produced ourselves. The *Gortday* would prove to be another milestone, pushing me into the playground of design and digital experimentation. It was a monthly 'zine with pictures, articles, drawings, reviews, poetry, and other writings, very local music oriented.

I took full advantage of the wee early hours of the morning at Kinko's, teaching myself Photoshop 3. I started haphazardly by scanning my face and spherizing it. It was fun! Not knowing how to draw in Photoshop, I scanned various drawings and pictures, spending weeks making very small refinements. My Gortday responsibilities included the layout and general graphic design, and the front and back covers. I didn't think of myself as a designer, more of a late night Kinko's junkie.

Kinko's itself was full of inspiration. Paper, highlighters, pens, scissors, whiteout, copiers, scanners, computers! It was a playground for ideas. I decided to document my 22nd birthday by making an animation using the industrial Xerox 5090 copier. I copied my face 250 times, moving around the glass making silly faces. My plan was to transfer the copies to individual super-8 frames, and have a copies-based animation. Again, looking to take something old and make it new. The project was successful, though I burned my retinas, and got written up by my boss. It was so worth it!

On a whim, I left Kinko's and ordered an iMac. Not only was I out of the box and on the Internet in 10 minutes, I put my first web page up on my included web space within 30. I was just messing around; it had tiled pictures of Yoda in the background, and said *Welcome to my Web Page!* The iMac is very significant, and I doubt I'd be doing any of this if it weren't for what was basically an impulse buy.

I always wanted to fly, though, and in an attempt to use garbage bags to their full potential, I took some time to build what became the first Garbasail. It was made up of 30 extra large garbage bags cut at two seams, duct tape, and nylon rope. I built it over a week, and had an unexpected first flight. I took it to the beach to see what would happen, held the rope, and let the Garbasail go. Instantly, I was pulled off my feet, and dragged across the sand at frightening speeds, just like that scene from *Raiders of the Lost Ark*. After about 12 seconds, I let go, and the sail fluttered out. I rolled over to face the sky, half buried in sand, dizzy and out of breath, with rope burn on my hands. All I could think was, "I just did this!". There were always modifications to make; lessons learned from the wind.

Throughout the next couple months, many Garbasail outings with friends and strangers took place, usually across from Golden Gate Park, always enjoying a breathtaking view. We made a second Garbasail too. The idea now was basically to ski across the sand, now with leather gloves and handlebars. Together we conceived new vehicles, like a mattress called the Garbapad, and a flat-bottomed skateboard. Kids always took turns sailing the Garba, making a day out of it. One time while this happy little boy was flying across the beach, his Dad told me how I could just get a cheap parachute, or get a large pre-cut tarp, instead of using garbage bags and duct tape.

I briefly explained to the gentleman that the point was to make it out of garbage bags and duct tape, to take something old and make it new. He seemed to understand.

The true driving force behind my adventures was my love of Datsuns. I had been a Datsun enthusiast for years, and I owned two of them, a 1970 240Z and a 1978 B210. There are few things I can think of more perfect than driving the open road in a classic Datsun. It's not just the innovative design and quality of the engineering, but the sentimental journey back to the 1970s, when a ride in the back of a Datsun 240Z was the adventure.

Web sites are very similar to cars - they run at different speeds, need maintenance, security and sometimes crash. You can enter and exit, modify, and personalize them. There are many different varieties of design and function, with various interface and audio elements. While some stand the test of time year after year, others have ongoing problems, but either way they need regular attention, and

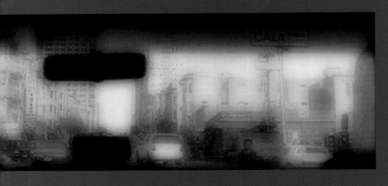

must be protected against break-ins. They also range from cheap to outrageously expensive, but both can take you to new places, where new adventures await!

Up to a point, I had used the Web solely for the purpose of searching for Datsun related web pages. I would print out every page of text, and print every JPEG image. For three years, that was the Web to me, piles of Datsun prints, and I was satisfied with that!

I began losing myself into the night making web pages on my iMac, with Claris Home Page. I made a personal homepage, a Classic Japanese Car/Datsun related web page, and a page for the Garbasail.

Following a gut instinct, I decided to move to New York City. Just before I was to move, my beloved Datsun B210 was towed away by the San Francisco Department of Parking and Traffic. It was total *Sophie's Choice*; I had to either bail out the B210, which accumulated an impressive number of tickets in its day, or move to NYC. I couldn't afford both. Guilt ridden, I let the Datsun go, not knowing its spirit would one day return.

I arrived in New York on my 27th birthday and was instantly taken by the complexity in the structures that line the streets of Manhattan. I loved the hard-lined edges to everything, so many perspectives, and never-ending depth. I even wrote a song, which summed up how I felt at the time.

A friend suggested I work in Silicon Alley, and I was like "Naaaah". All I had was a bunch of *Gortdays*, some web pages and drawings. Where would I fit in? I didn't see the Web as a landscape for big ideas, yet. He had mentioned something about Flash being the next big thing, and the upcoming market for Flash work. Thank God he had known, although I don't think he had even realized the scope of the boom that was to be. I had the Flash 3 trial on a CD that came with an issue of MacWorld, so I decided to check it out that night.

The next hours would prove to become a tremendous milestone. Flash would find me and take its hold. I felt scared, uneasy at first. I just told myself to go for it, check it out. Something drew me in. It made sense. I liked it.

I made some letters move, using the arrow keys and multiple keyframes, as opposed to tweening, which was unknown territory. I added sound, and put it on the Web. Up to that point, it was the coolest thing I ever made. I was *driven*.

On the Macromedia list of authorized training centers in NY, I found United Digital Artists, and registered for the next Flash class. It was most inspiring. The quality of the information really stood out. I was dreaming in class again, this time about making the future my own. I felt that anything I could imagine was possible with Flash.

It only took tweening, layers, basic actions, and movie clip symbols, to make me feel like a superhero. I became a Teacher's Assistant for classes at UDA, and did nothing but Flash projects during my spare time. I learned so much, and as Flash 4 had just arrived, it would be some time before I'd be pushing any boundaries.

One day, I happened to checked out yugop.com MONO*crafts. Disbelief. It was totally different, a new way of approaching motion and interactivity. I was so excited! Nobody told me about these actions! Where were they? ... or did I already know? My quest to explore Flash's boundaries had begun.

I began AlphaB2 Media in December of 1999. Alpha representing transparent and multi-dimensional, and B2 in memory of my beloved 1978 Datsun B210. I finally found some closure regarding the loss of that car. Running out of

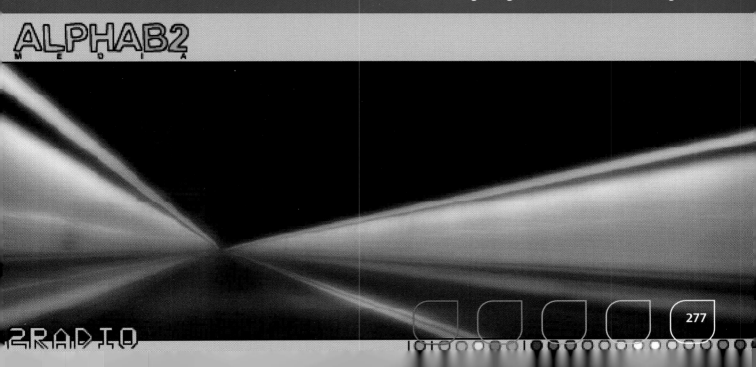

a bondi-blue iMac, my goal was to offer Flash development services while developing original content under the AlphaB2 identity, teaching classes simultaneously.

UDA was in the preliminary stage of preparation for the first ever flashforward2000 event at the time, and I was asked to do the web site for the Flash Film Festival. I was very happy to have no specific guidelines beyond the basic structure and copy of the web site, and I took it as an opportunity to push myself.

The loading animation is made up of one circle symbol to save file space. A digital photo of the inside of my cine Kodak 16mm movie camera is the only image used in the site, other than the 50 finalist buttons. I chose to go with an orange feel, which looks nice in hairline form. Building the design mathematically from top to bottom, it was just simple division from the center horizon. You'll notice that it's very symmetrical, vertically.

On stage, about to run the presentation of the first Flash Film Festival, I was listening to Sinbad's opening remarks. He was saying how amazing it was that all of us slackers who were always told to stop doodling, stop distracting ourselves with our own imaginations, ended up at the forefront of a revolution. He was right-on, and summed up the feel in the ballroom on that night, that something big was happening, right then.

Flash is magical because of the people behind it. The connection within the Flash community is based on the common ground we find having gone through some sort of awakening with this program. Even more beautiful is the fact that strung about the diversity of our journeys, lie interesting similarities. The first flashforward2000 event helped to set in motion a convergence of our experiences, all with the common goal to push the boundaries.

I continued to immerse myself in diverse Flash projects, including the first orange flashforward2000 web site for the New York event, and a Flash video for De La Soul's AOI tour.

The momentum behind Flash was thick in the New York City air, and I was training Flash classes for corporate clients on a regular basis. The students were yearning for information, and I was surprised by my own joy giving it to them. Teaching had become very gratifying. It hadn't been long since I had learned Flash, so I somehow could relate to their experience. I would talk openly to the students about overcoming confidence issues within the learning process. Flash is way more intimidating than difficult.

Teaching Flash felt so natural that I slowed down client work to a minimum, focusing primarily on teaching and original content creation. I consider myself as much an educator as developer, and this balance has been extremely satisfying. I learn, do, teach what I learn, show what I do, and pay my rent.

I think that the quality of my teaching comes from years of working with people. All the different experiences, from shooting super-8 films in restaurants to working at Kinko's, playing in bands at dive bars to searching for Datsuns in Southwest Utah. I enjoy communicating knowledge to others, for the purpose of revelation.

I'm just fascinated with everything and everybody. Regardless of how limitless my imagination, there's a boundlessness to life!

Flash is great because it gives us the ability to test a theory, represent an idea, convey a feeling, and tell a story as limitless as our imagination. My intersection with Flash and teaching was coincidental yet, when I look back at the journey, it seems like this was right where I was headed all along. Flash has given me a way to combine the things I love with my profession, plunging me into the depths of my creative ability.

If I have and idea, I just go for it. The fact that it may not work the first time creates a new challenge and a lesson learned. When I design, I just let it roll and find what works. I search my experiences, crazy fantasies, and random impulses in an attempt to convey a feeling.

"Work like you don't need the money.
Love like you've never been hurt.
Dance like nobody's watching."

Jessica Speigel
www.webstyles.net

305

Today

Ever since I was a little girl I wanted to be an artist. Most of the kids around me wanted to be firefighters, or something along those lines, but all I ever wanted to do was draw, paint, and make things. Everything around me inspired me, and rarely could I pay attention to one thing before another would come and whisk my interest away. My tastes changed faster than anything, and I always wanted to experiment with something new. I experienced a certain inexplicable feeling when I was creating something out of a space where there was nothing before. It made me feel alive, and that's something that I have carried with me my entire life.

My parents played a big part in shaping my artistic vision when I was young. They are such creative people themselves that it was hard not to be artsy. They were also extremely supportive of me, and even converted a spare bedroom into an art room for me, where I was allowed to do whatever I wanted, including painting on the walls. Whenever I wanted to try something new, they supported me, which played a huge role in my life.

My mother reminded me recently how I even used to cut up all my clothes and sew new clothes and bags out of them. I did that until I was about 16, which was, incidentally, when I started buying my own clothes.

Though the process of development has some consistencies, there is no formula, each project is unique and I approach them as such.

When I'm not thinking about Flash, I continue to relish in the splendor of my Datsun 240Z, and work on music and video projects. The Garbasail still flies, though now on the Jersey shore.

If you're going to get on the Web and represent yourself these days, unless you're an empty hole, Flash is a great way to do it. If you're a Photoshop and/or Illustrator person, Flash is the logical next step. Quicktime is getting more momentum these days, and Flash integration is getting there. Patience. HDTVs and fat digital cables delivering instant access to all digital content will be commonplace in 2 to 5 years. You can use Flash, video, shockwave, photography, DHTML, XML, canvas, clay, paper, wood, garbage bags, whatever. Regardless the tool, the content comes from you.

This is a great opportunity for all of us to be part of the innovation that will re-define our world. I think the trick is to just do it. What's with all this thinking *inside* or *outside* the box? There never was a box.

Driven

Flash is the paint, paintbrush, and canvas. You are the artist.

Knowing Flash at a bare bones level is to know what *actions* are available to you, where to find them, and what they do. Try not to see this as the challenge. It's only in the application of this knowledge, balancing Flash concepts with our inherent creativity and spirit, that innovation is born.

Complex worlds are made up of smaller pieces that can each be broken down into single elements. In the learning process, the 'world' of Flash can sometimes seem so complex; it becomes difficult to focus on the small things, the individual elements that make up a great effect.

Here I'll take you through the process to create one form of 3D object, by breaking down the individual elements within the effect. What appears to be one object is actually multiple identical movie clip symbols, constantly reproducing and removing themselves many times per second. The result is a seemingly 3D object. I will also show you how to integrate the sound object, which is new to Flash 5.

To summarize, we'll primarily use the `duplicateMovieClip` command within a looping action to create the illusion of a 3D interactive object. Once we've created a symbol and given it an instance name, we'll tell Flash to duplicate it, wait for its contents to animate, and then remove it, repeating this process 60 times per second. The object will follow the mouse with a pre-determined level of inertia, and the duplicates will form everywhere the object goes. The animation within the object seems to take place all at once in 3D. We'll also use variables to help process the calculations necessary to create the effect.

I suggest that you focus on the concepts I present, rather than just try to copy the code word for word. This is just one kind of 3D illusion that I came up with. You should run with these basic concepts here, combine and modify them, and make them your own. You might also want to view the final effect on the CD before starting this example, to see precisely what it is you're going to create.

The Structure
Let's begin by building the structure in the timeline, a scaffolding of blank keyframes. These act as holding cells, as they'll contain elements soon (the F7 key comes in handy here). There are three layers, and the movie is 600x600 pixels at a frame rate of 60 fps. I chose to use a dark background for this example (hex #333333). The actions layer is divided into three blank keyframes, and the movie clip layer is only one blank keyframe that lasts for three frames on the timeline.

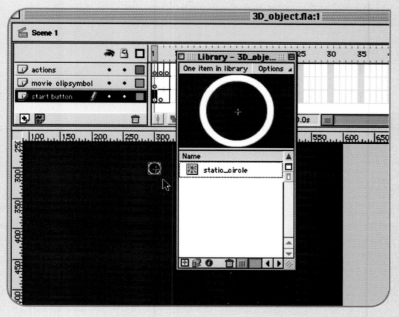

Using the Oval tool, create a small circle with a stroke only on frame 1 of the start button layer. Make sure there's no fill. If you want to match my example, make it 20x20 pixels. Center it on the stage by using the Align panel, or setting the *x* and *y* position of its center point to (300,300). This will be the only graphic element in the entire movie.

Put this live object inside a symbol by hitting *F8* Convert to Symbol. I suggest using movie clip symbols for all static objects. Movie clip symbols only differ from graphic symbols in the way animations run on the timeline. If the object is static, it should be a movie clip symbol, that way on a whim you can choose to make it targetable and/or a self-running animation. Name the symbol static_circle. You'll reuse this symbol again, on the movieclip symbol layer.

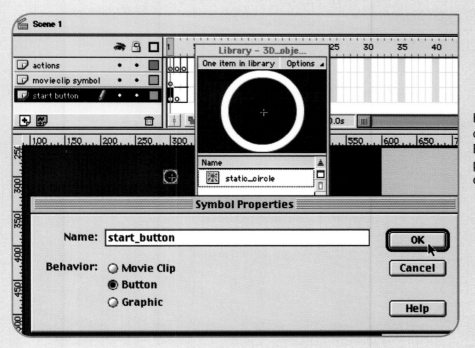

Hit *F8* again and put this symbol inside of a button. Call it start_button. Eventually, this button will tell the playback head to play, triggering the object to appear.

The Convert to Symbol command is a bit deceiving because you're not actually converting the static_circle symbol into a button symbol, you're simply housing it inside of one. Think of a set of Russian Matrushkah dolls, each one individual, one inside the other. The start_button symbol contains the static_circle symbol, which contains the original live object of the circle.

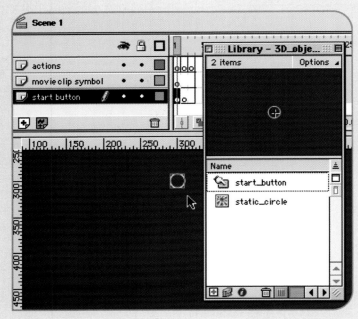

Now double-click on the button symbol on the stage to enter the timeline of the button and edit it in place. This is the edit mode that I prefer, as it allows you to see the stage and its contents, and where this specific instance lies on the stage.

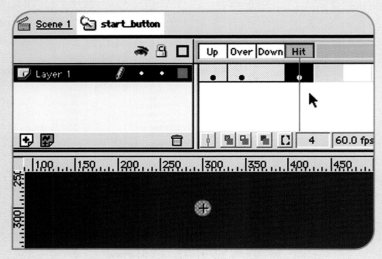

Create a keyframe for the Hit state, and make sure that it contains a filled circle, or else the button won't function correctly.

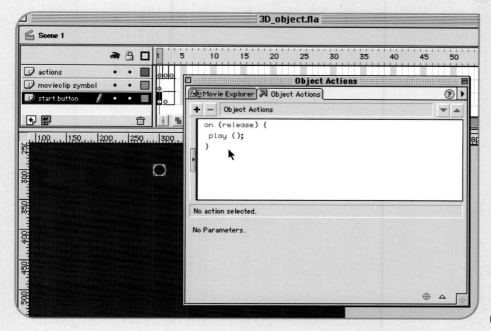

Highlight the button on the stage and open up the Object Actions panel. We'll be working in Normal Mode for this tutorial, so switch out of Expert Mode if that's your default. Hold down on the plus symbol to add a new item to the script, and choose Play from either Actions or Basic Actions. Note that on (release) automatically exists around the Play action. This will create a 'forgiving' button, the most common kind, which is why it appears by default. A forgiving button allows the user to press down on the button, then change their mind and drag off the button before releasing. The button forgives the user by not penalizing them with having to go to an unwanted destination.

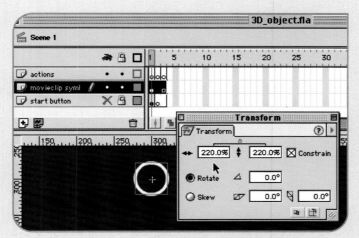

Hide the start button layer, and on the movieclip symbol layer, drag a new instance of the static_circle symbol out from your Library. Center it and resize it so that you can see it over the button, scaled to 220%.

283

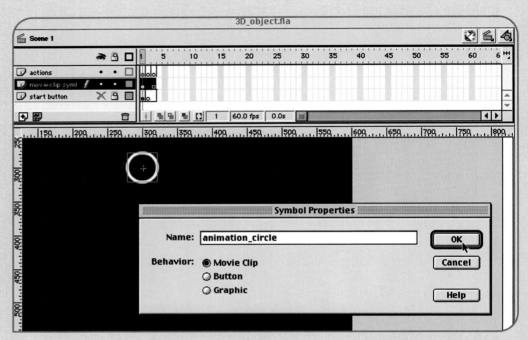

Select Convert to Symbol to place this instance of the static_circle inside a new movie clip symbol called animation_circle. Give the animation_circle movie clip the instance name object. If we give symbols instance names we can now program in a more object-oriented fashion, creating many instances of the same object, therefore allowing us to centralize and reuse code.

Creating Smooth Interactive Motion
Now the structure and symbols are in place, it's time to focus on the actions layer. We'll see how to divide distance to create the feel of inertia when interacting with objects.

Highlight frame 1 of the actions layer, and open the Actions panel. Add a Stop action to make the playback head stay put until the button is released and that Play command is activated.

Now you're going to set a variable. Choose setVariable from the Actions list. In the Variable field name the variable t for *target*. Almost all variable values will be expressions, so check the Expression checkbox next to the Value field. Place your cursor in the Value field and click on the bullseye in the lower right to bring up the Insert Target Path panel. Make sure that the Dots and Absolute radio buttons are checked. Click on the object movie clip icon and _root.object will appear in the Target field. This sets the target as the movie clip with the instance name object located in the root of the target path hierarchy (in other words, the main scene).

Remember that we set the variable name for the target as t. This variable is set on the first frame because it only needs to be declared once. Later we'll add a looping action that will make the movie constantly loop between frames 2 and 3 when the button is released. There's no need to remind the Flash player that t = _root.object every time it loops.

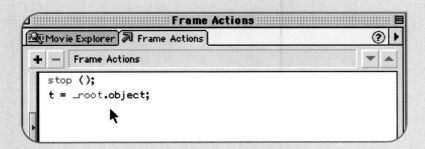

Keep in mind that this variable isn't absolutely necessary, although I use variables to represent targets all the time. It simply saves us the trouble of having to refer to the object as _root.object. When you're working with a large amount of code this is a good technique to reduce the amount of code you need to type in – and limit confusion!

Frame 2 of the actions layer will contain the engine of the effect. As I said just now, when the user releases the button the playhead will continuously loop between frames 2 and 3, so the only job for frame 3 is to send the playhead back to frame 2, and play.

Driven

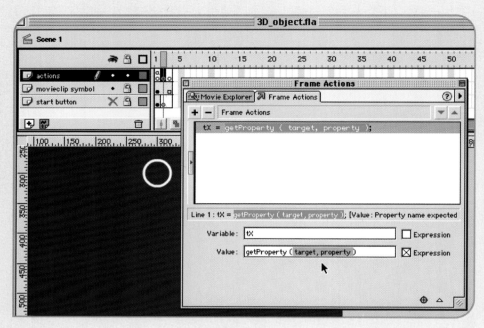

In frame 2 start by setting a new variable `tX` to represent the *x* position of the target, and choose getProperty from the Functions list. Within the `getProperty` statement, replace `target` with `t`, and replace the highlighted `property` with `_x`. Again, be sure to check the Expression box.

It's important to understand that `tX` doesn't represent the `getProperty` statement itself, but the value of the property that is ascertained. If the *x* position of the target is 300, `tX = 300`, because `tX` represents the *x* position of the target. Repeat the previous step to set the variable `tY`, representing the *y* position of the target.

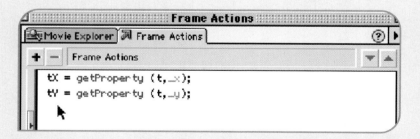

Now set a new variable, `difX`, to represent the difference between the *x* position of the target and the *x* position of the mouse. By subtracting the mouse's *x* position from the object's *x* position, you get the distance between the two in pixels. These are what we call *pre-set variables* representing the *x* and *y* position of the mouse, `_xmouse` and `_ymouse`. They are located in the properties list as well.

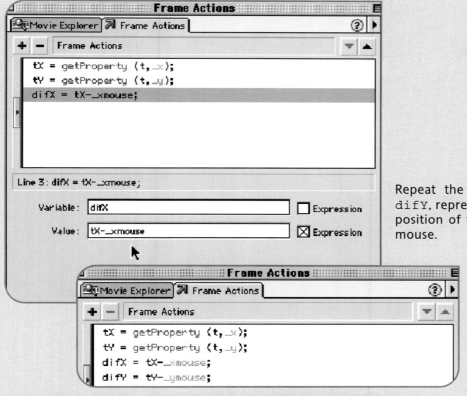

Repeat the previous step to set the variable `difY`, representing the difference between the *y* position of the target and the *y* position of the mouse.

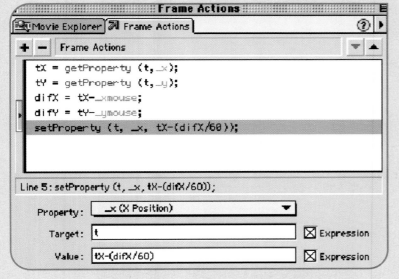

Now set the *x* and *y* positions of the object. It's because this frame will constantly be looping that these properties are constantly reset.

Choose setProperty from the list of Actions. First select the property you would like to set, which is `_x (X Position)`. Remember that `t` is the variable name we chose to represent the target `_root.object`. Enter `t` into the Target field, and check the Expression box.

Driven

This is the value is that you've been leading up to with all those variables. The effect is born when we take the distance between the target and the mouse, divide that distance into equal portions, remove the value of one of those portions from the distance, and repeat.

The value, $tX-(difX/60)$, states the target's current *x* position, minus 1/60th of the distance between it and the mouse's *x* position. The target moves 1/60th closer to the mouse. It's important to understand that 60 is an arbitrary number that I've chosen. Different numbers here will result in different rates of motion, in relation to a particular frame rate.

Repeat the previous step to set the *y* position of the object to be the value of its current *y* position, minus 1/60th of the distance between it and the mouse's *y* position.

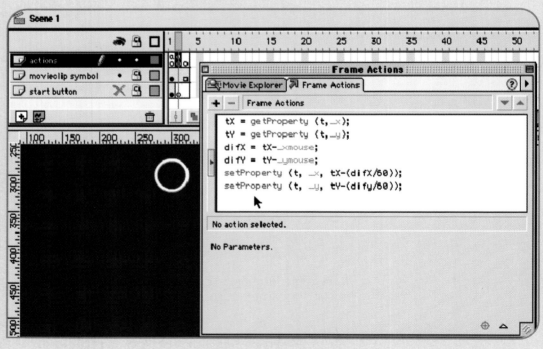

The final step is adding the looping action, `gotoAndPlay (2);` to frame 3.

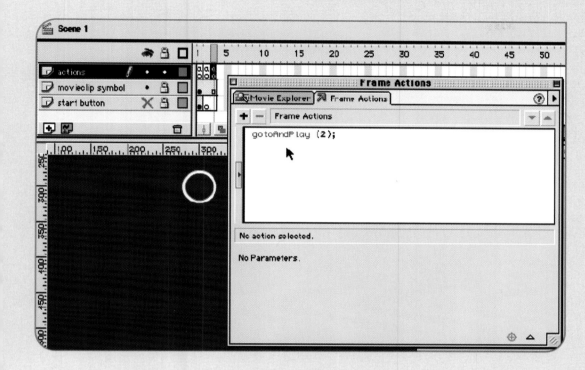

Now test your movie.

As you move the mouse, the motion of the object is smooth as it follows, slowing down as it nears the mouse's position because the distance being divided is shortening. This is the basic math and code for inertia-based effects. Try using *x* or *y* only for more constrained effects.

Panning with Inertia
The next step is to basically add a painting effect to the code. The target will be duplicated at the frame rate of 60 fps and, by default, each duplicate will appear in the same location as the original target. In a nutshell, the target drops a clone of itself everywhere it goes.

Driven

In frame 1 of the actions layer, set a new variable, n = 1. The variable n will be used next to automatically generate instance names for the duplicate symbols. This variable goes in frame 1 because its purpose is only to establish n's initial value.

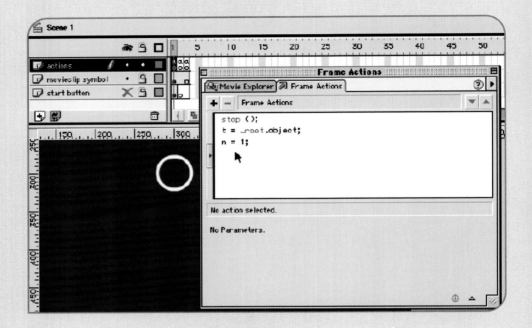

In frame 2 of the actions layer, choose duplicateMovieClip from the list of Actions. I think this is one of the coolest actions because of its many applications and lively results. It's also the most relevant to this effect.

First enter the target that you'd like to duplicate, t, into the Target field and check the Expression box.

The New Name field is where you enter the instance name of the duplicate being created. Once we get to the removal stage you'll want to be able to communicate with each of the duplicates individually, so each must have a unique instance name. This is where n comes in. You can create an expression that combines a string literal with the value of a variable. If n = 1, the expression ("duplicate"+n) is the same as the literal duplicate1. The + doesn't mean addition, it means *join the name* duplicate *with the value of* n. As n will change its value 60 times per second, each duplicate will have a unique name, duplicate2, duplicate3, and so on.

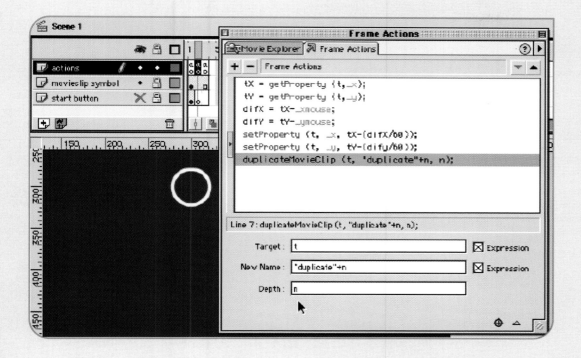

OK, on to the Depth field. Depth is just like arrangement within a layer, layers within a movie, and movies in multiple levels. Depth defines the arranged order, top to bottom, of duplicate symbols. The lowest depth is 1, although the duplicate symbol right at the bottom on depth 1 is above the contents of the topmost layer in your movie. Be aware that there can only be one duplicate symbol on a given depth. If a duplicate is placed on a depth that is occupied, the new one replaces the original.

Enter "duplicate"+n into the New Name field, and n into the Depth field. The first time the playback head hits this frame, the first duplicate created will be called duplicate1 and will be located on depth 1.

Driven

Now the final element of the painting stage. This is what tells n to increase its value by 1 every time the playback head loops. As you can imagine, the second duplicate symbol will be called `duplicate2` and will be located on level 2.

We could set a new variable, n = n+1, meaning the new value of n will equal the old value of n plus 1. Instead we'll use an `evaluate` action, which basically gives you an open-ended expression field where you say *do this*.

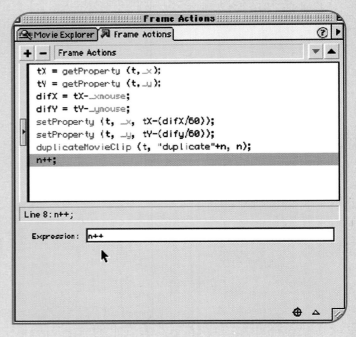

Choose `evaluate` from the list of actions, and type `n++` into the Expression field. By adding the operator `++` to the variable n, you're saying n = n+1.

You can now understand that n didn't need to equal 1 initially, but any number positive or negative. The purpose is to have a variable with a climbing value.

One shortcut here is to skip the initial variable declaration n = 1, in frame 1 all together. If you first refer to n in frame 2, within the n++ expression, or within an n = n+1 variable, n's initial value would default to 0. Test the movie.

This differs from a basic painting program because of the smooth motion of the object. If you'd like to just make a basic painting program, you could use this script:

Frame 1:

```
stop ();
    t = _root.target;
n = 1;
```

Frame 2:

```
setProperty (t ,_x , _xmouse);
setProperty (t ,_y, _ymouse);
    duplicateMovieClip (t ,"duplicate" + n, n);
n++;
```

Frame 3:

```
gotoAndPlay (2);
```

Paint with your object for a while, and you'll surely notice something. The motion becomes choppy, and the CPU slows and possibly crashes. There are just too many symbols. The code as it stands is too open-ended.

The first time I had this problem and looked for a way to limit the number of symbols that exist at any given time, was when I first discovered the skeleton of the 3D object.

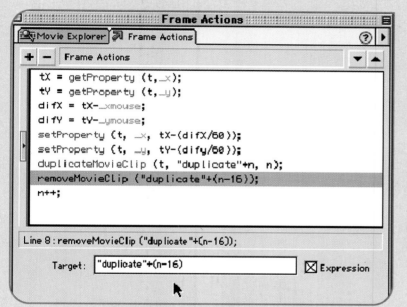

```
tX = getProperty (t,_x);
tY = getProperty (t,_y);
difX = tX-_xmouse;
difY = tY-_ymouse;
setProperty (t, _x, tX-(difX/60));
setProperty (t, _y, tY-(dify/60));
duplicateMovieClip (t, "duplicate"+n, n);
removeMovieClip ("duplicate"+(n-16));
n++;
```

Line 8 : removeMovieClip ("duplicate"+(n-16));

Target: "duplicate"+(n-16)   ☒ Expression

To limit the maximum number of duplicates, use the removeMovieClip action. This action can be used to remove any movie clip symbol with an instance name, but is primarily used in conjunction with duplicated symbols.

Choose removeMovieClip from the Actions list. In the Target field, place the name of the target to be removed, and remember this is happening 60 times per second. Type "duplicate"+(n-16). This means the duplicate that is 16 depths below the current one, or the one that was created 16 loops ago.

The very first time the playback head hits this action, n will equal 1, so the action would be read as being 1-16. As there would be no symbol with the name "duplicate(-15)", the action would be ignored. Once there are 17 duplicated symbols, the first one, duplicate1, will be removed.

Test your movie again and you'll see the beginnings of the 3D object in a tubular form.

3D Tweening

The 3-dimensional design of the object is a process I would call *3D tweening*. Whatever you create in a tween or linearly in the timeline of the animation_circle symbol will appear to tween backwards, into the screen.

Here's the animation that I created. You can copy it off the CD or make your own variation. It's basically two layers of animation, one circle getting larger while the other gets smaller. I also added some tint color effects.

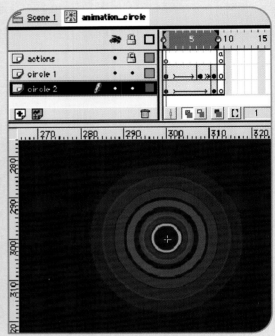

First take a look at how closely the onion skin of the entire animation resembles the motionless finished object. Because the duplicates are being created and removed so many times per second, the illusion is that the tween moves backwards, resulting in modifiable seemingly 3D objects.

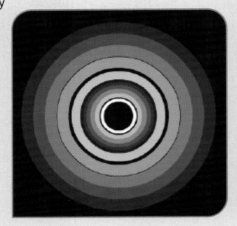

The number of maximum duplicates directly relates to the length of this animation. As this example uses (n-16) in the removeMovieClip action, it would not make sense to make this animation longer than 16 frames. A good rule is to match the maximum number of duplicates with the length of the animation.

Double-click on the animation_circle symbol on the movieclip symbol layer to enter the timeline of the symbol in edit-in-place mode.

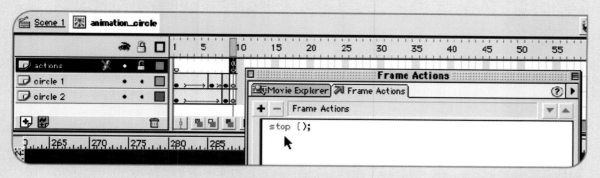

I recommend that you put a `Stop` action on the last frame so the animation doesn't start to loop before its container symbol is removed.

Some finishing touches to help bring the illusion to life. In the main scene, on frame 1 of the actions layer, you can add `fscommands` to make the movie full screen when off the Web, and disable scaling or modification via the Flash player menu.

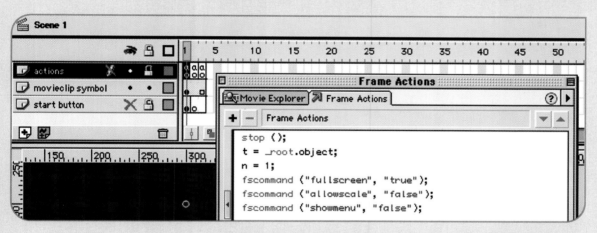

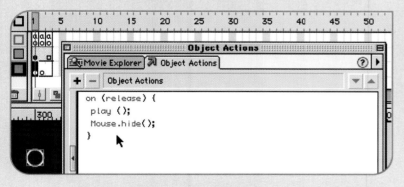

The final touch is to hide the mouse, which is an option found under the mouse heading in the objects list. Add this command to the Object Actions of the button on frame 1 of the start button layer. I find that this simple action adds a whole new level of illusion to the effect. When you can't see the cursor, your mind tells you that you're actually controlling the 3D object directly. You may make a huge figure 8 with your mouse,

295

but you *feel* like your just nudging in a small, soft figure 8. `Mouse.hide` works best in full screen mode, otherwise the illusion is rather spoiled each time the cursor moves out of the movie. Keep this in mind when you're putting your work on the Web.

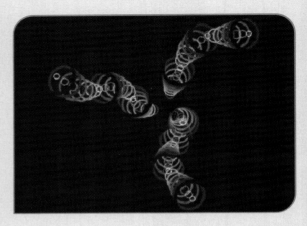

Adding the Sound Object

The sound object, new to Flash 5, enables you to add more realism still by setting the values of the volume and panning ratio, calculated from the motion of the object. This is done very similarly to the way you would set the *x* position property of a target for instance, but using different syntax.

We don't necessarily need to place sounds on the timeline anymore. Sound properties can be targeted if the sound file sits in an exported library.

Here you'll see how to export a sound file with the SWF, and how to call upon it and modify its volume and panning ratios based on the values of some new variables.

Import or drop a sound file into your Library; you can use mine if you want. Make sure the sound file is highlighted in your Library, and choose Linkage… from the Options menu.

Technically, when you have only one sound, you can skip this part of the process, but it's good to get in the habit of creating identifiers for all the sound files you intend to target with the sound object. If you want to target more than one sound file then this is an absolute must.

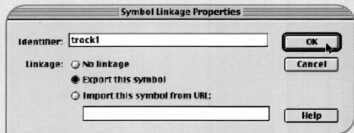

Keep the default identifier track1 in the Identifier field, and choose Export this symbol. This sound is now set up to be exported, and ready to target by its identifier name, track1.

We now need to introduce the sound object, linked to track1, and establish some initial values. We only want to establish these settings once, before the loop takes place, so we'll do this in frame 1 of the actions layer.

First set a new variable, sound. Add a value new Sound (), by clicking on new Sound in the Sound book under Objects. We're not setting a target here so delete target from within the brackets. This action initiates the sound object.

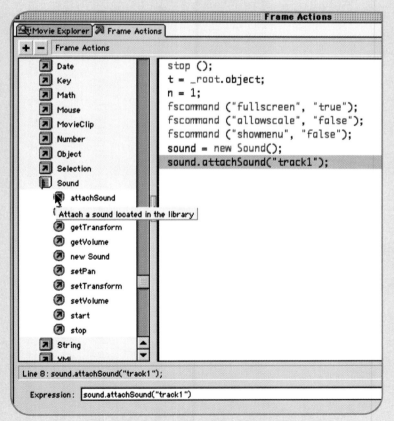

Next we'll attach the sound, track1, to the sound object. You can either choose evaluate first, or go directly to attachSound, in the Objects > Sound list. Add sound, the name of the variable representing track1, before the period in .attachSound in the Expression field. Within the brackets, replace the highlighted idName with the identifier name "track1". After all of this you should end up with:

```
sound.attachSound("track1");
```

You would follow this same process to attach other sounds.

This next piece of code starts the sound, and determines the number of loops. Choose start from the sound object list. Again, precede the first period with the variable name sound. Replace the highlighted secondsOffset, loops with 0,99999. The secondsOffset value refers to how many seconds before the sound is audible, and loop speaks for itself. This is what you should see:

```
sound.start(0,99999);
```

Lastly, set the initial volume for the sound, so it starts with no volume. Choose `setVolume` from the list and this time replace the highlighted `volume` with a `0`, meaning no volume:

```
sound.setVolume(0);
```

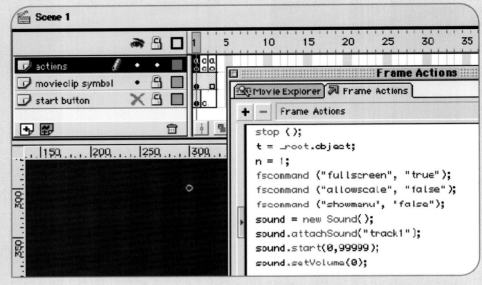

Now on frame 2 of the actions layer, we're going to set a new variable to represent the distance between the target's *x* position and the center *x* coordinate of the screen, which, based on the 600x600 pixel dimensions of the stage, is 300. Soon you'll be determining the sounds panning ratio based on this value. Call the variable `difXCenter`, and enter `tX-300` into the Value field.

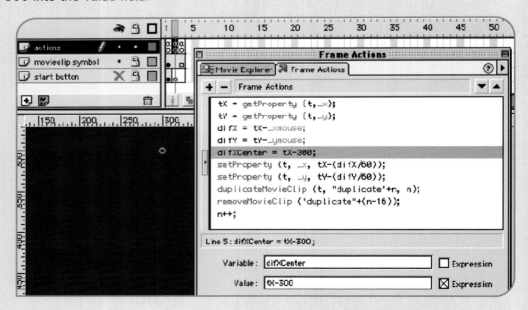

Let's take a closer look at that value for the `difXCenter` variable:

```
tX = getProperty (t,_x);
tY = getProperty (t,_y);
difX = tX-_xmouse;
difY = tY-_ymouse;
difXCenter = tX-300;
difAverage = (difX+difY)/2;
setProperty (t, _x, tX-(difX/50));
setProperty (t, _y, tY-(difY/50));
duplicateMovieClip (t, "duplicate"+n, n);
removeMovieClip ("duplicate"+(n-16));
n++;
```

Line 6 : difAverage = (difX+difY)/2;

Variable: difAverage ☐ Expression

Value: (difX+difY)/2 ☒ Expression

$$difXCenter = tx-300;$$

If the target's *x* position is 120, then `tX=120`. The equation `tX – 300` can be taken as 120 – 300 = (-180). This means that the object's *x* position is 180 pixels to the left of the center *x*-axis of the stage. If the value of `difXCenter` is positive, the object's *x* position must be to the right of the center. If the value is 0 (300 – 300 = 0), the object is at the center.

Now we'll set a new variable, `difAverage`, representing the average distance between the target and the mouse. The value is `(difX+difY)/2`, which is the sum divided by the number of values, the standard formula for averaging that you learned in high school math. If the difference between the *x* positions is 50, and the difference between the *y* positions is 200, the average distance is 125.

To make the sound seem to react to the motion of the object, you'll calculate the volume of track1 based on the value of `difAverage`. Volume will relate directly to distance; the larger the average distance, the louder the volume.

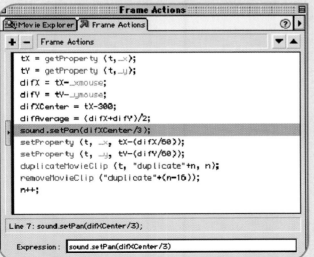

```
tX = getProperty (t,_x);
tY = getProperty (t,_y);
difX = tX-_xmouse;
difY = tY-_ymouse;
difXCenter = tX-300;
difAverage = (difX+difY)/2;
sound.setPan(difXCenter/3);
setProperty (t, _x, tX-(difX/50));
setProperty (t, _y, tY-(difY/50));
duplicateMovieClip (t, "duplicate"+n, n);
removeMovieClip ("duplicate"+(n-16));
n++;
```

Line 7: sound.setPan(difXCenter/3);

Expression : sound.setPan(difXCenter/3)

Now we'll put both of these new variables to work!

Choose `setPan` from the sound objects list. Again, precede the period with the `sound` variable. Replace `pan` with the value you would like the pan to be set to each time this frame loops. The extreme most panning values are (-100), panned all the way left, and 100, panned all the way to the right. 0 means equal sound levels are coming out of both speakers.

It's best to avoid a situation where the value of the pan goes beyond these extremes, meaning <(-100) or >100. We do this here by dividing `difXCenter` by 3. The longest distance possible between the object and the center of the screen in a

Driven

600-pixel box is 300. 300 / 3 = 100, and (-300) / 3 = (-100). Enter `difXCenter/3` in the brackets.

Now select the action `setVolume`. The volume of the `track1` will be calculated based on the value of `difAverage`. Amend the code so it reads `sound.setVolume(difAverage/10)`. The 10 is just another arbitrary number that determines the general loudness of the sound the object makes.

The extreme volume values are 0, being no volume, and 100, maximum volume. If the average distance between the object and the mouse is 420 pixels, the volume at that moment would be 42 (`difAverage` / 10 = 420 / 10 = 42). Don't set the arbitrary number too high, or you'll be setting the volume to a number greater than 100.

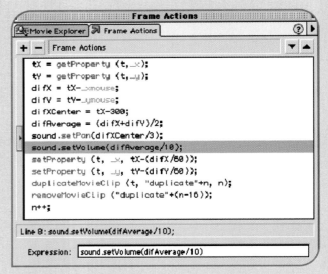

Conclusion

There are many ways you can use and modify the code in this example to take it further, find variations, or create something new. You can raise the number of maximum duplicates, and elongate your animation for a 'longer' object, but remember that larger amounts of duplicates at any given time lead to a decrease in the Flash player's performance.

You can also add a scale modification to the object over time, to create the illusion of forward or backward motion. I've created two examples to illustrate this: the parachute game, and the submarine, both of which are on the CD for you to play with, take apart and learn from.

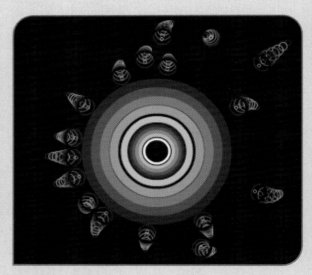

In the parachute game, the chute seems to begin high in the sky, and fall naturally to the earth, remote controlled by the mouse. This is the result of an increase in the x and y scale values of the object within the looping action. Because any modification to the original object will apply to each future duplicate, as the x and y scale values of the object increase, so do the duplicates. The object gets larger, appearing to move toward the viewer.

The submarine varies from the lesson in two ways. First, a decrease in the *x* and *y* scale values of the object over time, opposite to the parachute. Secondly, I set the initial value of n to be 999999, and I replaced n++ with n— in the looping action. The result is that the object forms back to front. The mouse doesn't tug on the back of the submarine, which is closest to the viewer, but the front of the submarine. Compare this to the reaction of the parachute.

Experiment with the timeline within your animation. The more spread apart the frames are, the more flexible and worm-like the object is. You can also create both flexible and rigid portions of the same object.

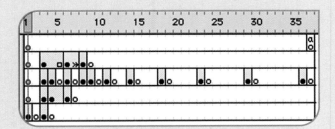

There's still much uncharted territory in the exploration of Flash. Take the helm of your sub and just explore, seek out new variations, and occasionally up-periscope to check out what's happening in the community.

Do what works for you.

Josh's piece starts out as that old Flash tradition – a mouse follower, but quickly develops into a fully-fledged game.

The beauty of Flash is the ability to start simple and build the effect up. Here's a few other ideas for the lowly mouse follower…

vary the input

Rather than a mouse follower, consider using other variables to define the movement. For example, a variaton of the parachute drop game might be to use percent loaded rather than mouse position; the closer to loading the swf is, the closer to landing the parachute will get.

By re-configuring the input you can re-engineer mouse follower effects for all sorts of things. By basing the accuracy of the drop on the number of correct questions answered, you even have the basis of something vaguely educational…

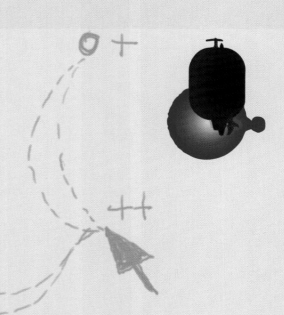

multiple inputs and flux effects

A recent and much prettier variation
of the humble mouse follower is the
flux effect, consisting of attractors
and repulsors.

By adding repulsors — points which
repel the followers — you enter a
much more dynamic set-up. Just like
real physical forces, you have a
number of attractive/repulsive forces
overlapping, and the motion becomes
much more complex.

By making your followers small
particles, you can even start to get
the patterns and curves you would get
by dropping iron filings onto a magnet,
or the arc effects you get on a plasma lamp.

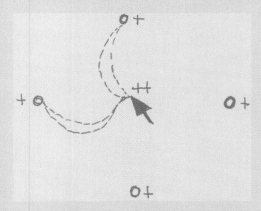

In this scheme, the 'standard'
mouse follower is a flux effect
with one attractor; the mouse itself.
The followers are attracted to the
mouse only, resulting in fairly
predictable motion. By adding
other stationary attractors you start
to get not just followers, but flow
effects, as the followers choose
what they want to be attracted to
based on proximity.

The sketch above shows a mouse that is twice
as attractive (++) than the point attractors (+),
and this would start to show arc effects. By setting
up the forces just so, you can generate not just
followers but oscillators and (if your math is up to it)
even chaotic motion...

Like all small children I colored, and played with Lego and Transformers, but when I was five years old my parents bought me the first Nintendo to hit the market – it came with one game, Super Mario Bros. In true 80s fashion, my young mind drew all its inspiration from that game. Of course, my parents were astounded when their little girl completed Super Mario Bros within a few short days. I loved how I could interact with the game, how the graphics would change based on what I was doing with the controller in my hand, and how different situations would occur depending on the decisions I made.

Controlling the intangible with the tangible fascinated me. This made for a natural leap into Flash when I got older. Shaping the experience that others will have when interacting with my work is the most important part of my design process. It's very important to me for people to be able to interact and play with my work. I want people to say to themselves, "Ooh wow, look what I can do if I move my mouse here!"

My tastes changed, I soon grew tired of video games and went back to more traditional art forms. I always have and always will draw and paint, but in the past five years I've developed a taste for decorating common household items and turning them into working pieces of art. It's more modern, usable sculpture than anything else, and a lot of fun. I would get a hold of old rotary phones from either antique or thrift stores, and cover them with friendly plastic (plastic strips that get soft and pliable when heated), fabric and anything else nearby. Picture frames are a lot of fun too! I suppose this hobby stemmed from my view that anything can be a canvas if you look at it the right way.

Having such a creative drive meant I also had very strong preconceptions about seemingly non-creative things, such as computers. I didn't have a lot of interest in technology until I got a little older. I remembered how much I enjoyed video games as a child, and thought it would be fun to be involved in the creation process of those games. I also thought that I could possibly turn that into a career. As I started down that path, I taught myself programming languages such as Visual Basic and C++. I was amazed at how I could control what was happening on my computer monitor with the code I was writing in the background, and it took me back to my video game days. I also realized that what I had originally thought of as non-creative was in fact very creative.

What I didn't realize at the time was how non-visual traditional programming is. In the beginning, I could deal with looking at text until I tested my program, but after a few months it started to be too much logic and not enough visual output, and I started to lose the feeling I got when I was working on more visual projects.

Today

I discovered Adobe Photoshop and Illustrator, and I was in heaven. I was amazed at how I could draw with my mouse, and see my work on the screen. Again, it took me back to my video game days, but in a much more visual way than programming had. I loved how I could create organic brushes in Photoshop and create in a digital medium; it gave me the same feeling as drawing and painting. I got my first Wacom tablet and started saving a lot of money on canvasses. I realized that graphic design was the field for me, and became a sponge for knowledge on the subject. I wanted to learn everything I could.

In my search for knowledge, I got online. It was then that I got my first taste of community web sites. I got involved with many communities, and was learning faster then ever. I was amazed that people would voluntarily share their years of experience with a young person just getting started in the graphic design world. It made me feel good to know that I had a support system that was always there to be used, and as soon as I knew enough to start helping other people, I jumped in with both feet.

To me, community is the most important thing the Internet has to offer. It provides an enormous network that like-minded people can use to discuss issues and share knowledge with others. It's like being at a conference all the time!

I saw Flash being discussed in the communities I was involved with, but I didn't think much of it until I saw it used for the first time on Hillman Curtis' site (www.hillmancurtis.com). I was in awe. I had never seen anything on the Internet like what I saw there. I bought Flash 3 and fell in love, using the online resources and the Flash community to learn the program. About three months after I picked up Flash 3, Flash 4 came out, and I got my first taste of ActionScript. I realized that the programming I had taught myself earlier laid a solid foundation of scripting for me, and right away I realized what could be done with the simple scripting engine Flash 4 introduced.

Today

Since I had learned Flash online, I felt that I had to give something back to the Flash community. Around two years ago, Aaron Adams and I founded We're Here Forums (www.were-here.com), a community resource site devoted to Flash. I wrote tutorials and articles, and Aaron took over the back-end and server maintenance tasks. Since then, We're Here has grown larger than either of us could have hoped. We're Here exists as a haven for Flash developers; they can ask questions and help others on the forums, better their skills with the tutorials, pick apart each others' files in the open-source FLA section, read interviews and reviews in the Articles section, download royalty-free music loops and effects in the audio section, find a new job or talent in the career center, and after they're done with work, play Flash games in the games section.

Currently, We're Here gets over ten million impressions per month, and has over twenty thousand community members. It has been great fun for me over the past two years; there's nothing more rewarding than watching a community grow and evolve. It's like a playground - people grow, learn, have fun, and also have squabbles! People come and go, and amazing friendships are formed. We're Here keeps me from getting into a rut with my work, by keeping me current with what's happening in the industry.

Around the same time, I landed my first full time design job creating a mix of static and Flash web sites for a design firm. My designs grew up at this point, and I came to realize what it takes to design a commercial web site. My design process also underwent drastic changes as I found myself needing to create highly attractive interfaces in extremely short periods of time. Dealing with the forced inspiration this job required took a lot out of me.

I've recently redesigned my personal site, webstyles.net. Version one was there to offer my services as a designer, and at the other end of the spectrum, version two is much more personal. I wanted version two to be a place where people could come to see my past work, learn about my history, download my experiments, and see what's currently happening in my life. Since I'm in a constant state of change myself, I wanted my web site to be the same way. I didn't want to finish the site and have it be 'done' because that's not the way my life is, so I made everything dynamic. I wanted the site to grow as I did. In that fashion, I added little things that I could change easily, and every day if I want to.

ome | articles | career center | tutorials | fla downloads | music loops | flash directory

www.were-here.com

We're Here Forums! > Mathematics (Moderated by: ahab)

The most common mistake people make about me is that I'm a programmer. Though I love ActionScript, programming is not what I'm interested in. I'm interested in making things beautiful with ActionScript, and making things work in a way that couldn't be achieved without ActionScript. Making an interface rich with interactivity is extremely creative, and not a purely programmatic activity. Because I didn't greatly enjoy learning C++ and Visual Basic, for me Flash is the perfect mix of visual output that can be intertwined with code.

I personally think the best part of Flash in its current incarnation is dynamic content support, and I'm sure it's only going to get better in future versions; this allows for the creation of applications with beautiful user interfaces, motion, and typography. Instead of being limited by what a browser can and can't do, Flash lets designers create a more fluid user experience. Another great thing about Flash's design and scripting flexibility is that it allows designers to create intuitive new applications inspired by classic applications. Later in this chapter I'll deconstruct a new type of calendar application. This will show how the standard features of a traditional application can be adapted and updated in ways that weren't originally possible in a static environment.

I'm one of those people that inspiration hits randomly, and while one type of thing might inspire me one day, the next it might mean nothing. Most of my inspiration lies in normal, everyday things. Whether I am walking through the city looking up through the skyscrapers, or looking out over the water, there is always something new to be seen. People have always told me that I'm extremely tangential, and this is why I think my inspirations lie in such common situations. When I see something, my brain goes off at a million miles a minute, and more often than not, I'm inspired not by what I see, but what I'm reminded of.

Every minute of every day can be an opportunity to be inspired, which is why I try to look at everything I can. This is one of the reasons I love living downtown; there is so much to look at! I can look outside my windows, and see people going about their daily lives, ferries coming into the wharf, construction, traffic, and buildings. (Of course, I see a lot of interesting things going on later in the evening as well!)

WE'RE HERE WHEREAREYOU?
****
IMAGINATION IS MORE IMPORTANT THAN KNOWLEDGE
KNOWLEDGE IS LIMITED. IMAGINATION
ENCIRCLES THE WORLD
- ALBERT EINSTEIN

Today

Looking at the world fascinates me, and most fine art inspires me for the very same reason. Being able to look at an artist's work and see the world the way they see it has an incredible impact on me. Artists such as Henri Matisse, Andy Warhol, and Dale Chihuly have had a great influence on me as an artist and as a person. I love Matisse's work because it has so much feeling; every brushstroke is filled with emotion. Andy Warhol's work triggers the same feeling I described above about ordinary objects. The way he takes normal things and transforms them into artwork is fantastic.

Flowers, 1964 Andy Warhol
© Geoffrey Clement/CORBIS

Nasturtiums with Dancers I, 1911 Henri Matisse
© Francis G. Mayer/CORBIS

Marilyn, 1964 Andy Warhol
© Burstein Collection/CORBIS

One art form that I find a lot of inspiration in is glassblowing. The act of shaping molten glass with the breath you need to live is very symbolic of the creation process for me. I'm a huge fan of Dale Chihuly's work; especially the Venetian series, the colors and shapes are absolutely beautiful! When I was younger, I had a chance to visit Dale Chihuly's studio, before it was closed to the public. It was an amazing experience for me, and something I'll never forget. Now, I can't walk by a glass show or gallery without stopping in.

Glass Blown Art Sculpture, Dale Chihuly
© Dave G. Houser/CORBIS

Glass works Dale Chihuly
© Kelly-Mooney Photography/CORBIS

I'm also exceptionally inspired by large scale sculpture, and this is one of the reasons I love living in Seattle; there are huge sculptures on a large number of blocks downtown. My favorite is the Hammering Man outside the art museum. Jonathan Borofsky's sculpture is 48 feet tall, 7 inches wide and weighs an immense 13 tons. His hammer is always in motion, striking four times a minute, from 7am to 10pm. The only time he isn't 'working' is Labor Day, his only day off. This union of movement and sculpture is a big inspiration to me.

Any art form that's executed on a large-scale inspires me greatly. I've always believed that creative power is much bigger than the person it's contained in, and to see large-scale art represents that in a very visual way for me.

Today

Like most people, I'm also very influenced by music. Artists like Dead Can Dance, Björk, and Sky Cries Mary really get my creative juices flowing. I can just sit with my eyes closed listening to soft, moody music such as this, and watch the imagery fill my mind. I think it's the beautiful female vocals that really get me rolling. Music like that is better inspiration for me when I need to concentrate, since it's soft and doesn't take my attention away from the task at hand. Since I grew up in the 80s, I also love the music that evolved from that decade. The music and disco of the 80s don't so much inspire me as get me pumped to create, and the radio in my office is almost always tuned to the local 80s station (96.5 for any other Seattle people out there). Some of my favorites are Depeche Mode, Talking Heads, Violent Femmes, Duran Duran.

If I had to choose one song that would serve as a 'theme song' for my life, I couldn't do it; I'm awful at making big decisions like that. One song I love and keep coming back to is Mathew Wilder's *Break My Stride*. Whenever I hear this song, it reminds me that I shouldn't let anything really get me down, because in the grand scheme of things, nothing is that big a deal. Another song that reminds me of myself is Talking Heads' *She Was*. The line "the world was moving, she was right there with it and she was" is so indicative of my life. There's nothing more enjoyable in life than not knowing what you are going to do, and just letting the current stream of events guide you. Again, this is why I love living downtown, everything is always moving, and it makes me feel alive. I can either watch what's happening from the inside, or go outside and be swept up in the flow of things.

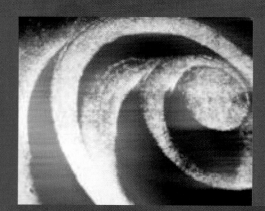

I'm also inspired by the work I see around the Web. Hillman Curtis, Todd Purgason, Matt Owens, James Paterson all shaped my outlook on design. Eneri.net had a big impact on me, and prompted me to redesign webstyles.net into a more personal work. My good friend Sam Wan continues to amaze me with his use of ActionScript, and his storytelling site samuelwan.com is incredible. Josh Davis (www.praystation.com) made me feel a lot better about not being a mathematician. I never understood math until it was put into context visually, and I was really happy to find that I wasn't the only person that didn't know physics and was using 'slam mathematics' in their ActionScript.

One person who inspired me more than anyone though is Aaron Adams, and I wouldn't be where I am today if it wasn't for him. He believed in me, supported me, and pushed me to go further and further with my artwork, no matter what. I think everyone has at least one person in their life that makes their creativity burn hotter and brighter than ever, and that's what Aaron does for me.

Now that you know what drives me in my Flash, in my design and in my free time, we can get busy with seeing some of it in action. My calendar will teach you about Flash, about PHP, about user interfaces and also about how to plan and organize your Flash projects. In fact, if you have a regular calendar on your wall or on your desk right now, take it down and scribble "Jessica's Tutorial" under today's date. Then I can have your full attention as I show you how to do it a better way!

To begin, let's talk a bit about my process. Everything in my Flash projects needs to be extremely organized (even though just about every other aspect of my life tends to be the opposite). Since I've always worked in a multi-designer environment, generally with dynamic content, this is a must. Disorganization coupled with dynamic content is an accident waiting to happen. My architectural practices may seem rigid at first, but they're extremely helpful in the long run, and make working in a multi-designer/programmer environment much more pleasant for everyone involved.

Before I even start a project, I make up a feature list; essentially a document describing each feature's solid functional requirements in detail. When I started this project, I wanted a calendar that could display events, and I figured a normal style of calendar was a little too boring for my personal web site. I also wanted to integrate the controls for changing the month and year into the functionality of the calendar, so I didn't have lots of buttons cluttering up the interface.

What I finally settled on was a design that integrated three draggable bars, one to change the year, one to change the month, and one to change the day. The bar that displayed the day would also display a truncated version of the event, and a clickable more button would show the user a detailed view of the event. To change the date, I wanted the user to be able to drag the different bars.

Of course, as the idea progressed, it turned into something more complex. By the time I was ready to start storyboarding the calendar, it was a database-driven application with a control panel that would let me add events easily. I also wanted the draggable bars to slide into place, and I wanted the calendar to initialize by sliding all the bars into their correct places to display today's date.

These were the main features that I needed to cement into the application:

1. Draggable controls to change the year, month and day.

2. Controls that slide into place to ensure a proper date has been selected.

3. A truncated version of the event shown in the day bar, with a detailed view that will allow the user to see the whole event.

4. External control panel to add events easily. Even though the control panel is only used behind the scenes, it's still a very important part of the application.

5. Database-driven event storing with PHP middleware.

If a project is large and/or contains multiple files, I also make a more detailed architecture document before starting any work in Flash, which can be shared between all the developers working on the project. For this calendar, however, I didn't find it necessary to create an architecture document, since it's only one file.

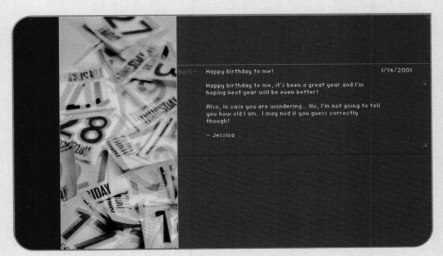

Another invaluable organizational aid is a storyboard. It helps squash bigger bugs (and oversights) before they ever make their way into the project. These help me mock up each screen the user will see when they interact with a project, and help plan the features, how they'll look and interact.

I can't emphasize enough the importance of creating storyboards and feature lists. Since Flash movies that interact with middleware to retrieve dynamic content are usually fairly complex and have lots of 'moving parts', the organization that comes along with this planning is very important.

When the time comes to open up Flash, there are a few rules I always stick to. I always put labels on their own in the top layer, so the entire label name can be seen. Labels make things easier to find in addition to their true function. I also put functions in their own layer, below the labels layer, and all in the first frame of the main timeline. This makes them easy to find instead of having to hunt all over the movie to find the function you're looking for. The Library is organized and all the symbols and folders are named descriptively. You'll see I tend to prefix symbols with their type (mc, bn, gr) so that they're grouped together and also so that I know what they are. This is much easier than having symbol1 through symbol534!

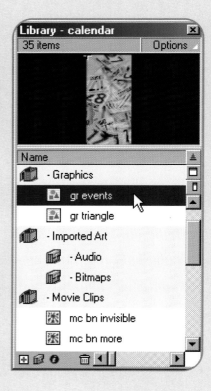

All the folders are pretty descriptive; I even have a fonts folder just to make it easier to find and replace fonts used in the movie. All these practices make other developers smile when they open up my files, because they're easy to work on and add to.

OK, let's get down to work and start looking at how this calendar project is built. We'll see that two of the basic building blocks are PHP and mySQL. If you're already using these you'll be able to work fine with `calendar.fla` on the CD. If you don't have them available, I've made a separate locally-run FLA called `calendar-local.fla` that you'll be able to run more easily.

We've established what main functions the calendar will need to work. I like to define these functions right in the beginning, but instead of writing all the actual code, include comments that explain what each function will do.

To start your calendar, put some placeholders in the Functions layer. We'll fill these in with code one by one later on:

```
// this function will initialize any variables the
// calendar needs to run.
function init () {
            }


// this function will return the number of days in
// the month passed to it and check for leap year
function getDays () {
      }


// this function will duplicate the movie clips
// needed for each bar.  It will space them out
// and put the correct text in the text field.
function buildCalendarView () {
            }
```

```
// this function will shorten an event to the
// correct number of characters.
function truncateEvent(event) {
          }

// this function will build a detailed view of
// of the event clicked on.
function buildDetailedView () {
          }

// this function will get a list of events from
// the server.
function getEvents () {
          }
```

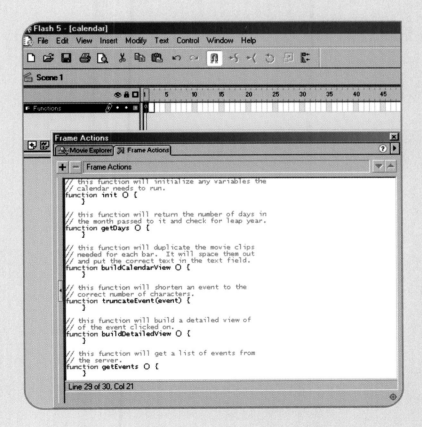

These functions will be the core functionality of the calendar. We can write the `init()` and `getDays()` functions now, and we'll come back to the rest in a minute. First, let's take care of `init()`:

```
function init () {
    initx = 280;
    currentDate = new Date();
    day = currentDate.getDate();
    month = currentDate.getMonth();
    year = currentDate.getFullYear();
}
```

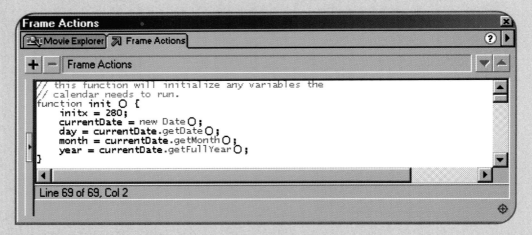

I find that 99% of my projects require an `init()` function just to initialize the variables that the project needs to run. The first line sets a variable `initx` to 280 – this is a useful reference point, and it's where the selected year, month and day are located on the screen. It's used all over the movie, so hard-coding it would be a big mistake. The second line creates a new `Date` object and the third stores the current day of the month in a variable `day`. The fourth line stores the current month in numeric format (January is 0, February is 1, etc...) in a variable `month`. The last line stores the full year in a variable `year`. `currentDate.getFullYear` will return 2002, whereas we'd see just 02 if we'd used `currentDate.getYear()`.

Now let's go on to the `getDays ()` function. Add the following code into the space we set aside a moment ago:

```
function getDays (year, month) {
    if (((year % 4 == 0) && !(year % 100 == 0)) ||
         ➥ (year % 400 == 0)) {
```

```
            var monthDays = new Array
➡   (31,29,31,30,31,30,31,31,30,31,30,31);
        } else {
            var monthDays = new Array
➡   (31,28,31,30,31,30,31,31,30,31,30,31);
        }
        return monthDays[month];
    }
```

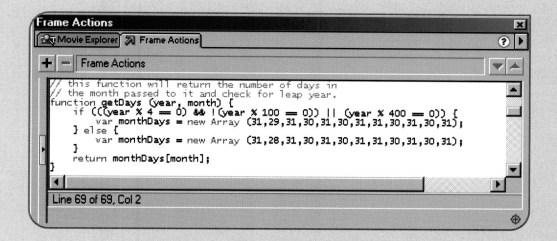

The first `if` statement looks really scary, but all it's really doing is checking to see whether the year passed to the function is a leap year, which is a handy function to have. If you were born on the 29th of February, you wouldn't want your calendar to forget your birthday, would you?

It works like this. If a year is divisible by four and the year isn't divisible by one hundred or the year is divisible by four hundred, it's a leap year! This function uses the modulo operator (the `%` symbol), which divides the first number by the second number and returns the remainder. The script then makes a new array that contains the number of days in each month. Finally, the function returns the days in the month for the month passed. At first glance, this function may look like it creates a new `monthDays` array object every time it's called, but it's actually just a local variable which is only present when the function is called. This saves memory by not keeping a long array around when it's not needed.

Now, let's start building the bits and pieces that will make it work. The first thing I did was to create the art for the interface, which was pretty basic: just two squares and the bitmap with the calendar pages. Then, I created the bars for day, month, and year. For your calendar, you would probably want to do the same – it's always best to get the artwork in place before you start on the code. Look at the illustration to see the main parts we need.

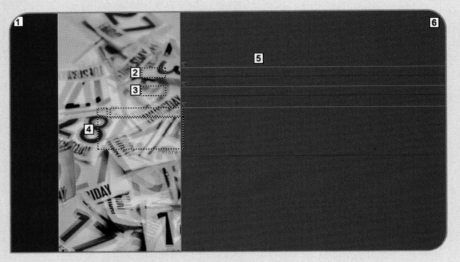

We begin with the empty movie clip vars, which holds events returned from the database – marked as **1** on the screenshot. Then we have movie clips to hold the years and months – instance names years **2** and months **3** respectively, and one for the days and events called days **4**. I have also added a mask layer **5** so that only the content in the bars shows through. Finally, a little question mark in the corner **6** displays the text click and drag the bars to change the date and browse events on rollover – just in case!

Let's take a look at the main timeline to see where all the interface elements fit into place.

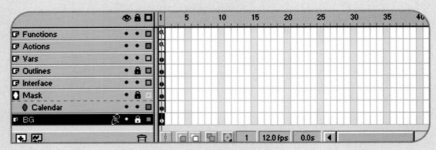

The first layer, Functions, holds all the functions we set up earlier that the calendar will use. This makes editing functions easy, because you don't have to hunt for them as you would if they were scattered around the movie.

The Actions layer calls the `init()` function. I put the Actions layer below Functions for a good reason. If it was stacked above the Functions layer, `init()` couldn't be called because, in Flash's mind, the function hasn't yet been defined. If you want to call functions in the same frame they're defined, the function call has to be below the function definition, because Flash reads ActionScript in different layers from top to bottom.

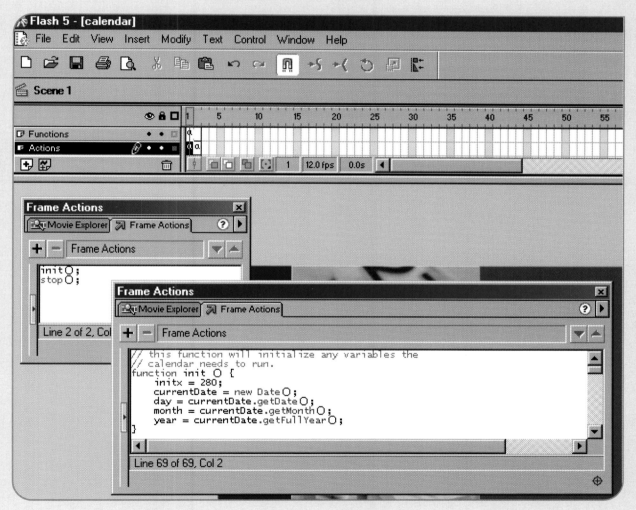

The Vars layer simply holds the vars movie clip. The Outlines layer holds 50% opacity white lines that encompass the entire interface plus the calendar pages bitmap. The Interface layer holds the three calendar bars, the arrows indicating the selected month, day, and year, as well as the help button. The Mask layer holds the mask which only lets the movie clips under the bars show through, and lastly the BG layer holds the background and the calendar pages bitmap.

Of course, there's something we're missing so far; the actual dates themselves. The years, months and days of the calendar are all built via duplicated movie clips. Before we take a look at the symbols, let's see how they should relate to each other once they're duplicated. Again, this kind of foresight is important and saves headaches later on.

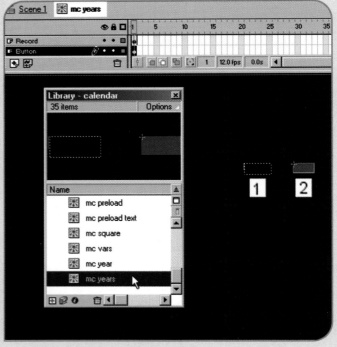

Each bar is a movie clip, within which all the individual items are duplicated. This makes it easier to move the whole bunch together.

To make the year bar, you need to create a new movie clip symbol with the name mc years, and then another new movie clip with the name mc year. The mc years clip will hold all the single year clips, which are duplicates of mc year.

The illustration shows you inside the mc years clip, and here's what the two main components do.

The dotted rectangle is an instance of movie clip mc year called item. This contains the bevel separating each year and a textfield with the variable name label. This is the movie clip that is duplicated to show each year.

Next we have mc bn invisible . This movie clip contains a button the same color as the background of the movie. It's scaled to the size of all the duplicated clips so the user's mouse turns into a hand symbol, prompting them to click and drag (we'll be scripting the click 'n' drag soon). This movie clip has two labels: in the first frame, on and in the second frame, off. The first frame has the button, and the second frame is blank.

You may be wondering why I didn't use a conventional invisible button for this project (a button with only the Hit state defined). It's because in the course of making this calendar, I found a small bug in Flash. If you try to scale a movie clip with an invisible button inside with ActionScript, the button's width and height revert to 0. This doesn't happen if there's something else in the movie clip with the button, or if the button has its Up state defined.

The clips for the months and days are almost identical to the mc years clip, although the mc days clip is slightly more complex. Like mc years, there are two movie clips inside, one for the day and one for the scalable button. Let's take a closer look at the individual mc day clip inside.

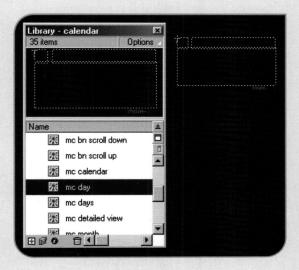

In the top left corner, **1** ,is a textfield with a variable name of label; this textfield will display the day. Next, **2** ,a textfield with the variable name title, which will display the title of the event for the day, if there is one. Area **3** is another textfield with variable name event, which will display the event for the day, again if applicable.

Lastly, **4** is a more button contained within a movie clip. When the user clicks this button they will be taken to the detailed view screen for the event. If there is no event or the event is less than 80 characters (and will therefore fit in the event box), the more clip will be invisible.

These are the main movie clips that make up the interface for the calendar. But it's the duplication of these which will build a recognizable calendar, so this is where the `buildCalendarView()` function comes in.

If you're building your own, add this code to the `buildCalendarView()` function in the Functions layer – the skeleton of which we wrote at the very start:

```
function buildCalendarView (clip, count, gutter) {
    for (i = 0; i < count + 12; i++) {
        _root[clip].item.duplicateMovieClip("item" + i, i);
        _root[clip]["item" + i]._x = gutter * i - 1;
        if (i < count) {
                _root[clip]["item" + i].label =
➥_root[clip].labels[i];
        } else {
            _root[clip]["item" + i].label =
➥Â_root[clip].labels[Icount];
        }
    }
    _root[clip].item._visible = 0;
    _root[clip].button._width = (count + 6) * gutter;
}
```

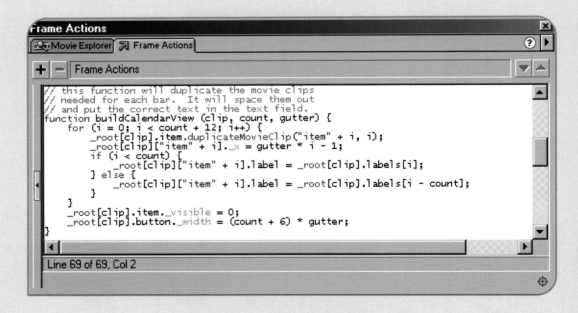

Since there are three movie clips that need to be duplicated a number of times, this function needs to be modular so we can use it on each clip with a different number of duplications, and a different number of pixels in between each clip (the gutter).

The `clip` argument is the instance name of the movie clip that the other clips should be duplicated inside (either days, months, or years), whilst `count` is the number of clips to be duplicated, and `gutter` is the number of pixels that should be placed in between each duplicated clip.

In the first line of the `for` loop (which duplicates the clips), you may notice that it loops until `i < count + 12`, but this isn't as strange as it may at first seem. If it were the 30th day of the month, for example, when the 30th clip is all the way to the left in the selected position, there would be blank space afterwards, which wouldn't be very nice. Instead of this, you duplicate twelve extra clips (twice the exact number that are visible at any one time). These display the first items again, then when the bar is dropped, the `_x` property can be checked and adjusted if necessary. These 'overflow' clips ensure that no blank space will be visible at any time.

regular clips	overflow clips

visible / invisible

If the regular clips are in the viewable area, the `_x` property stays the same.

regular clips	overflow clips

visible / invisible

When this happens, the total width of the regular clips is subtracted from the bar's `_x` property. This puts the bar back into its 'safe area' in the regular clips, with the same item in place, so it looks like the bar never moved.

The second line of the `for` loop sets the `_x` property of the newly duplicated clip to the `_x` of the last clip with the gutter added on. The `if` statement next checks to see whether `i` has reached `count`; this is needed to appropriately name the overflow clips. If it hasn't, the `label` textfield is set to display the corresponding item in the `labels` array.

To make the function modular, I stored an array of the values that were to be put in the labels of the duplicated movie clips in the parent clip. To make the labels start over at the beginning of the array, there needs to be a little fancy footwork in the `else` clause of the first `if` statement. Since the end of the `labels` array has been reached and we need to start over from the beginning, the `label` textfield is set to display the corresponding array item, minus `count`.

After the `for` loop has completed, the first `item` clip's visibility is set to false. Then, the `_width` property of the button movie clip is set to the number of items duplicated, multiplied by the `gutter` variable. This makes the button the same width as all the duplicated clips.

Now let's make the clips duplicate and build the calendar. Add the following actions to the instance of the `mc years` clip on the main stage:

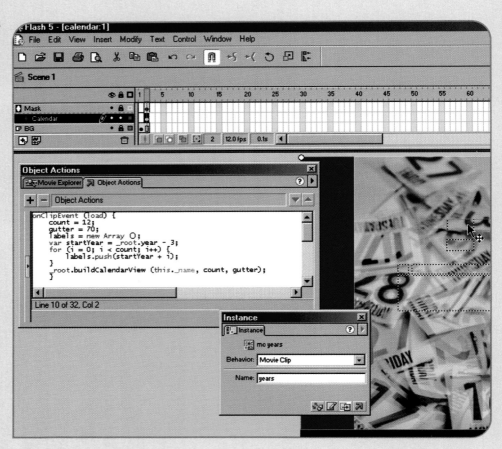

```
onClipEvent (load) {
    count = 12;
    gutter = 70;
    labels = new Array ();
    var startYear = _root.year - 3;
    for (i = 0; i < count; i++) {
        labels.push(startYear + i);
    }
    _root.buildCalendarView (this._name, count, gutter);
}
```

To start with, we define the count variable – for the years clip we want twelve in total. The gutter is defined as seventy pixels. Then the labels array object is created. The for loop afterwards populates the array with the twelve years, three years in the past, then the rest in the future. If you test the movie now, the years movie clip will be populated, and should look like this:

The load clip event for all the bars is very similar, except for a few variables. Let's take a look at the months load actions:

```
onClipEvent (load) {
    count = 12;
    gutter = 70;
    labels = new Array
("JAN","FEB","MAR","APR","MAY","JUN","JUL","AUG","SEP","OCT",
"NOV","DEC");
    _root.buildCalendarView (this._name, count, gutter);
}
```

In this case, only the labels array is different. The months bar looks like this once it's been duplicated:

Now, let's take a look at the days `load` clip event.

```
onClipEvent (load) {
    count = _root.getDays (_root.year, _root.month);
    gutter = 140;
    labels = new Array ();
    labels = new
➡Array(1,2,3,4,5,6,7,8,9,10,11,12,13,14,15,16,17,18,19,20,
➡21,22,23,24,25,26,27,28,29,30,31);
    _root.buildCalendarView (this._name, count, gutter);
}
```

Notice the `count` variable in this ActionScript calls the `getDays ()` function and passes the currently selected month and year. That function will return the correct number of days for the month and year. Also, the gutter is increased to 140 pixels to leave room for the events. Once duplicated, it looks like this:

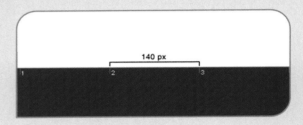

When the calendar first loads, each bar should slide into place at the current date. To do this, we need an `enterFrame` clip event:

```
onClipEvent (enterFrame) {
    if (move == 1) {
        var thisx = this._x;
        var diffx = endx - thisx;
        var movex = diffx / 5;
        if (Math.abs (movex) < .5) {
            move = 0;
        this._x = endx;
        } else {
            this._x = thisx + movex;
        }
    }
}
```

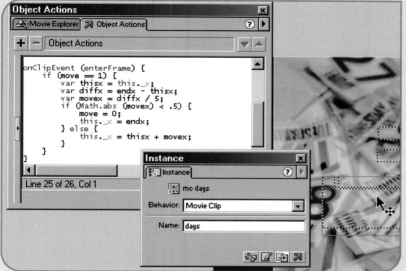

```
onClipEvent (enterFrame) {
    if (move == 1) {
        var thisx = this._x;
        var diffx = endx - thisx;
        var movex = diffx / 5;
        if (Math.abs (movex) < .5) {
            move = 0;
            this._x = endx;
        } else {
            this._x = thisx + movex;
        }
    }
}
```

Line 25 of 26, Col 1

Instance

mc days

Behavior: Movie Clip

Name: days

This piece of code is going to serve several purposes.

First, it's going to slide the bar into place, both initially and after the bar is dragged. The first `if` statement checks to see whether a flag (the `move` variable) is set to true, meaning the movement should take place. This code exists so the bar doesn't start floating into place while the viewer is dragging it. Then, the code sets a few variables. `thisx` is the current *x* position of the bar, `diffx` is the difference between `endx` (which hasn't been set, more on this in a second) and `thisx`, while `movex` is the distance the bar has to move.

The `movex` variable is calculated by taking `diffx` and dividing it by five, which gives the bar a nice slowdown effect. Once the variables have been set, a second `if` statement checks to see whether the absolute value of `movex` is less than 0.5. If it is, the code snaps the bar into its end position and sets the `move` flag to false again, telling the clip not to move anymore. I chose 0.5 as the limit, because it doesn't cause a noticeable jump when it snaps to the `endx` position. Otherwise, the code changes the *x* position of the bar to the value of `movex`.

You should add this code to all three of the movie clip instances: `days`, `months`, and `years`.

For this code to work, we need to add three lines of code after the `buildCalendarView` function call in the `load` clip events.

```
this._x = _root._width - this._width;
endx = _root.initx - gutter * 3;
move = 1;
```

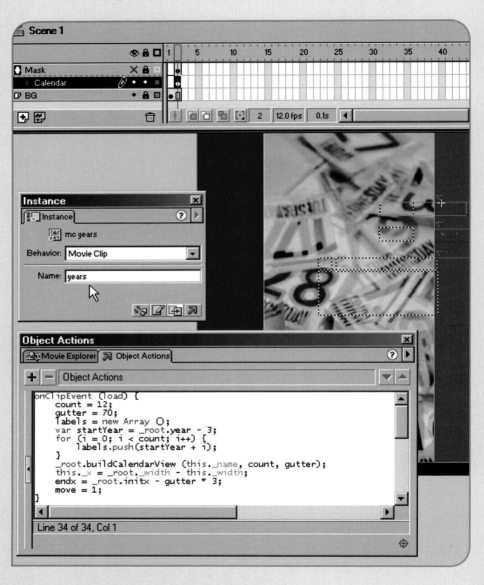

The first line of code sets the *x* position of the years bar so that its rightmost edge is at the edge of the interface, since there are twelve extra items at the end of the movie clip. This ensures that the bar will always move at least twelve positions to the right. The second line sets the `endx` variable that will be used in the `enterFrame` clip event. Finally, the third line of code sets the `move` flag to true, letting the `enterFrame` clip event work its magic.

This code is identical for all the bars with the exception of the `endx` variable. For the months bar `endx` is set to `initx - gutter * _root.month` and for the days bar, `endx` is set to `initx - gutter * (_root.day - 1)`.

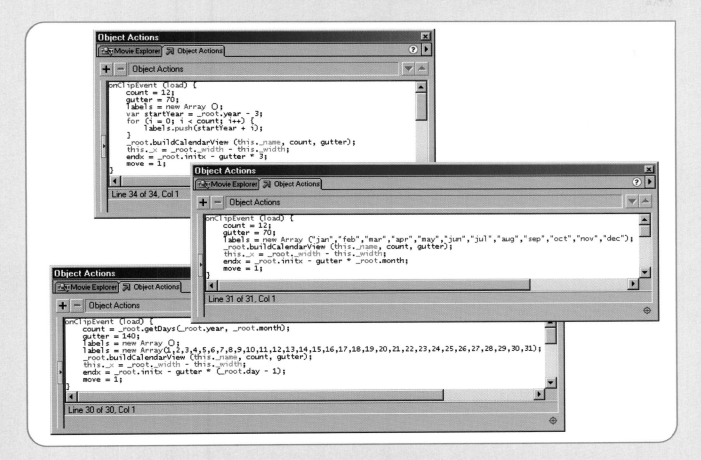

If you test the movie now, each movie clip will be populated, and scroll to today's date.

Now, to make the bars draggable! Double-click any of the bars to edit it in place, then double-click the button movie clip inside to edit it in place. Right-click, or command-click the button to bring up the Actions panel, and enter the ActionScript on the following page.

```
on (press) {
    lastx = _parent._x;
    var left = _root.initx - _parent._width;
    var y = _parent._y;
    var right = _root.initx;
    _parent.startDrag(false, left, y, right, y);
}

on (release, releaseOutside, dragOut) {
    _parent.stopDrag ();
    if (lastx < _parent._x) {
        _parent.endx = _parent._x - _parent._x %
➤_parent.gutter;
    } else {
        var decimalNumber = _parent.gutter -
➤Â(Math.abs(_parent._x) % _parent.gutter);
        _parent.endx = _parent._x - decimalNumber;
    }
    _parent.move = 1;
}
```

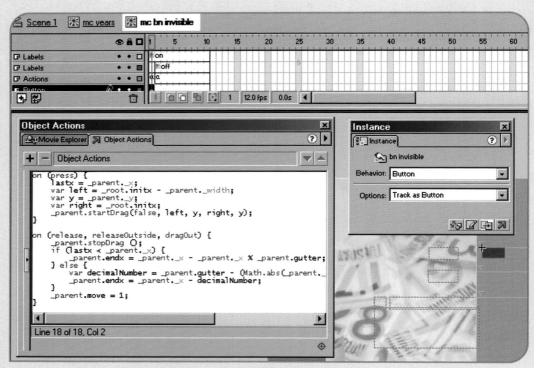

The `on (press)` code block starts the drag. The first line sets a variable `lastx` to the *x* position of the parent clip; this is used to determine which direction the clip should slide when it's released. The next lines set the variables that will constrain the bar to a bounding rectangle. The bar can be dragged only as far left as there are values, only as far right as its initial *x* position, and not up or down. The drag is then started with those values.

The second block stops the drag when the mouse is released, released outside the button, or if the mouse is dragged off the button. First, an `if` statement determines whether the bar should slide to the left or right, depending on which way the bar was dragged. Then we define the `endx` variable (which the parent clip uses to move the next position) for each direction. The equation to slide the bar to the right (if the first condition is met) uses the modulo operator (`%`), which calculates the remainder of the first number divided by the second. By subtracting the remainder of the *x* position of the parent divided by the gutter from the parent's *x* position, the parent automatically glides into place to the right. If the bar needs to move to the left, it gets a little more complex. First a local variable `decimalNumber` is set to the remainder of the gutter, minus the absolute value of the bar's *x* position divided by the gutter. The `endx` is then set to the bar's current `_x` position, minus the value of `decimalNumber`.

The `move` flag is then set to true, so the bar is moved to the correct position. Using this ActionScript, the bar always has a correct date selected. Test the calendar now, and throw the bars around.

We still have to modify the `enterFrame` clip events to customize them for each the years, months, and days movie clips. First, let's look at the final `enterFrame` code for the years clip:

```
onClipEvent (enterFrame) {
    if (move == 1) {
        var thisx = this._x;
        var diffx = endx - thisx;
        var movex = diffx / 5;
        if (Math.abs (movex) < .5) {
            move = 0;
            this._x = endx;
            var itemNum = (initx - this._x) / gutter;
            _root.year = this["item" + itemNum].label;
            if (itemNum >= count) {
                this._x += count * gutter;
            }
            _root.buildCalendarView ("days",
➥_root.getDays(_root.year, _root.month),
_root.days.gutter);
        } else {
            this._x = thisx + movex;
        }
    }
}
```

I've highlighted the new code as bold. The first line sets a variable itemNum to the number of the selected item. This math works since the enterFrame code moved the bar to the next item. The year variable on the main timeline is then set to the value of the label of the selected item. The next if statement checks to see whether itemNum is larger than count (this means the bar has reached the padding movie clips), and if it is, switches the x position to the equivalent position at the beginning of the years bar. Lastly the buildCalendarView function is called to rebuild the days bar. The only time this would actually change the number of days in a month is if February was selected, the current year isn't a leap year, and the new selected year *is*.

Now let's add the new code to the months bar:

```
onClipEvent (enterFrame) {
    if (move == 1) {
        var thisx = this._x;
        var diffx = endx - thisx;
        var movex = diffx / 5;
        if (Math.abs (movex) < .5) {
            move = 0;
```

```
        var itemNum = (initx - this._x) / gutter;
        if (itemNum >= count) {
            this._x += count * gutter;
            itemNum -= count;
        }
        _root.month = itemNum;
        _root.buildCalendarView ("days",
➦_root.getDays(_root.year, _root.month),_root.days.gutter);
        } else {
            this._x = thisx + movex;
        }
    }
}
```

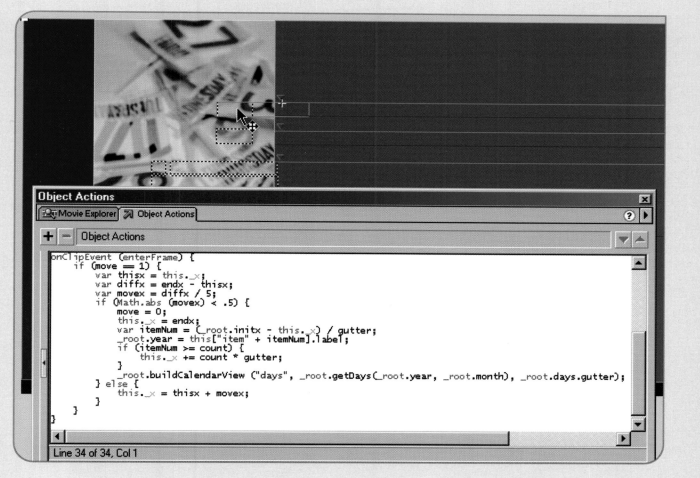

Object Actions

Movie Explorer | Object Actions

+ − Object Actions

```
onClipEvent (enterFrame) {
    if (move == 1) {
        var thisx = this._x;
        var diffx = endx - thisx;
        var movex = diffx / 5;
        if (Math.abs (movex) < .5) {
            move = 0;
            this._x = endx;
            var itemNum = (_root.initx - this._x) / gutter;
            _root.year = this["item" + itemNum].label;
            if (itemNum >= count) {
                this._x += count * gutter;
            }
            _root.buildCalendarView ("days", _root.getDays(_root.year, _root.month), _root.days.gutter);
        } else {
            this._x = thisx + movex;
        }
    }
}
```

Line 34 of 34, Col 1

This code is very similar to what we've just seen within the years clip, but a little different. Instead of setting the month variable to the *label* of the selected item, it sets the month variable to the item *number*. This is because the month needs to be in numeric format. The buildCalenderView function is called, passing the appropriate arguments to rebuild the days bar to the correct number of days for the selected month. Now let's take a look at the additional code in the enterFrame clip event for the days bar:

```
onClipEvent (enterFrame) {
    if (move == 1) {
        var thisx = this._x;
        var diffx = endx - thisx;
        var movex = diffx / 5;
        if (Math.abs (movex) < .5) {
            move = 0;
            this._x = endx;
            var itemNum = (initx - this._x) / gutter;
            _root.day = this["item" + itemNum].label;
            if (itemNum >= count) {
                this._x += count * gutter;
            }
        } else {
            this._x = thisx + movex;
        }
    }
}
```

This code is nearly identical to the years `enterFrame` code, except the `buildCalendarView` function isn't called. If you test the calendar now, you'll be able to drag all the bars anywhere you want to, and the days in the month change depending on what month and year are selected.

Now for the fun part, getting the events! First, let's define the `getEvents` function back on the Functions layer:

```
function getEvents (startYear, endYear) {
    vars.startYear = startYear;
    vars.endYear = endYear;
    vars.loadVariables("events.php", "GET");
}
```

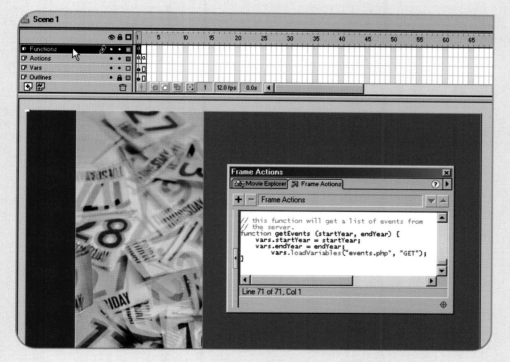

This function takes two parameters, `startYear` and `endYear`, which the PHP script takes as well. The first parameter, `startYear` defines the year for which it has to display calendar events. The second parameter, `endYear`, defines when to stop. This makes the function more flexible. The `startYear` and `endYear` variables are copied to the `vars` movie clip, and the PHP script is called.

To implement this function, we first need to build a data preloader. We'll need to move all the art that was in the first frame of the main timeline to the second frame, and the preloader will be in the first frame. After these modifications the main timeline looks like this:

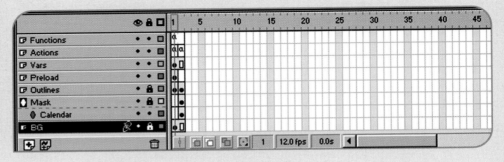

Now, let's add the actions to get the events to the preload movie clip. Right-(command-) click the mc preload clip to bring up the ActionScript window and add these actions:

```
onClipEvent (load) {
    var startYear = _root.year - 3;
    var endYear = _root.year + 8;
    _root.getEvents (startYear, endYear);
}

onClipEvent (enterFrame) {
    if (_root.vars.done == 1) {
        _root.nextFrame();
    }
}
```

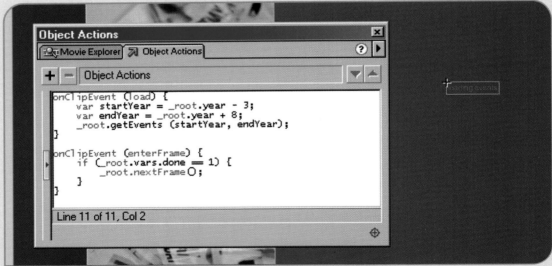

The `load` clip event first sets a local variable to the first year of the time period for which we want to see the calendar events, then another local variable for the last (`startYear` and `endYear`). Then the `getEvents` function is called, sending the two variables as parameters.

The `enterFrame` clip event has one `if` statement, which checks to see whether the `done` variable in the `vars` movie clip is true. If it is, it sends the main timeline to the next frame, launching the calendar.

Now that the events are loaded, the days need to be populated. Instead of making this code into a function, I decided to put it in the `load` clip event of the day clip inside the days bar. This automatically puts the event information in the movie clip when the clips are loaded, so it will fire each time the movie clip is duplicated. The main reason I chose to do things this way was because of the number of times the `buildCalendarView` function is called; a call to function would have to follow every call made to rebuild the days (which happens whenever the month and year bars are dragged).

```
onClipEvent (load) {
    for (i = 0; i <= _root.vars.count; i++) {
    if (_root.vars["year" + i] == _root.year &&
        ➥_root.vars["month" X + i] == _root.month &&
        ➥_root.vars["day" + i] == label) {
            title = _root.vars["title" + i];
            if (_root.vars["event" + i].length > 80) {
                event = _root.truncateEvent(_root.vars["event"
➥+ i]);
                more._visible = 1;
            } else {
                event = _root.vars["event" + i];
                more._visible = 0;
            }
            index = i;
            break;
        } else {
            title = "";
            event = "";
            more._visible = 0;
        }
    }
}
```

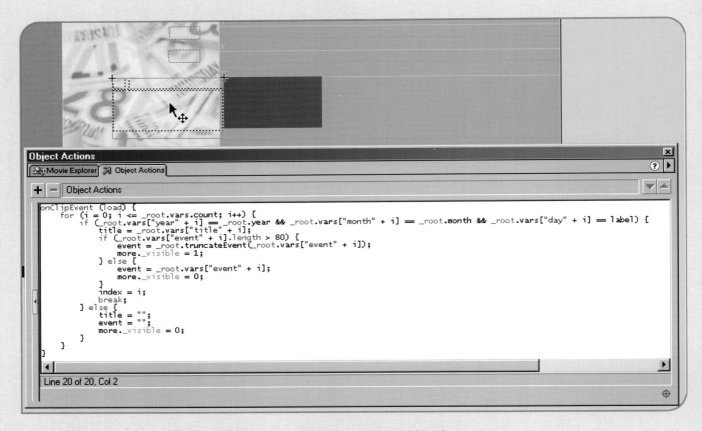

```
onClipEvent (load) {
    for (i = 0; i <= _root.vars.count; i++) {
        if (_root.vars["year" + i] == _root.year && _root.vars["month" + i] == _root.month && _root.vars["day" + i] == label) {
            title = _root.vars["title" + i];
            if (_root.vars["event" + i].length > 80) {
                event = _root.truncateEvent(_root.vars["event" + i]);
                more._visible = 1;
            } else {
                event = _root.vars["event" + i];
                more._visible = 0;
            }
            index = i;
            break;
        } else {
            title = "";
            event = "";
            more._visible = 0;
        }
    }
}
```

Line 20 of 20, Col 2

The first line starts a `for` loop that will loop through each event stored in the `vars` movie clip to determine whether there is an event for the specific date. The `if` statement checks to see whether the current month and year match the selected month and year and if the day matches the label – if all this is true, the code sets all the event variables and the loop is stopped using the `break` function. An additional variable, `index`, is also set. This contains the event number and will be used later in the `buildDetailedView` function. Then the `more` button movie clip's visibility is set to true if the event is more than 80 characters long. If there's nothing happening on that day, the variables are reset and the `more` button's visibility is set to false.

In the Functions layer on the main stage, notice how the `truncateEvent` function is used on the event:

```
function truncateEvent(event) {
    var i = event.lastIndexOf(" ", 80);
    return event.substr(0, i) + "..."
}
```

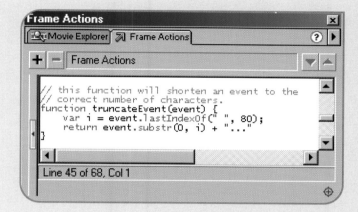

This function is short and sweet. The first line uses the `lastIndexOf` function to find the last space before the 80th character (the limit of the textfield) and stores the index in the local variable `i`. Then the function returns the substring of the event truncated at the space, with three periods added on.

If you test the calendar now, all the events should be in place. Now that we have events, we need the *more* button to work! The detailed view screen is contained within a movie clip on its own layer in the main timeline. First, let's take a look at what makes up that movie clip.

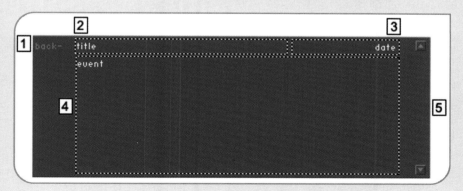

If you look at the figure, you'll see a back button to return to the calendar view . Next we have three dynamic textfields – one containing the variable `title` , another to contain the `date` , and a final one displaying the `event` variable . Finally, we have scrollbars, which are only visible if there is enough text to warrant it .

Now let's take a look at the main timeline now that the detailed view has been added:

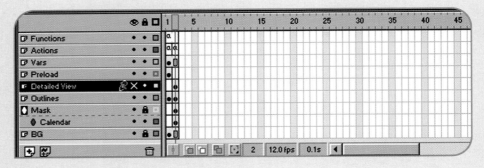

The `buildDetailedView` function will be called from the more button. Again, place this in the Functions layer, where we've reserved a space for it:

```
function buildDetailedView (date, title, event) {
    days.button.gotoAndStop ("off");
    months.button.gotoAndStop ("off");
    years.button.gotoAndStop ("off");
    detailedView.date = date;
    detailedView.title = title;
    detailedView.event = event;
    detailedView._visible = 1;
}
```

This function takes three parameters: `date`, `title`, `event`. First, the function sends all the buttons in the bars to their 'off' position. If the function didn't do this, the buttons would be active underneath the detailed view screen, which is not what we want for numerous reasons. Then, the textfields are populated with the parameters that were passed. Finally the mc detailed view movie clip's visibility is set to true.

Now, let's take a look at the ActionScript inside the more button:

```
on (release) {
    var date = _root.month + 1 + "/" + _parent.label + "/"
    ➥+_root.year;
    var title = eval("_root.vars.title" + _parent.index);
    var event = eval("_root.vars.event" + _parent.index);
    _root.buildDetailedView (date, title, event);
}
```

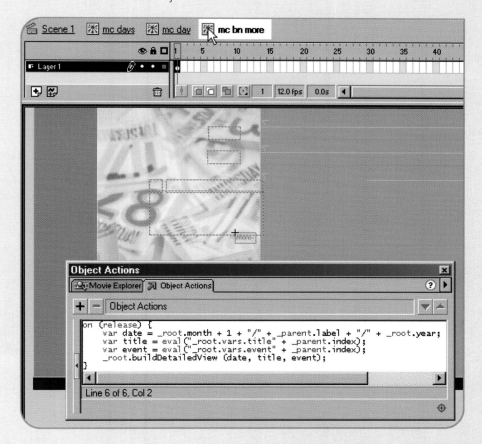

First, a local variable date is set to a formatted date using the currently selected month and year, and the label in the parent clip (the day). Then a local variable title is set to the correct title from the vars movie clip. This is determined using the index variable that was set during the setEvents function. The event variable is defined the same way as the title. Finally, the `buildDetailedView` function is called with the correct parameters.

On the detailed view screen, there are two scroll buttons. These need to scroll the text continuously when the button is pressed and disappear when they aren't needed. To accomplish both features, put the buttons into movie clips and add the following actions to their instances within the mc detailed view movie clip:

```
onClipEvent (enterFrame) {
    if (_parent.event.maxscroll > 1) {
        this._visible = 1;
    } else {
        this._visible = 0;
    }
    if (scroll == 1) {
        _parent.event.scroll++;
        updateAfterEvent (enterFrame);
    }
}
```

That's the code for the scroll down button. The code for the scroll up button is identical, except the scroll uses the decrement operator instead of the increment operator in the second `if` statement. The first `if` statement checks to see if the event textfield's `maxscroll` property is larger than one, this tells us whether or not the textfield needs a scrollbar, and sets the visibility appropriately. The second `if` statement checks to see whether the variable scroll equals true, and if it is, starts scrolling the textfield.

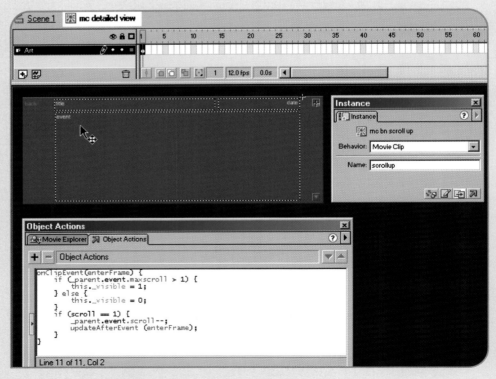

Now for the button actions.

```
on (press) {
    scroll = 1;
}

on (release, releaseOutside, dragOut) {
    scroll = 0;
}
```

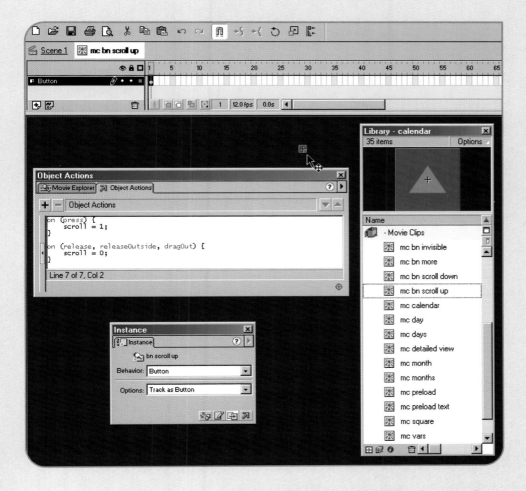

Easy enough! When the button is pressed, scroll is set to true, and when it's released in any way, scroll is set to false.

That wraps the calendar up, but we still need the control panel to add events. I made an HTML file in Dreamweaver that looked like this screenshot.

The filename is `controlpanel.php`. PHP is a blazing fast, server-side, cross-platform, HTML embedded scripting language but unless you have it along with Apache and mySQL installed on your computer, it's not going to work locally (I have provided a local version, `calendar-local`, on the CD).

For security's sake (so no one can enter events except for the person who knows the password), there is a username and password field. These are authenticated against the values set in `config.php`.

Despite the username and password fields, this really isn't incredibly secure. To protect it even more, I would recommend putting the control panel behind some sort of server-side authentication, which is the most secure. Another easy, but effective, method of securing the control panel is to rename it to something that would be difficult for anyone to guess.

Notice how today's date is already entered? This is the reason for the PHP extension; let's take a look at the HTML for the input field:

```
<input type="text" name="date" value="<?php echo (date
➡ ("Y-m-d")); ?>">
```

This is the great thing about PHP, it can be embedded anywhere; that one little line gets a formatted date, and the rest of the file is vanilla HTML. There is also a hidden field with the name `action`, and the value `add`. The PHP script uses this variable to set the action that the page will perform.

The file that takes care of adding the events from the control panel (as well as getting the events from the database and formatting them for Flash) is `events.php`. It's a short script, roughly 85 lines to do the whole job.

First, the file `config.php` is included. This has all the variables needed for connecting to mySQL, and which are used throughout the script. The script is made up of one big `if` statement. The first conditional checks to see whether the `action` variable equals `add`, and if it does, the `add` code is executed.

```php
// Security Check
if ($currentUser == $username && $currentPass == $password)
{
    // Prepare the data
    if (ereg ("([0-9]{4})-([0-9]{1,2})-([0-9]{1,2})", $date,
    ➥$regs)) {
        $year = $regs[1];
        $month = $regs[2] - 1;
        $day = $regs[3];
        $title = trim($title);
        $events = trim($events);
        if (get_magic_quotes_gpc() == 0) {
            $title = addslashes ($title);
            $events = addslashes ($event);
        }

        // Connect to MySQL
        mysql_connect($servername, $dbusername, $dbpassword)
        ➥or die(mysql_error());

        // Select database on MySQL server
        mysql_select_db($dbname) or die (mysql_error());
        // Formulate the query
        $sql = "INSERT INTO events (day, month, year,
        ➥title,event)VALUES ('$day', '$month', '$year',
        ➥'$title', '$event')";

        // Execute the query and put results in $result
        $result = mysql_query($sql) or die(mysql_error());

        // Notify the user the event was added
        echo "<html><head>\n";
        echo "<title>Calendar Event
        ➥Panel</title></head>\n";
        echo "<body bgcolor='#400020' text='#FFFFFF'>\n";
        echo "<font face='Verdana, sans-serif'
        ➥size=2><b>Thank you! XEvent added successfully!
        ➥</b></font>\n";
        echo "</body></html>\n";
    } else {
        echo "<html><head>\n";
```

(continues overleaf)

```
        echo "<title>Calendar Event Panel
    ➥</title></head>\n";
    echo "<body bgcolor='#400020' text='#FFFFFF'>\n";
    echo "<font face='Verdana, sans-serif'
    ➥size=2><b>Date format must be in YYYY-MM-DD format.
    ➥Please use your back button to try again
    ➥</b></font>\n";
    echo "</body></html>\n";
    }
} else {
    echo "<html><head>\n";
    echo "<title>Calendar Event Panel</title></head>\n";
    echo "<body bgcolor='#400020' text='#FFFFFF'>\n";
    echo "<font face='Verdana, sans-serif' size=2><b>
    The username and password you supplied were not correct.
    ➥Please use your back button to try again.
    ➥</b></font>\n";
    echo "</body></html>\n";
}
```

The first `if` statement checks to see whether the supplied username and password match the values taken from `config.php`, the matching `else` at the bottom gives the user an error message if the username and password are incorrect. The next `if` statement uses a regular expression to see whether the date is in the right format. The regular expression stores the numbers that make up the date in an array, and those values are then copied into variables. The `title` and `events` variables get any extra white space 'trimmed' off the beginning and end. Then, the `addslashes` function is used to escape any special characters before they're put in the database. A connection to mySQL is opened using the variables contained in `config.php`, and the correct database is selected. Then, the new data is inserted into the database, and the user is notified that the event was added successfully. If the date isn't in the correct format, the user gets an error message.

If the action variable isn't set, the script automatically views the events.

```
// Connect to MySQL
mysql_connect($servername, $dbusername, $dbpassword) or die
(mysql_error());

// Select database on MySQL server
mysql_select_db($dbname) or die (mysql_error());
```

```
// Formulate the query
if ($startYear == "" || $endYear == "") {
   $sql = "SELECT day, month, year, title, event FROM
   ➥events";
} else {
   $sql = "SELECT day, month, year, title, event FROM events
   ➥WHERE year>='$startYear' and year<='$endYear'";
}

// Execute the query and put results in $result
$result = mysql_query($sql) or die (mysql_error());

// Get number of rows in $result.
$count = mysql_num_rows($result);

// Use mysql_fetch_row to retrieve the results
for ($i = 0; $row = mysql_fetch_row ($result); $i++) {
   $output .= "&day$i=$row[0]";
   $output .= "&month$i=$row[1]";
   $output .= "&year$i=$row[2]";
   $output .= "&title$i=".urlencode(stripslashes($row[3]));
   $output .= "&event$i=".urlencode(stripslashes($row[4]));
}
$output .= "&count=$count&done=1";
mysql_free_result ($result);

echo $output;
```

First, a connection to mySQL is opened, then the database is selected. There is an `if` statement that checks to see whether either `startYear` or `endYear` was left blank. If they were, all the events in the database are returned. If not, the query to get the events uses the `startYear` and `endYear` variables passed to it. The `mysql_fetch_row` function is used to return the rows returned in array format. Then, a `for` loop is used to create an output variable which contains the URL encoded stream of text which will be the script's output for Flash. The `stripslashes` function is used to remove the backslashes in the title and event variables before they are URL encoded. Finally, the last two variables, `count` and `done`, are added to the output variable, the memory taken by the mySQL result is freed, and output is printed to the screen. You can call `events.php` right in the browser with the correct parameters, and see the output printed right in the browser window.

I've made an additional installation script that will automatically install `events.php` on your server so you can test it out. You can download this file from the friends of ED web site. To use it, first, put all the files found on the CD in the same folder on your server. Then, fill out `config.php` with the information to connect mySQL on your server. Call `install.php` in your browser, follow the prompts, and voila! It's important to only put the `install.php` on your server when you're ready to install the script, and delete it right away when you're done, since there isn't any authentication built into it.

There you have it – a calendar with a neat interface that also has some backbone. I really hope this tutorial has showed you how Flash can be used to build new web applications that are usable, useful, and still look great incorporating motion graphics.

Flash doesn't have to be just pretty pictures anymore. With a mix of ActionScript and a little bit of middleware, Flash can be the front-end to any application that needs to be intuitive and interactive!

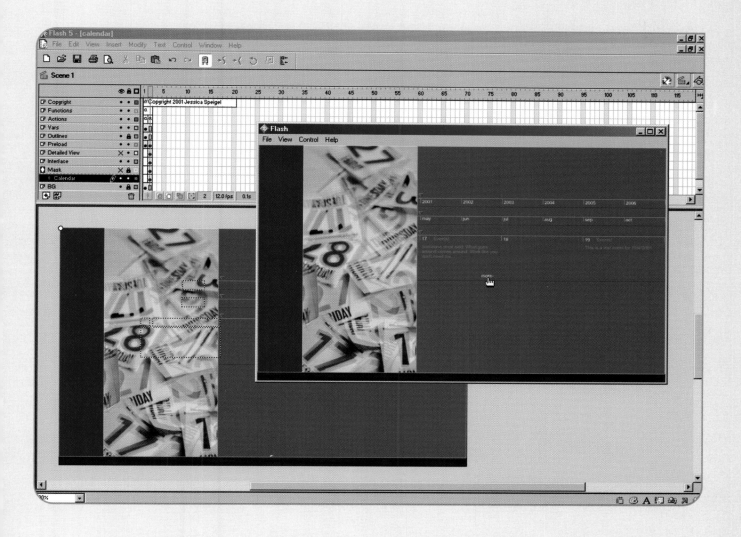

Server side applications and PHP files
don't have to be complicated or clever.
In fact there's a number of applications
that you can build up without the need
for databases and long server side scripts...

text files

By loading and writing variables
directly to text files you can create
simple things like counters and
guestbooks (which was in fact, one
of the target applications for PHP
when it first started out).

You can get more complicated,
such as creating a blank, content free
site and populating it with
content from a set of textfiles,
loaded in as string variables.

The advantage of this of course
being that the client can update his
own content simply by entering it
with a simple text editor.

Flash 5 can recognize a number
of HTML tags as well as just plain
text, so there's a fair bit of formatting
you can add if neccessary.

PHP/XML

The great thing about both XML and PHP is that they are both free. XML is integrated within Flash 5 ActionScript, and PHP is open source. The local server software to test either (IIS, Apache, etc.) are equally inexpensive, so if you haven't played with either yet, there's no excuse, particulary because there's a wealth of information out there on the Web to get you started.

Both XML and PHP as options for communications between Flash and a remote database or other application are becoming more and more popular as Flash is becoming a cool contender for dynamic content front ends.

Knowing one is an advantage, knowing both is a godsend for the ActionScript guru looking to make themselves future-proof.

"A magic trick is only magic until you find out how it works."

Hoss Gifford
www.h69.net

H 69

Think for a moment about the simple sum, 1 + 1 + 1 = 3.

Predictable but undeniably true – in the world of mathematics, that is. Well, what really turns me on is when 1 and 1 and 1 are carefully combined to equal 69. I'm not talking about when you've made an arse of evaluating your variables in ActionScript. I mean the clever combination of simple techniques to create a whole that is far more than the sum of its parts.

To do this you have to mess with your audiences' heads, and to do that you need to get inside and look around. So, thinking about what my creative influences are, I'd have to say the stuff that messes with my head.

I love to climb out of my head. Computer games provide my usual escape route. A good game takes all your senses hostage, and uses that 100% attention to mess with them. One way to measure the power of a game is by how much you begrudge pausing it to answer the doorbell or go to the toilet; the kind of game you'd rather wet yourself than tear away from.

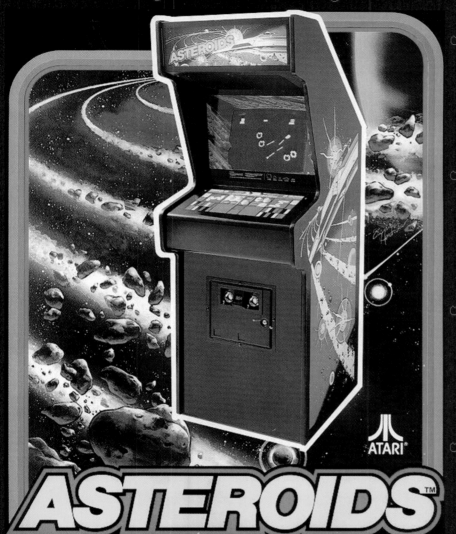

ASTEROIDS™

• Explosive rapid-fire space action • 1 or 2 players are challenged to destroy asteroids and enemy spacecraft • New Atari-designed QuadraScan™ display system • New personal high score table display • Optional "Hyperspace" • Optional coinage including Susan B. Anthony coin slot • Bonus play at 10,000 points.

© MIDWAY GAMES WEST INC.

I remember a holiday when I was wee, to Greece I think. The hotel we stayed in had an *Asteroids* cabinet, which I would give every penny I could squeeze out of my parents. I remember playing the game to death. But one day something miraculous happened – a man came to empty the cashbox inside.

When he opened the front of this amazing machine I looked inside and was stunned to see a mechanical contraption that took your money, and by putting my head nearly all the way inside, I could see a *telly*. It was then I realised that this was just a telly, a few buttons, and a joystick. This extraordinary contraption that defied belief was actually just a clever combination of simple elements.

I remember deciding that when we got home from holiday, I would make my own *Asteroids*® game with the portable telly in our kitchen. Sure, I was very naïve, but this concept of combining simple elements to trick the audience has always stayed with me. It's partly out of laziness, as it allows you maximum impact with minimum effort!

Trick

My next big revelation was with our trusty Sinclair ZX Spectrum 48k. (Think about that for a second – 48k of memory!) For years, the games on this small black block with its rubbery keys provided me with unhealthily long sessions with my nose two feet away from my portable television. After a year or so of playing these games I found out how to view the code that made some of them work.

The first time I looked at this code (called BASIC) I saw the line LET LIVES = 3. I remember thinking, "Surely it can't be that easy?" So I decided that LIVES would be much better off equaling 10. I was amazed to find it worked – I was hooked.

I temporarily lost interest in computer games and programming about the same time I discovered girls. For the next few years I did well at maths and physics at school, and then went on to study architecture, during which time I bought myself a Sega Megadrive. I've tried to maintain a healthy balance between games and girls ever since.

It was while studying modern architecture that I discovered my love for minimalism. I've never been a fan of history, especially not history of art, as it usually involved memorizing stuff from really long, detailed books. I've got a bad memory for stuff like that, and I'm not patient enough to read long books. One project, in my second year at University, had us writing an essay on an architectural book – my idea of hell. I looked through the list of books and chose the shortest one.

The book in question was *Towards a New Architecture* by Le Corbusier, and I absolutely loved it. It wasn't arty and up its own arse like other stuff I'd tried to read. It talked about an aesthetic derived from function; beautifully minimalist structures that were a combination of simple forms with dimensions dictated by function. This was my first joint encounter with art and science.

United Nations Secretariat Building
© G. E. Kidder Smith/CORBIS

Smith House
© Bettmann/CORBIS

I went on to study a house designed by the architect Richard Meier, called *Smith House*. The house is both minimalist and complex at the same time. Its platonic forms hide a complex relationship of spaces within. I love this house – simple ideas and concepts combined to what can't be that far away from perfection.

Another favourite of mine is the *Barcelona Pavilion* by Ludwig Mies van der Rohe – a small number of simple planes combined to create a very powerful space.

Room of The Mies Van Der Rohe Pavilion, Barcelona
© Francesco Venturi; Kea Publishing Services Ltd./CORBIS

Trick

After getting my degree in architecture, I started a graphic design agency. It was during this time that a client, for whom I was doing some identity work, asked if I did CD-ROMs. Work was thin on the ground, and I had just read a review of newly released Macromedia Director 5. I decided that was all the qualification that I required and I set about learning Lingo.

It was a sunny day in a park in Edinburgh. I was there with my dog, and my plan was to struggle from cover to cover of the Director manuals. It said something about how important it was for the designer to work closely with the programmer. "It doesn't get much closer than this," I thought "I'm going to have to do the lot myself." And, then something strange happened. Reading through the Lingo dictionary, I kept getting big time déjà vu. I knew this stuff. It was so weird. It was like visiting a foreign country and discovering that you already speak the language, albeit a slightly different dialect. All my ZX Spectrum coding days flooded back to me – I was onto

something here. I could control animation – provide interactivity. This was a total shock to my system and I loved it. This passion for making stuff happen with code has stuck with me and is still one of my biggest turn-ons. A few years ago I had the privilege of working with a guy called Toby Freeman. This provided me with my second joint encounter with art and science. I got on well with Toby, plus he was a 'proper' programmer – and that intrigued me. Toby also has a great eye for aesthetics (as I saw from his 3D work), but it wasn't until I saw his work on games and interfaces built in Director that I began to understand the power of computing in art.

I was seeing stuff that I had no idea how to create, but Toby is one of those great people who loves to share, and share he did. I learned how to treat complex projects as a series of mini-projects. Individually these elements are much easier to create, and then at the end you just have to combine them (which is often the hardest bit).

I had also gone through a phase at primary school of being into magic tricks. The wonderfully enigmatic Paul Daniels had a series of magic tricks that you could buy. My favourite was a mini-guillotine that miraculously went through your finger without cutting it. At first glance it is visually stunning – an impossible feat. But when I pulled it apart, I found it relied on a simple mechanism that distracted your mind from what was actually happening. It's that messing with your head stuff again!

I like to think of much of my work as being like those cheap Paul Daniels tricks – a brief hit of entertainment that you'd have to really analyze to work out what is actually happening, but you can't be bothered so you just accept it as something quite cool.

Another great inspiration for me is films. Like computer games, great films also take control of all your senses and whisk you outside the reality of everyday life. With this kind of control, a director can toy with your emotions making you laugh, cry, and feel genuine fear.

A firm favorite is *Willy Wonka and the Chocolate Factory*. It's not just the magical story that does it for me – it's the unadulterated creativity of lines like, "We are the music makers, and we are the dreamers of the dreams." Lots of people have seen this film as a kid, but it's only when you see it as an adult that you understand the message that a lot of what we do is pure imagination – and if you're looking for inspiration, this film has plenty.

During my time as a print designer I spent a lot of time with typography. Because a lot of the projects I took on didn't have budgets that allowed for photography or illustration, I'd use a combination of clever typography and minimalist design. It's only really within the last couple of years that I've started studying the history of typography and graphic design, and what I've found is that my approach isn't anything new – although I would have been very surprised if it had been. My experience of 'form follows function' comes from the world of architecture, but graphic design and typography went through a very similar revolution.

Reading up on typography has also exposed me to some stunning work that my dislike for history books had kept me away from in the past, most notably Josef Muller-Brockman. If you have any interest in typography, get the book on him called *Pioneer of Swiss Graphic Design* – it's a belter. I'm not as much of a purist as those original Swiss graphic design blokes though, as I think life's too long to devote yourself to working with just one font as some of those guys did.

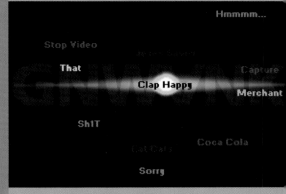

© Toby Freeman

© Paul Daniels 2000

Trick

Like many people, my first real encounter with the Internet was with porn sites. I've always found voyeur sites particularly interesting. I suppose it's like the time I looked up the skirt of the *Asteroids* cabinet – it's getting to see what is supposed to be hidden away. The porn industry itself has always fascinated me; it's a bit of a circus, with some fantastic characters. I'm a big fan of Ron Jeremy – mostly because he's an unattractive, short (in height, that is) and overweight bloke that gets paid to have sex with lots of attractive women. To me, Ron Jeremy is the ultimate triumph of function over form.

When Sony released their Nightshot feature on their latest camcorders a couple of years back, it was discovered that by putting the right filter on the camera you could use the nightshot feature during the day and it would make thin, dark material very transparent. I found this extremely inspirational – one camcorder + one filter + some creativity = one x-ray camera. The addition of elements to create a whole that is much more than the sum of its parts.

It was a shot taken using one of these cameras of Anna Kournikova that inspired one of the most popular exhibits on h69.net called *69-Sight*. Do you remember the wee adverts in the back of *MAD* magazine for x-ray glasses? They totally intrigued me when I was younger, and *69-Sight* gave me the opportunity to show what was going through my mind looking at that advert.

The homepage for h69.net is another example of a combination of simple ideas. When I explain to people how it's done they seem almost disappointed. They are expecting some amazing new bit of coding that's never been done before, when actually it's just a combination of proven techniques. I started with a simple mouse chaser, and threw in a couple of `if` statements to detect if the cursor is over a button, in which case the destination for the chasers is switched from the cursor to a fixed coordinate at the top left of the interface. Finally, one of the chaser movie clips contains an animation to reveal some text, and once it has reached its destination, it's told to play this animation. Simple, eh?

In 1986, Atari released the classic arcade game *Super Sprint*, which was responsible for me being broke for a few months. Hours were spent shoveling coins into the slot to keep a hold of that yellow Formula One car that I had customized up to level 5 in acceleration, top speed, and grip. I must admit that playing it on the arcade emulator MAME recently was a bit of a disappointment – I'd remembered it as being much more visually lush, but those sounds reminded me so much of my youth. When Flash 5 came out and I realized the power of the new version of ActionScript, I knew that the first thing I had to do was build my version of *Super Sprint*. Using the approach that I learned from Toby of breaking down the project into small components I first made the ice skater demo (available in the Lab section of flamjam.com).

The effect is just like an old Paul Daniels magic trick. People stare at it and have no idea how I've managed to do collision detection with the bitmap. And then I explain it and it loses its mystique and can be seen for the clever combination of simple techniques that it is. In general, most people starting out tend to bite off more than they can chew by attacking complex projects head on. My advice would be to split your objective up into wee bits and approach each bit individually. Just take it easy, gradually adding new strings to your bow, and improve and update your Flash creations as you go.

That's exactly how I'm going to take you through my tutorial – a breakdown of the Katakana Guestbook originally featured on h69.net. I never sat down and said

to myself, "Here we go – I'm going to create an all-singing, all-dancing online sketchbook." If that had been my original goal, I would have ended up down the pub after a few hours and it would have joined all those other "I've started but I'll not finish" projects that we've all got stashed away somewhere on our hard drives.

In the next section, you'll how see I created this guestbook – the most recent version of which you can see at katakanaguestbook.com – you'll see just how the guestbook was put together, from start to finish, and you'll get to see all the neat little tricks inside.

After all, a magic trick is only magic until you find out how it works.

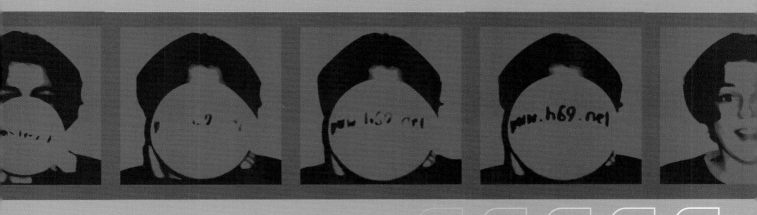

Trick

Before we set up Flammable Jam we all worked together at another agency, where one day a mate showed me an FLA he'd downloaded from one of the Flash resource sites (I think it was either flashkit.com or were-here.com), which drew a line as you clicked and dragged the mouse. I was having one of those days at work where I could get away without doing what I was supposed to do, so I pulled apart the code to see how it worked and put it back together in a way that was easier to understand, and less processor intensive.

Next, I had my 11 o'clock game of table football with Limmy (which I lost), and realized I could probably get away with skiving for the rest of the day. So I decided to start adding stuff to this little line drawing tool. The first thing I did was change the line to a fat brush stroke. Cool, I thought, it worked!

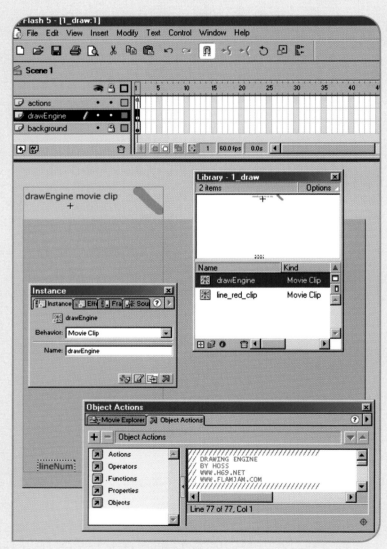

Take a look at `1_draw.fla` to see this first version of what would become Katakana Guestbook (although I didn't know this yet.)

Like a terrible magic trick, there's actually very little to this, but it's quite nice for a short while. Open the drawEngine movie clip and take a look at the code in the Actions panel.

Note how there's no code in the frames inside this clip. There is, however, another clip inside which is the base element – an instance called r that we duplicate and stretch, end to end, to give the illusion of a line being drawn (it's like a big fat red brush stroke).

That's it. Simple, eh? I'll run through the ActionScript on the drawEngine clip.

We start with this:

```
onClipEvent (load) {
    lineNum = 0; // NEXT LINE TO BE DRAWN IS LINE NUMBER 0
    brush    = "r"  // THE NAME OF THE MOVIE CLIP THAT
    ➡DUPLICATES
}
```

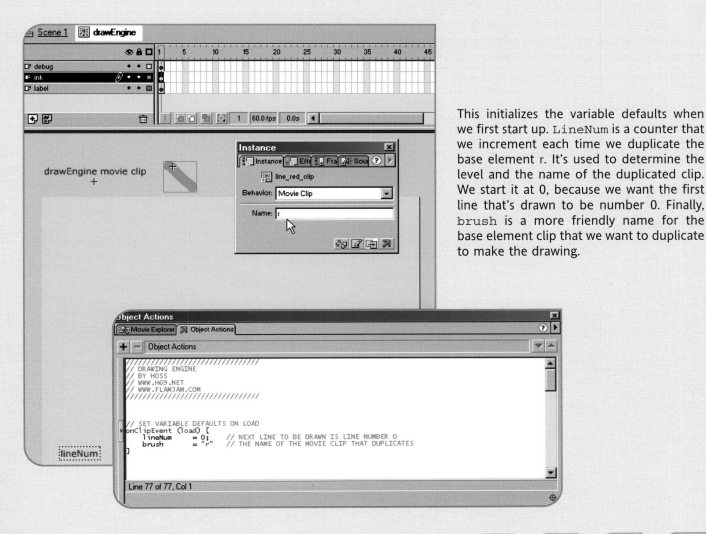

This initializes the variable defaults when we first start up. LineNum is a counter that we increment each time we duplicate the base element r. It's used to determine the level and the name of the duplicated clip. We start it at 0, because we want the first line that's drawn to be number 0. Finally, brush is a more friendly name for the base element clip that we want to duplicate to make the drawing.

OK, if you scroll down, the next chunk of code reads like this:

```
onClipEvent ( mouseDown ) {
    draw = 1; // SWITCH ON DRAWING TOGGLE
    x1 = 0; // RESET X1 TO SIGNIFY START OF DRAWING
}
```

Flash needs to know when to follow the mouse with a streak of paint, so this code waits for the mouse to be held down, in which case it will set the variables draw to 1 and x1 to 0. draw is a toggle (it either equals 1 or 0), to signify whether Flash should be drawing lines under the cursor or not. Setting x1 to 0 tells the main code that this is the first line of this click and drag. It would be slightly more efficient for draw, and the other toggles that we're going to be using, to be created as Booleans – but the saving is so small in this instance that I've just used plain old variables.

Next we look for the release of the mouse button, so that we can switch the drawing mode off by setting the variable draw to 0.

```
onClipEvent ( mouseUp ) {
    draw = 0; // SWITCH OFF DRAWING TOGGLE
}
```

Right, so it's all been straightforward so far – just a case of letting Flash know when brush hits canvas – but now it's time for the clever bit.

This is the code engine that actually duplicates the base element r to create the drawing. It runs on every frame of the SWF.

```
// ENTERFRAME CODE
onClipEvent (enterFrame) {

// *******************************
// ********* DRAW CODE *********
// *******************************
    if (draw) { // IF DRAWING (MOUSE IS DRAGGING)
        if (x1 == 0) {   // IF THIS IS THE FIRST BIT OF THE LINE
            x1 = Math.round (_xmouse);
            y1 = Math.round (_ymouse);
        } else {            // A LINE IS IN THE MIDDLE OF BEING DRAWN
            x0 = Math.round (_xmouse);
            y0 = Math.round (_ymouse);
            lengthSquared = ((x0-x1) * (x0-x1))  + ((y0-y1) * (y0-y1));
            if ( lengthSquared >= 4) {

                // CREATE NEW LINE
                lineName = "line" + lineNum;
                duplicateMovieClip (brush, lineName, lineNum+69);

                // POSITION AND SCALE THE NEW LINE
                this[lineName]._x       = x1;
                this[lineName]._y       = y1;
                this[lineName]._xscale  = x0-x1;
                this[lineName]._yscale  = y0-y1;

                // PREPARE VARS FOR NEXT LINE
                x1 = x0;
                y1 = y0;
                lineNum ++;
            }
        }
    }
}
```

I'll take it section by section and give you and overview of what's happening. To begin with, if the draw toggle variable is set to 1 then we draw:

```
onClipEvent (enterFrame) {
if (draw) { // IF DRAWING (MOUSE IS DRAGGING)
```

The first thing we need to do though is check to see whether x1 equals 0, which means that this is first part of the line, so we set a couple of variables up to get us going. The next time round x1 will equal something else and we run the code that duplicates the base element.

```
if (x1 == 0) { // IF THIS IS THE FIRST BIT OF THE LINE
     x1 = Math.round (_xmouse);
     y1 = Math.round (_ymouse);
   } else { // A LINE IS IN THE MIDDLE OF BEING DRAWN
     x0 = Math.round (_xmouse);
     y0 = Math.round (_ymouse);
     lengthSquared = ((x0-x1) * (x0-x1))  + ((y0-y1) * (y0-y1));
     if (  lengthSquared >= 4) {
```

Note that we check the current mouse position, and ensure that it's moved at least two pixels, otherwise holding the mouse down while not moving would just duplicate a movie clip too small to see.

Assuming that the mouse has moved this minimum amount we duplicate the base element r (stored in the variable brush). The new clip gets the name line0, the next line1 and the one after line2. We use the lineNum variable to do this:

```
// CREATE NEW LINE
   lineName = "line" + lineNum;
   duplicateMovieClip (brush, lineName, lineNum+69);
```

By measuring the distance the mouse has moved since the last frame, we position and stretch the duplicated element to join the two points. The cool thing about stretching the movie clip in this way is that when you draw with fast strokes, the movie clip is scaled up a lot to give big fat brush strokes. This is what gives us the brush and ink feeling:

```
// POSITION AND SCALE THE NEW LINE
   this[lineName]._x = x1;
   this[lineName]._y = y1;
   this[lineName]._xscale = x0-x1;
   this[lineName]._yscale = y0-y1;
```

Lastly we set up our variables for the next run through this code on the next line (and we close some brackets!):

```
        // PREPARE VARS FOR NEXT LINE
    x1 = x0;
    y1 = y0;
    lineNum ++;
      }
    }
  }
}
```

That's it! See – I told you there was nothing to it, but I still had a whole day of skiving ahead, so I started adding stuff – bit by bit.

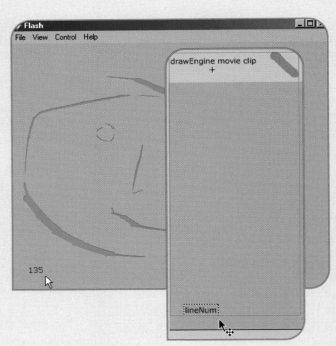

If you look again at the `1_draw.fla` you'll notice I've added an ink counter in the corner (from the variable `lineNum`). This helps us keep track of how much ink the artist is splashing around (and how much mess they're making!) This will come in handy later.

I felt that this could look a bit like brush strokes when you're drawing fast, probably because I'd been doing some night classes on Japanese (not for any reason other than I thought it would be cool. It is.) I'd started learning the alphabets and loved drawing them with brush and ink. I decided it would be cool to make this line tool draw with ink that faded.

This is a neat effect and a lot of people ask me how it's done, and I'm almost embarrassed to admit how simple a trick it is.

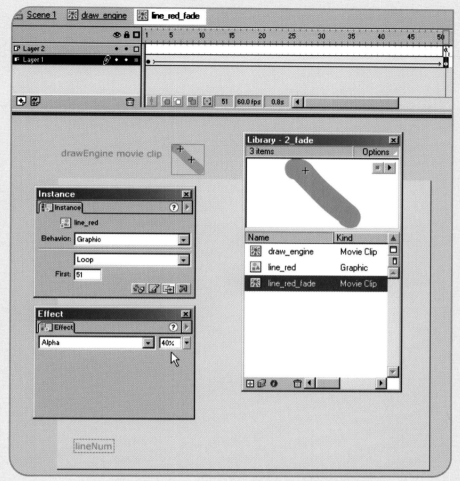

If you open up `2_fade.fla` you'll see that it's almost identical to `1_draw.fla`, but if you look in the base element – the instance `r` – you'll see a timeline animation that fades the graphic's opacity down over about fifty frames. Every time a line is duplicated, the new instance appears at the start of this fade animation and plays to the stop code at the end. This gives the illusion of the ink drying.

Lunchtime brought two pints of Beamish Red Ale, pie, beans, and chips in Bannisters – and chat about quitting our jobs to set up our own company. Arriving back from lunch, I avoided the dirty looks from the management for being half an hour late and I sat down at my desk to continue my R&D.

It's all very well drawing all these lines, but to get a clear screen I had to reload the SWF. So I set about adding an Undo button. You'll see that `3_undo.fla` has all the same stuff as `2_fade.fla`, but with the addition of this code:

```
if (undo) { // CHECK UNDO MODE IS ACTIVE
    // REMOVE LINE MOVIE CLIP INSTANCE
    lineNum —;
    lineName = "line" + lineNum;
    removeMovieClip (lineName);
    // OVERRIDE ANY REQUEST TO DRAW
    draw = 0;
    // DISABLE UNDO MODE IF ALL LINES ARE REMOVED
    if (lineNum == 0) {
        undo = 0;
    }
}
```

I also put a button on stage that sets the toggle variable `undo` to 1 when pressed and 0 when released. The `undo` code engine looks for this toggle equalling 1, at which point it uses the `lineNum` variable to workout the name of the last line duplicated and then deletes it. Each time the code runs, it decrements `lineNum` and deletes another clip. This gives a cool effect, which, as you can see, is easy to do.

I was fairly chuffed with myself making the `undo` work, so I had another game of table football with Limmy (I won this match by scoring repeatedly with my defenders). While enjoying my celebratory coffee, I decided it would be a good thing to add different colors of ink to the drawing tool.

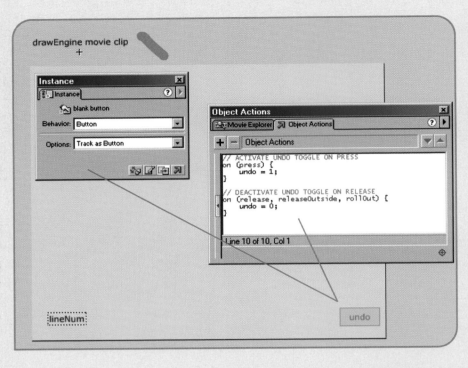

This was a doddle. Check out `4_colours.fla` to see how it's done. I created another four base element instances and named them b, g, o, and w. They're just like the original base element r, except they're blue, green, orange, and white respectively. If you remember back to the code engine that duplicates the base element to make the drawing, the line that actually does the duplication refers to the base element named in the variable `brush`. So all we need to do is change this variable to one of our other base elements and we get colored ink.

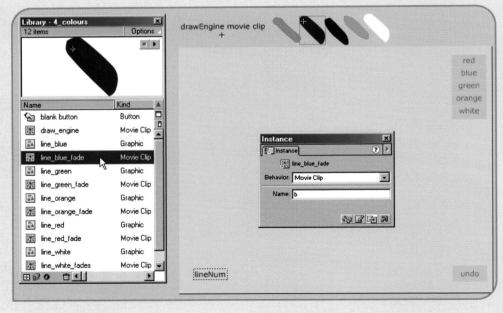

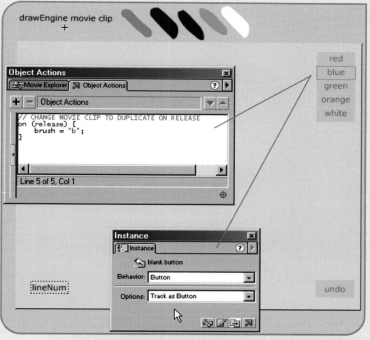

That's exactly what the color buttons on the stage do. The code looks like this:

```
on (release) {
  brush = "b";
}
```

This sets the ink color to blue by setting the movie clip to be duplicated as the blue-colored stroke.

I passed the file around the office to let people play with it. What struck me was how great some people's illustrations were – and it seemed a shame to erase them with no trace, so I set about working out how to save and load people's masterpieces.

The first thing I was going to have to do was record enough data on each line of the drawing to recreate it later. Back then I used fake arrays because I was using Flash 4, but if you look at 5_array.fla you'll see how it's done with proper arrays in Flash 5:

```
cArray = new Array();
xArray = new Array();
yArray = new Array();
wArray = new Array();
hArray = new Array();
```

This code initializes the five arrays that hold each of the required values for each line. The first is the color of the line to duplicate (cArray), the second the *x* coordinate of the line (xArray), then the *y* coordinate of the line (yArray), the width of the line (wArray), and the height of the line (hArray). Next I added this code to run every time a new line is drawn. It uses the lineNum variable to add the five bits of data we need to record to their respective arrays:

```
cArray [lineNum] = brush;
xArray [lineNum] = x1;
yArray [lineNum] = y1;
wArray [lineNum] = (x0-x1);
hArray [lineNum] = (y0-y1);
```

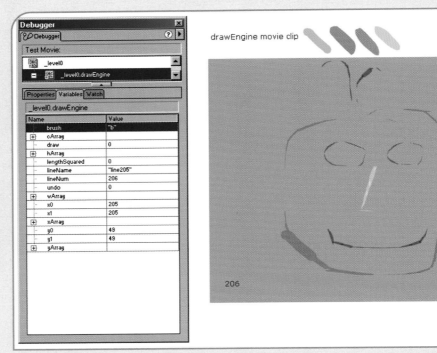

Take a look at the screen grab of the debugger – clicking the drop-down + menu beside `cArray` will display all the lines we've drawn (numbered 0, 1, 2…) along with their associated colors ("r", "w", "b" and so on). Now that I had a way of recording the lines in a drawing, it was a fairly straightforward task to be able to replay the drawings.

Take a look at how it's done in `6_replay.fla`. All I did was add a Replay button with the following code:

```
on (release) {
    // REMOVE ALL LINES OF THE DRAWING
    for ( i = lineNum; i >= 0; i — ) {
        removeMovieClip ( "line" add i
);
    }
    lineNum = 0;

    // CALCULATE NUMBER OF LINES
    numLines = cArray.length;

    // ACTIVATE REPLAY MODE
    replay = 1;
}
```

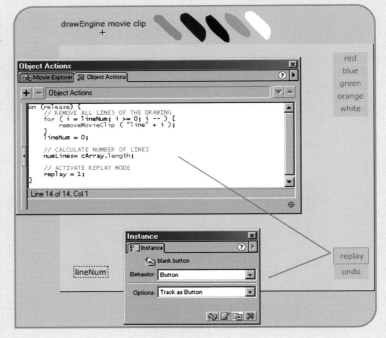

The first bit uses a loop to remove all the duplicated movie clips of the drawing, and then we store the number of lines that were in the drawing by measuring the length of the array holding the brush color data. Finally we set the variable `replay` to 1 to activate the replay code back in the draw engine.

This ActionScript sits at the start of the `enterFrame` code, before the undo code that I described earlier. I started by copying and pasting the ActionScript I wrote for the actual drawing of a line, because that's what I wanted to do, but in an automated way.

```
if (replay) {  // CHECK REPLAY MODE IS ACTIVE
   // CREATE NEW LINE
   lineName = "line" + lineNum;
   brush    = cArray [lineNum];
   duplicateMovieClip (brush, lineName, lineNum);

   // POSITION AND SCALE THE NEW LINE
   setProperty (lineName, _x, xArray [lineNum]);
   setProperty (lineName, _y, yArray [lineNum]);
   setProperty (lineName, _xscale, wArray [lineNum]);
   setProperty (lineName, _yscale, hArray [lineNum]);

   // PREPARE VARS FOR NEXT LINE
   lineNum ++;

   if (lineNum >= numLines) { // IF DRAWING IS FINISHED
      // DEACTIVATE REPLAY MODE
      replay= 0;
   } else {
      // OVERRIDE ANY REQUEST TO UNDO OR DRAW
      undo  = 0;
      draw  = 0;
   }
}
```

Trick

In the normal draw code we take a note of the mouse position and how much it has moved to work out the *x* and *y* coordinates, and the width and height. In replay mode we simply replace those measurements with the data stored in the array, and the line draws itself! The key to the replay working is that when we remove the lines from the drawing, we keep all the data in the arrays. This leaves us with one wee thing to fix. Remember the undo code from earlier? It simply clears the screen by removing the lines one at a time. To be a true undo, we need to add some code for it to also remove the data from each line from the arrays as it does so. So, as a final step, we add the following little update into the undo code:

```
cArray.pop ();
xArray.pop ();
yArray.pop ();
wArray.pop ();
hArray.pop ();
```

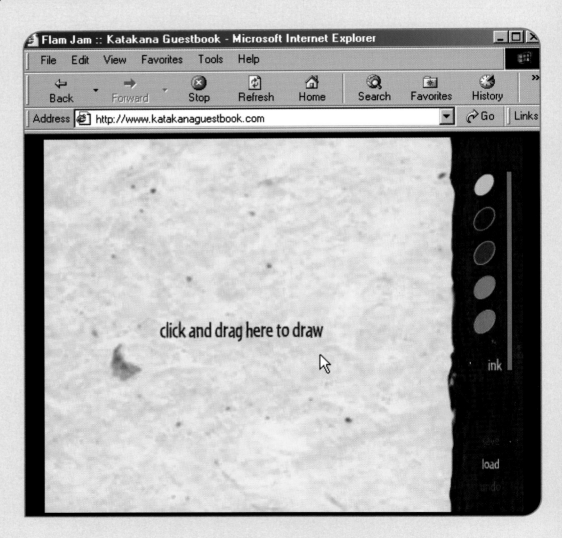

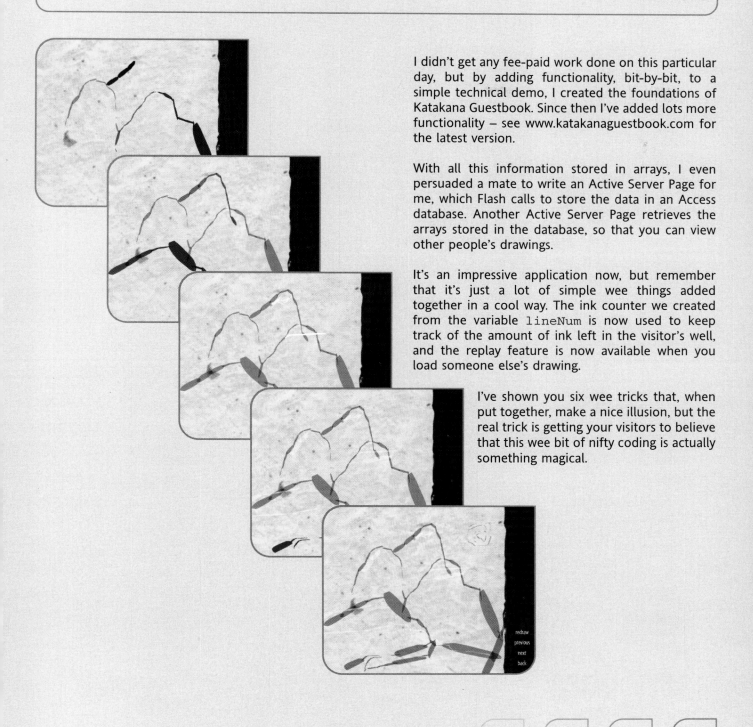

I didn't get any fee-paid work done on this particular day, but by adding functionality, bit-by-bit, to a simple technical demo, I created the foundations of Katakana Guestbook. Since then I've added lots more functionality – see www.katakanaguestbook.com for the latest version.

With all this information stored in arrays, I even persuaded a mate to write an Active Server Page for me, which Flash calls to store the data in an Access database. Another Active Server Page retrieves the arrays stored in the database, so that you can view other people's drawings.

It's an impressive application now, but remember that it's just a lot of simple wee things added together in a cool way. The ink counter we created from the variable `lineNum` is now used to keep track of the amount of ink left in the visitor's well, and the replay feature is now available when you load someone else's drawing.

I've shown you six wee tricks that, when put together, make a nice illusion, but the real trick is getting your visitors to believe that this wee bit of nifty coding is actually something magical.

The potential use of Flash to create interactive pieces like Hoss's has expanded via the addition of several new multimedia objects in flash 5. The key word here of course is interactive. The new sound and color objects allow direct user control of parameters that just are not accessible in Flash 4.

ink wells

Instead of a fixed color palette, use the new `color.setTransform(transformObject);` command to allow the user to vary the available colors. By using draggable ink wells, you could allow the user to add more red, blue or green to a particular ink color simply by dragging an inkwell over it.

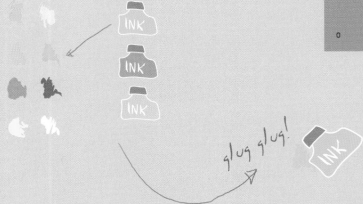

glug glug!

pen cursor

By using the `mouse.hide();` command, you can make the standard mouse pointer disappear. You can then replace it with any other graphic, such as the pen graphic shown.

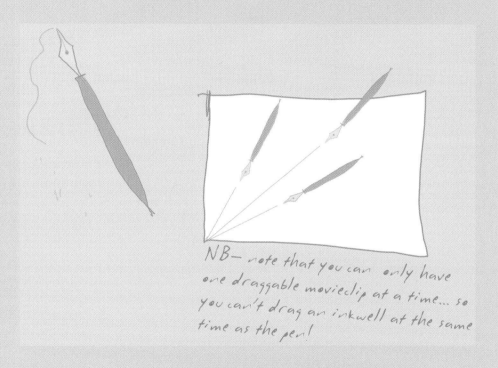

NB— note that you can only have one draggable movieclip at a time... so you can't drag an inkwell at the same time as the pen!

By making the pen always point to the same place, you can even simulate wrist movement as the artist moves around the canvas...

chapter 1

chapter 2

chapter 3

chapter 4

chapter 5

chapter 6

chapter 7

chapter 8

chapter 9

chapter 10

chapter 11

chapter 12

chapter 13

chapter 14

chapter 15

"I thought about frogs and grasshopppers
but that would make things a little too complex,
and I really didn't feel like doing more animals
at that time."

Manuel Tan
www.uncontrol.com

381

Flutter

I'd like to think that some well-known artist from some postmodern era inspired me to create all these experiments but that wouldn't be too truthful. Inspiration can come to me from a number of sources that may have nothing to do with the experiment I'm working on. You could be in a museum looking at Renaissance art or lounging on the couch in your friend's apartment.

I think about creating experiments all the time. I sometimes don't go to sleep until 2 a.m., thinking about what would happen if I tried this movement with that one. (I get so sleepy the next day that I've recently developed a bad habit of taking a catnap everyday at work, usually around 4:00.) At any given time I can give you a handful of ideas, most of which usually suck. Occasionally, though, one idea will bubble up and stay with me because it contains some interesting possibilities. It only becomes a good idea after plenty of refining.

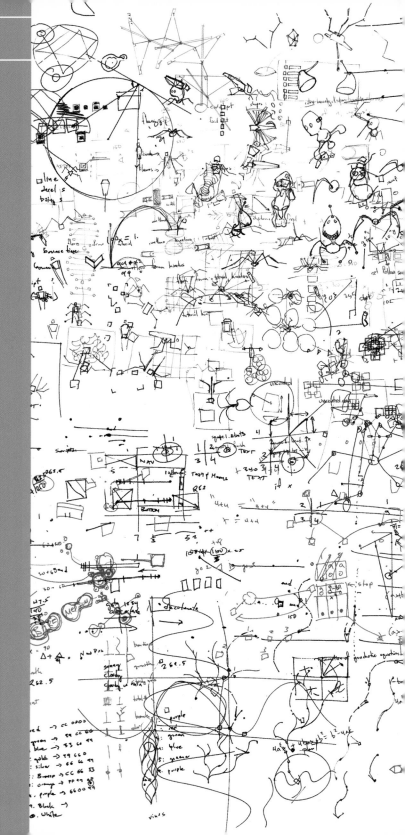

Manuel Tan

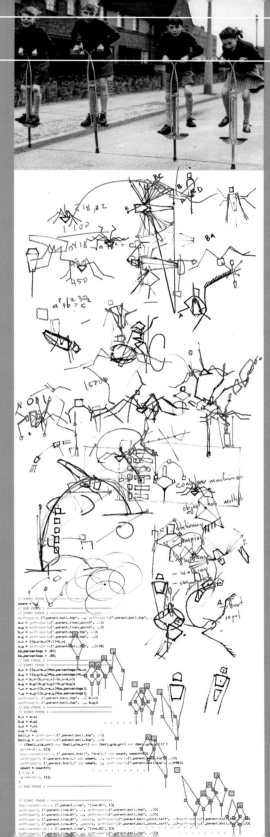

For a while I was obsessed with ideas involving the jumping action. I had just finished building some behaviors to create a sort of walking effect and I thought that developing things further to make something jump would be cool. I knew I could use one of my previous scripts to make it work but I got stuck on what to use as my subject. I thought about frogs and grasshoppers but that would make things a little too complex, and I really didn't feel like doing more animals at that time. A few months later, a co-worker and I were discussing hobbies and we ended up talking about vintage toys. Later on that week she gave me a vintage postcard of four little kids hopping around like madmen on pogo sticks and soon afterwards, I thought of that as the visual for the experiment. With that spark of inspiration from a postcard I created a Flash pogo stick. I sketched a generalization of how the pogo stick will jump around, wrote down any notes and flagged up things that may cause me problems later on. I created the Flash file from bits and pieces of my previous scripts until it vaguely resembled what I had in my head. I started to refine the movement and look, sometimes spending hours trying to find the right combination of variables and colors to make it react like a child.

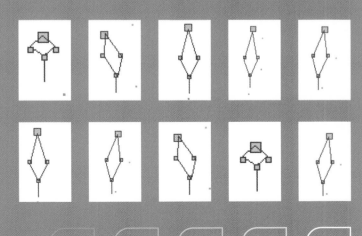

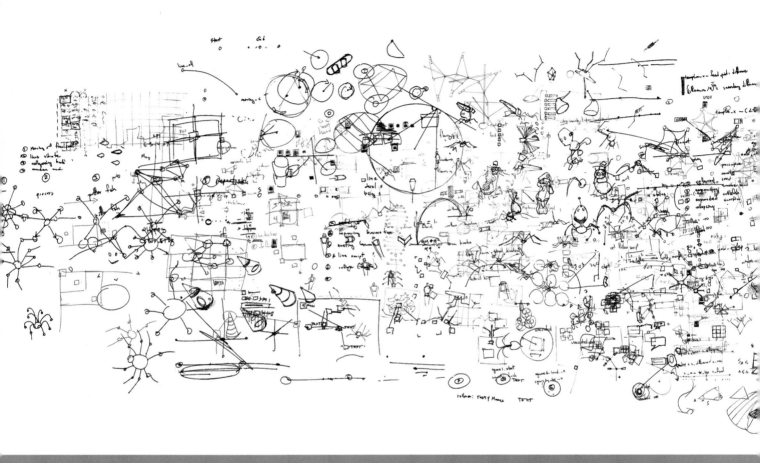

I think that one of the driving forces behind what I do is the idea of finishing what I started. I really think that most of us can continually come up with fairly good ideas, but the hard part is sticking with it until the ideas are finished and fully developed. I motivate myself to finish things by thinking that it won't matter if the idea is good if no-one can ever see it.

Inspiration can happen at any time, so that's why I have a sketchbook handy wherever I am and wherever I go. I usually use a large size sketchbook but it's a pain to carry with me at all times so I have five smaller our scattered

around, everywhere I go – at work, in my bedroom, my living room and even my bathroom. These are places where I spend most of my time, so if there's a sketchbook always at hand I can make the most of every spark of inspiration I get wherever I am. When I can't use my regular sketchbooks, I have a tiny one in my bag, just in case. Many of my friends and co-workers also carry sketchbooks (one even made a web site of it, called www.graphpaper.com), but unlike me they keep them very well taken care of, taping up a variety of things they would find, and then sketching on top of them with multicolored pens. As much as I want to do that with my

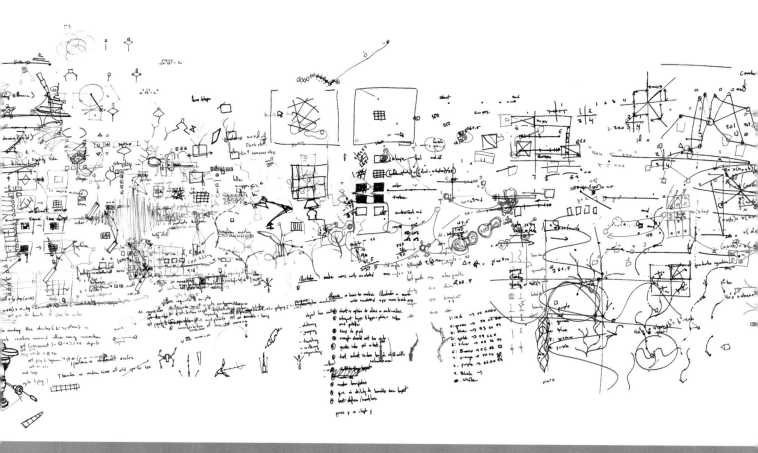

sketchbook, I don't because it's a real pain. I usually end up sketching a single idea using quick gesture drawings of lines, squares and circles using a blue Bic pen. I would draw the same object twenty times over until I'm finally comfortable with almost every stroke. I write short sentences to highlight key points of the experiment, its flaws and how to fix them. When I have an idea that I think is developed, I sometimes start writing out the code in simple terms on the sketchbook, just as a reference. Once I'm ready, I start to transfer all that into Flash ActionScript and all of a sudden, there it is - my finished experiment. As my scripts have begun to get more and

more complex, I've found it difficult to write out all the code by hand, so I've taken to drawing process maps. I see these process maps as a walking tour of how my code works, and that helps me concentrate on writing small parts of the experiment, instead of trying to figure out everything in one shot.

Rather than trying to quantify what inspires me, I'll just write about things I like and you can decide whether it's inspiring or not.

Flutter

One thing I like to do is watch a lot of television. I come home after work and sit in front of the TV and watch almost any show that's on for hours, from *Dateline* to RonCo's *Set It and Forget It* Showtime Rotisserie Oven thingy (that thing can cook four Cornish game hens, for Christ's sake!). I recently got cable television and an interesting phenomenon occurred. There were so many channels that I ended up watching everything and nothing at the same time. I would catch glimpses of shows; just enough to understand what was going on before I ended up changing the channel to something else. The good thing about TV is that it bombards you with a large quantity of information in a passive way. By constantly flipping the channel, you can soak in the most visual and audible impressions. The only drawback is that all this channel-flipping gives you a very low attention span. It's difficult for me to concentrate on anything for too long at a time. I'm actually having problems writing this chapter because I keep wandering around, writing the same line over and over again until it sounds good enough (the contents of this paragraph have changed three times over). Sometimes I treat writing code for my experiments the same way. I feel my experiments might not be as complex as others, because I can't continue on a single train of thought for a prolonged period of time, so I stop the first chance I get. Stopping midway while writing a script isn't a good thing, because if and when I come back to it, I forget what I was doing and I end up having to start all over again.

Another facet to TV is music videos. Everybody has their own opinions when it comes to videos that they like. Some people like them because of the music and the people that play the music. Others like them for their production quality. Bjork's *All is Full of Love* video directed by Chris Cunningham is one of the most stunning videos I've ever seen. Mixing her delicate profile onto a cold pneumatic, robotic body was utterly jaw-dropping. I can't wait until he directs Gibson's *Neuromancer* (which is also one of my favorite books; I had to read it at least three times to fully understand it.)

Another music video that didn't have a large production value but had an extraordinary simple concept was *Around the World* by Daft Punk. It juxtaposed the beats of the music with the movements of dancing quartets in curiously weird outfits. It's amazing how coordinatedly these quartets move across the circular stage without bumping into each other. (By the way, *juxtaposition* is one of those great words used only by designers. You should use it as often as you can.) I especially like the robot-space men. Try doing that dance at a club and see how many weird looks you get from other people.

If you know my work, I guess you'll have picked up the insect theme that runs through my experiments on www.uncontrol.com. When I was a kid, my dad bought for me the huge Audubon Society Encyclopedia of Animal Life reference book, filled with pictures and descriptions of a large variety of animals. I've had this book for over twenty years now, and I keep going back to it as my main resource for understanding everything I want to know about animals, and particularly insects. Insects aren't as complex as mammals. Their movements consist of simple and deliberate actions, so experimenting with that type of behavior is easier to do in Flash than trying to figure out the same behavior performed by a human being. My interest in insects has never stopped. A few months ago I bought the movie, *Microcosmos* . It shows animals, mostly insects, in motion, how they walk, eat, have sex, and so on. For me, *Microcosmos* has been a visual extension of the Audobon book. If you're bored, why not have some fun and rent this movie, mute the volume, turn off all the lights and listen to Underworld, Massive Attack or even White Zombie; basically any songs with strong bass – really sets your mind flying!

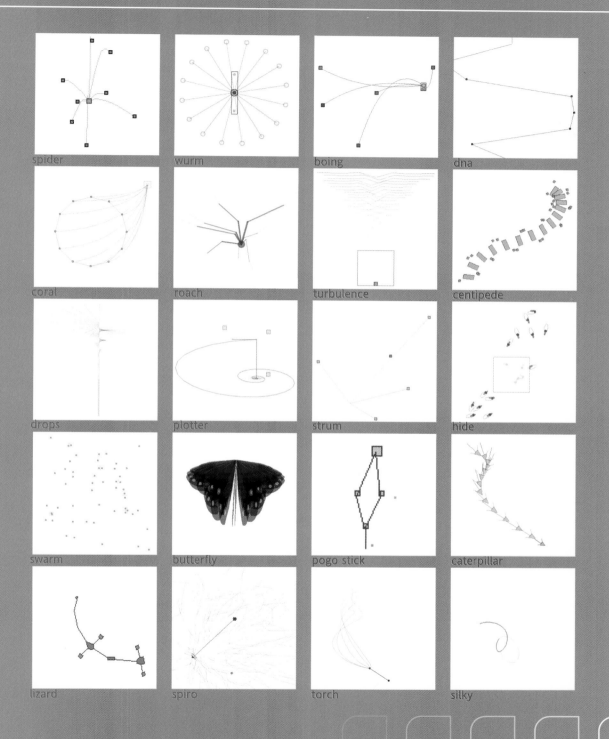

spider

wurm

boing

dna

coral

roach

turbulence

centipede

drops

plotter

strum

hide

swarm

butterfly

pogo stick

caterpillar

lizard

spiro

torch

silky

While I'm on the subject of the surreal, I also remember watching *Aliens* when it first came out. All I wanted was that big gun attached to the woman marine (I think her name was Chavez). I initially thought of using Lego sets to build it but the pieces were too small and not sturdy enough to create something that big. I did however have Construx. It was similar to Lego, except that all the pieces snapped together tight, allowing for more roughhousing. So for a week straight I experimented with creating new joint systems – something that the original pieces weren't intended to do. I ended up with something that was taller than I was at the time, and sturdy enough to withstand the pummeling of a ten year old. I'm twenty-five now and although I don't play with toys as much as I used to, I still love building them. Just like my Lego and Construx sets, I use Flash to build something out of my imagination. If you think about it, all my experiments are really just simple toys that I've made up to amuse others and myself. Play with them and they play back. And do you know why I make them all open-source? I want to share my ideas with others so they can build their own experiments for me to play with myself. This sounds really hokey but it's true.

In the rest of this chapter, I'll explain one of my little toys called *butterfly*. When I started ActionScripting, I began mimicking behaviors of simple walking creatures like the spider and roach. I always knew I wanted something that would fly, so my initial idea was of a bird flapping its wings. I imagined that as you played, you would be able to control the length of the wings and the speed at which a wing makes a full revolution. Gravity would be consistent and the bird would always be falling, so, depending upon how successfully you manipulated the controls, the bird would fly. After sketching this out about a billion times, I realized that that idea was a little too over my head. I couldn't quite figure out the relationship between the length of the wings and the speed at which it flutters and how it relates to the displacement of the bird's body. This meant that I put the idea on the back burner, waiting until I understood enough math and physics to make it fly.

Later on, I looked back at my sketchbook and found a simple chart I made to visualize the differences between a big bird and a small bird. The small bird was a hummingbird, with wings that would beat at such a fast pace you wouldn't be able to see them. Seeing this small bird suddenly made me switch from trying to recreate the motion of a bird to the motion of a small insect, the butterfly. After doing some sketches, I slowly focused my attention away from the flapping of the wings to the color and forms of a butterfly's wings. I looked up butterflies in my Audubon animal book and noticed that a single wing is based on the repetition of a single pattern over an area. As you'll see over the next few pages, with Flash 5's new color object this all became possible.

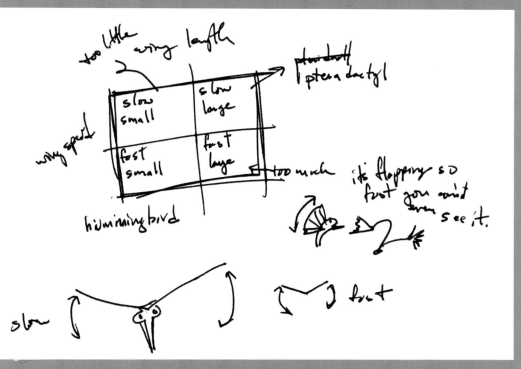

Before we start with the meat and potatoes of this section, you need to know what you're getting into. First off, there are no tweens in this chapter. Everything we do we'll do with ActionScript and recursive scripting, so you need to be comfortable with writing a few lines of code. You may be thinking "Well, why not just do it with keyframes and pre-built wing movie clips instead of all this long-winded scripting stuff?".

There are two main reasons for this. First, scripting usually results in smaller file size because the data is generated during runtime rather than having to be downloaded. Second up, we can change our butterfly to create new variations on the themes by changing our script parameters. Because we can change these dynamically, we can even get into random mutation and generate new species – something that's impossible with the more pedestrian graphical solution.

The other thing you should know before we start is that creating this butterfly was an iterative process. Before I made the butterfly, I created some experiments that used a simple script that moved objects around, called *Plotter*. This script is the basis for the creating and flapping of the butterfly wings.

To begin with, we'll go through a brief discussion on the progenitor of our butterfly, `plotter.fla`. You'll need to run it to see what it actually does – it creates pretty spirals.

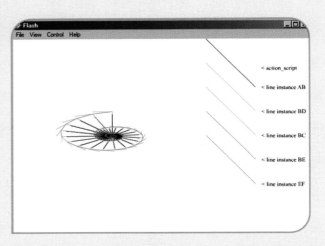

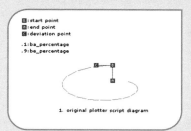

1. original plotter script diagram

This effect is built up stage by stage. First, I created the spiral by drawing an L shape ABC and then drawing subsequent versions of the same shape (that are always based on the last version).

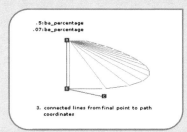

2. changed variables to create smooth path

Here you can see the path that the developing ABC shape actually traces out as I keep drawing scaled and rotated versions of the same L shape.

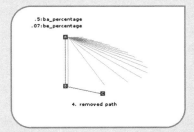

3. connected lines from final point to path coordinates

These next two figures show how I'm now no longer thinking in terms of an L shape, but a single line. You can see that the second is almost a skeleton version of the final wing shape; you only have to make the final jump of replacing the vector line 'bones' into full-blooded petals to see what I mean.

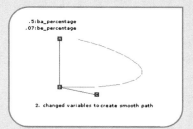

4. removed path

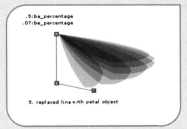

5. replaced line with petal object

Take a look at this.

If you want to look at the exact evolution of `plotter.fla`, take a look at the FLA on the CD with this book. For more explanation you can go to ww.friendsofed.com where you'll find a tutorial as a supplement to this chapter.

For now, back to our butterfly. So what exactly *is* a butterfly wing? Well...

From my observations (which might completely conflict with established laws of nature) I noticed that a butterfly is comprised of four wings which act very similarly. Each wing consists of a petal that is duplicated six times (six is just an arbitrary number). Each petal consists of four spots that change in color. We don't want to make a weird Technicolor butterfly that looks tacky, so all spots share the same color and size characteristics.

Let's quickly break down each observation into general components. The order might be weird but it's easier to start off with some simple components and work our way to the harder stuff:

1. Create a wing from petals.

2. Create a butterfly from four wings.

3. Flap the wings.

4. Create the petals from spots.

5. Use the color object.

6. Add the final touches

So we need to create a wing. As I've said, the wing is comprised of six petals. Each petal has the same *x* and *y* coordinates. What makes each one different is scaling. By scaling each petal along a different point of a curve you create the smooth wing. But where can we find a smooth curve? The answer to that is in the plotter script. The plotter is broken down into two parts; the first part initializes the variables and the second executes those variables continuously until told to stop. I wrote it here using `onClipEvents`. To get it working, you would need to attach this to a dummy blank movie clip on the stage at the same time as our petal movie clip.

```
onClipEvent (load) {
      x = 1;
a_x = 0;
a_y = 0;
b_x = 0;
b_y = 110;
c_x = 80;
c_y = 114;
ba_percentage = .05;
be_percentage = .7;
}

onClipEvent (EnterFrame) {
// ======================
// DRAWS OBJECT
// ======================
duplicateMovieClip ("petal", "petal" + x, x);
 ["petal" + x]._x = a_x;
 ["petal" + x]._y = a_y;
 ["petal" + x]._xscale = b_x-a_x;
 ["petal" + x]._yscale = b_y-a_y;
// ======================
// CALCULATES POSITIONING
// ======================
d_x = ((a_x-b_x)*ba_percentage)+b_x;
d_y = ((a_y-b_y)*ba_percentage)+b_y;
e_x = b_x-(b_x-c_x)-(b_x-d_x);
e_y = b_y-(b_y-c_y)-(b_y-d_y);
f_x = e_x-((b_x-e_x)*be_percentage);
f_y = e_y-((b_y-e_y)*be_percentage);
// ======================
// SWITCHES VARIABLES
// ======================
b_x = e_x;
b_y = e_y;
c_x = f_x;
c_y = f_y;
x++;
}
```

Flutter

```
Object Actions
  Object Actions                                                    ? ►
 + -  Object Actions                                             ▼ ▲
onClipEvent (load) {
    x = 1;
    a_x = 0;
    a_y = 0;
    b_x = 0;
    b_y = 110;
    c_x = 80;
    c_y = 114;
    ba_percentage = .05;
    be_percentage = .7;
}
onClipEvent (enterFrame) {
    //======================================
    // DRAWS OBJECT
    //======================================
    duplicateMovieClip ("petal", "petal"+x, x);
    ["petal"+x]._x = a_x;
    ["petal"+x]._y = a_y;
    ["petal"+x]._xscale = b_x-a_x;
    ["petal"+x]._yscale = b_y-a_y;
    //======================================
    // CALCULATES POSITIONING
    //======================================
    d_x = ((a_x-b_x)*ba_percentage)+b_x;
    d_y = ((a_y-b_y)*ba_percentage)+b_y;
    e_x = b_x-(b_x-c_x)-(b_x-d_x);
    e_y = b_y-(b_y-c_y)-(b_y-d_y);
    f_x = e_x-((b_x-e_x)*be_percentage);
    f_y = e_y-((b_y-e_y)*be_percentage);
    //======================================
    // SWITCHES VARIABLES
    //======================================
    b_x = e_x;
    b_y = e_y;
    c_x = f_x;
    c_y = f_y;
    x++;
}
                              I

Line 39 of 39, Col 1
```

At first glance this looks intimidating, but don't worry – it really isn't that bad. The `onClipEvent (Load)` requires you to input a simple series of numbers. They are:

The starting points of the petal `b_x` and `b_y`.

The ending points of the petal `a_x` and `a_y` – so the line that forms the 'skeleton' of our petal is the line joining the points `b_x`, `b_y` to `a_x`, `a_y`.

The deviation direction points `c_x` and `c_y`.

The distance/increment between each object (or the distance the curve would spiral on every iteration in `plotter.fla`); `ba_percentage`.

The deviation amount of the curve or a measure of how much the spiral curves; `be_percentage`

`x` – a simple counter

The `onClipEvent (EnterFrame)` takes these numbers and plots them into a scary looking equation. Understanding that chunk of code is a chapter in itself, so all I'll say here is that we just need to mess with the *draw object* part of the script.

OK, so how do we incorporate this into the butterfly? It will take a little massaging to make it work. First off, we need to create a way out of this loop. We could use a `gotoAndStop()` to proceed to the next frame to exit the `onClipEvent(EnterFrame)`, but I find that a little on the sloppy side because the ActionScript would require using redundant frames. We could also just let it run and nest it within a loop, or something similar, but that means it would be processing still and you'd be wasting valuable CPU cycles. Instead, I prefer reverting back to using frame-based ActionScript techniques.

```
Frame 1:
stop ();

Frame 2:
x = 7;
a_x = 0;
a_y = 0;
b_x = 0;
b_y = 110;
c_x = 80;
c_y = 114;
ba_percentage = .05;
be_percentage = .7;

Frame 3:
// =======================
// DRAWS OBJECT
// =======================
duplicateMovieClip ("_parent.petal", "petal" + x, x);
_parent["petal" + x]._x = a_x;
_parent["petal" + x]._y = a_y;
_parent["petal" + x]._xscale = b_x-a_x;
_parent["petal" + x]._yscale = b_y-a_y;
// =======================
// CALCULATES POSITIONING
// =======================
d_x = ((a_x-b_x)*ba_percentage)+b_x;
d_y = ((a_y-b_y)*ba_percentage)+b_y;
e_x = b_x-(b_x-c_x)-(b_x-d_x);            (continues overleaf)
```

```
e_y = b_y-(b_y-c_y)-(b_y-d_y);
f_x = e_x-((b_x-e_x)*be_percentage);
f_y = e_y-((b_y-e_y)*be_percentage);
// =====================
// SWITCHES VARIABLES
// =====================
b_x = e_x;
b_y = e_y;
c_x = f_x;
c_y = f_y;


Frame 4:
if (x<=1) {
      gotoAndStop (1);
} else {
      x--;
      gotoAndPlay (3);
}
```

If you're not familiar with the fact that you can actually insert variables in a path by enclosing them in [] brackets, you could be forgiven for thinking I'm doing something odd with arrays or some other long-winded Flash 4 technique. I promise you, I'm not. Rather, I'm using Flash 5's new feature of adding square brackets into the path to tell Flash '*This part of the path is a variable*'. In Flash 4, we used to have to mess about with all sorts of tricks to achieve the same effect, but no more!

We dropped the Stop frame in at the beginning so it will only run when something else targets it to go to frame 2. To repeat the object six times, we use a simple counter. I reversed the counter from 7 counting back to 1 because the final outcome looked prettier to me when I originally created the butterfly. If you're uncomfortable with this, you can switch it back by counting up instead of down – simply set x to 1, change the if/else statement to x>=7 and change x–to x++.

So we've got this far, now what? Well for starters, we haven't even made a Flash file yet, so let's do that right now. Create a new movie at 60 frames per second – which essentially means 'run as fast as you can'.

Rather than create versions of all the following movie clips on the stage, we'll create all the following symbols in the Library. This is because our butterfly wing will be created in real time from an initially blank screen, pulling in the required symbols dynamically from the Library (rather than us having to position everything manually).

You might not have done something like this before, which is all the more reason to try it. Here goes...

Create a movie clip called duplicate_petal_object_script and drop our code (the four frame script that we've just seen) inside it.

Now create another movie clip in the Library called petal and draw a simple wing that looks like this:

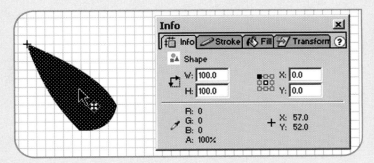

Using the Info panel, select the entire wing so that its absolute position is at the (0,0) coordinate and its width and height are 100px. Don't worry if the wing isn't exactly at the 100px mark. As long as it's no bigger than 100px you should be OK. This is because our code will scale the petal based on a 0 to 100% value, and making our petal 100 pixels square means we can easily see what the outcome will be.

Create another movie clip called wing and make sure you have two layers. The top layer is for the Stop action and the bottom is for our movie clips. Drag the petal and duplicate_petal_object_script clips into the layer, positioning both instances on the (0,0) coordinate. Name the instances in line with their movie clip names – give petal the instance name petal, and so on.

Set the alpha of wing to 25% so we can see all the petal iterations; without it, it would look like one big glob.

On the main timeline, mirror the situation in the wing movie clip by having a top layer for the Stop action and a bottom layer for movie clips. Whenever I create a new symbol, I have a tendency to put Stop actions in because I'm always afraid that the movie clips will interfere with the processing power. I'm not sure if it even affects anything, but it's better to be safe than sorry.

Finally, drop our wing movie clip in onto the stage for an initial test run and name the instance wing. To give it a test run, let's create an invisible button and put that into the main timeline.

Here's the ActionScript:

```
on (release) {
// ACTIVATES duplicate_wing_object_script ============
wing.duplicate_petal_object_script.gotoAndPlay(2);
}
```

When you publish the movie and click on the invisible movie clip, a butterfly wing should emerge. Cool huh?

Creating a butterfly from four wings

Now that we've created a wing, let's make three more. All we have to do is duplicate the existing wing, set the *x* and *y* coordinates to the same points for each wing and scale appropriately. Instead of using the duplicateMovieClip action, let's use a new action called attachMovie(). It works the same way as duplicateMovieClip but there's no need to have a master symbol on the timeline. It automatically links from the Library (as I said it would earlier), making things much cleaner. Delete everything on the stage from the last step.

The first thing we need to do is declare the wing symbol as a link. Right-click or CTRL-click on the wing movie clip in the Library and select Linkage.

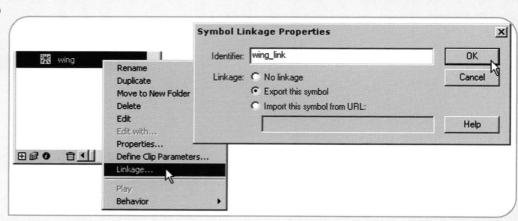

Click on Export this symbol and make the Identifier wing_link. That's about it. Now let's write the code. Since this is a one-time load, we can probably add the script on the main timeline on frame 1 of the first layer. Above the existing Stop action, write:

```
// =========================================================
// THIS SCRIPT CREATES THE 4 WINGS OF THE BUTTERFLY
// =========================================================
butterfly_xpos = 200;
butterfly_ypos = 100;
// =====================
// TOP LEFT
// =====================
attachMovie ("wing_link", "wing_top_left", 4);
wing_top_left._x = butterfly_xpos;
wing_top_left._y = butterfly_ypos;
wing_top_left._xscale = -100;
wing_top_left._yscale = 100;
// =====================
// TOP RIGHT
// =====================
attachMovie ("wing_link", "wing_top_right", 3);
wing_top_right._x = butterfly_xpos;
wing_top_right._y = butterfly_ypos;
wing_top_right._xscale = 100;
wing_top_right._yscale = 100;
// =====================
// BOTTOM LEFT
// =====================
attachMovie ("wing_link", "wing_bottom_left", 2);
wing_bottom_left._x = butterfly_xpos;
wing_bottom_left._y = butterfly_ypos;
wing_bottom_left._xscale = 60;
wing_bottom_left._yscale = 160;
// =====================
// BOTTOM RIGHT
// =====================
attachMovie ("wing_link", "wing_bottom_right", 1);
wing_bottom_right._x = butterfly_xpos;
wing_bottom_right._y = butterfly_ypos;
wing_bottom_right._xscale = -60;
wing_bottom_right._yscale = 160;
// =====================
stop ();
```

Flutter

```
// this script creates the 4 quadrants of the butterfly

butterfly_xpos = 200;
butterfly_ypos = 100;

// top_left

attachMovie ("wing_link", "wing_top_left", 4);
wing_top_left._x = butterfly_xpos;
wing_top_left._y = butterfly_ypos;
wing_top_left._xscale = -100;
wing_top_left._yscale = 100;

// top_right

attachMovie ("wing_link", "wing_top_right", 3);
wing_top_right._x = butterfly_xpos;
wing_top_right._y = butterfly_ypos;
wing_top_right._xscale = 100;
wing_top_right._yscale = 100;

// bottom_left

attachMovie ("wing_link", "wing_bottom_left", 2);
wing_bottom_left._x = butterfly_xpos;
wing_bottom_left._y = butterfly_ypos;
wing_bottom_left._xscale = 60;
wing_bottom_left._yscale = 160;

// bottom_right

attachMovie ("wing_link", "wing_bottom_right", 1);
wing_bottom_right._x = butterfly_xpos;
wing_bottom_right._y = butterfly_ypos;
wing_bottom_right._xscale = -60;
wing_bottom_right._yscale = 160;

stop ();
```

Since the *x* and *y* coordinates are the same for all the wing parts (butterfly_xpos and butterfly_ypos), the first thing we've done here is declare these variables. Changing the *x* and *y* scale requires some minor fudging, but the key is to make sure you use opposing numbers. If you change the xscale of the right wing to 100%, you have to change the xscale of the left wing to -100%. So now we have a boring-looking butterfly. It's not really doing anything right now. Let's make the wings flap!

Flapping the wings

How do we make the wings flap? There are two ways of doing this. We can use sine and cosine to create the flapping motion, but that might be overkill for something like this. If you're interested, here's the code snippet::

```
[wing._xscale = Math.sin(x/Math.PI/speed)*radius + offset]
```

where speed, radius, and offset are variables and x is a counter.

Another way is to use the plotter script. I found out that changing a few variables of the plotter script creates a similar flapping motion. Instead of duplicating an instance along a path, the plotter script will move an instance over time along that same path. This is a good time to use the onClipEvent handlers because the flapping motion goes on indefinitely.

First, create a new blank movie clip in the Library and name it on_clipevent_object. Place it on the first layer of the main timeline (the movie clip layer) and attach the following script:

```
onClipEvent (load) {
  x_scale_offset = 150;
  a_x = 200;
  a_y = 200;
  b_x = 200;
  b_y = 190;
  c_x = 201;
  c_y = 190;
  ba_percentage = .001;
  be_percentage = 1;
}
onClipEvent (enterFrame) {
  // ============================================
  // CREATES FLAPPING MOTION FOR EACH WING
  // ============================================
  _parent.wing_top_left._xscale = (b_x-x_scale_offset)*-1;
  _parent.wing_top_right._xscale = b_x-x_scale_offset;
  _parent.wing_bottom_left._xscale = (b_x-
  ➥x_scale_offset)*.65*-1;
  _parent.wing_bottom_right._xscale = (b_x-
  ➥x_scale_offset)*.65;
  // =====================
  // CALCULATES POSITIONING
  // =====================
  d_x = ((a_x-b_x)*ba_percentage)+b_x;
  d_y = ((a_y-b_y)*ba_percentage)+b_y;
  e_x = b_x-(b_x-c_x)-(b_x-d_x);
  e_y = b_y-(b_y-c_y)-(b_y-d_y);
  f_x = e_x-((b_x-e_x)*be_percentage);
  f_y = e_y-((b_y-e_y)*be_percentage);
  // =====================
  // SWITCHES VARIABLES
  // =====================
  b_x = e_x;
  b_y = e_y;
  c_x = f_x;
  c_y = f_y;
}
```

There are three things to notice. The first is that we're only scaling along one axis (flapping actions only occur on one plane – in our case it's *x*), so we don't have to bother with *y* anymore (I left the *y* script within the code because it doesn't really affect the outcome.)

The second thing is the appearance of the x_scale_offset. If I didn't add it, the wings would look like they were scaling out even more than they are now. Fiddle with the offsets if you want to see for yourself.

The third thing is the direction in which each wing flaps. By multiplying the left wings by -1, they reverse the direction from left/right to right/left. The bottom wings shouldn't come out too much, so I reduced the wing motion to 65% of the wings up top. You can change this number to whatever you want. I chose 65% because I thought it was visually appealing. When you publish the FLA and click on the invisible button, we have a butterfly flapping its wings.

```
Object Actions
Object Actions
+  -  Object Actions
onClipEvent (load) {
    x_scale_offset = 150;
    a_x = 200;
    a_y = 200;
    b_x = 200;
    b_y = 190;
    c_x = 201;
    c_y = 190;
    ba_percentage = .001;
    be_percentage = 1;
}
onClipEvent (enterFrame) {
    //===============================
    // CREATES FLAPPING MOTION FOR EACH WING
    //===============================
    _parent.wing_top_left._xscale = (b_x-x_scale_offset)*-1;
    _parent.wing_top_right._xscale = b_x-x_scale_offset;
    _parent.wing_bottom_left._xscale = (b_x-x_scale_offset)*.65*-1;
    _parent.wing_bottom_right._xscale = (b_x-x_scale_offset)*.65;
    //===============================
    // CALCULATES POSITIONING
    //===============================
    d_x = ((a_x-b_x)*ba_percentage)+b_x;
    d_y = ((a_y-b_y)*ba_percentage)+b_y;
    e_x = b_x-(b_x-c_x)-(b_x-d_x);
    e_y = b_y-(b_y-c_y)-(b_y-d_y);
    f_x = e_x-((b_x-e_x)*be_percentage);
    f_y = e_y-((b_y-e_y)*be_percentage);
    //===============================
    // SWITCHES VARIABLES
    //===============================
    b_x = e_x;
    b_y = e_y;
    c_x = f_x;
    c_y = f_y;
}

Line 38 of 38, Col 1
```

Depending on your computer processor, the butterfly is probably flapping really slowly. The problem is that as the browser is constantly rendering the object. Flash is also telling it to anti-alias the edges, making it look very smooth and real pretty. This hogs up processor time and slows down the overall speed of the movie. A quick fix is to go into the Publish Settings of the movie and set the movie quality to low. That way it can spend all its processing power on the script and nothing else. It's pretty plain right now, so let's start adding some color.

Creating the petals from spots

A real butterfly wing is made up of several colored areas that I'll call *spots*. In our virtual butterfly wing, each spot will read a series of variables that tell it which color to use and how large or small it should be. So first we need to create those spots. The best way to do this without disrupting any of the other code is to do it at the petal level. This way the rest of the code doesn't see any difference between a wing with spots and a wing without them, and will quite happily cause them to flap in either case.

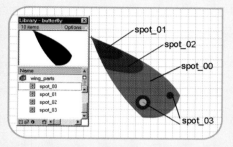

First, go into the Library and grab the petal movie clip. We need to chop up the single colored vector drawing into four movie clips, representing the different spot areas.

The largest spot area is the wing background, which I've called spot_00. Then comes an inner and outer band of color, which I've called spot_01 and spot_02. Finally, there are the butterfly dots, which I've called spot_03. If we vary the colors of these four currently gray areas, hopefully a fully-fledged colored butterfly wing will emerge.

The quickest way to do this is to convert the existing drawing to a movie clip. Select the object and go to Insert > Convert to Symbol. Name this spot_00 and declare it a movie clip. The dumb thing about Flash is that when you convert an object to a movie clip, it repositions the registration point of that object to the center. We need to reposition the movie clip instance to the (0,0) point and then we need to go into spot_00 and reposition the drawing back to the (0,0) point.

A really good habit to pick up in Flash is to understand where the registration point is for all movie clips that you create. In the case of the butterfly, all objects move and pivot at one specific point on the screen. Through trial and error, I found it easier to code by simply positioning the registration point on the top left of each object (you can see this by looking at the spot_00 to spot_03 movie clips in the Library of the finished `butterfly.fla`).

So we have this new movie clip symbol called spot_00. Now duplicate the symbol three more times so we have a total of four movie clips, called spot_00, spot_01, spot_02, and spot_03 respectively. We then need to start cutting up each movie clip to reflect the colored areas as I showed you in the last diagram.

I decided that spot_00 should be the base of the petal. This way, no matter how extravagant each spot becomes, it will still resemble a butterfly shape. A quick thing to note about the color of the spot is that the color action will create a color relative to the color of the spot now. If you have a light gray spot and set the color action to a red, you'll end up with a light red color. It gets even screwier and more unreliable when you start using a color like blue for the spot symbol. The only reliable way to create color actions is to use a black symbol, which gives us the widest spectrum (0-255) and completely accurate color. What does this all mean for the butterfly? We simply have to make the spot areas black when we've finished creating them.

OK, so now we have our four spots. Let's put them within the petal symbol. Delete what's already there, that is the spot_00 instance. It should now be a completely blank movie clip. Again, set it out so there are two layers: a top layer for the `Stop` action and a bottom layer for the movie clip instance.

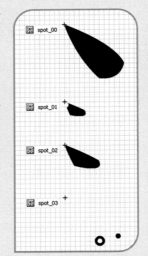

Drop all four movie clips into the bottom frame and change the alpha of all four instances to 50%, just so we can see it (later on, we'll refine the alphas of each spot). We need to make sure all spots are exactly positioned at the (0,0) coordinate points and that they are stacked numerically so that spot_00 is on the bottom and spot_03 is on top. Once again we give each instance the name of its corresponding symbol. Unless the symbol has weird properties, I usually do this as a force of habit to name instances the same as the symbol — for me it avoids confusion.

Using the color object

We now have everything set up for the scripts. Changing the color of each spot happens only once, so using an `onClipEvent(Load)` is a good way to start. We'll put this script onto the spots themselves, but we first need to make sure that the code works.

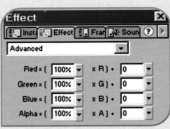

The values that you can use in color object transformations are identical to the six sliders you see on the Effect > Advanced panel, so playing about with them manually gives you an idea of what's possible dynamically with the color transform object and method.

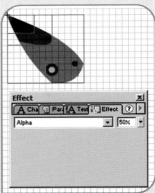

Here's the code. The color `setTransform` method allows you to specify values for all eight sliders, but my transformations will only look at three: the red, blue, and green offsets `rb`, `gb`, and `bb`.

```
onClipEvent (load) {
  // =============================================
  // color object of spot 00
  // =============================================
  // declares color object
  wing_color_spot_00 = new Color(_parent.spot_00);

  // populates color object
```

```
new_color_spot_00 = {
    rb:0,
    gb:0,
    bb:204
};

// sets color of object
wing_color_spot_00.setTransform(new_color_spot_00);
// ==============================================
}
```

The first line of code creates a new color object (in this case I've called it wing_color_spot_00). The second line is an object with methods rb, gb, bb – which corresponds to the actions of the xR, xG and xB sliders in the Effect panel above. If you're interested, you can access the other slider functionalities by adding additional methods to new_color_spot_00 of ra, ga, ba (corresponding to the Red, Green, Blue sliders) and aa and ab (which does the same as the two alpha sliders at the bottom of the panel). If you read the ActionScript dictionary, you'll see Macromedia's 'official' descriptions of the methods (but you may prefer to play about with the panel sliders to see what they *do* rather than what they *are*).

> ra is the percentage for the red component (-100 to 100).
> rb is the offset for the red component (-255 to 255).
> ga is the percentage for the green component (-100 to 100).
> gb is the offset for the green component (-255 to 255).
> ba is the percentage for the blue component (-100 to 100).
> bb is the offset for the blue component (-255 to 255).
> aa is the percentage for alpha (-100 to 100).
> ab is the offset for alpha (-255 to 255).

As I've said, all we needed to use was the rb, gb, and bb in our array. All the other parameters just overcomplicate matters. I used a specific color (dark blue, actually) for now. We're just testing to make sure this will work. The last line of code uses the setTransform() action to set the color to spot_00. When we publish the FLA and click on our invisible button, it works. The color of the wings becomes blue. Notice, however, that we get a rather light blue, instead of the dark blue that should be there. To make it look right, we just need to change the alpha of the wing instance from 25% to 100%.

But now there's only one color being used. How can we dynamically change the color? Well, we have a button on the main timeline that creates the wing from the petals.

We could just add the color changing scripts there:

```
on (release) {
  // ACTIVATES duplicate_wing_object_script =============
  wing_top_left.duplicate_petal_object_script.
  ➥gotoAndPlay(2);
  wing_top_right.duplicate_petal_object_script.
  ➥gotoAndPlay(2);

wing_bottom_left.duplicate_petal_object_script.gotoAndPlay(2);

wing_bottom_right.duplicate_petal_object_script.gotoAndPlay(2);
  // COLOR_VALUES SPOT_0 ================================
  red_spot_00 = Math.random()*255;
  green_spot_00 = Math.random()*255;
  blue_spot_00 = Math.random()*255;

}
```

If we do things this way, the spot color script will grab the color values from the main timeline. Now we need to revise the color object script:

```
onClipEvent (load) {
  // ==========================================
  // color object of spot 00
  // ==========================================
  // initializes color object
  wing_color_spot_00 = new Color(_parent.spot_00);

  // populates color object
  new_color_spot_00 = {
      rb:_parent._parent._parent.red_spot_00,
      gb:_parent._parent._parent.green_spot_00,
      bb:_parent._parent._parent.blue_spot_00
  };

  // sets color of object
  wing_color_spot_00.setTransform(new_color_spot_00);
  // ==========================================
}
```

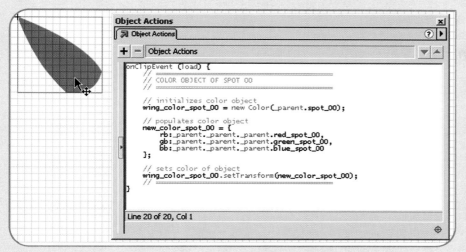

If you noticed, instead of using the `_root` action, I used `_parent` three times. Although it might be difficult to write at first, it pays off in the long run because in the future, you might have to embed this movie into another movie, thus screwing up the levels. If you use `_parent`, it's guaranteed to work no matter how deep you embed this movie.

Publish this and click on the invisible button. The butterfly constantly changes colors. Cool, huh? Now let's just add the color object action to all the other colors, making sure to change any instance of 00 to 01, 02, 03 respectively. Here's the updated code for the button on the main timeline:

```
on (release) {
  // ACTIVATES duplicate_wing_object_script =============

wing_top_left.duplicate_petal_object_script.gotoAndPlay(2);

wing_top_right.duplicate_petal_object_script.gotoAndPlay(2);

wing_bottom_left.duplicate_petal_object_script.gotoAndPlay(2);

wing_bottom_right.duplicate_petal_object_script.gotoAndPlay(2);
  // COLOR_VALUES SPOT_0 ================================
  red_spot_00 = Math.random()*102;
  green_spot_00 = Math.random()*102;
  blue_spot_00 = Math.random()*102;
  // COLOR_VALUES SPOT_1 ================================
  red_spot_01 = Math.random()*255;
  green_spot_01 = Math.random()*102;
  blue_spot_01 = Math.random()*102;
  // COLOR_VALUES SPOT_2 ================================
  red_spot_02 = Math.random()*153;
```

(continues overleaf)

407

```
green_spot_02 = Math.random()*153;
blue_spot_02 = Math.random()*153;
// COLOR_VALUES SPOT_3 ================================
red_spot_03 = Math.random()*255;
green_spot_03 = Math.random()*255;
blue_spot_03 = Math.random()*255;
// ====================================================
}
```

Object Actions

Movie Explorer | Object Actions

Object Actions

```
on (release) {
    // ACTIVATES duplicate_wing_object_script =============
    wing_top_left.duplicate_petal_object_script.gotoAndPlay(2);
    wing_top_right.duplicate_petal_object_script.gotoAndPlay(2);
    wing_bottom_left.duplicate_petal_object_script.gotoAndPlay(2);
    wing_bottom_right.duplicate_petal_object_script.gotoAndPlay(2);
    // COLOR_VALUES SPOT_0 ================================
    red_spot_00 = Math.random()*102;
    green_spot_00 = Math.random()*102;
    blue_spot_00 = Math.random()*102;
    // COLOR_VALUES SPOT_1 ================================
    red_spot_01 = Math.random()*255;
    green_spot_01 = Math.random()*102;
    blue_spot_01 = Math.random()*102;
    // COLOR_VALUES SPOT_2 ================================
    red_spot_02 = Math.random()*153;
    green_spot_02 = Math.random()*153;
    blue_spot_02 = Math.random()*153;
    // COLOR_VALUES SPOT_3 ================================
    red_spot_03 = Math.random()*255;
    green_spot_03 = Math.random()*255;
    blue_spot_03 = Math.random()*255;
    // ================================================
}
```

I changed the random amount for the variables associated with spot_00 and for spot_02 because I wanted those to be a lot darker than the others. You can go nuts by changing the random amounts for any of the four colors, but alas, this is a tutorial. You can change all this later. Although the values should be whole numbers, the random values shown here will be decimal. Flash doesn't seem to mind, but, if you do, all you have to do is add a Math.round into the color values, like this, for example:

```
red_spot_00 = Math.round(Math.random()*102);
```

Final touches

The butterfly is basically finished, but we need to add some finishing touches. First off, make sure the invisible button in the main timeline spans across the entire movie clip. This way, wherever you click on the movie, the butterfly will change color. You can adjust the alphas of our spot instances to make it richer in color or more opaque, depending on your preference.

I'm not going to go too in-depth with any added touches because I really want you to figure it out for yourself. A couple of things you could think about include maybe changing the direction of the butterfly dynamically or even making it move and wander about.

So where does this leave us? At one level we have a butterfly that can change its color, but more fundamentally, we've defined our butterfly wings in purely mathematical terms. There are a number of side effects of this, and we have only used one of them: the ability to dynamically change color. We can also change anything else, be it wing shape, size, or another variable. In fact, by changing our iterative 'build a wing' equations, we could just as easily create colored beetles or birds of paradise.

That's the beauty of controlling everything by scripting – you can make slight changes to the code which can have profound effects on the final graphics and what they do. So now it's your turn to pull the code apart and put in new values and create new life forms, or even something totally abstract.

Because that's what Flash is all about...

Emulating butterflies may not be web design in the strictest sense, but Flash experiments are one of the best ways to hone your scripting prowess. All the Flash masters do this, from the regular experiments posted on Praystation to the strange dancing surrealism of James Paterson.

The thing is, if you do enough of these little trials, some new idea or direction usually falls out, and you have the basis for something practical.

Manuel concentrates on natural structures in his butterfly scripting experiments, but nature is a much bigger stage than that...

So what use is coding this up?

Who wants an ActionScript tree generator? Well, the tree parent-branch:daughter-branch relationships are found in all sorts of other programming structures because it's a definite hierarchy.

Code the tree up, and XML parsing gets slightly easier when you come to it...

preconceptions of trees

Look at a tree. We expect it to be a random collection of trunks and branches, but nothing in nature is ever haphazard, which is a good thing, because it allows us to re-create it

If the trunk splits into two branches, then the thickness of the trunk, a, is equal to the thickness of the two new branches, b+c.

Also, the angles that the two new branches make is largely dependent on the tree species. The rules that define the tree structure are the same at every level; a split at the trunk is the same as a split at the topmost twigs.

This means that you could build a tree-like structure by applying the same few simple rules again and again at every level of the tree.

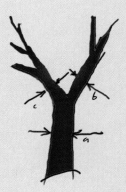

variety of species
Once you understand the butterfly wing construction, there is a plethora of other things you can also create...

A peacock tail is really no different. Instead of petals, you have feathers. Once you can create a single feather, consisting of a quill, feather shape and 'eye', you can arrange them into a tail.

Instead of flapping, you can create a peacock tail's opening/closing motion. Same goes for everything else from a flowerhead to a fish. Once you've sketched out the details of the way nature does it, it's just a question of getting the ActionScript to do the same.

"I won't try to instantly create a 'masterpiece', but rather structure a platform that embeds potential for further exploration."

Amit Pitaru
www.pitaru.com

413

Flux

How do we perceive Flash? Is Flash a production tool or an explorative one? Initially, Flash was created as a production tool for the purpose of creating motion-driven and interactive web content. Today, we're all dealing with usability issues that Flash raises in that regard, as we are collectively learning what are the best uses of Flash towards transmitting content onto the screen.

Growing up as a jazz musician, my first impression of Flash was slightly different; I wasn't driven by its original purposes as a production tool, but rather interested in its value as an explorative tool – a tool that provides interesting grounds for the exploration of ideas and concepts. Sometimes, these ideas are derived from the potential of the tool itself, but I also use the capabilities of Flash to answer questions that involve other fields, such as physics, biology, music, anthropology, and even raw emotions. In this respect, my production process of Flash content is similar to the improvisational techniques I use in jazz; during performance, a good jazz musician won't produce music for the audience, but rather lets the audience witness his explorations. Through the same concept, I consider my Flash work to be evidence of an exploration rather than a result of a predetermined production process. For me, a good SWF file is like a clear snapshot taken during a successful expedition that I began in order to explore an idea and to express particular emotions, just as I do with my music.

Realizing the correlations, I evolved my Flash skills in the same way a musician learns to freely improvise on an instrument. I would like to share with you some of the concepts that I borrowed from jazz to better express myself with Flash. For this purpose, let's first take a journey into the mind of a jazz musician, and than apply some of the knowledge back into our own realm.

Before we do though, let's preview how Flash production methods may relate to the notion of improvisation in jazz.

The connection exists in four main areas:

- The state of mind that initiates the improvisational process.

- The way in which musicians establish a structure that allows improvisation.

- The training and knowledge that produces the ability to successfully improvise through this structure.

- The outcome: the ability to constantly re-invent through knowledgeable creative exploration.

To shed light on these correlations, we should first reach a basic understanding of the foundation of jazz music. I'm aware that this may temporarily divert our attention from Flash, but it's also my hope that this 'detour' will pay off towards the second segment of this chapter. The full scope of the jazz language is a subject for an entire book, and indeed, several adequate books have been written on the subject. The following isn't meant to be a complete guide to jazz improvisation, but rather an introduction to the subject as it relates to this chapter. Throughout the chapter I'll provide 'in depth' insights, which, although not necessarily crucial to the overall purpose of this chapter, provide other key aspects of improvisation as well as reference for further resources. For a more fluid reading experience, I suggest disregarding these In depth segments during the first read.

The three disciplines of music

The three fundamental disciplines of the musical form are rhythm, melody, and harmony. A work of music can be deconstructed according to its rhythmic patterns, melodic motion, and harmonic composition. All three disciplines can be conveyed on paper, using musical notation language and staff paper.

I'll give you a brief description of how each discipline plays a fundamental part in music.

Rhythm

One of the basic properties of a piece of music is its tempo, or in other words speed, often indicated by an exact metronome marking. Using a metronome, tempo is measured in beats per minute (bpm), and is analogous to the frames per seconds (fps) value in Flash. Bigger fps values provide potential for faster movement in Flash, as frames move faster on the timeline, providing smaller units of time-segments. Just as fps and the frames on the timeline create the time-grid for Flash, tempo and 64th duration notes create the time-grid for music.

In depth: swing

While tempo is a universal aspect of music, jazz has a unique rhythmic feel that is impossible to describe analytically – it's called *swing*. Swing refers to the way jazz musicians divide the time-grid as they perform a piece of music. Swing can't be conveyed on paper, as it's not a clear static division of time measurements, but rather one that is in constant flux according to the dynamics of the music. While not as noticeable to the untrained ear, 'playing with swing' may probably be the hardest task that a jazz musician will face. For more information on swing, visit www.outsideshore.com/primer/primer/ms-primer-3.html#Swing

Melody

When we're singing or whistling a song we're really performing its *melody*. Melody can be defined as a change of a single note over time. As most of us can only sing one note at a time, we're confined to producing melody through our voice. In Flash, you could compare melody to the tweening of a single object between two keyframes. In music, this change would be applied to a single note and, in Flash, to a single graphic element. In both the change would occur over time.

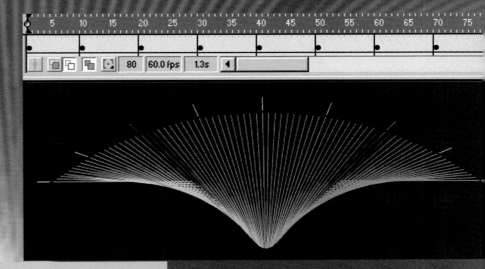

Right: a line, tweened over 80 frames, and viewed in multiple frames mode.
Below: a melodic sequence of notes

Pleasing time-based intervals in music and Flash:
A musical scale and a tweened object viewed in multiple-frames mode.

In depth: intervals

Melody and harmony are both derived from one origin: note *intervals*. An interval is simply the distance between two notes. Mathematically, it would mean a distance in frequencies (Hz). In music, the distance is measured in 'whole steps' or 'half steps' rather than actual frequency values. The difference between melodic and harmonic intervals lies in the factor of time: melodic intervals occur when two notes are played over time, while harmonic intervals occur when two notes are played simultaneously.

In this regard, melodic intervals may relate to time-based visual change such as animation, while harmonic intervals relate to a static visual composition. In both cases, our aesthetic senses differentiate between 'pleasing' intervals and 'disturbing' intervals, in the same manner that our minds register certain visuals as aesthetically 'pleasing', and others as 'ugly'. For more information, visit www.outsideshore.com/primer/primer/ms-primer-4-1.html#Intervals

Harmony

While a singer can only produce one note at a time, piano players can use all ten fingers at once. Playing several notes at once is called playing a *chord*. When piano players accompany singers, they play the right chords at the right time lining up with the singer's melody. By playing the right chords of the song, a piano player will produce the proper context for the singer's melody. Another term for the sequence of 'right chords' that are played during a song is *chord progression*. This provides the harmonic structure of the song. In Flash, we sometimes use multiple layers on one timeline, creating a composition of elements on the screen that are placed one on top of the other. We can compare the composition effect of multiple visual elements shown at once to the harmonic effect that chords produce.

Hidden connections – the structure

When a singer isn't conforming to the chords that the piano is providing, we say that he/she is singing 'out of tune'. Even without musical education, most of us feel that something is wrong. How does this happen?

Remember – the piano player is playing a sequence of chords throughout the song. In order to obtain the right tune, a singer has to use notes that 'fit' the specific chord that is played at that moment. If the singer is singing a pre-written melody, it's up to the songwriter to compose music with a 'fitting' chord-melody relationship, and up to the singer to accurately perform these notes.

Left: three elements placed vertically in 'layers', creating a visual composition.

Right: three notes, placed vertically to produce a musical 'chord' (harmony).

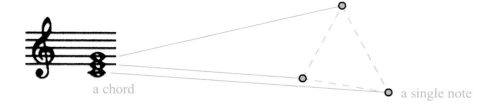

a chord

a single note

There are several musical rules that determine which notes fit a specific chord, and which don't. For starters, as each chord is actually a set of notes played simultaneously, it makes sense that these notes can also be used for the melody when the chord is played. Here's a visual example: suppose that I draw three pixels on the screen and ask you to imagine a triangle. I now ask you to place your mouse on a pixel that potentially 'belongs' to this triangle – anywhere on the imaginary delineating lines. Your best shot would be to place the mouse on one of the dots that originally defined the triangle. This is similar to singing one of the notes that make up the chord.

In addition to the notes that make up the chord, a songwriter could also use notes that are derived from the chord. These notes can be seen as an extension of the chord, and are called *scale notes*. How does this translate visually?

In our triangle, you could also choose to place the mouse anywhere between the points – on the connecting lines delineating the triangle. This would be similar to singing the scale notes that a chord allows.

In depth: scales

In reality, a composer may start with a melody, then choose chords to accompany it, and then re-adjust the melody according to the new chords. This cycle can repeat itself many times until the harmony and melody are meshed to the composer's satisfaction.

There are several musical rules that connect harmony and melody. These rules determine which notes may 'fit' a specific chord, or through the mirrored angle – which chord progression may 'fit' a specific melody. The key to this connection is a musical grid – the scale, or a group of eight notes. In theory, any group of notes can be named a scale, but over the years, we've learned to identify 'successful' scales as ones that are very useful towards composition due to the nature of the intervals in between each of the notes. For more information on chord-scale relationships, visit www.outsideshore.com/primer/primer/ms-primer-4.html

Flux

As you can see, there is a mathematical connection between the chord and the 'fitting notes', and apparently our brains can naturally do the math and figure out whether a singer is confirming to these rules. See the In depth section on intervals.

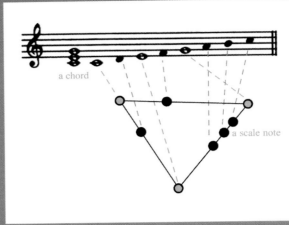

Improvising
As I've said, a song consists of a set of chords that play out in sequence (chord progression). Each one of these chords carries many fitting notes, and with them a vast array of opportunities for melody. A good songwriter will find an interesting 'path' of notes as the melody for his/her tune.

Using our triangle analogy, we can illustrate the song's chord progression like this:

In depth: improvisation
The improvisation method described in this chapter is called 'playing changes', as musicians use the harmonic change of the chord-progression towards developing new melodies.

Playing changes is considered the most basic improvisational technique, while more advanced methods enable greater freedom of exploration. These techniques include the use of special 'synthetic' scales that are not chord-related, as well as the use of rhythmic modulations, which provide an entire new dimension to explore. For more information on improvisational techniques, visit www.outsideshore.com/primer/primer/ms-primer-5.html

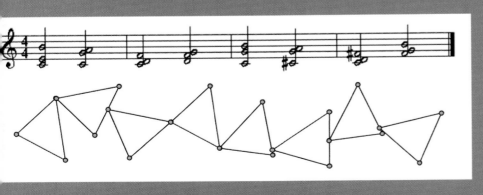

The song's melody will 'travel' through fitting notes of the chord progression:

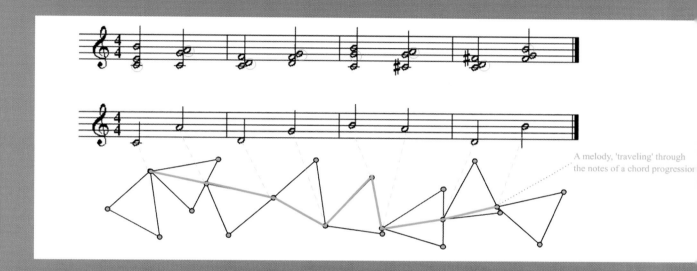

A melody, 'traveling' through the notes of a chord progression

Jazz musicians take pre-written songs (jazz standards), and improvise on their chords by inventing new paths. In other words, improvisation is a deviation from the pathway of fitting notes that was originally written for the song. Musicians will usually refer back to the original path while they're improvising. Here's how it would look visually:

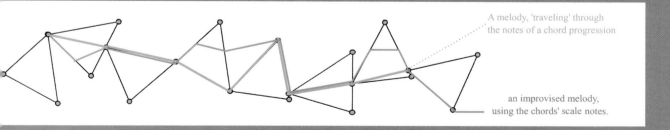

A melody, 'traveling' through the notes of a chord progression

an improvised melody, using the chords' scale notes.

Flux

Working with Flash

We've just witnessed the way that musicians establish a structure that allows improvisation, and also observed the knowledge that produces the ability to successfully improvise through this structure.

Let's see how these concepts may apply to Flash.

When jazz musicians choose a song to improvise on, they will either write it themselves, or more often pick an existing song that is known to be a good 'playing ground' towards improvisation. There are over a hundred songs that have been repeatedly picked by jazz musicians over the years for this purpose, called *jazz standards*. If we look at these, we can see that many of them aren't necessarily an 'accomplished masterpiece', but rather an adequate 'playing ground' towards improvisation. Of course, it helps to have a beautiful song to play on, but their significant strengths often lie in the interesting melodic/harmonic/rhythmic aspects, which provide a flexible structure towards improvisation.

I use a similar method during my Flash production process: when I start to structure a new Flash file, I won't try to instantly create a 'masterpiece', but rather structure a platform that embeds potential for further exploration. I would aim for a SWF file that provides fundamental quality as a standalone piece, yet welcomes change and modification without losing its core functionality. With this flexible structure at hand, I will start exploring its potential.

In jazz, the true potential of a song is materialized as musicians improvise on its harmonic structure – deviating from the basic melody of the song, while referring back to it. In the same way, I explore the potential of my work by modifying and extending the existing code of my file, then react to the outcome of my changes and repeat the cycle through further modifications. This cycle is the core process of improvisation, and to fluently perform throughout it, one must be well trained.

As we've learned, musicians train by learning how to use the harmonic structure of the song as a 'road map' towards deviating from its melody. When doing so, their ability to improvise relies on their harmonic, melodic and rhythmic skills applied to their specific instrument. In other words, regardless of the instrument a musician plays, for the purpose of improvisation he is required to train in all three disciplines of music. In the same way, I feel that it's important to acquire the adequate skills in Flash, by recognizing and mastering all that it has to offer. This is easier said than done, especially if you've never intended to deal with aspects of programming before. How do musicians deal with the need to study several different disciplines that are not all natural for them to begin with? Musicians don't confuse learning the disciplines of music and mastering an instrument. A piano player will study rhythm, not for the purpose of becoming a drummer but in order to enhance his musicianship. By the same token, people shouldn't confuse learning programming with becoming a programmer. A Flash designer should learn programming in order to compliment his overall Flash design skills, and not in order make a career change.

I think that this state of mind can release much of the pressure we may feel when we're covering new ground. It releases unrealistic comparisons to full time programmers, and focuses on the notion of extending knowledge through familiar territory. I found that the best way of starting out with ActionScript was to try to incorporate programming into my existing work, towards my current interests and needs. Any of us can learn ActionScript in small isolated portions that we can instantly apply to visual content on the stage. When we're starting out, many of these portions don't require comprehensive knowledge of programming, but rather an intuitive focused study on a specific subject of interest. Of course, not all code is accessible at first – and there's no way out of eventually learning basic concepts such as the dot syntax, and what variables are. But in general, if you're a visually oriented person, it's best to start with code that directly relates to visual elements. By getting an immediate visual response to your code you can actually 'see' yourself improve. After a while, you'll gain basic familiarity with ActionScript, which will prepare the grounds for the learning of more complex programming concepts. This learning method is similar to the manner of which pianists learn the higher levels of rhythmic patterns, and drummers learn concepts of harmony, all for the purpose of improvising on their own instruments.

To conclude, improvisation is a journey that involves unpredictability, which can be the thing that makes it so rewarding. Surely, it would be much easier to plan things ahead when you're performing in front of a judging crowd, but for jazz musicians, it's not the outcome, but the process itself that is of most significance. Under the pressure of performance, during these unpredictable moments hidden treasures surface as musicians test their capabilities. When we're exploring with Flash, we can also revolve our attention around the process rather than the outcome. By learning how to produce flexible structures, and later skillfully exploring them, we can also produce situations that, although unpredictable at first, may lead to surprisingly innovative results.

In the next section I'll take you through a deconstruction of one of my recent experiments: FLUX. As we go, I'll refer back to the issues that this chapter has raised so far regarding the correlations of jazz improvisation and experimentation with Flash. This segment will demonstrate how theory turns into tangible lines of code. Armed with the proper context through the previous segment, you'll be able to recognize the general logic of process that exists beyond this specific example. I believe that this is the best way for me to transfer knowledge in a manner that you could later superimpose onto your own work.

Usually, my work process starts off by dealing with a subject of interest through a specific angle. As a subject matter, lately, I've been interested in the methods in which we perceive systems in nature, and specifically the notion of a truly random phenomenon. For our expedition today, perhaps the following thought may provide a good angle to explore: as we discuss the manner in which humans perceive the creations of nature, maybe there is something to be learned from starting 'closer to home' – the way in which we perceive the creations of our own kind, for example, a work of art. Notice that I will not try to answer the 'dangerous' issue of judging art , but rather use it as a 'spring-board' towards the '_parent' concept.

When we're listening to music, or viewing an animation, our mind searches for the inner logic of the work. This inner logic doesn't have to be logical in the intellectual sense, nor even definable. Whether conscious or inspirational, this inner logic produces noticeable patterns in the work. We usually define these patterns as the artist's style and the work's overall flow.

Although flow is a time-based term, it may refer to all art forms, because regardless of the medium, all art forms embed a time-based production process. A work of art is constructed of many production cycles. In each cycle, a decision is made that changes the state of the work. If these decisions are driven by inner logic, then the sequence of changes will embed a flow.

Flux

What happens when we don't recognize such patterns (or flow) in a work of art? As these patterns are our evidence towards the inner logic of the work, not recognizing such patterns may lead us to define the art as random and arbitrary. Throughout our history, we've dismissed numerous genius artists during their lifetimes, because they were slightly ahead of their time. We didn't possess the intellectual ability or cultural consensus to perceive their work (in many cases, political and religious reasons, as well as other cultural consensus, have 'blinded' us from recognizing patterns). Failing to notice these patterns, we've wrongfully concluded that there is no inner logic to their work.

When extending this notion to nature, some questions come to mind. If we miss patterns in the work of our own species, we may be scoring very low points when it comes to recognizing patterns in the chaotic environment of nature – where systems interweave in a much more 'borderless' manner. Through extending our perception by using technology, we're moving at a fast pace towards finding inner logic in systems that were once considered random, and even non-existent. But examine the other side of the coin: could we identify a truly random phenomenon if we saw one? If a phenomenon is indeed random, how would we prove it? You could always claim that we simply can't see the patterns of its inner logic, in which case the phenomenon isn't random at all.

So, does true randomness exist, or is randomness just a measurement that indicates our failure to perceive the inner logic of a system? Perhaps flow and randomness are two opposite measurements on the spectrum of our perception. We say that something flows when we can clearly recognize the patterns that the inner logic produces. We define something as random when such patterns elude our human perception.

It would be interesting to explore this notion in a controlled environment, by creating a system that works through a defined inner logic, and can flux in and out of recognizable patterns – creating effects of both flow and randomness. While not attempting to prove a theorem, such a system may provide us with the experience of witnessing the borderline (threshold) of our ability to perceive inner logic, as it moves in and out of recognizable patterns.

With this in mind, it's time to turn to Flash. Let's start by connecting our concept to elements in Flash. I usually do so by asking myself a set of questions:

Firstly, what is the core of the concept as it relates to Flash? Here, the core concept is to produce a system that generates the effects of both flow and randomness, while working through a definable and consistent set of rules

(inner logic). Unlike a human artist's inner logic, Flash's inner logic can't be 'spiritual', but instead has to be clearly defined, as we don't yet posses the power to create 'spiritual machines'.

We now have a concept, but how can Flash produce the effects of randomness and flow? The easiest way for us to experience either flow or random effects is by physically witnessing something changing over time. Another way would be by witnessing the static result of a production process. For example, while a painting is a static image, producing the work is a time-based process, which embeds change – from an empty canvas to a complete work of art, and all the stages in between. In simple terms, Flash needs to produce some sort of changing environment, and either output the process in real-time, or output the final result of the process.

So, we need a changing environment, but how can Flash produce this? In art, a painter may create an oil painting using numerous brush strokes. Consider each brush stroke to be a production cycle that changes the current state of the painting. In Flash, each production cycle will include the execution of ActionScript code, rather than a brush stroke. The recurring execution of these production cycles will produce the changing environment that we're seeking.

The next question I ask myself is whether I can simplify and separate the functional elements that this system relies on. Yes I can! The system relies on two elements: change, and recurrence/repetition. Each production cycle will produce some sort of change to the environment, and executing the production cycle repeatedly will produce the overall process.

But which ActionScript/structuring elements relate to the concepts of change and recurrence/repetition in Flash? Let's start with the concept of recurrence/repetition. There are looping frames on the timeline (repetitive execution), the EnterFrame movie clip event (repetitive execution), and for statements (repeating a set of commands a defined number of times).

Now let's take a look at the concept of change. Bear in mind that in order to witness change, it must be applied to an object. We have a movie clip, which is an object to apply the change to, and instance properties provide the 'changeable' facets of the object. The Time/FPS rate provides us with a way to witness change through time – think of melody in music. The ability to duplicate movie clips provides a way to witness change through comparison of multiple objects, and relates to harmony in music. For future reference, let's call these elements the *building blocks*.

My final question is to ask myself how we can use these building blocks towards materializing our original concept. We can use the building blocks to help structure a file that conforms to our concept's guidelines of creating a system that works through production cycles to produce change whilst maintaining the system's inner logic. Throughout the production cycles, the engine will have to retain its original set of rules, always applying the same type of change.

With this in mind, let's get to work.

OK, first off, we want this project to have some kind of structure:

1. In the heart of the work, there will be a movie clip object, which will act as the subject of the applied change. To start with, this movie clip will be a simple visual object.

2. In general, I'll apply change to instances of this movie clip by modifying some of their properties (`_xscale`, `_yscale`, `_x`, `_y`, `_rotation`).

3. These changes will be noticeable by having many instances of the movie clip on stage, each with unique properties. Duplicating the original instance of the movie clip many times over will do this.

4. Just as in art, the overall process will be constructed of several production cycles. In each cycle, a new instance will be created, and then modified to a unique state.

Next, I've applied these four structuring notes to a Flash file. I've included this file, `flux_1.fla` on the CD. You may want to look at the relevant FLAs as we go through the tutorial.

Here's a screenshot of `flux_1.fla`. It displays the code that exists on the second frame of the timeline (this is the only code that currently exists in this file). Notice that I've defined our building blocks, which we'll refer to from now on as Area 1, Area 2. Area 3 and Area 4. Area 1 is the basic movie clip that will be the subject of all the changes we make. Areas 2-4 show the ActionScript split to coincide with the structure notes 2, 3 and 4 above. Take a minute and compare each Area with the correlating structuring note, and try to identify the different building blocks that are used to bring our original concept to life.

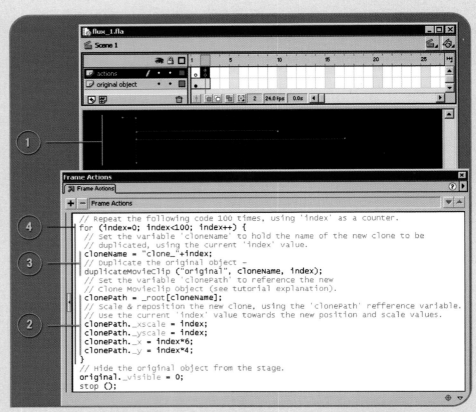

```
// Repeat the following code 100 times, using 'index' as a counter.
for (index=0; index<100; index++) {
    // Set the variable 'cloneName' to hold the name of the new clone to be
    // duplicated, using the current 'index' value.
    cloneName = "clone_"+index;
    // Duplicate the original object -
    duplicateMovieclip ("original", cloneName, index);
    // Set the variable 'clonePath' to reference the new
    // Clone Movieclip Object (see tutorial explanation).
    clonePath = _root[cloneName];
    // Scale & reposition the new clone, using the 'clonePath' refference variable.
    // Use the current 'index' value towards the new position and scale values.
    clonePath._xscale = index;
    clonePath._yscale = index;
    clonePath._x = index*6;
    clonePath._y = index*4;
}
// Hide the original object from the stage.
original._visible = 0;
stop ();
```

Let's go through this code line by line. Area 4 begins with a `for` loop:

```
for (index=0; index<100; index++) {
```

For the purpose of creating production cycles, I'm using this `for` statement, and the variable `index` as a counter towards looping a set of commands 100 times. Area 4 holds all the actions that will be executed in each production cycle.

First, the counter (`index`) is set to 0. As long as the `index` value is less than 100, all the commands within Area 4 are executed. (Once the index value reaches 100, the loop stops.) Once all the commands within Area 4 have been executed, the counter (`index`) is increased by 1 and the loop starts again.

Now let's get down to the details. The first line within Area 3 is:

```
cloneName = "clone_" + index
```

This command will be executed 100 times as it's part of the `for` command. With the future intention of duplicating the original instance (see next code line), this command prepares a unique instance name for each new duplicated instance. It does so by setting the variable `cloneName`, which will later be used by the `DuplicateMovieClip` command.

Notice how I'm using the variable `index` to construct the name of the new instance. As `index` is actually the counter in the `for` command, each new instance will be named according to the production cycle in which it was created.

```
duplicateMovieClip("original",cloneName, index);
```

As part of the `for` command, this will also be executed 100 times. In each execution (production cycle), it will duplicate the instance `original` (that movie clip in Area 1), and name the new duplicate as `clone_1`, `clone_2`, `clone_3`, and so on, due to the aforementioned `cloneName` command.

```
clonePath = _root[cloneName]
```

If you're not familiar with the `[ ]` array access operator, in essence, it replaces the Flash 4 `eval()` function. Here's an alternative (yet not preferred) method of writing this line:

```
clonePath = eval("_root." + cloneName).
```

This command will again be executed 100 times, as it's part of the `for` command. A new and powerful feature of the Flash 5 ActionScript, this command will enable us to easily change the properties of the newly duplicated instance. We do so by setting the value of the `clonePath` variable to an actual movie clip (instead of a string or numeric value type). My friend Colin Moock calls this method *MovieClip Object Reference*.

Let me give you an overview of what MovieClip Object Reference is. You may be familiar with the concept that variables can hold different types of values, the most common being *string* ("My Name is Amit"), and *numeric* (1,-5, 8.9). Beyond string and numeric values, variables in Flash 5 can hold additional value types, one of them being a MovieClip Object Reference. It's called so because the variable holds a *reference* to a movie clip object. This might be a bit confusing at first, as we're used to variables that hold a real value, such as a string, or a number. But in this case, the variable acts as an alias to a movie clip object. A nice comparison may be to the concept of a Shortcut icon (PC), or Alias icon (Mac), which serves as a reference to the original file on our computer. By clicking on the Shortcut icon, we actually activate the original file.

In Flash, we can later use the variable in a path, towards changing the properties of the referenced movie clip. For example, suppose we have a Flash file with one movie clip instance on stage, named `instance_1`. Now, let's define the variable `refVar` to serve as a *reference* to `instance_1`:

```
refVar = _root.instance_1
```

In this case, the following two lines of code will produce similar results, setting the `_alpha` property of `instance_1` to 50 percent:

```
_root.instance_1._alpha = 50
refVar._alpha = 50
```

The first line of code refers to `instance_1` in a direct manner. It's therefore *static*, and cannot be modified during the execution of our file. This means that this code will forever affect `instance_1`.

On the other hand, the second line of code is dynamic – by changing the value of `refVar` (for example to `instance_2`), we can at any time reuse this code towards affecting other movie clips (for example: `instance_2` instead of `instance_1`).

The entire benefits of this method are beyond the scope of this chapter, but as shown above, it enables us to reuse the same line of code toward changing more than one object (by dynamically resetting `refVar`). In addition, it enables us to avoid the usage of the `eval()` function, and string evaluations in general, as Flash 5 is known to have a slow execution of such commands. It also provides easy modifications of the object you wish to affect (much like the `With` and deprecated `TellTarget` commands).

Returning to our code, we're setting the `clonePath` variable to dynamically *reference* the newly duplicated instance, and later use `clonePath` towards changing the properties of that instance:

```
clonePath._xscale = _root.index;
clonePath._yscale = _root.index;
clonePath._x = _root.index * 6;
clonePath._y = _root.index * 4;
```

Notice how each line uses the variable `index` to change one of the new clone's properties. As `index` changes with each cycle, each clone will be reset with a unique set of property values. I've chosen to multiply the `_x` and `_y` properties by 6 and 4, in order to evenly spread the elements on a 600*400 stage.

Export `flux_1.fla` and you should see something like I've shown here.

Flux

At this infant stage, I'm not interested in producing a masterpiece, but rather in achieving a flexible structure. This structure should enable further exploration, without losing its core functionality. In our case, there are two aspects that produce this flexibility, and thus provide future potential – simplicity and dependencies.

The more details we include in a file, the more details there are to adjust for further modifications. In our case, all the code is localized on one frame so far, which eliminates the need to consider other elements during modifications. This is a small matter that may have larger implications further on. In other words, simplicity is vital.

In our file, *all* the functionality revolves around, and is therefore dependent on, the `index` variable. `index` defines the number instances to clone (on the `for` statement). `Index` is used to define the names that the new clones are given (on the `duplicateMovieClip` function), and `index` is part of the property modifications that are made to each clone.

With this in mind, let's capitalize on the vast impact that `index` has on our work. One of the simplest ways of doing so is by using `index` to change more of the object's properties. For example, let's play around with the `_rotation` property of the object, by adding the following line of code to our work:

`_rotation = _root.index`

This can alternatively be written as `_rotation = index`. We can insert this into the Area 2, like this:

```
Frame Actions                                                           ×
[Movie Explorer] [Frame Actions]                                      ? ▶
+  -  || Frame Actions                                              ▼ ▲
// Repeat the following code 100 times, using 'index' a
for (index=0; index<100; index++) {
    // Set the variable 'cloneName' to hold the name of
    // duplicated, using the current 'index' value.
    cloneName = "clone_"+index;
    // Duplicate the original object -
    duplicateMovieClip ("original", cloneName, index);
    // Set the variable 'clonePath' to reference the new
    // Clone Movieclip Object (see tutorial explanation)
    clonePath = _root[cloneName];
    // Scale & reposition the new clone, using the 'clon
    // Use the current 'index' value towards the new pos
    clonePath._xscale = index;
    clonePath._yscale = index;
    clonePath._x = index*6;
    clonePath._y = index*4;
    clonePath._rotation = index
}
// Hide the original object from the stage.
original._visible = 0;
stop ();

Line 17 of 22, Col 29
```

Exporting `flux_1b.fla` should produce the following result:

Now take a minute to explore other rotation values, such as:

rotation=_root.index*2

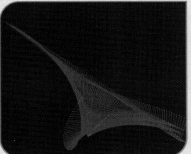

rotation=_root.index*4

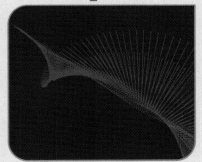

rotation=_root.index*(-10)

rotation=_root.index*math.PI

rotation=_root.index*(-5.4)

rotation=_root.index*(-1.1)

Let's examine where we stand regarding our original concept. We've started out by establishing the need for a changing environment, which will enable us to witness the effects of randomness and flow. We've also concluded that there are two ways in which we may experience this changing environment: either view the change in real-time, or view the final result of the process (like a painting – a result of a time-based production). So far, we've used the second method, as our final output is a static image. To do so, we've used one of our building blocks – the duplicateMovieClip command.

Let's see if we can now incorporate the other method, real-time change, towards further exploring our engine. If you think back to the building blocks that I mentioned at the end of the last section, you'll remember I said that time/fps rate provides us with a way to witness change through time.

To incorporate this building block into our existing structure, we should take one of the elements that are currently executed once through the frame, and move it into a time-based situation. But, which element should we move, and where exactly should we move it to?

I suggest moving the element that has produced the most interesting results – the _rotation function. As all clones will need to be affected by this change, it makes sense to modify the original instance.

This screenshot demonstrates the new code that I've added to the original instance's Object Actions.

You can find this file on the CD as flux_2.fla. Exporting the file should produce the constant rotation of all instances on stage.

From this stage on, the functionality of our file may become CPU-intensive, resulting in a clunky execution of the rotation. To put this right, I've defaulted the file to low quality mode by adding the _quality command on the first frame of the main timeline, as well as resetting the HTML setting in the Publish Settings window. On slower machines, you may also decrease the number of clones by changing the index value in the for statement from index < 100 to index < 50.

 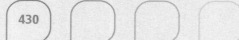

Once again, we can capitalize on the fact that our file's functionality revolves around the variable `index`. Let's try to incorporate the `index` variable in the new `_rotation` command that we've just added to the `original` instance. To do so, we'll need to focus on the connection between `index` and the `original` instance. The deepest implication of this connection lies in the fact that each clone of the `original` instance is created by a unique production cycle, and is also named according to the cycle's `index` value. Let's re-examine the way this is done:

```
cloneName = "clone_" + index
duplicateMovieClip("original", cloneName, index);
```

```
onClipEvent (load) {
  // Set Variable 'my_id' according to the 'index' portion of the instance name.
  my_id = number(substring(_name,7));
}
onClipEvent (enterFrame) {
  // Constantly rotate, using 'my_id' as a factor
  _rotation += my_id/10;
}
```

Each clone is given a unique instance name, which starts with the word `clone_`, and ends with a unique value that is set by `index`. The `for` statement increases the value of `index` by one with each execution, which produces the following instances: `clone_1`, `clone_2`, `clone_3`, and so on. In fact, the `index` value is always present in the same location, starting from the seventh character, as the first six characters of the name are static: c, l, o, n, e, _ (six characters altogether).

In theory, if each instance clone could look at its own name and derive the `index` value, it could then potentially use `index` towards the new `_rotation` function. This shot demonstrates this concept as it's applied to our system (you can see it in `flux3.fla` on the CD).

Let's go through this code line by line:

```
my_id = number(substring(_name,7));
```

Flux

In general, this command will derive the `index` value from the instance name, and place it in the `my_id` variable. Using the `substring()` command, we trim the instance name to include only characters starting from the seventh position on the string, hence dropping the `clone_` part of the name. For example, `clone_99` will be trimmed to `99`, revealing that this instance was created in the 99th production cycle. As instance names are string values, we use the `number()` function to ensure that the new value of `my_id` is of a numeric type. This will enable us to later use `my_id` for mathematical purposes.

```
_rotation += my_id/10
```

Embedded in the `enterFrame` event handler, this line uses the previously attained `index` value (`my_id` variable), towards constantly modifying the rotation property of the instance. This line can also be read as follows:

```
_rotation = _rotation + (my_id / 10)
```

Why did I choose to divide `my_id` by 10? After experimenting with several different settings, I found that this expression will produce results that work well with the 360-degrees system. After 360 degrees, the rotated object completes a cycle, hence the values 361 and 1 will have the same effect on it.

Exporting this file should produce some interesting results. It's fair to say that at this point we have successfully translated most of our initial concept into the Flash environment. We've produced a process that's constructed of many production cycles, and we've made sure that these cycles are driven by a definable and consistent set of rules, or inner logic. When exporting this engine, it's apparent that patterns emerge through the change, and as a result we experience *flow*. Take a couple of minutes and observe the different patterns of flow that this engine produces.

After a short observation, you may notice that the flux is actually repeating itself, as every ten seconds, a three-dimensional field forms on the screen, then peaks are created as this field twists and finally breaks apart into a less definable form. During these phases the flow is most apparent, as the inner logic of our engine is creating recognizable visual forms. Afterwards, the flow is still apparent, but to a lesser degree. Perhaps, with a bit more control over the flux, we can extend the scope of our system from shifting through several degrees of flow, to shifting between flow and randomness.

If you look up the definition of *flux* in the dictionary, you'll find that it also bears meaning as a term in physics: 'the rate of flow of particles or energy on a field'. In our case, the rate of flow is actually determined by the rotation speed of the instances. Perhaps we can gain more real-time control over the flow by adding a slider that will dynamically affect the speed of the rotation.

I've incorporated such a slider into `flux_4.fla`, and modified our file to include the output of this slider.

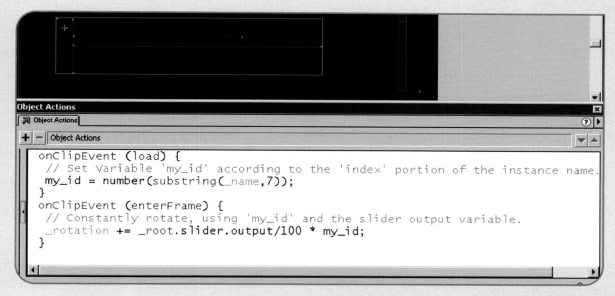

```
onClipEvent (load) {
  // Set Variable 'my_id' according to the 'index' portion of the instance name.
  my_id = number(substring(_name,7));
}
onClipEvent (enterFrame) {
  // Constantly rotate, using 'my_id' and the slider output variable.
  _rotation += _root.slider.output/100 * my_id;
}
```

I've added a slider object, which outputs a number from 0 to 100 according to its handle position. This value is stored in a variable inside the slider, named `output`.

Next, I've modified the `_rotation` value on the `original` instance to include the `output` variable as a factor. I've experimented with several different settings before choosing the current expression:

`_rotation += root.slider.output/100 * my_id`

In general, this expression will produce results that work well with the 360 degree system that the `_rotation` value works through. Experiment with this slider and you'll notice a general rule – the slower the flux, the easier it is to perceive the flow.

And now for the final touch, let's see how the visual content (movie clip) impacts our perception of flow. In `flux_5.fla`, I've modified the original movie clip into

433

Flux

a less definable visual form. I've done so by removing the lines and all but two dots from the `original` instance:

Export this file and position the slider on 5; the flow should be clearly apparent. Now move it down all the way to 100; the dots *seem* move in a random manner throughout most of the cycle.

Next, slowly move the slider up, until you feel you've reached a balance that brings our initial concept to life: creating a system that works through a defined inner logic, and can flux in and out of recognizable patterns, creating the effects of both flow and randomness. I've found the value 20 to produce the most satisfying result.

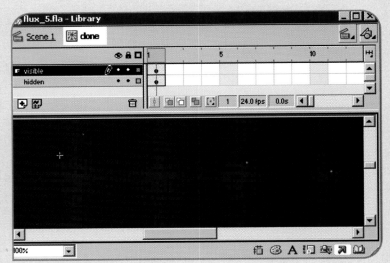

Here are two screenshots that demonstrates two polar instances of this phenomenon:

In the left image, we can see the dots in two separate lines, which seem to cross each other on the top. The distribution of the dots in the image on the right doesn't seem to produce a clear pattern, but rather to imply a random phenomenon.

If you remember, during the conceptualization of this experiment, I said that such a system may provide us with the experience of witnessing the borderline (threshold) of our ability to perceive inner logic, as it moves in and out of recognizable patterns.

With that in mind, look at the file and try to notice the exact moment in which you recognize a pattern formed in the distribution of the dots – at that moment you've crossed the borderline (threshold) of your ability to perceive inner logic. Next, notice the exact moment in which the pattern was lost – at that moment, the border was crossed once again, as you've returned to the realm of randomness.

Interestingly, after spending some time with the file, I've stated to notice that my threshold has slowly started to shift, as I start to recognize patterns sooner than before, and for a longer period of time once they've showed up. In other words, I had an unpredictable learning experience.

How did this happen?

One possible explanation may be the sheer fact of spending time with the system: as my brain was repetitively exposed to the cycles of the system, it trained itself to recognize hidden patterns.

This magical learning ability is an inheritance of our neural net system. Another reason may lie in our devising of a tool that could control the flux. Using the slider, I could slow down the flux, and recognize patterns in a process that seemed random when viewed at a higher rate. Upon returning to the faster rate, I knew what to expect of the system.

At this point, I've satisfied my initial curiosity. What started as an abstract concept is now visually dancing on my monitor. Of course, there is much left to explore (even more than when we started), but I'll leave the rest up to you, as you should now have the proper tools to further explore and materialize your inspirations. In case you're interested, I'll post any further developments to this experiment at www.pitaru.com/flux.

paint daubs

Replace the geometric lines in flux.fla with some simple paint brush strokes as shown.

When you now run the FLA you will see some colorful patterns emerging. Certain values will produce a screen full of dancing paint daubs.

NB— try using a pressure sensitive pen

 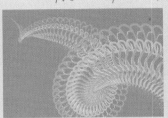 

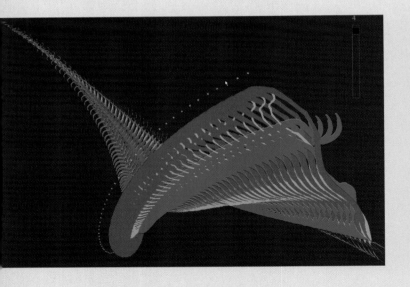 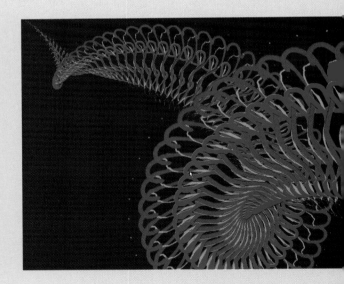

slider input values

The use of sliders as a graphical input method can be more intuitive than entering numeric values; the user isn't worried about the actual value, but rather its effect on the emerging pattern or effect.

Sliders can also be used during development to fine-tune site parameters, and this is especially useful for advanced interfaces and games. If the slider values are written to a text file, they will be available the next time the FLA is opened. Once the FLA is fully developed, simply make the slider layers guides, and you are done.

Some developers use a slider system in developing the final 'playability' factor into Flash games because it allows real time feedback on the effects of changes on gameplay whilst the game is actually running...

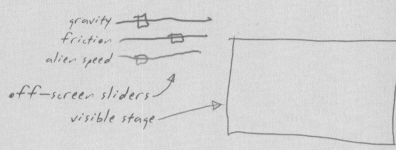

"Imagination is what makes us all different."

Ross Mawdsley
www.ikda.co.uk/simian

I love escapism. Always have. Ever since I was a young kid, I have always made fantastic, brave new worlds in my head. Whether they were brought to life by Playmobil toys, Star Wars figures, or toy soldiers it didn't matter, the outcome was always the same to create other worlds, to escape, to use my imagination. The most powerful tool I have is my imagination. It doesn't matter if you're the world's best artist, or the world's best at ActionScripting. If you don't have an imagination, you don't have anything.

Untitled (1958) Mark Rothko
© Christie's Images/CORBIS

Whether I get it from books, music, films, art or comics my love for escapism has pretty much influenced everything in my life, including my style of work today. Art has always been a big part of my life. Paintings like the *Mona Lisa* or Van Gogh's *Sunflowers* have never interested me. Never turned me on. But Jackson Pollock's *Autumn Rhythm* or *Yellow, Grey, Black* or Mark Rothko's work, like *White over Red*, plus *Lettre a* by Antoni Tapies – this is what I call *real* art. Art that you can get your teeth into. Strange, surreal, makes you think, "What the hell is that about?" That's what I like. You have to think, make up your own mind what it's saying. The artist gives you some hints, but then it's up to you. And that's what I like to do with my Flash work. Steer the user in a certain direction, then it's up to them. Don't make it too obvious. Let them decide what's going on. Let them use their own imagination. I think there's too much Flash out there saying nothing more than "This is it, this is what it does, that's it."

As a contrast, sites like Matt Owens' volumeone.com, Joshua Davis' once-upon-a-forest.com or requiemforadream.com, make you use your imagination. These sites make you think.

Talk

If you've seen any volumes of Simian, you'll know that music and sound play a large part in creating the right atmosphere or mood. Well, music also plays an important part during the creative process of the piece. I find that if I sit in front of the computer with no music on in the background, I can't work. Nothing happens. Music makes my mind work. It turns my mind on. I think the type of music you listen to determines the type of work you produce, or at least its general flavor.

Music and art have always crossed over into each other. Just think about music videos: the music can make the video, and vice versa. One of the best music videos ever has to be *Rabbit in Your Headlights* by U.N.K.L.E (directed by Jonathan Glazer). This is amazing. The atmosphere and mood created are just awesome. I just love the look of it, as well as the strangeness. I think this one video has had a major influence on me - or at least it has steered me in a certain direction.

I tend to listen to all sorts of music, old and new, but at the moment I am into David Holmes, U.N.K.L.E, DJ Shadow, Amon Tobin, Goldie, Mogwai, and Underworld. As with everything in my life, things have to create the right atmosphere. Pop music just wouldn't create the same atmosphere that these bands/artists do for me. I think I like the darker, grittier, seedier side of life – feelings that some of this music invokes. Again, this is escapism. My life isn't dark, seedy or gritty. Probably the exact opposite. But this sort of music can make me escape into this world for a while. Try it out – have a little dabble in it, and then when you turn the stereo off, you're back in your own comfy, safe world.

Films have always played an important part in my life, and, looking back, I can see how they've shaped me, and more importantly, my style. I remember, when I was about ten or eleven, watching *Blade Runner* for the first time. My God! It blew me away! I think the opening scenes of the movie are amazing - you know, the bit where the car is flying around the city, with all the neon and video screens. I love that sort of vision of the near future. It's not really all that different from now, but everything is just exaggerated, bigger, more in your face, more gritty.

Around the same time, I watched *Dark Star* and *Silent Running*. Again, visions of the not-too-distant future. These films had a gritty realism about them, and again evoked feelings of escapism. They also had humour (albeit dark humour). Around this time I also saw *Planet of the Apes* for the first time. This had a major influence on me. I remember as a kid having the same dream all the time: gorillas on horseback, rounding up humans. This of course is a scene from the film (you know - the bit where the astronauts first see the apes), but it obviously stuck with me. I still get shivers when I watch that scene now. I like this feeling. It means it has moved me in some way. I would love to achieve this feeling with my work. Hopefully one day I will. I think it's this that drives me, pushes me to keep creating, trying to achieve my goal.

Some people might think I'm a bit strange, but I like to watch foreign films without the subtitles. Because I don't know the language, I have to work out for myself what's going on. I think this is a really useful exercise. It makes you use your brain. It forces you to be imaginative. I remember watching the French film *La Haine*. If you read the subtitles, you know that the film's about dissatisfaction, uprising, tension etc. But without the subtitles, you can *still* tell it's about dissatisfaction, uprising, tension. This means that the images are stronger than the words. This type of exercise taught me an important lesson: to make sure you make your work visually strong, to try to get across the feeling, mood, atmosphere of a piece without telling someone directly what it's about. If you can crack this, you're half way there.

Planet of the Apes, 1968
© Bettmann/CORBIS

Planet of the Apes, 1968
© Bettmann/CORBIS

Talk

Through my love of art/sci-fi/escapism, I got heavily into comics when I was a kid. *2000 AD* was my favorite. I used to get it delivered on a Saturday morning with my Dad's newspaper. I remember always looking forward to reading it. Beautiful artwork, amazing storylines, it was fantastic. Stories about distant worlds, war-torn planets and futuristic mutant bounty hunters.

My favourites were *Strontium Dog* and *Rogue Trooper*. Once I got to about fourteen, I started to drift away from comics, but I got back into them as I got a bit older, with the likes of Frank Miller's *Batman – The Dark Knight Returns*, and, even more recently, *The Invisibles*. I think comic art is amazing. Better than most of the art out there at the moment. I would much rather go to an art gallery full of comic covers than one full of pickled sheep and unmade beds.

All images on this page courtesy of 2000 AD Magazine, 2000ad weekly and www.2000adonline.com
2000AD Designer Steve Cook
Artwork by Cool Beans Productions, Mark Harrison, Cliff Robinson, Siku

The appeal of comic art to me is similar to my love of graffiti artists. I've been hooked ever since I got a copy of *Subway Art* for my birthday, sometime back in the mid 80s. It inspired me back then, but even more so now. If you look at the work of people like Banksy, Twist, She One, Mr Jago, Ben Drury and, of course, my hero Futura, it blows you away. A lot of things I talk about in this section are interconnected in some way. Futura does the artwork for the U.N.K.L.E record covers. This is probably how I first came across his work. This guy is a genius. His work inspires me so much; it's hard to put into words. Talk about escapism, this guy has created his own alien world order (look at the cover on the U.N.K.L.E album *Psyence Fiction*). I think his work is a modern version of Jackson Pollock (if you look at Futura's *Violent Treasure* and compare it to one of Pollock's paintings, for example, *Number 22* you'll see what I mean).

Number 22, 1949 Jackson Pollock
© Christie's Images/CORBIS

Violent Treasure
© Futura

The art I've talked about is all quite dirty and messy. I think this is why I like it so much. I don't like clean things; I like things messed up. If ever I do a drawing or painting that I want to scan into the computer to use as a background, I'll rip it up and Sellotape it back together, or spill coffee on it, or rub it in some soil. I like things dirty, weathered, used. I think this goes back to when I was a kid playing with Star Wars toys. I used to cover them with soil, or burn parts of them (to give them that weathered, war-torn look). I've still got the Millennium Falcon now, with a huge hole on the side, with burn marks on it. In my imagination this is probably where a laser from the Death Star hit it (actually it was a large stone and a box of matches).This sort of weathered, dirty look is probably why I like the work of the artist/illustrator Ralph Steadman. If you look at his work, particularly the illustrations for *Fear and Loathing in Las Vegas* by Hunter .S. Thompson, they are excellent: black ink, splashes of colour, ink splodges – superb.

As a designer, a lot of influences come from your contemporaries / peers / heroes. I really admire the work of David Carson. It was about the time I was working for *Linedancer* magazine when one of the other designers brought in a copy of *Raygun*. I remember looking at it and thinking, "Why can't I do this type of work?" His layouts

were fantastic. Text all different sizes, all over the place, photocopy upon photocopy. (Needless to say my proposed redesign for *Linedancer* magazine was turned down on the spot. Philistines!)

Another designer I worked with introduced me to the work of Tomato. He had a copy of the book *Mmmm...Skyscraper I love you*. This was a book made up of snippets of conversations overheard in New York, and the text was laid out like buildings and skyscrapers. I thought this was brilliant, and so I started to source out more Tomato work. I wasn't disappointed. Their work appeals to me in the same way as David Carson's does. I think it's safe to assume that I like 'dirty' graphics. I do like clean design, and there's obviously a place for it, but give me a dirty, messy design any day. Attik is another design company I love. About two years ago I bought one of their books (*no3*, you know, the one that came in a metal sleeve), and I probably still look at it at least once a week. I love the way they mix up 2d and 3D pictures. I also like the 3D work of the guys from *me company's* 3D work (for Nike, and the firetrap dogs).

Ideas and inspiration come to me all the time - but very rarely when I'm sitting in front of the computer, desperately trying to think of something. I will sit there

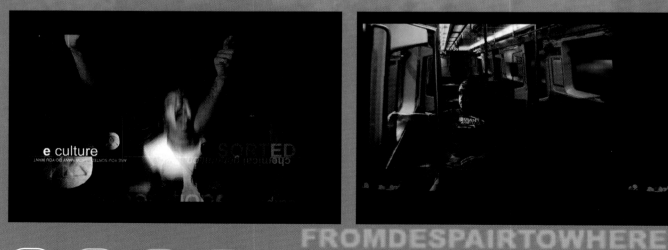

FROMDESPAIRTOWHERE

staring at the blank screen for ages, and usually nothing will happen. Whereas if I am in the supermarket, buying some vegetables for example, I will suddenly get an idea for a Flash piece. It just pops into my head from nowhere. Probably my best ideas come from when I'm about to go out on a Friday or Saturday night. I'm ready to go, but I'm waiting for my girlfriend to finish getting ready (don't we all?). So I'll have a beer and a cigarette, and pop some music on. I don't know why, but ideas just come into my head from nowhere. I'll suddenly just think of something, and think, "That would look great in Flash". This happens all the time. Have you found that as soon as you start designing in Flash, your mind tends to picture everything in a 'Flash' mode. Or is it just me?

Getting into Flash is probably the best thing I've ever done. It's opened my eyes to a whole new world. It enables us to bring life to our work. It enables us to get our ideas across in an amazing and fascinating way. Looking back over the years, I'm glad I was born when I was.

Growing up as a child of the Seventies in the suburbs of Liverpool has shaped me and made me into what I am today. Back then we didn't have Playstations or videogames, there weren't half as many toys as there are today, and of course there were no home computers or the Internet, and so you had to rely on your imagination to have fun. If it weren't for your imagination, you would live in a very dull, grey, boring world. Imagination is what makes us all different. Imagine what it would be like if we were all the same, we all tried to look the same and like the same things. Boring – that's what.

Imagination gives us our own tastes, likes and dislikes.

Never be afraid to do something your way. Developing your own style, and letting that style grow is very important. Strive to be different. Use your best tool – your imagination – to the full.

You might not like my work, or some of my influences, but I do, and that's all that matters. I probably don't like some of the things you like. Well that's OK, we're all different. Flash has given us the opportunity to express our feelings, thoughts, styles, and ideas in a way we haven't been able to do before. It's opened up our way of thinking to a whole new level. And of course, the Internet has opened up our work to a whole new audience – the world.

To me Flash, is the most important piece of software that I've ever had. Couple this with the most important tool we all have – our imaginations – and the possibilities are endless.

Talk

In this section, I'll show you how to build up the main elements of one of my narrative Flash pieces. This will illustrate the type of motion and layering effects that I tend to use in most of my Flash work, especially with my Simian work. The piece I will use to demonstrate these effects and techniques is called *Communication Decline*. This particular piece doesn't involve complicated ActionScripting. I prefer to use Flash to explore more artistic/graphic avenues than to use a lot of cold coding, so I tend to stick to my strengths and concentrate on making my work look slick and cool. I use a lot of transparencies and alpha channels, and build up movie clips using lots of layers and symbols, thus creating a rich and aesthetic-looking piece. In this chapter, we'll concentrate on building up a movie using various movie clips, which will interact with each other. They will contain motion graphic sequences that will work whilst moving (floating) over the top of each other and the background.

To see what we're trying to achieve take a look at the finished piece `communicationdecline.fla` on the accompanying CD. Concentrate on the man videophone – the larger of the two. Study what it does, watch what happens to it when you click on the video screen and drag the videophone across the screen.

We'll first look at how to create most of the images used in the Flash file, and then we'll have a brief look at the sound files used. We'll then combine these in Flash, to produce the finished piece.

Anyway, enough spiel, let's get down to business!

I'm sure I'm not the first person to say that I never begin a project without having gone through those preliminary planning stages. This always sounds good in principle, but when you're working on a Flash piece, 99% of the time it will change, evolve, and mutate into something other than your original plan. However, in this case, the finished Flash movie contains lots of imported graphics, which are essential to the smooth working and running of the movie, and most of these are created before you even open Flash. I use Adobe Photoshop, and will refer to it in this chapter, but you should use whatever graphics package you're comfortable with.

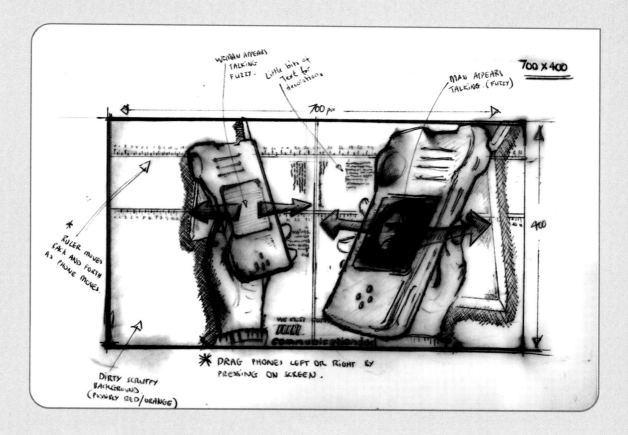

Here's how I sketched out my ideas first.

Once I've sketched the idea, I recreate it in Photoshop. I work to the same dimensions as my planned Flash movie, in this case, 700 pixels wide and 400 pixels in height. On this document I create all the different elements of the movie; in other words, the two videophones, the background image, and the motion graphics sequences of the man and the woman that will be shown on the video screens of the phones.

I'll now go into a bit more detail on how to create these various images.

I build up the background image using lots and lots of different layers with several different layer filters, such as Soft Light, and Screen. Next, I add little bits of text, scratches, and other little touches until I think it looks right. Finally, I flatten it and save it as a bitmap. I could save it as a GIF, but I like to use BMPs because they're generally smaller in file size. When I export my Flash file, I can set the quality of images, so I can reduce the quality of the images I've used if I need to keep the file size down (this applies to BMPs and JPGs, but not GIFs).

Next, I start by cutting out the videophone using paths, remembering to cut out the screen section. That leaves me with a background layer and a layer with the cut out videophone. This is essentially the videophone that I'll be using in Flash, so I need to save it exactly as it will appear in the final Flash effect. I'll show you how I do this by using an alpha channel.

First, select the areas that you want to be transparent, which is everything other than the videophone. Use the magic wand, paths, or any other way you're used to, to achieve this.

Then, in the Layers window, select Channels and click on the save selection as channel button. This creates an alpha channel, which shows up as red. These red areas are what will be transparent when you import it into Flash. You need to save it as a PNG, making sure that the exclude alpha channels box is *not* ticked.

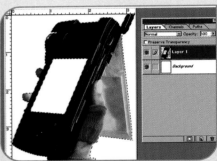
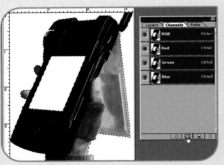
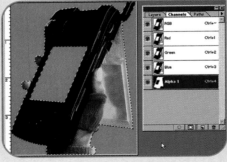

For the footage that will appear on the videophones, you need to create a series of images which, when played one after another, will give the impression of blurry, disjointed video footage. Once you have your series of images all set up in a Photoshop document, you need to make them look a bit more blurry, messy, more like video. To achieve this effect I use the filter Halftone Pattern. This adds a series of small lines to the image, which is perfect. I also want the images to have an orange tint to them, just for aesthetic reasons. The bottom layer of the document is orange, so for each particular image I use the layer filter Hard Light to give me the effect I want.

Now you need to go through the process of saving each individual image. The way I do this is to save the main document, then flatten it, cut the image, create a new document, and paste in the image. I save it as a BMP, and then go back to the main document and revert to saved. Once you've done this for one, start again with the next image and repeat the process. Keep doing this until you have a full set of images – man1.bmp through man12.bmp.

There are two videophones in the movie, one showing a man speaking and the other a woman. I've named them rather unoriginally man phone and woman phone. Both phones basically do the same thing, so I'll only show you how to create one – the larger of the two, man phone.

In the movie, when you keep the mouse pressed over the screen of the videophone, you'll see a face appear on the screen and hear a voice soundtrack over the top of the background music. Later on we'll add some actions that call in two SWF files, manvoice.swf and womanvoice.swf for those two voices. Each is fifty frames long and has two layers, sound and actions.

On the actions layer we add a Stop action on the last frame (50), to stop the movie from repeating itself. On the sound layer, we import the sound file at frame 20, and in sound properties set loop to a large number, let's say 10. This means that the sound file will play ten times and then stop. For a closer look at the sound files, you can find both manvoice.fla and womanvoice.fla on the CD.

Now on to the best bit – combining the images and sound in Flash to create the finished movie. If you're going to be following this tutorial by creating a replica, it's best to import the `communicationdecline.fla` Library using the Open as Library function. Ready? OK then, let's make that movie!

Firstly, open up Flash 5 and create a new movie. Set the dimensions to 700 pixels wide and 400 pixels high, set the frame rate to 30 fps, and the background color to red. Call the movie communication decline. You need to have two scenes. The first scene is the 100 frame pre-loading scene, which I named preloader. The second scene is the main scene of the movie, simply called main.

In the main scene, create a layer, call it background, and onto this layer import the main background image, `background.bmp`, from the Library. Position it in the center of the movie (cut and paste it, or use the align function).

Make a keyframe at frame 480, so that the background image is visible for the whole movie. Now we'll create the main object of the movie, the videophone.

Create a new graphic symbol, call it manphonegraphic and rename the default layer man phone graphic. From the imported Library, place the image `manphone.png` onto the exact center of the stage. I'm using a PNG file because it recognizes alpha channels. Due to the techniques we employed in Photoshop (the masks and alpha channels), we can move the phone around freely in the movie, and have images appear through the screen of the phone. You can also achieve this mask effect using a transparent GIF, or alternatively creating a mask in Flash itself. The transparent area of a GIF will still appear when it's in Flash, but I find the edges a bit scrappy and ragged, so I prefer to use a PNG image because I find it has a much cleaner and smoother edge.

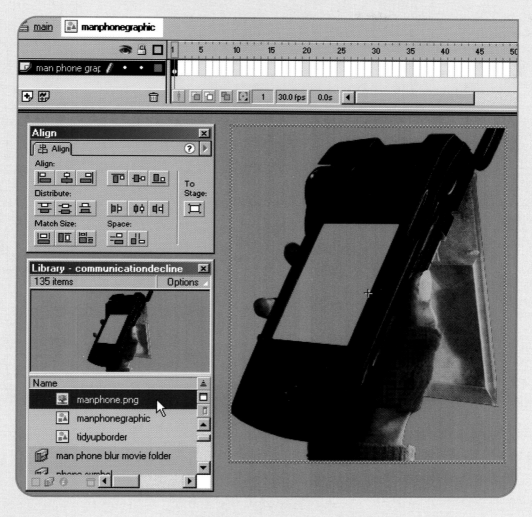

Talk

Add another layer above man phone graphic and call it tidyupborder. Onto this layer, pull the graphic symbol tidyupborder from the Library and position it over the video screen of the phone. This will tidy up the edges of the video screen for when we put a movie clip behind it.

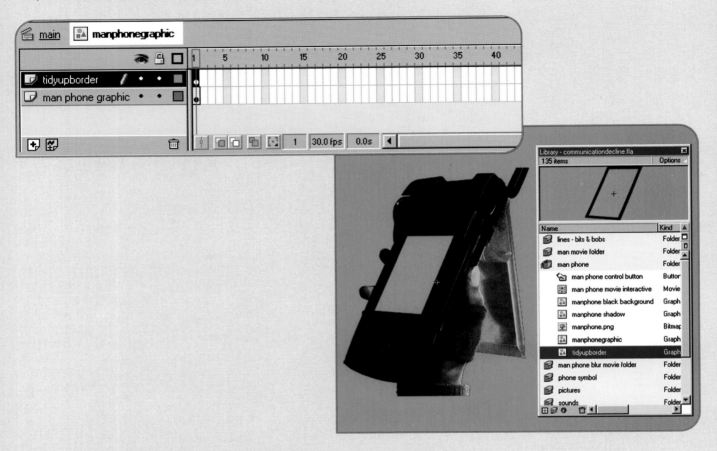

Now that we've made the symbol manphonegraphic, we need to make the videophone look like it blurs into the movie at the start. We could just put the phone on the first frame of the movie, so that when you open the movie the phone is already there – but that's boring! Let's make the phone look like it merges or blurs out from the background.

To do this, we'll use a series of four Photoshop images of the man videophone in different stages of a motion blur – `manblur1.bmp` to `manblur4.bmp`. You'll find these images in the imported Library. Create a graphic symbol using `manblur1.bmp`, and another graphic symbol using `manblur4.bmp`, and call these manblurgraphic1 and manblurgraphic4, respectively.

Now create a movie clip and call it man phone blur movie. Call the first layer manblur 1-5, and on frame1, put the symbol manblurgraphic1 right in the center of the stage (use the align function).

Make another instance of this symbol at frame 4, and put a motion tween between these two instances. Change the alpha of the symbol on frame 1 to 0%. This makes the symbol manblurgraphic1 fade in from 0% to 100%.

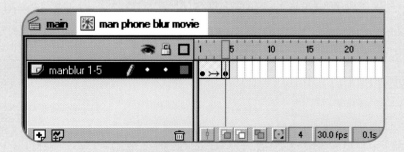

Talk

On the same layer, at frame 5, put the image `manblur2.bmp` exactly in the same place as the image on frame 4. Put `manblur3.bmp` on frame 6, again in exactly the same place as the previous image. Now put the symbol `manblurgraphic4` on frame 7. Again – you've guessed it – in exactly the same place as the others. Make another instance of this at frame 11, and put a motion tween between them. This time make the alpha of the instance on frame 11, 0%. This now means that the symbol `manblur4` fades out to 0%. We've now created a great effect where the images will seamlessly fade in and out. Create a keyframe at frame 12, and add a `Stop` action to it.

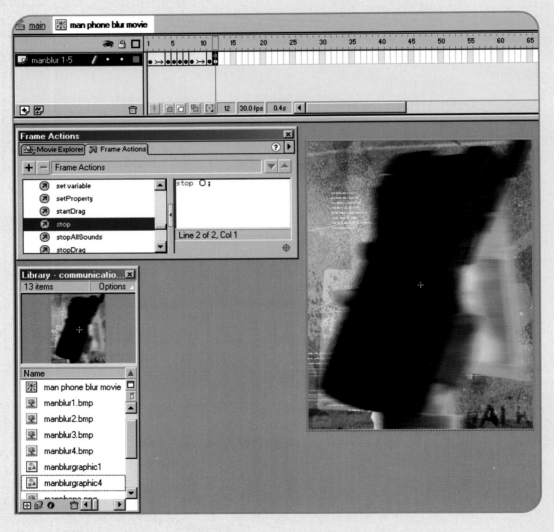

Still in man phone blur movie, make another layer and call it manphone graphic. At frame 7, put the symbol, manphonegraphic (we made it earlier). Again, put it exactly over the image below. Sorry to keep saying this, but it's very important that all the images are in the same place, so they seamlessly blend over each other.

Talk

The last step within this movie clip is to add the symbol manphone black background in a new layer. Call this layer man phone black BG and place it between the layers manblur 1-5 and manphone graphic. Put the manphone black background symbol on frame 7 and position it behind the phone screen. We do this because the symbol manphonegraphic has a transparent screen area. We need the symbol manphone black background to act as the blank video screen. To help with the placement, it's a good idea to hide the manblur 1-5 layer.

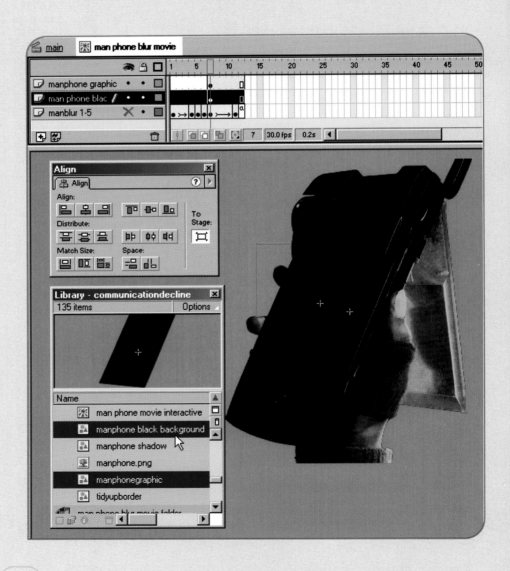

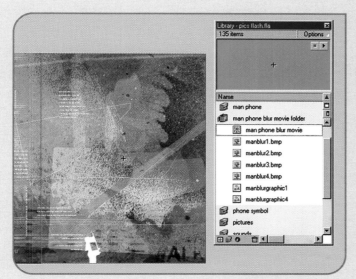

Now we can position the movie clip man phone blur movie onto the main scene of the movie.

Create a layer on the main scene, and call it man phone blur. Make a keyframe at frame 42, and place man phone blur movie onto the stage. Make sure you position it in the right place, so that the background image and the movie clip correspond exactly with each other. (Use Align right edge, and Align vertical center.) You need to position this exactly right. If it's slightly wrong, it will look terrible because the image will move as well as fade, thus destroying the smooth transition.

Insert a blank keyframe at frame 51 on the man phone blur layer. Next, we need to make a layer above this called man phone graphic. Make a keyframe at frame 50, and put the symbol manphonegraphic exactly over the movie clip man phone blur movie, aligning as before. This now means the phone blurs in from frame 42 to frame 50, and at frame 50 the manphonegraphic symbol appears, thus making the transition seamless. At frame 51 the symbol manphonegraphic is being used on its own, and the background can be seen through the screen. So we have to use the symbol, manphone black background again. Make a layer under the man phone graphic layer, and call it man phone black BG. On this layer, at frame 50, place the symbol manphone black background, and position it under the symbol manphonegraphic. We've now created the blank movie screen again.

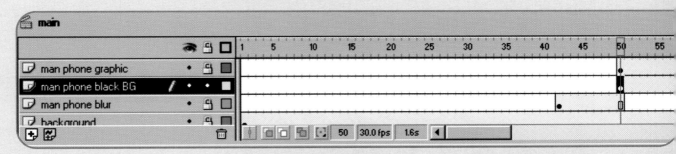

Talk

This first picture shows the effect *without* the manphone black background, and the second with.

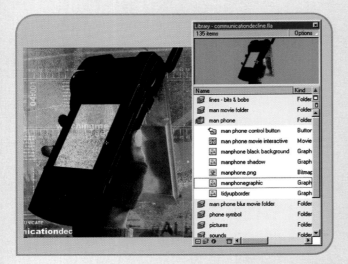

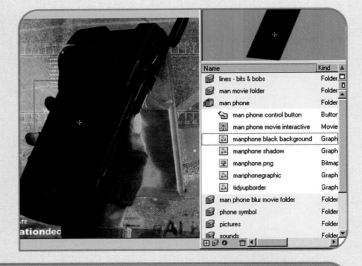

To make the videophone look even cooler, we now add a layer under the man phone black BG layer, and call it man phone shadow.

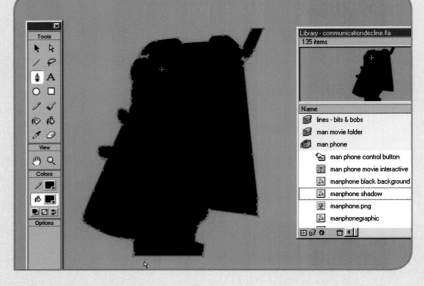

On this layer, at frame 50, add the symbol manphone shadow, and position it under the videophone, wherever you think it gives the best shadow effect. (I created manphone shadow using the Bezier tool to trace round the videophone image, thus

creating an outline of the phone. I then filled it with black.) Change the alpha of this symbol to 30%, thus emphasizing the shadow effect.

From this point (frame 50 to frame 110), we want the videophone to move horizontally back and forth across the scene. We'll do this so that the viewer will realize that the phones move - it's a bit of a prompt. Move the phone a little to the left, then 10 frames later, a little to the right. 10 frames later, move it again to the left a little, and so on. Add motion tweens between these frames. Do exactly the same with the symbols on layers man phone black BG and man phone shadow.

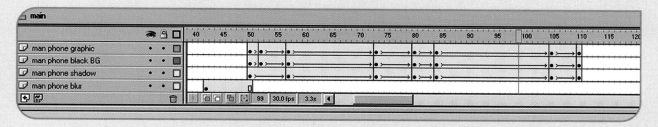

This means that the videophone, the black screen, and the shadow all move in situ. As I've said, this movement is done as a bit of a prompt, to show the viewer that the phones move, so prompting them to click on the phone.

Because we're building the Flash movie up in layers, using lots of different symbols and movie clips, which are essentially meant to be the same thing (the videophone), we need to make sure that they line up exactly. This will make for a seamless transition, so that the user can't tell we've used lots of different symbols and movie clips.

At frame 110, we want the videophone to become active; in other words, let the user be able to drag the phone and see the video footage. So make a new layer above the man phone graphic layer, and call it man phone movie (interactive). On each of the previous three layers, make a blank keyframe at frame 111. On the man phone movie (interactive) layer, we're going to put the videophone that the user can actually use on frame 111.

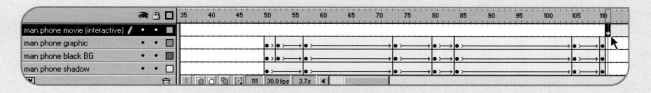

Before we create the movie clip man phone movie interactive, we need to add a `Stop` action to the main scene to stop the movie. Once we've done this, we can add movie clips after this point and call them later using `GoTo` actions. Create a new layer and call it actions. Make a keyframe at 222, and on this frame add the `Stop` action.

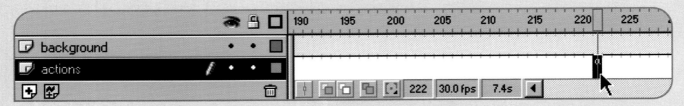

We can now build the movie clip man phone movie interactive, which will go on frame 111 of the man phone movie (interactive) layer. This is the main movie clip of the videophone, which allows the user to drag the videophone to the left or right, and sets off a series of effects when they activate the videophone by holding the mouse over the video screen.

Create a movie clip symbol and call it man phone movie interactive. Call the first layer actions, and make a keyframe at frame 16. Then create five further layers: control button, manphonegraphic, man movie, background, and shadow.

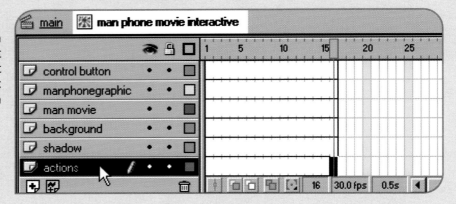

Place the symbol manphonegraphic onto the manphonegraphic layer, and align it in the center. On the background layer, position the manphone black background symbol behind the videophone screen, thus making the screen appear blank. Place the manphone shadow symbol on the shadow layer, making sure you position it in relation to the videophone the same as you did on the main scene. Remember to reduce alpha to 30%.

At this point you've recreated the same image that appears at frame 110 on the main timeline. The first picture here shows the image formed by man phone movie interactive so far, and the second, the same set of images on the main timeline.

We now need to create the movie clip that will be placed on the man movie layer. This is the sequence of images that appear on the screen of the videophone when it's activated.

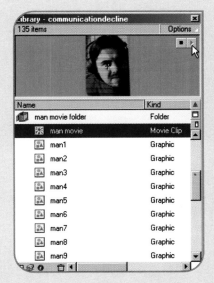

Create a movie clip symbol and call it man movie. Make it 139 frames long. We'll be using the images man1.bmp through man9.bmp, and manintro.bmp through manintro7.bmp. The first thing we need to do is to create a symbol for each of these images. We don't want to use the images as they are, because we want to add motion tweens and alpha effects to them, so they need to be turned into symbols. So use man1.bmp and turn it into a graphic symbol called man1, turn man2.bmp into man2, and so on until you have nine symbols named man1 through man9. Do the same with the images manintro1.bmp through manintro7.bmp, thus creating symbols manintro1 to manintro7.

Create a layer in this man movie movie clip, and call it fuzzy intro. On frame 2 of this layer, place the symbol manintro1 in the center of the scene (using the align function). Make another instance of this at frame 8. Create a motion tween between these two frames and set the alpha of the symbol at frame 2 to 0%. Remember I said before that we fade in this image just to make it a smoother transition.

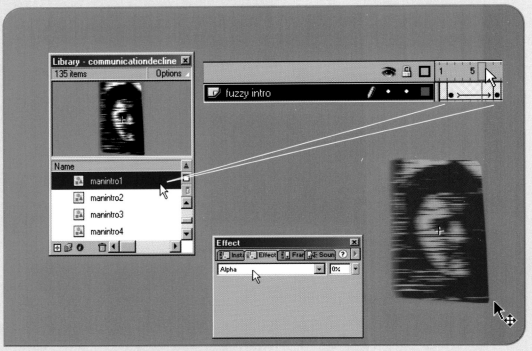

I've recommended that you put the first instance of the symbol manintro1 at frame 2, and not at frame 1, because very occasionally when a movie clip is used, Flash can skip the first frame. It's not meant to, but it can happen.

Now, on the same layer, put the symbol manintro2 on frame 9, in the center. Then, making sure that each image is aligned in the center of the stage, put symbol manintro3 on frame 10, manintro4 on frame 11, and so on and so on, until you get to manintro7 in frame 14. Then start repeating some of the symbols until you've filled right up to and including frame 25. We've done this just to prolong the fuzzy intro bit.

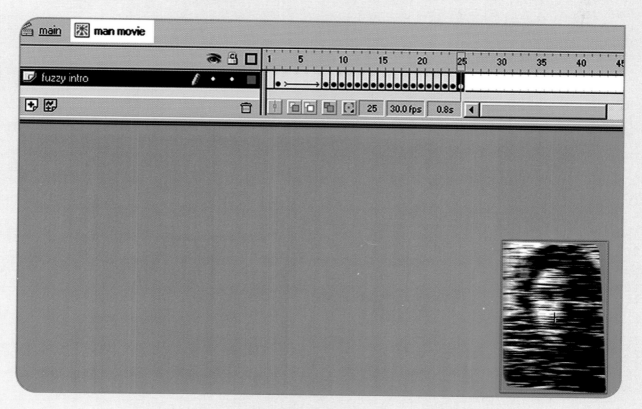

On frame 26, place the symbol manintro7, and make another instance of it at frame 41. Add a motion tween between these two frames and set the alpha of the symbol on frame 41 to 0%. (This fades out the last image of fuzzy intro.) Make frames 42 and 139 blank keyframes.

Create a new layer below the fuzzy intro layer and call it motion blur 1. On this layer, place the symbol called man1 on frame 26, directly under the image on the fuzzy intro layer. (Use the align center function.) Place another instance of this symbol at frame 42. (So far the sequence of fuzzy intro images plays through and fades out to reveal the first clear image of the man.)

Create a layer above motion blur 1, and call it motion blur 2. At frame 46 on this layer, place the symbol man2 directly on top of the image on the motion blur 1 layer. Create another instance of this symbol at frame 53. Change the alpha of the man2 symbol on frame 46 to 0% and add a motion tween between the two frames.

Create a new layer above this one, and call it motion blur 3. On this layer, place the man3 symbol at frame 53, directly on top of the image on the layer motion blur 2.

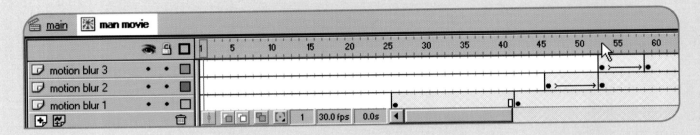

Create another instance of this symbol at frame 59. Change the alpha of the symbol on frame number 53 to 0%, and again add a motion tween between the two frames. Now if you play this movie clip, the fuzzy intro images play through to reveal the man images, which seem to blur into each other, making it look like video footage.

Repeat this process with the remaining symbols (man4 to man9), putting each different symbol on a different layer (put symbol man4 on a layer called motion blur 4, man5 on layer motion blur 5, and so on, until you have nine motion blur layers).

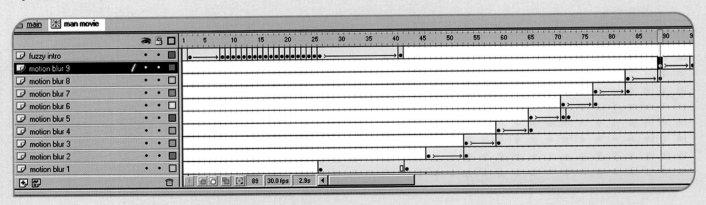

Now we'll repeat the above process, but this time in reverse.

There are two techniques that you could use to achieve this. Firstly, you can just copy and paste the frames on the timeline, and then reverse them. Alternatively, starting on the layer motion blur 9, make another instance of the symbol man9 at frame 96, and then another one at frame 102. Add a motion tween between them, and set the alpha of man9 at frame 102 to 0%. This now makes the image fade out, not fade in like before. Make a blank keyframe at frame 103 to clear the rest of the layer. On layer motion blur 8, make another instance of the symbol man8 at frame 102, and another one at frame 108. Add a motion tween between them and set the alpha of the symbol man8 at frame 108 to 0%. Repeat this process on the remaining layers, motion blur 7 to motion blur 1.

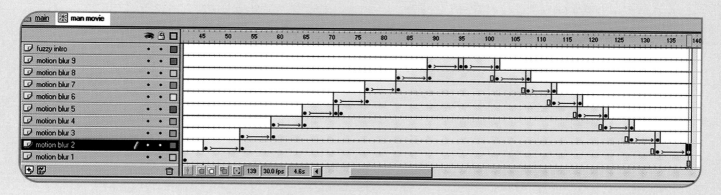

Now play back the movie clip and watch how the video sequence works. The fuzzy intro images run through to reveal the man images, which appear to blur into each other. We now need this movie clip to repeat itself, but without playing the fuzzy intro bit again. We don't know how long the user will keep the mouse pressed down on the videophone, so we need to make the sequence of the man symbols play again and again, if necessary.

Create a layer at the very bottom, and call it actions. On that layer, first add a label at frame 46, resume playing. (Just to recap, frame 46 is where man1 fades into man2.) At frame 139, where the last image fade occurs (man2 fades out to reveal man1), create a keyframe and add this action to it:

```
gotoAndPlay ("resume playing");
```

This will make sure that if the movie clip repeats itself, it appears seamless.

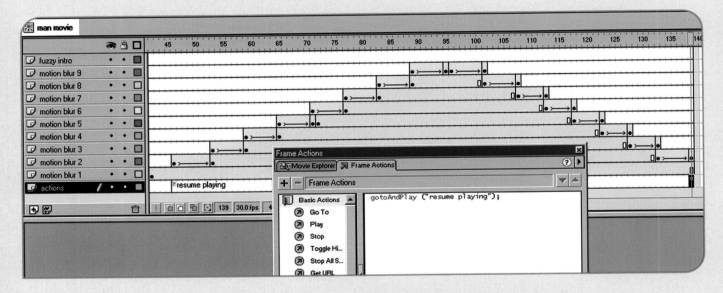

The last thing to add to the man movie movie clip is the fuzzy intro sound effect, which sounds a bit like a radio being tuned. Create a layer above all the others and call it sound layer. Create a keyframe at frame 2, and assign the sound file mainsound3.wav to this frame. This means that when this movie clip plays, there's a fuzzy sound effect when the fuzzy intro images are playing. If the movie plays over and over again, because the sound file is on frame 2 it won't keep playing the sound because of the action gotoAndPlay ("resume playing"), which we added before.

Now we've made the movie clip man movie, we can go back to finishing off the movie clip called man phone movie interactive, so reopen this movie clip. We're currently using three of the six layers.

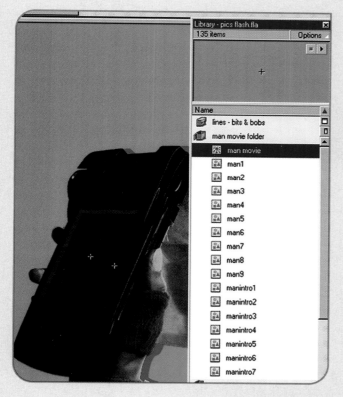

On the layer man movie, make a keyframe at frame 2. Place the movie clip symbol man movie on this frame. Make sure to position it so that it appears in the screen area of the videophone.

Having trouble doing this? Yeah, so did I! The first frame of the movie clip man movie doesn't contain an image, so you can't see it properly to position it correctly. The way I got round this was to re-open the movie clip man movie and make a new temporary layer. On this layer, copy any one of the symbols used in this movie, for example man1. Place this symbol on frame 1 of this layer in exactly the same place as it appears in the movie clip. This means now that when you're positioning the movie clip man movie in the movie clip man phone movie interactive, you can now see what you're trying to position. You may need to scale and rotate the clip so that the images appear correctly on the video screen. Once you've positioned it in the right place, reopen the movie clip man movie, and delete the layer containing the copied image.

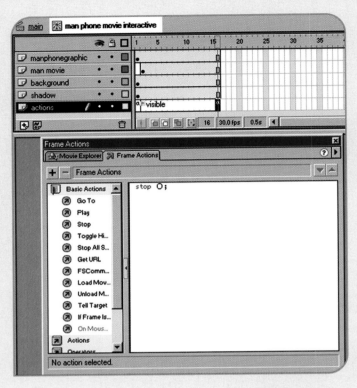

Now you've got man movie in the right place, in frame 1 of the actions layer add a Stop action. Do the same in frame 16.

This means that the movie clip won't play past frame 1 until it's told to do so. When it does, it won't repeat itself, but will stop at frame 16. We've added these actions because they're necessary for the control button, which is the next thing that we'll create. This control button adds an important element of interaction to the movie – giving the user a sense of control and providing a way for them to activate the videophone by clicking on the screen within it.

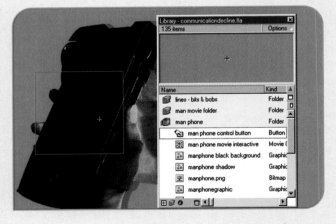

First, create a skewed solid square, the shape of the video screen, and make it into a button symbol. Call it man phone control button and position it exactly over the videophone screen. Hide the background layer to see the screen area easier. Now change the alpha of the button to 0%, making it transparent. Alternatively, of course, you could use ActionScript to create an invisible button. Whichever way you make it, once you've finished, place it at frame 1 of the control button layer.

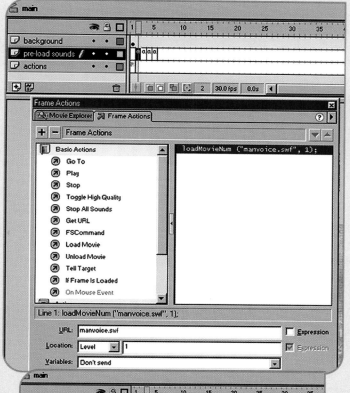

Before we add the actions to the button, we need to add some actions and movie clips to the main timeline, which the button will call when the user presses it. First we need to add a couple of actions, which preload the voice sound files for the phones. This will mean that when the control button activates the videophone, the voice that you hear on the phone has already loaded in, so you don't have to wait ages for it. Create a layer on the main scene and call it pre-load sounds. Position this layer above the actions layer. Create a keyframe at frame 2 and add this action:

```
loadMovieNum ("manvoice.swf""", 1);
```

This action loads `manvoice.swf` onto level 1.

Then create another keyframe at frame 3, and add this action:

```
unloadMovieNum (1);
```

This action unloads `manvoice.swf` from level 1. We don't want to use this yet, so we get rid of it, but it's now stored in the cache memory. It will load in immediately when it's called later. Frames 4 and 5 repeat this same process, but instead load and then unload `womanvoice.swf`. Make a blank keyframe at frame 6.

Now we need to drop a movie clip into the main scene, which the control button will call. This clip is the pieces of text that fade in when the videophone is activated, and then fade out when the videophone is deactivated (the control button is released).

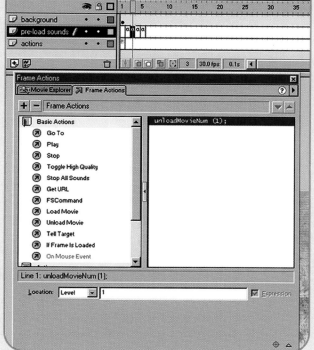

471

Talk

The movie clip is called man phone text movie 1. It's all pretty straightforward stuff - just bits of text that fade in, then fade out, on a loop - so I won't take your time showing it to you here. If you need to, take a closer look at the movie clip before you drag it onto the stage.

Create a layer in the main scene and call it man phone text. To make sure that the text appears behind the complete videophone, place this layer beneath all the layers containing videophone elements.

On the actions layer place a `Stop` action at frame 222. On the man phone text layer create a keyframe somewhere after the frame 222 (I've used frame 240) and add the man phone text movie 1. This means that if the user doesn't activate the phone, the movie stops at frame 222, and so doesn't bring in the movie clip man phone text movie 1 until the phone is activated.

Now add a `Stop` action frame 297 of the actions layer to stop the movie with the movie clip man phone text movie 1 still playing over and over again (until it's told not to).

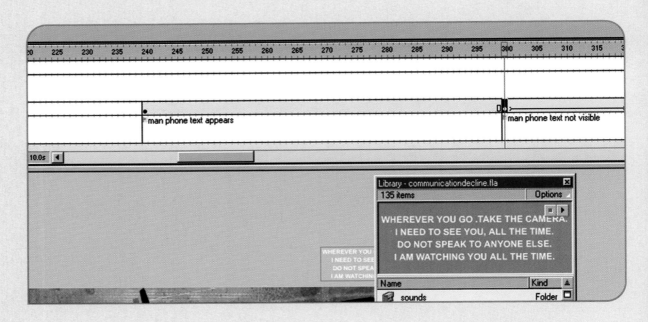

To enable the movie clip man phone text movie 1 to fade out (stop) when the user releases the control button, make further instances of the movie clip at frame 300, and at keyframe 321, with a motion tween between them. Set the alpha of the instance on keyframe 321 to 0%. At frame 321 on the actions layer, add a Stop action. This means the movie clip man phone text movie 1 has now faded out, and the main scene has stopped here. Make frame 322 a blank keyframe.

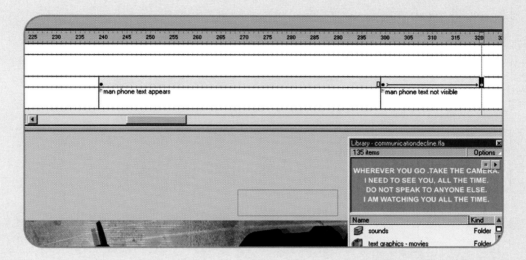

We'll now go back to the movie clip man phone movie interactive, and add the actions to the control button to tie everything together and give the whole movie the wow factor. The actions that we're about to add will tell the movie to play at frame 240 when the user presses the button and go to frame 300 when the button is released, thus fading out the movie clip man phone text movie 1. The main scene will stop here, but when the videophone is activated again the actions we add to the control button tell the main scene to go back to a certain point and play again. Remember that we already added a Stop at frame 222 right at the beginning to stop the movie playing all the way to the end.

Reopen the man phone movie interactive. At frame 2 on the actions layer, add a blank keyframe, and label it visible. Select the control button on the stage and add this action:

```
On (press) {
gotoAndPlay ("visible");
```

Talk

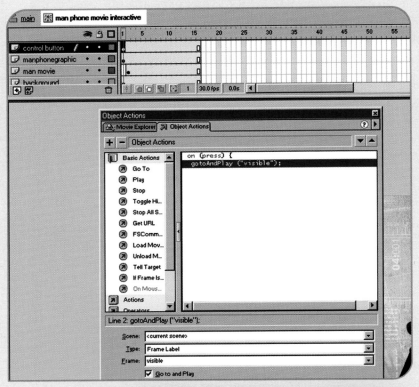

When the user clicks on the invisible button over the screen of the videophone, this will send the movie to frame 2, which if you remember contains movie clip man movie. The movie clip will start to play and the videophone starts to receive a call.

Now add this action:

```
startDrag ("", false, 50, 200, 700, 200);
```

This allows the viewer to click and drag the videophone a certain distance to the right and left, but not up and down.

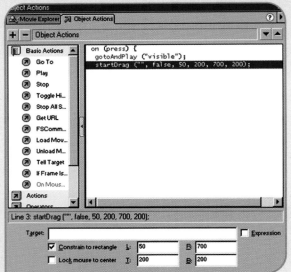

Now, before we add the next action, we need to go back to the main movie and add another label. In the main movie scene, add a label at frame 240, which reads man phone text appears. Quite logically, this is where the movie clip man phone text movie 1 kicks in.

Back at the control button, add the action:

```
_level0.gotoAndPlay ("man phone text appears");
```

This tells the movie to go to level 0 (which is the main movie scene) and to play from frame 240. The movie clip is situated on frame 240, but remember we have a pre-loading scene, which has a total of 100 frames. This means that if we were using a frame number rather than a label within this ActionScript, we'd have to add these to the total, (100 + 240 = 340) and direct the movie to frame 340.

Next, add this action:

```
LoadMovieNum ("manvoice.swf", 1);
```

This action loads manvoice.swf, onto level 1, above the main movie. Remember that we've loaded this movie before, so it's in the cache, and therefore plays straight away.

That's it for the actions on the videophone control button. Let's recap. When we click on the screen of the man videophone, the videophone picks up the call (the fuzzy intro), the man starts talking, and will continue to do this while we drag the phone around. Text fades in and moves around behind the phone. We can drag the woman videophone under the man videophone whilst the images are still playing on the screen.

Now we have to deal with what happens when we release the control button. At frame 16 of man phone movie interactive add a label, notvisible.

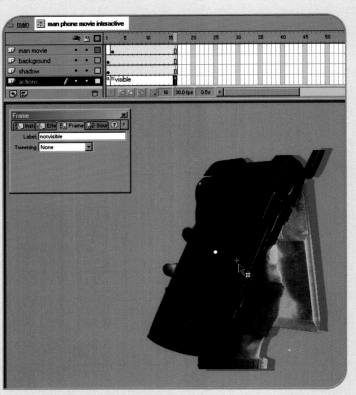

Back in the Actions window add the ActionScript:

```
On (release) {
gotoAndStop ("notvisible");
```

to send the movie to that frame and make man phone movie interactive **disappear**.

Now add this action:

```
_level0.gotoAndPlay("man phone text not visible");
```

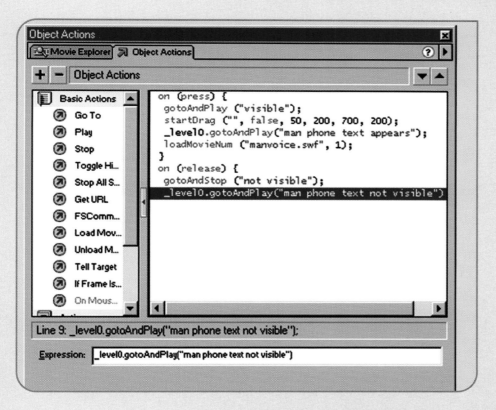

This tells the movie to go to level 0 (the main movie scene), and go to and play frame 300, labeled man phone text not visible. This is the frame where the movie clip symbol, man phone text movie 1 starts to fade out, so now, when the button is released the text that's floating around behind the phone fades out and disappears.

Next, add this action onto the control button:

```
unloadMovieNum (1);
```

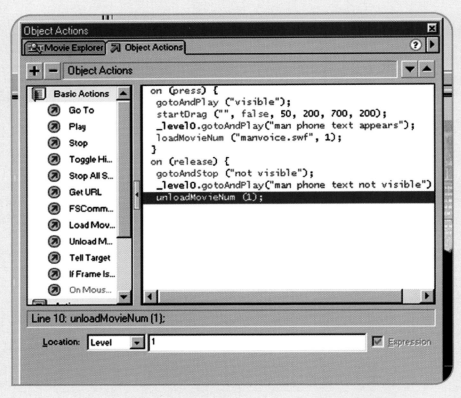

This unloads `manvoice.swf` from level 1, which means that when you release the control button, the sound of the man talking will stop, no matter where it is. This is the only way I've found to stop a sound in mid-flow (which is notoriously difficult to do). If you use the `stopAllSounds` action, it does exactly that - it stops all sounds, not just the one you want to stop. However, because we preloaded the sounds into separate levels from the main movie, we can stop the sound in mid-flow like this by unloading the movie.

Now add this final action:

```
stopDrag ();
```

This stops the videophone moving until we activate it again by repressing the control button, which starts the whole process over again. Finally, place the man phone movie interactive clip onto the main scene at frame 111 of the layer that we set aside for it earlier - man phone movie (interactive).

And that's pretty much that. The main elements of this Flash movie are now complete. There are other elements in this Flash movie, but they're all pretty much the same as those I've described here. Rather than explain things over and over again, I'll leave you to explore things for yourself. Now you know how the main effects and techniques work, you can apply them to your own work, or open up the FLA file on the CD and see how they've been applied to other elements in this movie. You may be familiar with some of the techniques I've discussed over the last few pages, but I hope I've at least given you a new angle on how you can combine things in a different way to produce effects that you haven't tried before. This is what I hope will give your Flash movie the **wow** factor. Good luck in standing out from the crowd.

Headnotes

Although we're told that Flash
is a vector-based engine and doesn't
like bitmaps, there's a lot of digital
artists out there who carry on regardless.
As long as we keep our bitmaps small
or don't move them much, and especially
so long as we don't try to scale them or
use alpha transitions, Flash seems to
cope rather well on a medium-powered
computer.

So here's a few thoughts for the
bitmap renegades...

www.bluemondo.com   *www.2advanced.com*

static interface
Because Flash doesn't slow
down when the bitmaps aren't
being moved around the screen,
many top designers use small
bitmaps in place of vectors for
interface elements such as fascias,
buttons and incidental graphics.

If the bitmaps aren't scaled
up either, they look better than
the same vector-based versions.

For inspiration of this look no further than
some previous New Masters; Blue Mondo and
2Advanced being good example sites.

the digital sketchbook

With things like camcorders and digital cameras now being affordable, they are becoming a new and different way to form 'sketches' or record ideas for the web designer/graphic artist.

If something interests you, or if you like a design out there in the real world, simply take a snap of it. Back in the lab it's only a quick trip to Photoshop (via firewire) to add a mask or resize the bitmap to get the size down, and then import it into Flash to start playing. Trace it (manually or automatically) or use it directly...

Example
I am writing a space combat video game and need to build a fighter cockpit... This will consist of a glass canopy and lots of struts, so I take some footage of a bicycle(!)

These headnotes themselves were created in this way (along with that other vital digital artist's tool, a pressure sensitive pen). There's no longer any need to search out expensive picture reference material (such as the phones and man/woman images in communication decline); just find it for real and press the red button.

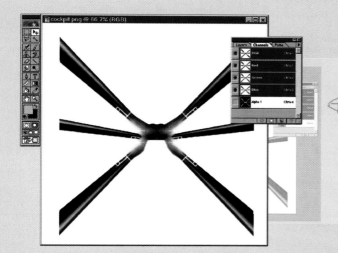

The tubes of the bike are transformed and composited together in Photoshop, and exported with a mask as a PNG file.

Because the png file doesn't move, it takes no CPU time to display it in the finished game...

481

"This mentality to dissect, evaluate,
and evolve through reconditioning has been the
overwhelming theme to my own explorations."

Erik Natzke
www.natzke.com

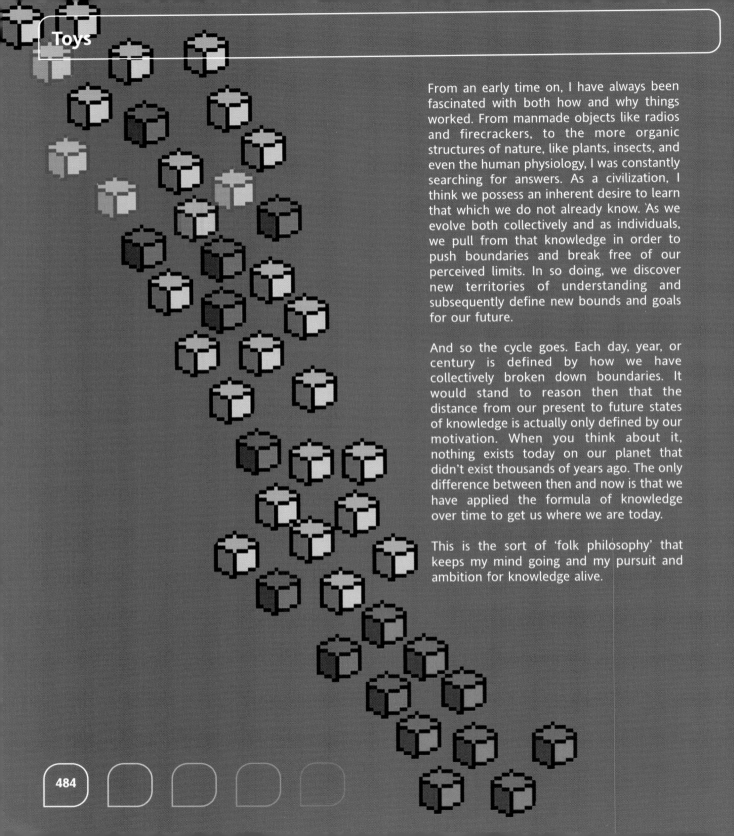

From an early time on, I have always been fascinated with both how and why things worked. From manmade objects like radios and firecrackers, to the more organic structures of nature, like plants, insects, and even the human physiology, I was constantly searching for answers. As a civilization, I think we possess an inherent desire to learn that which we do not already know. As we evolve both collectively and as individuals, we pull from that knowledge in order to push boundaries and break free of our perceived limits. In so doing, we discover new territories of understanding and subsequently define new bounds and goals for our future.

And so the cycle goes. Each day, year, or century is defined by how we have collectively broken down boundaries. It would stand to reason then that the distance from our present to future states of knowledge is actually only defined by our motivation. When you think about it, nothing exists today on our planet that didn't exist thousands of years ago. The only difference between then and now is that we have applied the formula of knowledge over time to get us where we are today.

This is the sort of 'folk philosophy' that keeps my mind going and my pursuit and ambition for knowledge alive.

I can trace my own inquisitive roots back to a time where I was constantly taking things apart. One event in particular stands out in my mind above all the rest. This was when I got it in my head to dissect an Atari joystick. At the time I couldn't have been more than seven or eight, so I should have been satisfied with simply playing with the console, but that wasn't the case. Curiosity ruled the day, and out came the screwdriver and needle-nose pliers. Unsure as to what sort of mechanics lay beneath, I was almost dumbfounded to discover that its construction was quite simple. Essentially it used only five buttons; four that controlled the directional movement and one that functioned as the 'firing' button. To see whether I had properly interpreted the structure and function through the process of dissection, I made out to build a joystick of my own. This time I was going to do it a little bit differently though. Using the original plug, a small piece of plywood, some foam padding, a spool of wire, and a bunch of staples, I set out to make a touchpad version of the controller. When it was complete, the results weren't exactly optimal for the gaming experience. The staples had made poor conductors and an eight-year-old had made a poor engineer. But it did work.

This mentality to dissect, evaluate, and evolve through reconditioning has been the overwhelming theme to my own explorations. Be it communication design, interactive development, or artistic expression, understanding the various structures and behaviors of everyday items and systems has had a tremendous influence on where I take my own work.

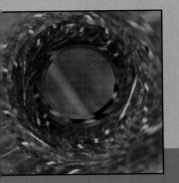

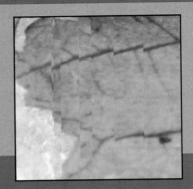

When I started college I has no idea what I wanted to do for a career. Having an appreciation for knowledge and a desire to learn about our natural environment, I started out majoring in biology. This later evolved into medicine, which strangely enough progressed into design, but that's is a whole other story. Throughout that period of my education, my appreciation and understanding of organic structures grew. It was almost like you could continually dissect structures until each component was comprised of many different parts, and each part was made up of even more components, and so on. Conversely, when you pull back from a subject, you realize how species relate to one another and how entire ecosystems emerge. You begin to realize that the characteristics and behaviors of organic structures are the result of the relationships that have formed both internally as well as externally.

Now, how to relate this to designing interactive structures? There's a tremendous amount of power and control that programming now lends to how we're able to control objects. In order to bring life to those objects, we need to pull in those ideas and concepts of interrelation that we observe in nature. Properties and attributes of smaller parts characterize the behavior of the elements they're nested in. Thus, we can create structures that have relationships to one another. We can then allow for these elements to adapt and react to outside forces or environments.

Regrettably, when I was in school, math was the subject I gave the least amount of attention to. I mean, "who is really ever going to use math in the real world?"

How naive I must have sounded to my teachers. If only I could have taken a glimpse into what I'm doing now, I might have paid a little more attention in class. Well, probably not, but I'd like to think I would. Now I resort to a number of books I have that relate to math, science, and physics. Often I'll thumb through them searching for answers, looking for challenges, and on occasion looking for inspiration.

Going back to the idea of relationships, numbers provide a means for objects to relate easily with one another on a programmatic level of structure and logic. Many times it's the most simple calculations or numeric relationships that complete these bonds or patterns. Take for example the Variable Typography tutorial that I've prepared for this book. In order to get the letters to line up so we can see

the word they're spelling, each object needs to understand where it was supposed to go. By assigning numbers to the names of each movieclip, we in essence define the pattern of position that they would need to follow when that action was targeted.

The power of math goes beyond simply relating objects to one another. Many of the formulae I use to control object motion are a return to many of the things I learned in physics class. Using values of speed, acceleration, and friction, I've been able to incorporate the fundamentals of gravity, inertia, tension and so on into a number of my studies. I think the more that I'm able to relate the work that I do online with the environment that we're accustomed to, the more attached the viewer is able to become to the work.

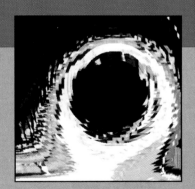

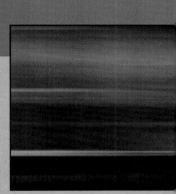

Toys

I'd be the first to admit that I'm not a programmer, but I also don't think you need to have gone to school for computer science to begin developing ideas with code. Similarly, I don't think you need to be a photographer to take pictures or be a designer before you can start laying things out on a page. Most of the things that I've learned were out of motivation to create, control, and understand whatever tool or set of knowledge that was required for me to execute an idea.

One of the first things I ever tried to do with code was to control the movement of an object by assigning variables to properties and then controlling it all by manipulating those variables. Once I was comfortable with controlling its movement, I would then see if I could change its scale, then its rotation, and then I would add fifty objects to the stage and see what happened. Many of my early stage studies weren't pretty. In fact, they were quite atrocious. But the point of them wasn't to be pretty, it was to learn. It was just like when I was younger and I had to take things apart to understand them better. Throughout each stage I would play with the code. Testing to see if I had properly understanding what was going on before moving ahead.

As my comprehension of the language increased, so too did the level of imagination that I've started to incorporate with it. The way I see it, Flash and ActionScript provide a means, but it's the concept and creativity that you enlist along the way that make the biggest differences. The best place to originate a concept is as far away from the code as possible. Usually thinking outside of the code will force me to think of new ways to solve problems and in most situations will even lead me into more new ideas. Each time adding another element to my skill set and constantly raising that bar for myself.

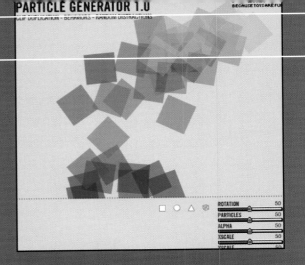

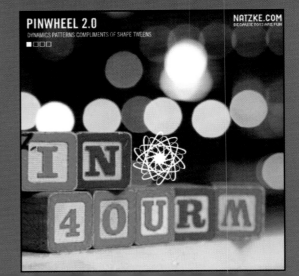

Erik Natzke

Photography is a hobby that has slowly become an addiction. I never really took any formal training in it, nor do I have any inclination to make a career out of it, but there is a certain amount of joy that I get out of capturing images. We all have our own take on life or point of view and photography provides me with a powerful way to express mine. About a year ago I bought a digital camera, thereby eliminating all the cost of developing and the time required for scanning. Now my motivation is the only thing to blame for not getting shutter-happy, so about every other week or so I make it a point to go out on what I have characterized as a photo scavenge hunt. Sometimes I look for specific subject matter like fire escapes or flowers, and then other times I just go for a walk and see what manages to catch my eye.

The subject matter or techniques I use are as varied as my mood. As I never want to see myself having a unilateral view of the world, the same holds true with how I choose to capture it. Sometimes I get in close for an insect's view of a flower, while at other times I take a more observational stance of things like architecture or modes of transport. I am also constantly experimenting with different angles, apertures, and shutter speeds. The only objective I have is to explore compositions that relate to how I view or think about the things around me.

Toys

At the moment I live in a rural town about thirty minutes north of Milwaukee, Wisconsin. Across the road from my home is a cornfield and behind my backyard is a decent-sized marshland. Both serve as excellent resources to capture and observe nature on a seasonal basis. Each passing month brings with it new plants, palettes, and creatures to find. All serve as continued sources of inspiration.

Playing is a word that I commonly use to associate how I approach many things I do in life. Never trying to take anything too seriously, I try to exhibit a playful nature, whatever situation I am in. Even when I decided to publish my own explorations on natzke.com, the emphasis is on exploring the combinations of code and imagination to create playful experiences, because toys are fun.

I only wish more things in life were as fun and rewarding as the experience that I get from both learning and sharing with those around me. To that extent, I would also have to say that I have been quite blessed.

One of the first things I ever did when I was exploring how to use Director and Flash was to play around with typographic motion, at first using keyframes and tweens to control motions, progressions, and transitions. As my knowledge of scripting grew, I began to develop typographic engines that would allow me to pull individual letters from strings and develop particle systems of structured random motion. What interested me most about doing all this was the ability to work with both the element of a word (which brings with it the inherent values of language) and also the actual letterforms (which centers more on values of aesthetics and composition).

Recently I had the good fortune to be invited to contribute a piece for www.bornmag.com, an online design and literature collaborative magazine, which you can see at bornmag.com/projects/walking. I was given a poem by Chris Green with the intent to design an interface that would allow the viewer to interact with the piece. Seldom do occasions arise where you are given such creative freedom, especially with content that carried with it a great deal of emotion. Without going into vast amounts of detail, I took the opportunity and ran with it, allowing the words themselves to tell the story, while using imagery and typographic transitions to relate to the poem.

On a technical level, the piece ended up being quite simple to structure, but from a labor perspective, the project took a tremendous amount of time to produce. With the concept that I wanted to carry out, I needed to have a certain amount of control over the movement and final placement of the letters in each section – the result being that I had to hand-tween some 100+ layers of type

over an 800 frame timeline! To cut a long story short, this is how I spent my Christmas break.

Now, we aren't all blessed with a tremendous amount of time in the day. Even if we were, chances are we wouldn't spend it hand-tweening keyframes. In the case of that project it was a self-imposed challenge that I required of myself, but after this experience it got me thinking again about how to build typographic engines. The goal would be to create a structure whose motion, transition and actions were solely dependent on code and not keyframes. We could then retrieve its text value from a variable and thereby allow for the ability to reuse that structure as information is updated.

So, in part, this is what we're going to try and accomplish throughout the process of my tutorial over the next few pages. Over a series of eight FLAs and sections, we'll try to deconstruct and understand a number of concepts relating to the variable typography study that I've provided.

To get started, if you look on the CD that accompanies the book, you'll find a series of FLAs. These correspond to the sections that this tutorial has been broken down into.

Without further delay, let's begin.

01:Pulling names from an array
Refer to `VarTypog_01.fla`.

We'll start things off pretty simple by making a *generic movie clip* containing a button that we'll use to pull string values from an array.

What is a generic movie clip? Well, this is the term that I use to describe a movie clip with a button nested inside that operates based on the instance name of the movie clip. I do this so that I can create multiple instances of a button whose actions are based on the name of the clip it's nested in.

In this project we have sixteen generic movie clips on the stage, all named RollOver followed by a unique number from 1 to 16 (RollOver1, RollOver2...). This number is what we'll use to target and pull a value from an array. The following code inside each clip is what we'll use to perform this task:

```
on (rollOver) {
    n = Number(_name.substring(8));
    _root.Name = _root.Titles[n-1];
}
```

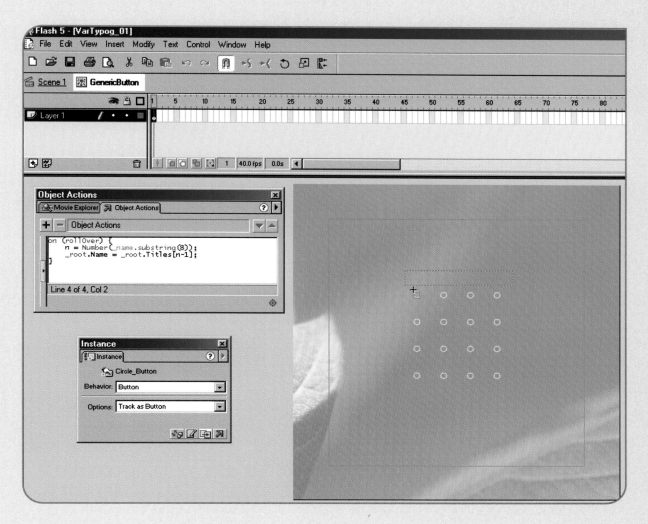

Toys

The first thing that will happen as we roll over this button is for it to determine what number was assigned to its instance. We can do this using the substring() function.

For example, say the name of this particular clip is RollOver12. The information that we want to extract is 12, which is a value that begins on the ninth character of this string. So in using substring() with our target _name and our starting point on a zero scale (in this case it's 8), we're then able to extract all characters beyond that index point of 8. Since we're going to use this number in a later calculation, we need to also convert this string into a numeric value by using Number().

In our example, the code would work out as follows:

```
// the equation
n = Number(_name.substring(8));

// in this instance
_name = "Rollover12"

// the result is then
n = 12
```

The second line in our rollOver event will then assign a value to _root.Name from the _root.Titles array that was defined in the first frame of our movie. Since arrays are also based on a zero scale, we use [n-1] to acquire values of 0-15.

A variable textfield called Name has been placed on the stage so as you roll over the various buttons you can see how that variable is changed to reference the value it's targeting in the array.

The array itself is defined at the top of the script:

```
Titles = new Array("FOURM", "INFOURM", "MINIML",
"SOUNDOFDESIGN", "GOINGONSIX", "PRATE", "HUNGRYFORDESIGN",
"PRESSTUBE", "VOLUMEONE", "WIREFRAME", "PRAYSTATION",
"FIFTHROTATION", "K10K", "BORNMAG", "DECONCEPT",
"UNCONTROL");
```

This defines the titles that n will index on.

02:Duplicating/removing movie clip and assigning *x* and *y* positions
Refer to `VarTypog_02.fla`.

Before I deconstruct the next file I should quickly touch on *functions*. Functions are a beautiful way to organize your ActionScript into reusable modular elements. All the functions we'll use throughout this tutorial will be defined on the first frame each movie and called on by an `onClipEvent (enterFrame)` that's attached to the background image movie clip (named `ActionClip`).

The `onClipEvent` code goes like this:

```
onClipEvent (enterFrame) {
  _root.Population();
  _root.LetterFlight();
}
```

The two functions we define in this movie are `Population` and `LetterFlight`. First, let's take a look at `Population`.

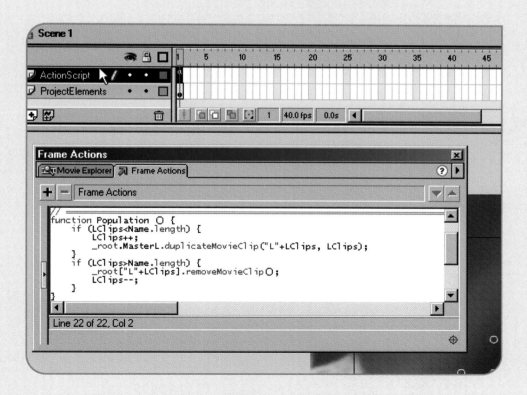

```
function Population () {
  if (LClips<Name.length) {
    LClips++;
    _root.MasterL.duplicateMovieClip("L"+LClips, LClips);
  }
  if (LClips>Name.length) {
    _root["L"+LClips].removeMovieClip();
    LClips—;
  }
}
```

In the previous section we were changing the value of Name in our root. Now, based on the string length of that variable, we'll duplicate and remove movie clips as needed.

To do so, we have two if statements and a new variable (LClips). As the length of the string for Name increases and decreases, so too will the value of LClips (incrementally (++) or decrementally (—), whichever the case may be). For example, say the string value for Name is MINIML. The Name.length would then equal 6 (the number of characters in MINIML). This would enlist our first if statement which incrementally increases the value of LClips and duplicates our MasterL movie clip along the way. If we were then to change Name to equal K1OK (whose character length is 4), that would enlist our second if statement which removes our excess clips and decrementally changes the value for LClips.

The whole process is shown in the following commented code:

> **Name = "MINIML"**
> **Name.length = 6**
>   //Number of MovieClips created = 6
>   //(L1,L2,L3,L4,L5,L6)
> **LClips = 6**
>
>   //Going from "MINIML" to "K1OK" >>
>
> **Name = "K1OK"**
> **Name.length = 4**
>   //Number of MovieClips removed = 2
>   //(L5,L6)
>   //Number of MovieClips remaining = 4
>   //(L1,L2,L3,L4)
> **LClips = 4**

Note how if the number of letters equals the current number, the length (and therefore LClips) remains unchanged. Also, the value of LClips is incremented/decremented by 1 each frame, and not all in one go (as would occur in a loop).

Now that we've controlled the number of movie clips that we're duplicating or removing from the stage, we need define their position and the letter they will carry. We'll do this with another function called `LetterFlight` which is written like this:

```
function LetterFlight () {
    for (c=1; c<=Name.length; c++) {
        this["L"+c]._x = XPosStart+(c*Kern);
        this["L"+c]._y = YPosStart;
        this["L"+c].L = Name.substring(c-1, c);
    }
}
```

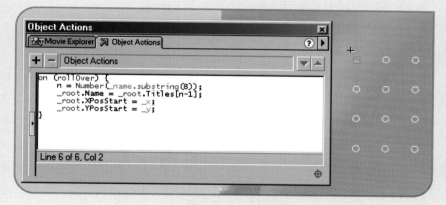

In this function, we'll use a `for` action to cycle through the various movie clips on the stage. This means that each time the movie passes by this segment of code it will initialize a variable (`c=1`) and execute the statement contained repeatedly (`c++`) until the condition (`c <= Name.length`) is satisfied. In this case, our statement will target the `_x` and `_y` properties as well as our variable `L` inside of each clip which is the name of our text field. Before we dissect this statement further, let's take a look at a few lines that were added on the `rollOver` of our buttons:

```
on (rollOver) {
    n = Number(_name.substring(8));
    _root.Name = _root.Titles[n-1];
    _root.XPosStart = _x;
    _root.YPosStart = _y;
}
```

Depending on which button you roll over, the value of `XPosStart` and `YPosStart` will correspond to the `_x` and `_y` placement of the movie clip that it resides in.

If we look again at our `LetterFlight` function, we can then see how the `L` movie clips will begin to position themselves based upon these coordinates. At the top of the script we've also added the variable `Kern` (set to 10), which will control the spacing of these movie clips.

Notice that we're using `substring()` again, but this time to pull a single letter from our string.

```
this["L"+c].L = Name.substring(c-1, c);
```

Let's pick a moment in time to demonstrate how this formula works. Say that `Name` now equals `GOINGONSIX` and the `for` statement is cycling through with `c` equal to 7.

```
Name = "GOINGONSIX";
c = 7
this["L" + 7].L = Name.substring(7 - 1, 7);
L7.L = Name.substring(6,7);
L7.L = "N"
```

To give us another visual reference of how `substring()` pulled that value, look at the graphic which illustrates this instance in time.

```
// the equation
this["L" + c ].L = Name.substring(c - 1, c);

// in this instance
c = 7;
Name = "GOINGONSIX";

// calculations would then follow
this["L" + 7 ].L = Name.substring(7 - 1, 7);
L7.L = Name.substring(6, 7);
L7.L = "S";
```

03: Programmatic motion
Refer to `VarTypog_03.fla`

Programmatic motion enlists the use of ActionScript to control the placement of objects on the stage. Instead of using keyframes and tweens we reference variables and properties and control their placement over time with equations. In essence, we already did a portion of this in the previous section when we assigned values for the x and y coordinates of our movie clips, but the illusion of motion was not really achieved. This is where equations come in.

From the standpoint of a movie clip, if you know where it is (`_x,_y`) and you know where it is heading (`Xn,Yn`), it's then a matter of implementing an equation that will chart a path over time leading to the destination (`Xn,Yn`).

If you look at how we've altered our LetterFlight function for this particular section, you'll notice how we've begun to implement this strategy with code:

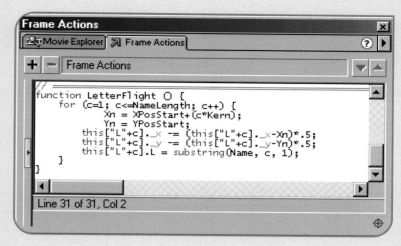

```
function LetterFlight () {
    for (c=1; c<=NameLength; c++) {
        Xn = XPosStart+(c*Kern);
        Yn = YPosStart;
        this["L"+c]._x -= (this["L"+c]._x-Xn)*.5;
        this["L"+c]._y -= (this["L"+c]._y-Yn)*.5;
        this["L"+c].L = substring(Name, c, 1);
    }
}
```

Line 31 of 31, Col 2

We've added two new values (Xn and Yn). In the case of Xn, it's actually taking on the value we used to define the _x property in the previous section. We then use that value in our equation to establish the ultimate destination of our movie clip. We've also added a new variable, NameLength, which is set in our Population function. We'll eventually want to control this value so that it's not solely dependent on the string length of Name, but for now it's only important to know that NameLength equals Name.length.

Let's simplify things and take a look at our equation without all the other evaluations.

$$x = (\_x - Xn) * .5$$

Let's expand this even further so we can input values easier.

$$x = x - ((\_x - Xn) * .5)$$

Each time this line runs, it evaluates the difference between the current position (_x) and its destination (Xn). It then multiplies that value by 0.5, halving it (generally in scripting, multiplication is faster than division). What then occurs is that each time we run this line of code, our movie clip repositions itself half way between its current position and its destination value. To make things clearer, let's take a look at this equation in action with a few values.

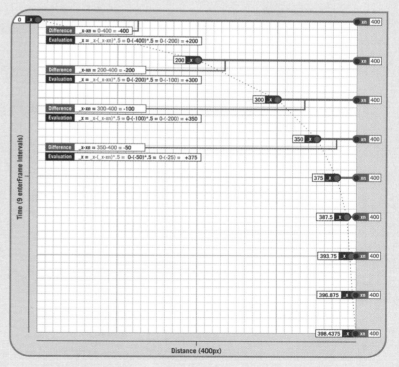

In the illustration, we gave our movie clip a placement of origin for $\_x$ of 0 and we gave it a destination (Xn) of 400. What's interesting about this particular equation is that it creates an easing effect as it approaches its destination. It would be like you were standing 20 feet from a wall and continued to move so that you were half way between yourself and that wall. In theory you should never hit the wall, but in reality, when you get to the point where you're half an inch away and you are about to move to a quarter of inch away, you might as well just say you are at the wall.

A quick note before we move on. In this and all the remaining sections, we've added the `MasterLetter` function:

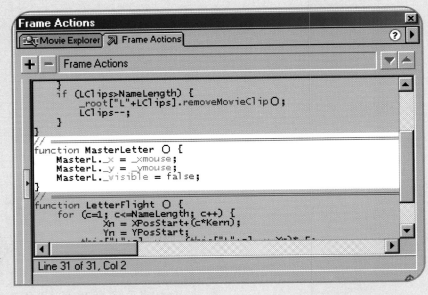

```
function MasterLetter () {
  MasterL._x = _xmouse;
  MasterL._y = _ymouse;
  MasterL._visible = false;
}
```

I did this so that as movie clips were being duplicated they would originate from the mouse instead of some arbitrary place off the stage.

04: Active and non-active states of motion
Refer to `VarTypog_04.fla`.

Having added programmatic movement to our movie clips, we now need to put them into 'flight'. We can do this by establishing Active and Non-active states of motion. The Active state is defined whenever we roll over a button and, conversely, Non-active is defined when we roll out. In the Active state we want all the movie clips to line up so we can read our text and in the Non-active state we want to have these movie clips move around the stage independently of one another. Let's first take a look at how the `LetterFight` function has evolved in this section:

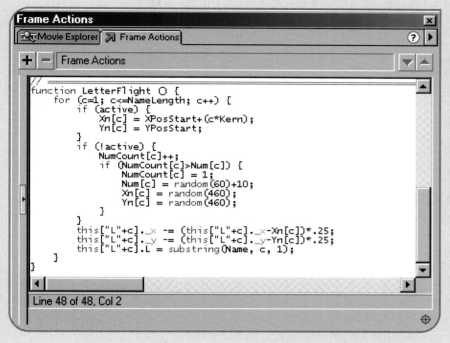

```
Frame Actions                                            ×
 Movie Explorer   Frame Actions                         ?  ▶
 +  −  Frame Actions                                 ▼  ▲
//
function LetterFlight () {
    for (c=1; c<=NameLength; c++) {
        if (active) {
            Xn[c] = XPosStart+(c*Kern);
            Yn[c] = YPosStart;
        }
        if (!active) {
            NumCount[c]++;
            if (NumCount[c]>Num[c]) {
                NumCount[c] = 1;
                Num[c] = random(60)+10;
                Xn[c] = random(460);
                Yn[c] = random(460);
            }
        }
        this["L"+c]._x -= (this["L"+c]._x-Xn[c])*.25;
        this["L"+c]._y -= (this["L"+c]._y-Yn[c])*.25;
        this["L"+c].L = substring(Name, c, 1);
    }
}
Line 48 of 48, Col 2
```

Right away you should notice how we've divided our statement into two conditions (`active` and `!active`). If you're unfamiliar, the exclamation point means false, or not active. The Active state carries the same values of `Xn` and `Yn` as our previous section, but now we're writing these values to an array. In order to do this, we must first define the arrays before we can write to them. We did this by adding the following few lines to the beginning of the main script:

```
Xn = new Array();
Yn = new Array();
Num = new Array();
NumCount = new Array();
```

Arrays are necessary because the value of the destination is now toggled between an Active state and a Non-active state, where the movie clips are in a random flight. Since this Non-active state assigns random values of destination, we then use arrays to store those values over time.

Two other values that have been added to our script as a result of this Non-active state are `Num` and `NumCount`. Both are dependent on the movie clip that they're assigned to, so we'll use an array for each to store their values through time. `NumCount` is a value that incrementally (`++`) counts itself up until the condition (`NumCount >Num`) is achieved. When that condition is achieved, the timer resets the `NumCount` to 1, a new random value is set for `Num`, and new random destination values for `Xn` and `Yn` are given.

```
on (rollOver) {
    n = Number(_name.substring(8));
    _root.Name = _root.Titles[n - 1];
    _root.XPosStart = _x;
    _root.YPosStart = _y;
    _root.Active = true;
}
on (rollOut) {
    _root.active = false;
    for (c = 0; c <= _root.NameLength; c++) {
        _root.NumCount[c] = _root.Num[c];
    }
}
```

We've also added a few more lines to our nested button that correspond to this Non-active state. Look specifically at the last three lines:

Setting the `NumCount` to equal `Num` thereby resets our random timer, giving us new values for destination and the random timer itself.

The following is an illustration that shows that moment between Active and Non-active states. The red dots along the dashed lines represent positions to which the clips will plot themselves over time.

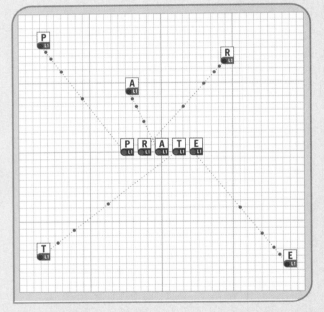

05:Refining our programmatic motion
Refer to `VarTypog_05.fla`

Now that we've gone over most of the principal concepts relating to a variable typography engine, the next few sections are simply going to refine and add a few features. The first will be to adjust how we're controlling the motion of our movie clips.

The bottom section of our `LetterFlight` function now goes like this:

```
function LetterFlight () {
    for (c=1; c<=NameLength; c++) {
        if (active) {
            Xn[c] = XPosStart+(c*Kern);
            Yn[c] = YPosStart;
            if (Mn[c]<.8) {
                Mn[c] += .1;
            }
        }
        if (!active) {
            NumCount[c]++;
            Mn[c] -= .0008;
            if (NumCount[c]>Num[c] or Mn[c]<-.1) {
                Mn[c] = .01;
                NumCount[c] = 1;
                Num[c] = random(60)+10;
                Xn[c] = random(460);
                Yn[c] = random(460);
            }
            if (this["L"+c]._x>460 or this["L"+c]._x<0 or this["L"+c]._y>460 or this["L"+c]._y<0) {
                Mn[c] = -Mn[c]*4;
            }
        }
        this["L"+c]._x -= (this["L"+c]._x-Xn[c])*Mn[c];
        this["L"+c]._y -= (this["L"+c]._y-Yn[c])*Mn[c];
        this["L"+c].L = substring(Name, c, 1);
    }
}
```

We've added another array value (`Mn`) that reads, writes, and stores a number that we use to multiply the difference between our current position and our destination. `Mn` starts out having a value of 0.01. As long as the condition of (`!active`) is satisfied, it will then equal itself minus 0.0008.

Mn will then reset itself to 0.01 when either the NumCount is greater than Num or Mn has a value of minus 0.1. We've also added a bounding condition that states if the movie clip moves off our stage, it will equal itself times 4. You will also note in the Active state, if Mn is less than 0.8, it will equal itself plus 0.1.

A few more extra lines were then added to the rollover of our generic movie clip:

```
on (rollOut) {
    _root.active = false;
    for (c=0; c<=_root.NameLength; c++) {
        _root.Xn[c]  = random(460);
        _root.Yn[c]  = random(460);
        _root.Sn[c]  = .4;
        _root.NumCount[c]  = _root.Num[c]-3;
    }
}
```

Instead of initializing our random timer again, we set the random destination values for all the movie clips, give Mn a value of 0.2 to speed up the motion, and set our NumCount equal to 5 less than Num so that the random timer will rest itself in after a count of 5.

So what does all this mean?

Well, to deconstruct all these variables and actions properly would take a good amount of explaining. To put it simply, having Mn change its value over time, in different ways, under different circumstances, will result in a variety of motion attributes. In the case of the Non-active state, it will move in the direction of its destination as long as its value is positive. Once that value turns to a negative it will then come back on itself. In the Active state, the movie clips will move faster to their destination. The result is that when I roll over a button it will quickly snap the letter into place, and when I roll out it will set in motion a variety of random 'flight' motions that are constrained to the size of our movie.

06:Removing clips when out of bounds
Refer to VarTypog_06.fla.

Remember when I mentioned that we created the variable NameLength so that it's not solely dependent on the string length of Name. Well, this is where that independent association comes into effect. Let's take a look at what our Population function does for this section of our tutorial.

```
function Population () {
    if (_xmouse>50 && _xmouse<410 && _ymouse>50 && _ymouse<410) {
        NameLength = Name.length;
    } else {
        NameLength = 0;
    }
    if (LClips<NameLength) {
        LClips++;
        _root.MasterL.duplicateMovieClip("L"+LClips, 1000 + LClips);
    }
    if (LClips>NameLength) {
        _root["L"+LClips].removeMovieClip();
        LClips--;
    }
}
```

The first `if` statement says that if my mouse is within the defined bounding area around a particular button, set `NameLength` to equal the string length of `Name`; otherwise set `NameLength` to 0. The result of this would mean that if I move my mouse outside that defined area (Left:50, Right:410, Top:50, Bottom:410), because `NameLength` equals 0, it will remove all remaining movie clips.

Why would we want to remove all of our movie clips?

Well, the direct need to do so in this study isn't great, but in a large project where many things are going on all around, it is always good to unburden the load you place on the processor. In developing studies or client-driven projects, I generally try to incorporate this concept of focus, the idea being that if you have a number of elements or programmatic structures, they enlist or unburden themselves depending on the current focus of attention by the user. In this case, it happens to be that number of movieclips we populate to our stage.

07:Joining lines with a linked library movie clip
Refer to `VarTypog_07.fla`.

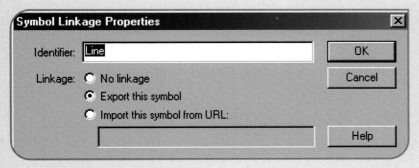

As if we haven't learned enough already, now we'll quickly go over one of the (in my view) 'coolest' features of Flash 5. That is, being able to pull and attach linked library objects into your project.

To do this, go to the Library and select Line Clip. Pull down the Options menu and select Linkage.

We need to select the Export this symbol checkbox and give it an Identifier value of Line. We can now reference this symbol in our movie as if it were an object on our stage.

Before we go into the script, let's go over a few things about how to connect a line in Flash from one point to another.

First draw a line at a 45-degree angle with a height and width of 100.

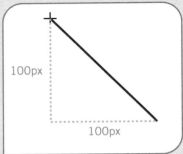

This next diagram will show you how we're going to connect A and B with a straight line by referencing the _x and _y values of both objects and defining the scale of our line as being the difference between the two:

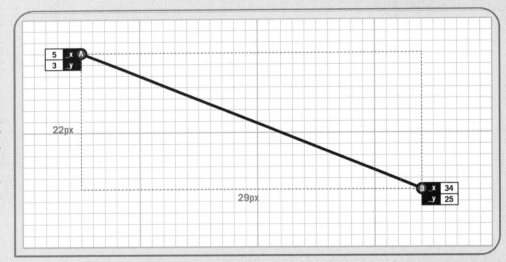

Let's look at the code behind this:

```
//the equation
Line._x = A._x;
Line._y = A._y;
Line._xscale = B._x - A._x ;
Line._yscale = B._y - A._y ;

//the result in this instance
Line._x = 5;
Line._y = 3;
Line._xscale = 29;
Line._yscale = 22;
```

Let's now look at the `LineDraw` function that we introduced to this section.

```
function LineDraw () {
    if (Lc>=LClips) {
        _root["Line"+Lc].removeMovieClip();
        Lc—;
    }
    if (Lc < LClips) {
        Lc++;
    }
    for (c=1; c<LClips; c++) {
        _root.attachMovie("Line", "Line"+c, 100+c);
        this["Line"+c]._x = this["L"+c]._x;
        this["Line"+c]._y = this["L"+c]._y;
        this["Line"+c]._xscale = this["L"+(c+1)]._x-
this["L"+c]._x;
        this["Line"+c]._yscale = this["L"+(c+1)]._y-
this["L"+c]._y;
    }
}
```

The first few lines act very similar to our `Population` function. The only difference here is that we're using the `attachMovie` to pull a linked symbol from our Library, instead of using `duplicateMovieClip` to duplicate an object on our stage. The remaining few lines function the same way as our previous example on how to connect a line, but now with the inclusion of evaluations to determine the positions for `_x` and `_y`, as well as the `_xscale` and `_yscale` values. The reference image below shows how these lines will connect from one another in a chain. Also note how we have nine movie clips, but only eight lines connecting them.

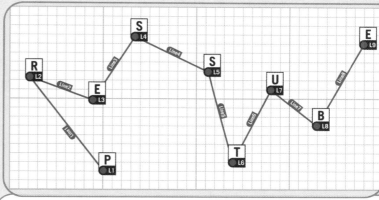

```
//in this instance
Name = "PRESSTUBE";
LClips = 9;
        //number of Letter MovieClips
        // (L1, L2, L3, L4, L5, L6, L7, L8, L9)
Lc = 8;
        //number of lines
        // (Line1, Line2, Line3, Line4, Line5, Line6, Line7, Line8)
```

08:Adjusting our LineDraw function to draw more line segments
Refer to `VarTypog_08.fla`

All the functions that we've used up until now have strictly held nuggets of code that we're calling on later. In this final section we'll alter our `LineDraw` function so that it will include an argument which will allow us to reuse that function to perform several tasks. Arguments are placeholders for values, which we use in our function and are given a value when we enlist that function to change how it operates for that condition. The argument we use in the following bit of code is `OffSet`. It appears in the parentheses following the function name and throughout the statement.

```
function LineDraw (OffSet) {
   if (this["Lc"+OffSet]>=LClips-OffSet) {
   _root["Line"+OffSet+this["Lc"+OffSet]].removeMovieClip();
      this["Lc"+OffSet]—;
   }
   if (this["Lc"+OffSet]<=LClips-OffSet) {
      this["Lc"+OffSet]++;
   }
   for (c=1; c<=LClips-OffSet; c++) {
      _root.attachMovie("Line", "Line"+OffSet+c,
➡(100*OffSet)+c);
      this["Line"+OffSet+c]._x = this["L"+c]._x;
      this["Line"+OffSet+c]._y = this["L"+c]._y;
      this["Line"+OffSet+c]._xscale =
➡this["L"+(c+Number(OffSet))]._x-this["L"+c]._x;
      this["Line"+OffSet+c]._yscale =
➡this["L"+(c+Number(OffSet))]._y-this["L"+c]._y;
   }
}
```

It's important to look at how we enlist that function. The following is the `onClipEvent` that we've attached to our background image movie clip:

We see that we've enlisted the `LineDraw` function three times, with three different values for our argument (1, 2, and 3). Basically, what this means is that any time `OffSet` appears in our statement, it will be replaced with this argument. As in the previous section, we enlisted this function to help draw connecting lines between the movie clips, but now we want to add more lines.

```
onClipEvent (enterFrame) {
   _root.MasterLetter();
   _root.Population();
   _root.LetterFlight();
   _root.LineDraw(1);
   _root.LineDraw(2);
   _root.LineDraw(3);
}
```

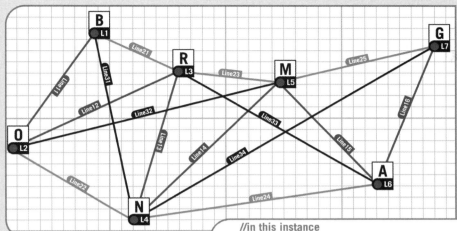

`OffSet` was structured and placed in such a way that it will determine how many lines to produce, where to connect them, what name to give to the line movie clips, and what level they will appear on. In the this next diagram I've color-coded the line segments to help deconstruct what's actually occurring: red shows `LineDraw(1)`, green shows `LineDraw(2)`, and blue shows `LineDraw(3)`:

```
//in this instance
Name = "BORNMAG";
LClips = 7;
        //number of Letter MovieClips
        // (L1, L2, L3, L4, L5, L6, L7)
Lc1 = 6;
        //number of lines (w/ an offset of 1 - shown in red)
        // (Line11, Line12, Line13, Line14, Line15, Line16)
Lc2 = 5;
        //number of lines (w/ an offset of 2 - shown in green)
        // (Line21, Line22, Line23, Line24, Line25)
Lc3 = 4;
        //number of lines (w/ an offset of 3 - shown in blue)
        // (Line31, Line32, Line33, Line34)
```

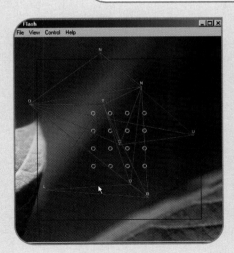

That's about all I can teach you about my text effect; all that's left is for you to go away and play with the FLAs and dabble with the ActionScript.

You've now seen stage-by-stage how I built the effect, and you can find the final completed FLA on the CD as `VarTypog_Final.fla`. The lessons you've learned through the eight stages of this tutorial will hopefully be of use to you in many different projects in the future and I'd like to think I showed you that there's nothing 'static' about static text.

Type seems to be added as almost an afterthought in many sites. By adding various effects and transitions that control how text appears on the stage, you can add a more dynamic feel to the main message, making sure it stands out...

can you read me

can you read me

can you read me

can you read me

can you read me

can you read me

can you read me

can you read me

can you read me

can you read me

unreadable text
A recent Flash fashion is to make text as small as possible. Although small text looks cool, it does have the unfortunate side-effect that no-one can read it.

This may bother Mr. Nielsen, but not us. Simply create a type engine that magnifies text based on its closeness to the mouse and you have a cool space-saving menu system, as used in the wild by people like Joshua Davis. Extend the idea to your main text as well and see what happens.

surface.yugop.com

ActionScript only text engines

We can talk about text engines until the cows come home, but if you want to see what the undisputed ActionScript master can come up with, check out Yugo's new site...

text transitions

Now that Flash has a proper array object, coupled with some cool string handling, it is much easier to separate the individual letters of your message and make them fly in and out of place with ease. Simply create a movie clip with a one character dynamic text field in it. Then, by separating out your text into individual characters and displaying each one in a duplicate of your dynamic text movie clip, you can use scripting to do whatever you want.

An ActionScript version of the**void**'s text effect (from the original New Masters Book) might be a good example to practice the technique with...

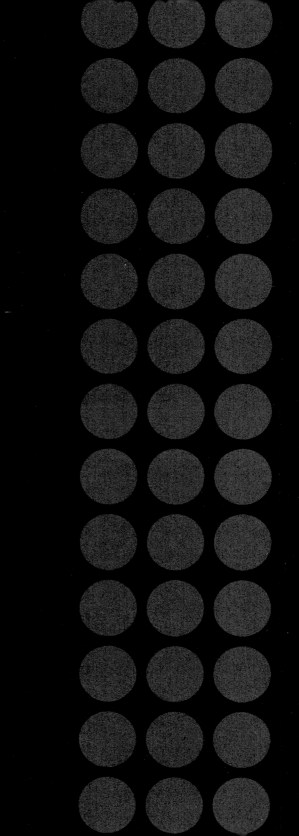

The index is arranged hierarchically,
in alphabetical order, with symbols preceding the
letter A. Many second-level entries also occur as first-level
entries. This is to ensure that you will find the information
you require however you choose to search for it.

Index

Index

Index

Index

Index

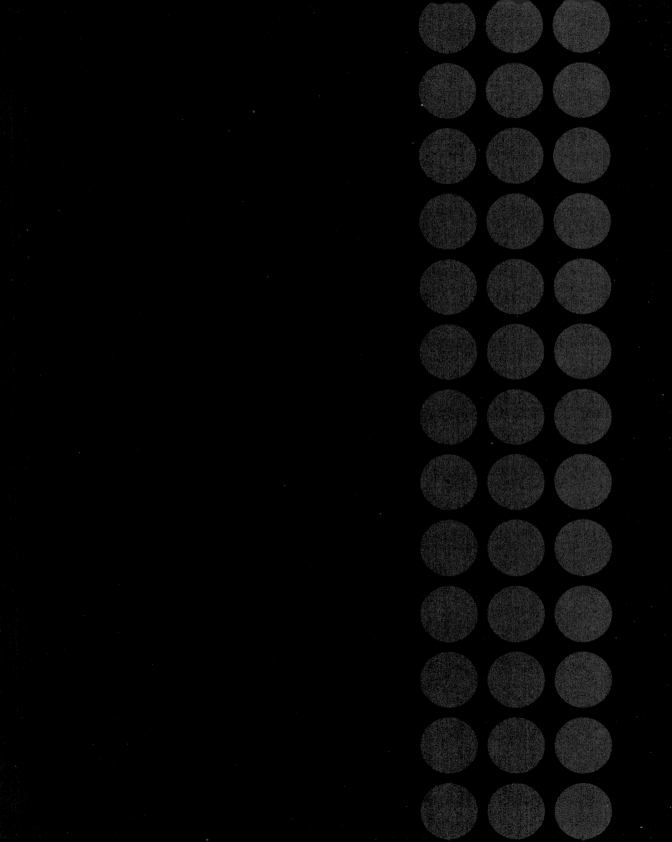

Be inspired.

New Masters of Flash

New Masters of Flash
The 2002 Annual

friendsof
DESIGNER TO DESIGNER™

Flash 5 Studio

Flash 5 Dynamic Content Studio

Flash 5 ActionScript Studio

Foundation Flash 5

Foundation ActionScript

Foundation Dreamweaver UltraDev 4

Foundation Director 8.5

Foundation JavaScript

OUT: JULY 2001

Flash 5 Games Studio

OUT: AUGUST 2001

Director 8.5 Studio

OUT: AUGUST 2001

Foundation Flash XML

OUT: SEPTEMBER 2001

The New Masters Series – Advanced – *Showing it*

Where can you find out what inspires the top designers? Where can you learn the secrets of their design techniques? New Masters is the ultimate showcase for graphics pioneers from around the world, where they write about what influences their design and teach the cutting-edge effects that have made them famous.

The Studio Series – Intermediate – *Doing it*

The essence of the studio is the collective – a gathering of independent designers who try out ideas and explore techniques in finer detail. Each book in the studio series assumes that the reader has learned the fundamentals of the topic area. They want to grow their skills with particular tools to a higher level, while at the same time absorbing the hard-won creative experience of a group of design experts.

The Foundation Series – Starting out – *Learning it*

Every web designer benefits from a strong foundation to firmly establish their understanding of a new technology or tool. The friends of ED foundation series deconstructs a subject into step by step lessons – stand alone design recipes that build together into a complete model project. Practical, intuitive – a must-have resource.

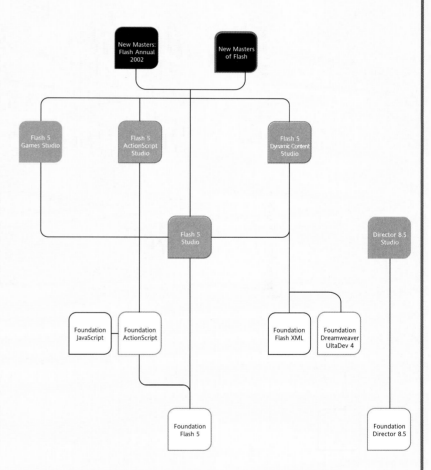

The CDRom was designed and built by

The New Media Works Ltd.
3rd Floor, Lupus House
11-13 Macklin Street
Covent Garden
WC2B 5NH

Tel: +44 207 8313391
Fax: +44 207 4044320

Email: info@newmediaworks.co.uk

DESIGNER TO DESIGNER™

friends of ED writes books for you. Any suggestions, or ideas about how you want information given in your ideal book will be studied by our team. Your comments are always valued at friends of ED.

Free phone in USA 800.873.9769
Fax 312.893.8001

UK Telephone 0121.258.8858
Fax 0121.258.8868

feedback@friendsofed.com

New Masters of Flash: The 2002 Annual – Registration Card

Name ....

Address ....

....

....

....

City .... State/Region ....

Country .... Postcode/Zip ....

E-mail ....

Occupation ....

How did you hear about this book? ....

☐ Book review (name)..

☐ Advertisement (name) ....

☐ Recommendation ....

☐ Catalog ....

☐ Other ....

Where did you buy this book? ....

☐ Bookstore (name) .... City..........

☐ Computer Store (name)..................................

☐ Mail Order...

☐ Other..

What influenced you in the purchase of this book?

☐ Cover Design

☐ Content

☐ Other (please specify)..........................

....

How did you rate the overall content of this book?

☐ Excellent   ☐ Good

☐ Average   ☐ Poor

What did you find most useful about this book? ....

....

What did you find the least useful about this book? ....

....

Please add any additional comments ....

....

What other subjects will you buy a computer book on soon?

....

What is the best computer book you have used this year?

....

Note: This information will only be used to keep you updated about new friends of ED titles and will not be used for any other purpose or passed to any other third party.

friendsof

DESIGNER TO DESIGNER™

N.B. If you post the bounce back card below in the UK, please send it to:

friends of ED Ltd.,
30 Lincoln Road, Olton,
Birmingham, B27 6PA. UK.

**NO POSTAGE
NECESSARY
IF MAILED
IN THE
UNITED STATES**

BUSINESS REPLY MAIL

*FIRST CLASS MAIL   PERMIT*64   CHICAGO,IL*

POSTAGE WIIL BE PAID BY ADDRESSEE

**friends of ED.
29 S. LA SALLE ST.
SUITE 520
CHICAGO IL 60603-USA**